BETTER CRICKET STATS

A New Statistical System
& Review of Cricket History

2022 Edition

compiled & edited by

R.B. BANFIELD

www.rbbanfield.com
www.storiesfrommyhead.com

Also by R.B. Banfield:

The New Covenant; Reference Edition
The New Covenant: Modern Style Edition

Better Movie Awards
Revelation in Harmony

Novels:
Against the Night
Easy Say They
The Great Assumption
The Man Who Flew Too Much
To Sail the Stars
Until All Their Dreams Faded
The Writer

The Burning Star Series:
Shadow
Companion
Dawn
Horizon
Bright
Legend
Glow
Rise
Birth

ISBN: 9798817480511
Imprint: Independently published

INTRODUCTION

Cricket has no right or wrong statistics, only misleading ones, occasionally misleading ones, outdated occasionally misleading ones, and new ones designed to get to the truth of the matter—such as the ones presented here. These new stats are simple and easy to calculate, as the game should not be held hostage by longwinded calculations, such as the ridiculous Duckworth-Lewis thing. Why would an international sport, with a highly profitable yearly turnover, and players who can become millionaires, rely on a system of statistics that were primitive even in Victorian times? Yes, there are attempts to show modern things, like run rates and strike rates, but they don't show a player's full range, because in Test cricket it simply doesn't matter how fast runs or wickets are made or taken. The most important skill for a Test player is the ability to play well consistently. Sporadic success is a sign that the player is out of his class and relies too much on luck.

Supporters and fans want their team to win, but the game's purists want more than that; the pleasure of watching the great players. With the exception of the rare exciting finishes, what stays in the memory of old cricket observers are the great shots, the great bowling, the great catches, and the great characters. Batsmenship, bowling artistry and athleticism are what sets the great players apart from the good ones, and it's what causes the crowds to endure through a game that can have periods when it is deadly dull. It's the beginning of the game that is the most interesting, when the players are fresh and no one knows what may happen—when the result is obvious, that's when the interest can wane. Cricket is about performance more than result, the same as it's about individuals rather than teams. The crowds watch through the dull times to catch glimpses of brilliance; that wonderful drive, that stupefying catch, that great fightback that changes the course of a match.

Along with providing better stats for the cricket world, this book focuses on the great players of every recorded era of the game. By that we can see how cricket was played throughout the years and what took the imagination of the crowds. The intention is to preserve the history of the game in the face of ever-present corporate media nonsense and commercially-driven bluster that chokes the modern game. Cricket's history is formidable and vast, yet how easy it is to find that the great players of the past are quickly forgotten. There is a strange modern attitude towards the early versions of the game, that has the opinion they were not playing real cricket, or that the games were not competitive. Cricket has always been played hard and tough, right from the seventeenth century when it came under the thumb of gamblers.

A neglected part of cricket history is that the sole reason for the game becoming a game for adults was that the English, being the English, put money on the outcome. Games were played with full teams of eleven, or just one of per side, attracting huge roaring crowds and huge profit for the organisers. This led to violent on-field behaviour, such as batsmen bashing fielders with their bats, to outright cheating. Laws were passed, some players were kicked out of the game, other players became rich, and the game eventually became mannered.

It is rightly said that leading players in one era of the game would be leading players in another era. Just because a certain cricketer played at a time when the bats were curved and the ball was rolled along bumpy turf, when they all wore funny clothes, and were continually polite, doesn't mean that it was below the level of today's players; the pampered era of supercharged bats on flat pitches with short boundaries. The game's greatest players, dominating above everyone else of their generation, were Bedle, Waymark, Beldham, Beauclerk, Grace and Bradman. Most of these names have long been forgotten, and only one played Test cricket from a young age, but that doesn't make any of them lesser players.

ABOUT THE STATS

Stats play an important role in every professional sport in the world except for cricket. For reasons of snobbery and ignorance, the system used for mid-nineteenth century cricket prevails today. A batsman's innings is not regarded as finished until he is dismissed, even if it's in another match, weeks or even months later. The bowler is judged not on how many wickets he takes during an innings, but on how many runs he concedes. The most vital players in the game, the all-rounders are judged on ... nothing at all. Fielders taking catches are judged on ... nothing at all. The brilliance of a wicket-keeper is judged not on how well he takes a catch or how fast he can make a stumping, but how many dismissals were lucky enough to come his way. In this book the batting, bowling and all-rounders are addressed (but regrettably, it remains to be seen how fielding and wicket-keeping can ever be fairly measured).

Because of the ineffectiveness of cricket's stats, today's media analysis is fixated with telling us the total amount of runs and wickets each player has. This is in an age of non-stop cricket, when a regular player can get through one hundred Tests in ten years, and a poor player can get to thirty Tests without anyone noticing. Not only does this obsession with the "most" completely ignore all the great players of the past, it gives the impression that they weren't really great players at all. The truth is that most of the cricketers of any past age, had they had the toys available today, would not only compete with today's bunch, they would annihilate them. In the old days they hit the ball harder and bowled better than anything seen today. Has anyone ever been faster than Charles Kortright, who alleged to have bowled a ball that went for six byes in 1893? We know that no player has hit a six at Lord's further than Albert Trott in 1899. The only real difference in skills is in fielding, in which today's players are expected to throw themselves around to save a run, but that is not to say that the past had no great fielders, because they most certainly did.

This book's new stats work in three ways. The first is the most obvious, a simple way to critique a player through the actual performances; runs scored and wickets taken. The second is perhaps a little contentious, but is needed to compare players of different eras, with an adjustment of runs in the days before World War One, when pitches were poor and runs were harder to get and wickets easier.

The third is the most contentious, that some Tests should never have been labelled Tests at all. In the 1890s the weak South Africa teams that played touring English teams were given Test status for no merit at all. All touring teams from England at that time were privately organised, and featured only a few leading players, and only those that toured Australia played against equal opposition. The quality of their South African opposition, and how representative they were of their cricket at that time, remains a mystery. Had the earlier English touring party to North America met a team representing the U.S.A., then that would now be called the first Test. But the biggest lunacy of all was in 2005 when the I.C.C. decided, for reasons of self-aggrandising, that an invitation team playing an Australian team should have Test status, despite the fact that none of the so-called "World" players were interested in playing the game, and were certainly not representing their countries. Such mindless decisions from the I.C.C. skewer the game's stats and make a mockery out of the game's history.

The First Part to the New Stats

Concerning the most important aspect of the new stats is the simple analysis of a player's performance on the field on a game-to-game basis. The old system of judging a batsman's worth by how often he was dismissed allows for tail-enders to have inflated numbers since they have far more chance of being "not out" at the end of an innings, and someone like an opener little chance. Most openers, since they bat at the most difficult part of an innings and need to have good techniques to survive, have averages around 5 runs below middle order batsman simply for that reason, that they make few "not outs", which is hardly a fair system.

The system used for bowling averages gives the appearance that it is fair, by calculating how many runs were conceded by how many wickets were taken, but it does not show at what frequency the wickets were taken. It also does not take into account the fact that most spinners concede more runs but take slightly more wickets than fast bowlers, giving them higher averages. A part-time bowler, who may only bowl three or four overs per match, and takes a wicket every ten matches or so, can have a better average than a frontline bowler who does most of the work, which is hardly fair. The excuse given for this is that we must analyse the stats and identify who is a part-time bowler and who is a main bowler, or what is a good average for a spinner as opposed to a fast bowler. Or we could have a system that clearly shows us who the pretenders are.

The formula for RWI (runs per wickets per innings) is simple:

Innings Bowled ÷ Wickets × (Runs ÷ Wickets)

If one bowler finished an innings with figures of 5-40, and another had 1-8, it is obvious that the first did more for his team. Under the usual system both bowlers get an average of 8.00, but their RWI shows the true picture; the first bowler's RWI is 1.60, to the second bowler's RWI of 8.00.

A bowler who routinely has figures of, say, 3-38 (giving an RWI of 4.22), is better than a bowler who takes wickets irregularly but has a good average, because the bowler who can routinely take three wickets an innings is of more value to his team.

The handy part-time bowler is useful to any team, but their average should not be compared with the frontline bowlers. If they get a wicket every three or four innings, their RWI shows that. A bowler who has figures over three matches of 0-17, 1-10, 1-14, 0-10, 0-5, 1-8, would have an average of 21.33, which most average bowlers would kill to have, but the RWI is the more accurate 42.66. Since the bowler took a wicket every two innings, the bowling average has doubled for RWI. If a bowler takes two wickets per innings, the average is halved for RWI. Over their career, most of the great bowlers will average two or three wickets per innings.

Allan Border and Bob Holland both bowled spin and both have near-identical figures, but one was a specialist spinner and the other a part-timer:

	runs	*wkts*	*ave*
AR Border	1525	39	39.10
RG Holland	1352	34	39.76

But when the number of innings bowled is applied, we get the true picture with RWI:

	ib	*runs*	*wkts*	*ave*	*rwi*
AR Border	99	1525	39	39.10	99.25
RG Holland	17	1352	34	39.76	19.88

The following English bowlers from the 1990s are ranked by Average:

	runs	*wkts*	*ave*
RK Illingworth	615	19	32.36
GC Small	1871	55	34.01
MA Butcher	541	15	36.06
PCR Tufnell	4560	121	37.68

And now by their RWI:

	ib	*runs*	*wkts*	*ave*	*rwi*
GC Small	31	1871	55	34.01	19.16
PCR Tufnell	70	4560	121	37.68	21.79
RK Illingworth	13	615	19	32.36	22.14
MA Butcher	30	541	15	36.06	72.06

Mark Butcher, who was a top-order batsman, took a wicket every two innings he bowled, which is good for a part-timer but bad for a main bowler, so his RWI should show that. Despite Phil Tufnell's average being 5.32 runs higher than Richard Illingworth's, their RWI is very close. This shows that Tufnell went for more runs but took more wickets than Illingworth, which is why he was a better bowler and played more Tests.

Michael Bevan has a better bowling average than the late Shane Warne, but no one would ever claim that he was anywhere near as good a bowler:

	runs	*wkts*	*ave*
MG Bevan	703	29	24.24
SK Warne	17924	702	25.53

With the RWI applied, there is no confusion.

	ib	*runs*	*wkts*	*ave*	*rwi*
SK Warne	271	17924	702	25.53	9.85
MG Bevan	21	703	29	24.24	17.55

It is also interesting that Glenn McGrath's average is a noticeable 3.85 runs better than Warne's, but because Warne took slightly more wickets per innings, their RWI was very close.

	ib	runs	wkts	ave	rwi
GD McGrath	241	12144	560	21.68	9.33
SK Warne	271	17924	703	25.53	9.85

Five of England's better fast bowlers, ranked according to Average:

	tests	ib	runs	wkts	ave
M Hendrick	30	54	2248	87	25.83
JA Snow	49	93	5387	202	26.66
D Gough	58	95	6503	229	28.39
IT Botham	102	168	10878	383	28.40
GOB Allen	25	45	2379	81	29.37

All good bowlers, except that Darren Gough took more wickets per innings than the others, and Mike Hendrick the least. Under this system Hendrick and John Snow are the best bowlers. While Snow was England's leading bowler when he was at his peak, Hendrick was merely a good player and not better than the likes of Gough and Ian Botham, who could both be match winners on their good days.

Now the same players ranked according to RWI, which rewards the wicket takers:

	m	ib	runs	wkts	ave	rwi
D Gough	58	95	6503	229	28.39	11.77
JA Snow	49	93	5387	202	26.66	12.27
IT Botham	102	168	10878	383	28.40	12.45
M Hendrick	30	54	2248	87	25.83	16.03
GOB Allen	25	45	2379	81	29.37	16.31

Both Gough and Botham's average are higher than Snow's, but because they took their wickets more frequently, their RWI is very close together. Hendrick and Gubby Allen are also similar in RWI, despite having differing averages.

The general guide for judging a player's RWI is as follows:

Great bowlers: less than 10
World-class bowlers: 10 to 15
Very good bowlers: 15 to 19
Good-enough bowlers: 20-24
Struggling to be a top bowlers: 25-29
More than useful change-bowlers: 30-49
Useful part-timers: 50 to 100
Anything over 100 is not quite good enough.
Anything over 1000 and the guy shouldn't be bowling.

The batting RI (runs per innings) is simpler than the bowling, and also sorts out the pretenders. A good example is in 1953 when Bill Johnston, a bowler for the touring Australians, topped the English first-class season averages with a whopping 102.00. His highest score was 28 and he was only dismissed once, having compiled 102 runs in 17 innings. This outcome must have been hilarious to everyone, and the source of much merriment within the Australian touring party, but it hardly served to provide an accurate list of the best batsmen of the season.

1953 English Season Top 10 First-Class Batting Averages

	m	*i*	*no*	*runs*	*ave*
WA Johnston	16	17	16	102	102.00
RN Harvey	25	35	4	2040	71.60
L Hutton	27	44	5	2458	63.02
L Livingston	24	36	6	1710	57.00
KR Miller	24	31	3	1433	51.17
PBH May	34	59	9	2554	51.08
R Subba Row	30	46	10	1823	50.63
WJ Edrich	32	60	6	2557	47.35
RT Simpson	33	60	5	2505	45.54
D Barrick	26	38	7	1530	49.35

It is difficult to see how someone who made a mere six runs per innings can be rewarded with an average of over a century and the honour of topping the season averages. What does such a system prove, other than showing that Johnston didn't get out very much in England in 1953? Also worth pointing out is that had Johnston not been dismissed on that one occasion, he would not have had any average for the season at all, and therefore not been on any of the statistical lists. It's time to move on to something more accurate.

The same 1953 players ranked according to RI:

	m	*i*	*no*	*runs*	*ave*	*ri*
RN Harvey	25	35	4	2040	71.60	58.28
L Hutton	27	44	5	2458	63.02	55.86
L Livingston	24	36	6	1710	57.00	47.50
KR Miller	24	31	3	1433	51.17	46.22
PBH May	34	59	9	2554	51.08	43.28
WJ Edrich	32	60	6	2557	47.35	42.61
RT Simpson	33	60	5	2505	45.54	41.75
D Barrick	26	38	7	1530	49.35	40.26
R Subba Row	30	46	10	1823	50.63	39.63
WA Johnston	16	17	16	102	102.00	6.00

Not only has the pretender dropped to the bottom, but it shows how Raman Subba Row's average was inflated due to his ten "not outs", and Bill Edrich deserved to be placed nearer to Peter May. To make over fifty runs per innings, as Neil Harvey and Len Hutton did in 1953, is something only the great players can do.

The Second Part to the New Stats

The adjusted stats according to era. Run-scoring in world cricket has basically remained consistent since the 1920s. Even allowing for the odd "sticky wicket" when the game was played without the need to cover it up when it rained, there is not much difference between today's scores and those of yesteryear's. Before the First World War the pitches were not great, but they were wonderful when compared to the early nineteenth century, back when it was a bowler's game and a two-innings match could be completed in one or two days.

years	*credited runs*
1895-1914	+5
1890-1894	+10
1880-1889	+15
1870-1879	+20
1860-1869	+25
1730-1859	+30

The Third Part to the New Stats

The non-Tests. The following Tests are rejected as being at a true Test level:

South Africa pre-1900 (#31, 32, 37, 47, 48, 49, 58, 59)
Australia vs I.C.C. XI (#1768)

It can be argued that perhaps New Zealand after World War Two, Zimbabwe from 2004 until today, the early years for Bangladesh, the current West Indies team, and the new Ireland and Afghanistan teams, lack the quality we want in Test cricket, but for the sake of making this less complicated than it could be, we will overlook their shortfalls. How long we can continue to overlook them is another matter.

England left-arm spinner Johnny Briggs was famous for being the first to 100 Test wickets. 21 of those wickets came in two "Tests" against South Africa. Facing someone like Briggs on a poor pitch, they were never to last long.

To remove the South African Tests from his record, Briggs' stats go from:

tests	*runs*	*ri*	*wkts*	*ave*	*rwi*
33	815	16.30	118	17.75	7.37

to:

tests	*runs*	*ri*	*wkts*	*ave*	*rwi*
31	809	16.85	97	20.55	9.53

Now his RI and RWI show that he was a fairly useful batsman, say a good number eight or nine, and an RWI that is still world-class. If we apply the "adjusted" formula, based on the average runs made at the time in which he played, a clearer picture of Briggs' cricketing abilities emerge:

tests	*runs*	*ri (adj)*	*wkts*	*ave*	*rwi (adj)*
31	809	16.85 (26.95)	97	20.55	9.53 (14.39)

This shows that Briggs was a very good lower order batsman, as he was described by contemporaries, a number seven or even number six, but too good to be as low as eight or nine. His bowling was very good, but not in the "great" category.

ODI and T20 Stats

One Day International cricket (ODI), which usually consists of two innings of 50 overs, is such a different game to Test and First-Class cricket, that the stats need to be more detailed. The even shorter format of twenty overs per innings (T20), also benefits from more detailed stats. At this point in the game's history the cricketing luminaries who run the game use the typically dull system of Strike Rate for batsmen and Run Rate (recently changed to "Economy") for bowlers. Strike Rate is what a batsman scores, on average, every 100 deliveries. The Run Rate/Economy is how many runs are scored off every six deliveries, because that is a bowler's over. But batsmen don't typically face 100 deliveries, so where did that number come from? Why not have the runs per over for the batsman, like with the bowler? That way it could easily be seen if they score 5 or 6 runs per over. Or why not have the bowler's runs conceded per 100 deliveries, like with the batsmen? Under the current system, during a run chase and a team wants something like 8.50 runs per over to win, we would need to know that a batsman's stats were around the required Strike Rate of 141.66. The team's required run rate is never calculated and televised for the audience in the format of Strike Rate, so why have that in a batsman's stats at all?

New ODI Batting System: RIRB (Runs ÷ Innings) × (Runs ÷ Ball)

If a batsman scores at a run per ball, his RI remains the same; over a run a ball and the RI increases, less than a run a ball and it decreases. A batsman who can score very quickly, say at 10 per over, but only makes low scores, is not as useful to his team as he may appear. 10 per over is a Strike Rate of 166.66. If that batsman has an RI of 10.00, then his RIRB would be 16.66. (10.00 × 1.66). If another batsman is a slow scorer but makes decent scores, with an RI of 30.00 but an RB of 0.55 (which is a Strike Rate of 55) then the RIRB is 16.50. So deciding who is the better player does not matter. The first one makes small but quick scores, and the second is too slow but makes good scores. Neither of them are all that great and they would need to have other skills to give value to their team, but statistically they are identical. When looking at career stats there is no room to determine minute details. Perhaps one day we will be able to look at player's performances at the beginning, middle and end of ODI innings, but for the time being that is out of the scope of this book.

In a more extreme example, a player who has an RI of 6.00 but a Strike Rate of 200 (RB of 2.00), would have an RIRB of 12.00. Another player with a great RI of 40.00 but a Strike Rate of only 30 (RB of 0.30) also has an RIRB of 12.00. In a low scoring game, the batsman who can get runs, with the 40.00 RI, is the better player. But in the frenetic last overs of an innings, the second player, who could get the quick runs, would be better.

One of the greatest ODI batsman was Viv Richards, who played 187 games and made 6,721 runs at a 40.24 RI. He faced 7,451 deliveries and had a Strike Rate of 90.20. His runs per delivery was 0.902, so therefore his RIRB was 36.21. Of Richard's contemporaries, there were three others who had similar RIs: Zaheer Abbas, Glenn Turner and Gordon Greenidge:

	odis	*i*	*runs*	*ri*
Zaheer Abbas	62	60	2572	42.86
CG Greenidge	128	127	5134	40.42
IVA Richards	187	167	6721	40.24
GM Turner	41	40	1598	39.95

But if they are ranked according to their RI multiplied by how fast they scored, their RB, we have this:

	odis	*i*	*runs*	*ri*	*b*	*rb*	*rirb*
IVA Richards	187	167	6721	40.24	7451	0.90	36.21
Zaheer Abbas	62	60	2572	42.86	3033	0.84	36.00
GM Turner	41	40	1598	39.95	2348	0.68	27.16
CG Greenidge	128	127	5134	40.42	7908	0.64	25.86

The Strike Rate favours the successful lower order thrashers, so let's take a look at some. The leading Strike Rate stats for players who played at about the same time as Richards is listed below. No one in their right mind would suggest any of them were better than Richards. Anyone studying the numbers would need to factor in his superior batting average, but since that is a stat that does not exist, it becomes difficult to compile any sort of list.

	odis	*i*	*runs*	*ri*	*b*	*sr*
BL Cairns	78	65	987	15.18	941	104.88
IDS Smith	98	77	1055	13.70	1061	99.43
Kapil Dev	225	198	3783	19.10	3979	95.07
C Sharma	65	35	456	13.02	504	90.47
IVA Richards	187	167	6721	40.24	7451	90.20

When RIRB is applied to this group, it becomes clear who is the best.

	odis	*i*	*runs*	*ri*	*b*	*rb*	*rirb*
IVA Richards	187	167	6721	40.24	7451	0.90	36.21
Kapil Dev	225	198	3783	19.10	3979	0.95	18.14
BL Cairns	78	65	987	15.18	941	1.04	15.78
IDS Smith	98	77	1055	13.70	1061	0.99	13.56
C Sharma	65	35	456	13.02	504	0.90	11.71

The bowling stats need to be a little more complicated. A great ODI bowler not only keeps the runs down, he also takes wickets, so there must be a system that incorporates the rate of wickets taken, and the cost of those wickets, and the amount of runs given up. Current cricket analysis has no system for this at all. There is only Average and Run Rate/Economy, and they cannot be combined with any validity.

New ODI Bowling System:
RWIRB (Innings Bowled ÷ Wickets × (Runs ÷ Wickets)) × (Runs ÷ Ball)

	odis	*ib*	*runs*	*wkts*	*ave*	*rwi*	*b*	*rb*	*rwirb*
RM Hogg	71	67	2418	85	28.44	22.41	3677	0.65	14.56
GF Lawson	79	79	2592	88	29.45	26.43	4259	0.60	15.85
SP O'Donnell	87	87	3102	108	28.72	23.13	4350	0.71	16.42
PR Reiffel	92	92	3096	106	29.20	25.34	4732	0.65	16.47
MG Hughes	33	33	1115	38	29.34	25.47	1639	0.68	17.31
PAJ DeFreitas	103	103	3775	115	32.82	29.39	5712	0.66	19.39
SJ Harmison	58	57	2481	76	32.64	24.48	2899	0.85	20.80
BA Reid	61	61	2203	63	34.96	33.85	3250	0.67	22.67
JR Thomson	50	50	1942	55	35.30	32.09	2696	0.72	23.10
RJ Sidebottom	25	25	1039	29	35.82	30.87	1277	0.81	25.00
LE Plunkett	34	34	1578	45	35.06	26.48	1603	0.98	25.95

In the above example (a collection of similar bowlers from England and Australia) the RWIRB shows that Rodney Hogg was an outstanding ODI bowler. Hogg had the best Average, RWI and RWIRB, and rightly heads the table. By contrast, Geoff Lawson had high RWI but a very low RB, so he comes in at number two. Simon O'Donnell had a high RB but a good RWI, because he took wickets with good frequency, so he deserves to be at number three. Bruce Reid had a low RB but he was not a big wicket taker, so he is in the middle of the table. Steve Harmison was expensive in his RB, but had a good RWI, which also puts him middle of the table. Liam Plunkett's good RWI was offset by his poor RB, putting him last on the table.

Economy Rate, Average or even RWI fails to clearly show how these players should be ranked.

RECORDS

The Best Test Cricket Batsmen

(Qualification: retired, 2000+ runs, 45.00+ RI)

		team	*years*	*tests*	*runs*	*ri (adj)*
1	DG Bradman	Aus	19	52	6996	87.45
2	JB Hobbs	Eng	22	61	5410	53.03 (55.44)
3	RG Pollock	SA	6+	23	2256	55.02
4	ED Weekes	WI	10	48	4455	55.00
5	GA Headley	WI	24	22	2190	54.75
6	H Sutcliffe	Eng	11	54	4555	54.22
7	KC Sangakkara	SL	15	134	12400	53.21
8	KF Barrington	Eng	13	82	6806	51.95
9	BC Lara	WI	15	130	11912	51.79
10	WR Hammond	Eng	19	85	7249	51.77
11	CL Walcott	WI	12	44	3798	51.32
12	L Hutton	Eng	17	79	6971	50.51
13	GS Sobers	WI	20	93	8032	50.20
14	SR Tendulkar	Ind	24	200	15921	48.39
15	Mohammad Yousuf	Pak	12	90	7530	48.26
16	V Sehwag	Ind	11	103	8503	47.76
17	AD Nourse	SA	16	34	2960	47.74
18	JH Kallis	SA	18	165	13206	47.50
19	Younis Khan	Pak	17	118	10099	47.41
20	SM Gavaskar	Ind	16	125	10122	47.29
21	GS Chappell	Aus	13	87	7110	47.08
22	IVA Richards	WI	16	121	8540	46.92
23	DPMD Jayawardene	SL	17	149	11814	46.88
24	Javed Miandad	Pak	17	124	8832	46.73
25	SM Nurse	WI	9	29	2523	46.72
26	RS Dravid	Ind	15	163	13265	46.70
27	RT Ponting	Aus	16	167	13278	46.58
28	ML Hayden	Aus	14	102	8437	46.35
29	AB de Villiers	SA	13	114	8765	45.89
30	GC Smith	SA	11	116	9253	45.58
31	MEK Hussey	Aus	7	79	6235	45.51
32	RB Kanhai	WI	16	79	6227	45.45
33	KP Pietersen	Eng	8	104	8181	45.19

It is astounding that Don Bradman averaged 32.01 more runs per innings better than the next man, Jack Hobbs, especially when the difference between 2 and 12, Hobbs and Len Hutton, is only 4.93 runs. Four runs may not seem many, but such numbers make all the difference when comparing players; enough to separate the great from the plain very good. There are a lot of players with an excellent RI of over 40.00, but there are few who can get into the 50.00s. Four outstanding players, Ken Barrington, Wally Hammond, Brian Lara and Clyde

Walcott averaged over 51 with only 0.63 between them. Knowing that so small a margin separates these players, to see that Bradman made 32 runs more than the great Hobbs is beyond comprehension. The man was simply playing a different game.

Current Leading Test Cricket Batsmen

(Qualification: active player, 2000+ runs, 45.00+ RI)

		team	*years*	*tests*	*runs*	*ri*
1	M Labuschagne	Aus	3	26	2390	53.11
2	SPD Smith	Aus	11	85	8010	53.04
3	KS Williamson	NZ	11	86	7272	48.48
4	V Kohli	Ind	11	101	8043	47.03
5	JE Root	Eng	9	109	9278	46.39
6	DA Warner	Aus	10	94	7753	45.07

The remarkable Marnus Labuschagne, who came from nowhere into the Australian team, has slowed just a little but still scores runs by the truckload, passed 2000 runs and makes his first appearance on this list at number one. All other players on the list have declined from last season.

Best Test Cricket Batting Record Overall

(Qualification: 60.00+ RI)

		team	*tests*	*runs*	*ri (adj)*
1	AG Ganteaume	WI	1	112	112.00
2	VH Stollmeyer	WI	1	96	96.00
3	DG Bradman	Aus	52	6996	87.45
4	H Wood	Eng	2	142	71.00 (86.00)
5	RE Redmond	NZ	1	163	81.50
6	BA Richards	SA	4	508	72.57
7	KR Patterson	Aus	2	144	72.00
8	DP Conway	NZ	7	767	63.91
9	Abdullah Shafique	Pak	5	547	60.77

The 20 Worst Test Cricket Batsmen, 10+ innings

		team	*tests*	*i*	*runs*	*ri*
1	Ebadot Hossain	Ban	14	22	8	0.40
2	CN McCarthy	SA	15	24	28	1.16
3	CS Martin	NZ	71	104	123	1.18
4	MB Owens	NZ	8	12	16	1.33
5	M Mbangwa	Zim	15	25	34	1.36
6	DT Dewdney	WI	9	12	17	1.41
7	Mohammad Akram	Pak	9	15	24	1.60
8	Imran Khan	Pak	10	10	16	1.60
9	Abu Jayed	Ban	13	22	36	1.63
10	DA Renneberg	Aus	8	13	22	1.69
11	CBRLS Kumara	SL	24	32	56	1.75
12	GI Allott	NZ	10	15	27	1.80
14	MI Black	WI	6	11	21	1.90
14	H Ironmonger	Aus	14	21	42	2.00
15	BP Bracewell	NZ	6	12	24	2.00

16	Naseem Shah	Pak	11	14	29	2.07
17	BS Chandrasekhar	Ind	58	80	167	2.08
18	D Olivier	SA	10	12	26	2.16
19	IJ Jones	Eng	15	17	38	2.23
20	Enamul Haque, jr	Ban	15	26	59	2.26

Featuring current players Ebadot Hossain, Abu Jayed, Lahiru Kumara, and Naseem Shah. Imagine if they all played for the same team. That's some tail.

The 10 Worst Test Cricket Batsmen, 30+ innings

(Qualification: 30+ innings)

		team	*tests*	*i*	*runs*	*ri*	*wkts*
1	CS Martin	NZ	71	104	123	1.18	233
2	CBRLS Kumara	SL	24	32	56	1.75	70
3	BS Chandrasekhar	Ind	58	80	167	2.08	242
4	Manjural Islam	Ban	17	33	81	2.45	28
5	PCR Tufnell	Eng	42	59	153	2.59	121
6	Maninder Singh	Ind	35	38	99	2.60	88
7	ST Gabriel	WI	56	84	221	2.64	161
8	Nuwan Pradeep	SL	28	50	132	2.64	70
9	BA Reid	Aus	27	34	93	2.73	113
10	AL Valentine	WI	36	51	141	2.76	139

A good way to tell if a cricketer generally can't bat is if the number of runs equals the number of wickets. In the case of **Chris Martin** (1974), he almost had almost two wickets for every run. Martin really was one of a kind. Every other player managed to gain even a little bit of confidence after playing over thirty innings, and discover unique ways of making runs, but Martin only succeeded in getting worse.

The Best Test Cricket Bowlers

(Qualification: retired, 100+ wickets, -11.00 RWI)

		team	*years*	*tests*	*wkts*	*ave*	*rwi (adj)*
1	SF Barnes	Eng	12	27	189	16.43	4.34 (5.66)
2	M Muralitharan	SL	17	132	795	22.67	6.50
3	CV Grimmett	Aus	11	37	216	24.21	7.50
4	WJ O'Reilly	Aus	14	27	144	22.59	7.52
5	RJ Hadlee	NZ	17	86	431	22.29	7.75
6	CTB Turner	Aus	8	17	101	16.53	4.90 (8.34)
7	MD Marshall	WI	12	81	376	20.94	8.40
8	AA Donald	SA	9+	72	330	22.25	8.69
9	C Blythe	Eng	8	19	100	18.63	6.89 (8.74)
10	DK Lillee	Aus	12	70	355	23.92	8.89
11	FS Truman	Eng	13	67	307	21.57	8.92
12	DW Steyn	SA	14	93	439	22.95	8.93
13	Imran Khan	Pak	20	88	362	22.81	8.94
14	J Garner	WI	10	58	259	20.97	8.98
15	AK Davidson	Aus	9	44	186	20.93	9.05
16	BA Reid	Aus	6	27	113	24.63	9.15
17	CEL Ambrose	WI	12	98	405	20.99	9.27

18	HJ Tayfield	SA	10	37	170	25.91	9.29
19	GD McGrath	Aus	13	123	560	21.68	9.330
20	NAT Adcock	SA	8	26	104	21.10	9.332
21	Fazal Mahmood	Pak	9	34	139	24.70	9.41
22	JC Laker	Eng	11	46	193	21.24	9.46
23	CEH Croft	WI	5	27	125	23.30	9.69
24	AV Bedser	Eng	9	51	236	24.89	9.70
25	Waqar Younis	Pak	13	87	373	23.56	9.72
26	SK Warne	Aus	15	142	691	25.53	9.85
27	Mohammad Asif	Pak	6	23	106	24.36	10.11
28	R Peel	Eng	11	20	101	16.98	5.88 (10.13)
29	Wasim Akram	Pak	16	104	414	23.62	10.32
30	JH Wardle	Eng	9	28	102	20.39	10.39
31	Saeed Ajmal	Pak	5	35	178	28.10	10.57
32	MA Holding	WI	11	60	249	23.68	10.74
33	RJ Harris	Aus	4	27	113	23.52	10.82
34	PM Pollock	SA	8	28	116	24.18	10.83
35	H Trumble	Aus	13	32	141	21.78	8.80 (10.94)

Current Leading Test Cricket Bowlers

(Qualification: active player, 100+ wickets, -11.00 RWI)

		team	*years*	*tests*	*wkts*	*ave*	*rwi*
1	PJ Cummins	Aus	10	41	197	21.27	8.52
2	R Ashwin	Ind	10	86	442	24.13	8.84
3	K Rabada	SA	6	52	243	22.41	8.76
4	JJ Bumrah	Ind	4	29	123	21.73	9.89
5	Yasir Shah	Pak	6	45	235	30.83	10.88

The 10 Best Test Cricket Bowling Records Overall

(Qualification: -5.00 RWI)

		team	*tests*	*ib*	*wkts*	*ave*	*rwi (adj)*
1	W Barber	Eng	2	1	1	0.00	0.00
2	BAG Murray	NZ	13	1	1	0.00	0.00
3	AN Hornby	Eng	3	1	1	0.00	0.00
4	PD Lashley	WI	1	1	1	1.00	1.00
5	CS Marriott	Eng	1	2	11	8.72	1.58
6	SM Boland	Aus	3	6	18	9.55	3.18
7	AR Patel	Ind	6	12	39	12.43	3.82
8	J Benaud	Aus	3	1	2	6.00	3.00
9	Azhar Khan	Pak	1	2	1	2.00	4.00
10	LJ Johnson	Aus	1	2	6	12.33	4.10

In the 1935 Test at Headingley, Leeds, England's Wilf Barber bowled only two deliveries when the match was about to finish in a draw, and caused a stumping. New Zealand opening batsman Bruce Murray, despite playing 13 Tests, bowled only one over, in a 1968 Test that India was about to win, and got a lucky wicket.

At Melbourne in 1879, England's AN Hornby bowled 28 deliveries for no runs. West Indies opening batsman Peter Lashley bowled three overs in a Test at Leeds in 1966 and removed the famously stubborn batsman Geoff Boycott.

The Worst Test Cricket RWI

(Qualification: 1000.00+ RWI)

		team	*tests*	*i*	*runs*	*wkts*	*ave*	*rwi (adj)*
1	SM Gavaskar	Ind	125	29	206	1	206.00	5974.00
2	Naeem Islam	Ban	8	14	303	1	303.00	4242.00
3	M Vijay	Ind	61	18	198	1	198.00	3564.00
4	KLT Arthurton	WI	33	19	183	1	183.00	3477.00
5	RS Bopara	Eng	13	10	290	1	290.00	2900.00
6	AH Jones	NZ	39	14	194	1	194.00	2716.00
7	JB Hobbs	Eng	61	11	165	1	165.00	1815.00 (1870.00)
8	KR Rutherford	NZ	56	11	161	1	161.00	1771.00
9	S Shivnarine	WI	8	10	167	1	167.00	1670.00
10	CA Davis	WI	15	20	330	2	165.00	1650.00
11	ME Trescothick	Eng	76	10	155	1	155.00	1550.00
12	TW Graveney	Eng	79	9	167	1	167.00	1503.00
13	RGCE Wijesuriya	SL	4	5	294	1	294.00	1470.00
14	Hanif Mohammad	Pak	55	13	95	1	95.00	1235.00
15	GN Yallop	Aus	39	10	116	1	116.00	1160.00
16	CS Nayudu	Ind	11	12	359	2	179.50	1077.00
17	Rajin Saleh	Ban	24	16	268	2	134.00	1072.00
18	MA Atherton	Eng	115	14	302	2	151.00	1057.00
19	Tareq Aziz	Ban	3	4	261	1	261.00	1044.00

The more they bowled and the less wickets they took, the worse it all got for them. These are mostly players who fancied themselves as useful change-bowlers, but who perhaps should have let someone else have a go. Sunil Gavaskar's sole wicket, coming at a cost of nearly six thousand RWI runs, was Pakistan's leading batsman Zaheer Abbas.

The Most Test Cricket Innings Bowled Without a Wicket

(Qualification: 7+ ib)

		team	*tests*	*ib*	*runs*	*wkts*
1	K Srikkanth	Ind	43	16	114	0
2	GA Headley	WI	22	14	230	0
3	TM Head	Aus	26	12	124	0
4	Sadiq Mohammad	Pak	41	11	98	0
5	V Kohli	Ind	101	11	84	0
6	MC Cowdrey	Eng	114	10	104	0
7	HP Tillakaratne	SL	83	10	25	0
8	Habibul Bashar	Ban	50	9	217	0
9	RB Kanhai	WI	79	9	85	0
11	CJ Barnett	Eng	20	8	93	0
12	MW Goodwin	Zim	19	8	69	0
13	Sabbir Rahman	Ban	11	7	98	0
14	MS Dhoni	Ind	90	7	67	0
15	AL Wadekar	Ind	37	7	55	0
16	Taufeeq Umar	Pak	44	7	44	0
17	RB Richardson	WI	86	7	18	0

It looks like Virat Kohli has given up on getting that elusive wicket, but Travis Head now plays as Australia's backup spinner, so he must get one soon, right?

The Most Test Cricket Innings Bowled With Under 10 Wickets

(Qualification: 25+ ib, -10 wickets)

		team	*tests*	*ib*	*wkts*	*rwi*
1	ML Jaisimha	Ind	39	51	9	521.95
2	S Chanderpaul	WI	164	43	9	468.74
3	RC Fredericks	WI	59	43	7	480.86
4	GC Smith	SA	116	37	8	511.61
5	Azhar Ali	Pak	94	37	8	358.99
6	RT Ponting	Aus	167	36	5	397.44
7	Mominul Haque	Ban	51	35	7	397.44
8	Yuvraj Singh	Ind	40	35	9	236.37
9	MP Vaughan	Eng	82	35	6	545.41
10	IJL Trott	Eng	52	33	5	528.00
11	MEK Hussey	Aus	79	32	7	199.81
12	MW Gatting	Eng	79	32	4	634.00
13	Younis Khan	Pak	118	31	9	187.89
14	Saleem Malik	Pak	103	30	5	496.80
15	SM Gavaskar	Ind	125	29	1	5974.00
16	M Leyland	Eng	41	27	6	438.75
17	Shoaib Mohammad	Pak	45	26	5	176.80
18	Nasir Hossain	Ban	19	25	8	172.65
19	MR Ramprakash	Eng	52	25	4	745.31

India's Motganhalli Jaisimha bowled some form of off-break. England's Kevin Pietersen would have been at number one on this list, with 58 innings bowled, but somehow he went and took a tenth wicket just before he was kicked out of the England team.

The Best Test Cricket All-Rounders

(Qualification: retired, 1000+ runs, 50+ wickets, RI 15+ runs higher than RWI)

		tests	*runs*	*ri (adj)*	*wkts*	*rwi (adj)*	*diff*
1	GS Sobers	93	8032	50.20	235	23.02	27.18
2	GA Faulkner	25	1754	37.31 (42.10)	82	13.93 (16.56)	25.54
3	Imran Khan	88	3807	30.21	362	8.94	21.27
4	KR Miller	55	2958	34.00	170	12.83	21.17
5	IT Botham	102	5200	32.29	383	12.45	19.84
6	G Giffen	31	1238	23.35 (34.49)	103	11.30 (15.20)	19.29
7	JM Gregory	24	1146	33.70	85	15.39	18.31
8	CL Cairns	62	3320	31.92	218	14.02	17.90
9	AW Greig	58	3599	38.69	141	21.23	17.46
10	JH Kallis	165	13206	47.50	291	30.27	17.23
11	TL Goddard	41	2516	32.25	123	15.98	16.27
12	RJ Hadlee	86	3124	23.31	431	7.75	15.56
13	MH Mankad	44	2109	29.29	162	13.96	15.33

The stats for all-rounders is simply the run differential between their RI and RWI. The greater the gap, the more effective the player. Another way to gauge an all-rounder is to divide the RI by the RWI (in which case Imran Khan would be the best, with 3.37, way ahead of anyone else), but this system favours the bowlers and punishes the batsmen. In the case of Garry Sobers, who was by far the best *batsman*-all-rounder, he would be equally rated with Jack

Gregory, which is not accurate of his value to a team. Under the differential system Sobers rightly takes the top position, and the great South African player Aubrey Faulkner is not far below him.

Not only was Sobers the leading batsman for his team, and the world, he could also open the bowling and later bowl left-arm spin. There has been a fair bit of modern opinion that the recently retired Jacques Kallis was the equal of, or better, than Sobers, judging only from their career numbers. They both seem close under the old tired system of "average":

	tests	*i*	*runs*	*ave*	*ib*	*runs*	*wkts*	*ave*
GS Sobers	93	160	8032	57.78	159	7999	235	34.03
JH Kallis	165	278	13206	55.48	270	9497	291	32.63

Since their bowling average was near-identical, it is assumed that they were of the same standard, but this doesn't take into account Sobers' higher rate of wicket taking (23.02 RWI to Kallis' 30.27). Only a simple viewing of their records reveals how much better Sobers was; Kallis played 64 more Tests and made 4,745 more runs, but took only 28 more wickets. Kallis' all-rounder differential was 13.90, a little more than half of what Sobers achieved.

Current Leading Test Cricket All-Rounders

(Qualification: active player, 1000+ runs, 50+ wickets, RI 15+ runs higher than RWI)

		team	*tests*	*runs*	*ri*	*wkts*	*rwi*	*diff*
1	Shakib Al Hasan	Ban	59	4029	36.06	215	14.41	22.44
2	RA Jadeja	Ind	59	2396	27.54	242	11.31	16.23

The Best ODI Batsmen

(Qualification: 50+ odis, 1000+ runs, 35+ RIRB)

		team	*odis*	*runs*	*ri*	*rb*	*rirb*
1	Babar Azam	Pak	86	4261	50.72	0.90	45.64
2	JM Bairstow	Eng	89	3498	43.18	1.05	45.33
3	V Kohli	Ind	260	12311	49.04	0.92	45.11
4	AB de Villiers	SA	228	9577	43.93	1.01	44.36
5	JJ Roy	Eng	98	3658	39.33	1.07	42.08
6	Q de Kock	SA	129	5658	43.86	0.95	41.66
7	Fakhar Zaman	Pak	56	2427	43.33	0.95	41.16
8	DA Warner	Aus	128	5455	43.29	0.95	41.12
9	HM Amla	SA	181	8113	45.57	0.88	40.10
10	S Dhawan	Ind	149	6284	43.04	0.93	40.02
11	GJ Maxwell	Aus	116	3230	30.47	1.25	38.08
12	JC Buttler	Eng	148	3872	31.47	1.18	37.13
13	RG Sharma	Ind	230	9283	41.62	0.89	37.04
14	JE Root	Eng	152	6109	43.02	0.86	36.99
15	IVA Richards	WI	187	6721	40.24	0.90	36.21
16	Zaheer Abbas	Pak	62	2572	42.86	0.84	36.00
17	F du Plessis	SA	143	5507	40.49	0.88	35.63
18	AJ Finch	Aus	135	5255	40.11	0.88	35.29
19	V Sehwag	Ind	251	8273	33.76	1.04	35.11
20	SR Tendulkar	Ind	463	18426	40.76	0.86	35.05

The Best ODI Bowlers

(Qualification: 50+ odis, 50+ wkts, -10 RWIRB)

		team	*odis*	*ib*	*runs*	*wkts*	*rwi*	*rb*	*rwirb*
1	J Garner	WI	98	98	2752	146	12.64	0.51	6.44
2	AME Roberts	WI	56	56	1771	87	13.09	0.56	7.33
3	DK Lillee	Aus	63	63	2145	103	12.73	0.59	7.51
4	SE Bond	NZ	82	80	3070	147	11.36	0.71	8.06
5	RJ Hadlee	NZ	115	112	3407	158	15.28	0.55	8.40
6	MA Holding	WI	102	102	3034	142	15.34	0.55	8.43
7	Saqlain Mushtaq	Pak	169	165	6275	288	12.47	0.71	8.85
8	AA Donald	SA	164	162	5926	272	12.97	0.69	8.94
9	GD McGrath	Aus	249	247	8354	380	14.28	0.64	9.13
10	CG Rackemann	Aus	52	52	1833	82	14.17	0.65	9.21
11	Saeed Ajmal	Pak	113	112	4182	184	13.82	0.69	9.53
12	M Muralitharan	SL	350	341	12326	534	14.73	0.65	9.57
13	BAW Mendis	SL	87	84	3324	152	12.08	0.80	9.66

The Best ODI All-Rounders

(Qualification: 50+ odis, 15+ RIRB, -30 RWIRB, +diff)

		team	*odis*	*runs*	*rirb*	*wkts*	*rwirb*	*diff*
1	A Flintoff	Eng	141	3394	24.47	169	12.52	11.95
2	Shakib Al Hasan	Ban	221	6755	26.50	285	16.67	9.83
3	IVA Richards	WI	187	6721	40.24	118	29.42	6.79
4	GS Chappell	Aus	74	2331	24.27	72	18.15	6.12
5	SR Watson	Aus	190	5757	30.65	168	25.28	5.37
6	AD Russell	WI	56	1034	28.60	70	24.25	4.35
7	Kapil Dev	Ind	225	3783	18.14	253	14.62	3.52
8	Imran Khan	Pak	175	3709	17.68	182	14.31	3.37
9	L Klusener	SA	171	3576	23.22	192	19.95	3.27
10	JH Kallis	SA	323	11550	27.28	269	26.42	0.86
11	JP Faulkner	Aus	69	1032	20.63	96	19.80	0.83
12	IT Botham	Eng	116	2113	15.74	145	14.93	0.81
13	Shahid Afridi	Pak	398	8064	25.56	395	25.02	0.54

The Best T20I Batsmen

(Qualification: 20+ innings, 40+ RIRB)

		team	*t20is*	*i*	*runs*	*ri*	*rb*	*rirb*
1	V Kohli	Ind	97	89	3296	37.03	1.37	50.73
2	Babar Azam	Pak	74	69	2686	38.92	1.29	50.20
3	KL Rahul	Ind	56	52	1831	35.21	1.42	49.99
4	DP Conway	NZ	20	17	602	35.41	1.39	49.21
5	DJ Malan	Eng	36	35	1239	35.40	1.37	48.49
6	AK Markram	SA	20	18	588	32.66	1.47	48.01
7	Mohammad Rizwan	Pak	56	45	1662	36.93	1.28	47.27
8	KP Pietersen	Eng	37	36	1176	32.66	1.41	46.05
9	E Lewis	WI	50	49	1423	29.04	1.55	45.01
10	AJ Finch	Aus	89	89	2741	30.79	1.44	44.33
11	C Munro	NZ	65	62	1724	27.80	1.56	43.36
12	BB McCullum	NZ	71	70	2140	30.57	1.36	41.57
13	MJ Guptill	NZ	112	108	3299	30.54	1.36	41.53

14	F du Plessis	SA	50	50	1528	30.56	1.34	40.95
15	CH Gayle	WI	61	57	1656	29.05	1.40	40.67
16	DA Warner	Aus	88	88	2554	29.02	1.40	40.62
17	Q de Kock	SA	61	61	1827	29.95	1.35	40.43

The Best T20I Bowlers

(Qualification: 20+ innings, -17 RWIRB)

		team	*t20is*	*ib*	*runs*	*wkts*	*rwi*	*rb*	*rwirb*
1	PWH de Silva	SL	35	33	784	57	7.96	1.06	8.43
2	BAW Mendis	SL	39	39	952	66	8.52	1.07	9.11
3	Kuldeep Yadav	Ind	24	23	605	41	8.27	1.17	9.67
4	Imran Tahir	SA	38	38	948	63	9.07	1.12	10.15
5	Nasum Ahmed	Ban	20	20	416	26	12.30	1.07	13.16
6	GP Swann	Eng	39	38	859	51	12.54	1.06	13.29
7	Al-Amin Hossain	Ban	31	29	730	43	11.44	1.18	13.49
8	Saeed Ajmal	Pak	64	63	1516	85	13.21	1.06	14.00
9	Umar Gul	Pak	60	60	1443	85	11.97	1.19	14.24
10	YS Chahal	Ind	21	21	646	35	11.07	1.32	14.61
11	DW Steyn	SA	47	47	1175	64	13.47	1.15	15.49
12	Abdur Razzak	Ban	34	33	838	44	14.28	1.14	16.27
13	JR Hazlewood	Aus	27	27	772	40	13.02	1.25	16.27
14	IS Sodhi	NZ	26	25	696	36	13.42	1.23	16.50
15	MA Starc	Aus	35	35	911	47	14.43	1.15	16.59
16	LM Jongwe	Zim	22	21	611	33	11.77	1.41	16.59
17	JP Faulkner	Aus	24	24	684	36	12.66	1.32	16.71
18	DL Vettori	NZ	34	34	748	38	17.60	0.95	16.72
19	RE van der Merwe	SA	24	23	546	29	14.92	1.13	16.85

The Best T20I All-Rounders

(Qualification: 20+ innings batted and bowled, rirb rwirb +diff)

		team	*t20is*	*runs*	*rirb*	*wkts*	*rwirb*	*diff*
1	Yuvraj Singh	Ind	58	1177	31.37	28	23.07	8.30
2	Shakib Al Hasan	Ban	96	1908	23.89	119	17.61	6.28
3	SR Watson	Aus	58	1462	37.84	48	32.04	5.80

WORLD XIs

To be selected for all-time world cricket elevens, a player must have completed ten years for his country in Tests, and be retired from the game at the highest level. The teams consist of two openers, three top order batsmen, two all-rounders, one wicket-keeper, three bowlers—usually one spinner and two fast. This is a bias-free selection with the players' performances on the field being all that matters.

The Openers

Batsmen who open the innings have always had a problem with the traditional average statistic, as they will record far less not-outs than the others. With the RI system there is no confusion. There are only around forty players who were regular openers with an RI of over 40.00. Usually a team's best batsmen will shy away from facing the new ball, which is probably better for the team, but some great players were keen to bat straight away, such as WG Grace and Jack Hobbs. The only weakness in Hobbs' batting was that he became bored after getting a hundred, and thought that someone else should have a go. Blessed with perfect technique that no one has bettered, Hobbs made his runs on poor pitches and made more hundreds than anyone else in first-class cricket history.

The Batsmen

Protected from the hostility of the new ball, the best players usually played at number three or four. Every period of the game has seen its share of great batsmen. Cricket is all about how many runs are scored, so a batsman who is dull and plodding, who gets his runs in a professional manner, is of more value to his team than a player who is flamboyant and elegant, or flashy and egotistical. We would, however, all much rather watch an entertaining and graceful player, who can hit the ball like no other, who leaves memories implanted in the mind. The flowing hook, the savage pull, the crisp on-drive, the unbelievable cover-drive, the brutal cut—these are what brings in the crowds and has them cheering. The exciting shots played by Victor Trumper were remembered a long time after he died. Or the joyful flamboyance that went into every shot played by Garry Sobers. The almost sleepy way in which David Gower could waft the ball through the cover field defied belief and made people think he wasn't really trying. The high bat-swing, exceptional balance and perfect execution by Brian Lara made batting look easy. But Lara had something else, his desire to make runs, and then make more runs. Like Lara, WG Grace and Don Bradman, two of the very best batsman in cricket history, shared the one thing in common: they hated getting out—really hated it. If they made a hundred runs they wanted another hundred, and then a hundred more. Such players are a rare breed.

The All-Rounders

All-rounders come in two types, one who is more of a batsman, to bat at six, and one who is more of a bowler, to bat at seven. Some all-rounders are no more than "useful" at either batting or bowling (say an RI of 23.00 for a bowler, or an RWI of 23.00 for a batsman), and most will favour one skill over the other. To be classed as a "batting" all-rounder, the RI should be over 33.00, and the RWI at, say 30.00. To be classed a "bowling" all-rounder then the RWI would be that of a genuine bowler, such as 15.00, and his RI around 20.00. This is not as easy as it looks. There are currently only nine players in Test history with an RI of 28.00 or over and an RWI of less than 20.00. It is usually accepted that the best all-rounder was Garry Sobers, but he was a "batting" all-rounder, since he was one of the few players who achieved an RI of over 50.00. Of all the players to make over 8,000 Test runs, only three did so at over 50.00 an innings (the others were Brian Lara and Kumar Sangakkara), but Sobers was also a bowler of both pace and spin, with an RWI of 23.02.

The Wicket-Keeper

The selection of wicket-keeper presents a difficulty. There was a time when a player like Bert Strudwick, who had a career RI of 5.47 (and a first-class RI of 7.71), was the first choice for his country, but any player like that today would not get beyond club level, no matter how good a gloveman he was. The criteria for selection is that of genuine wicket-keepers, not batsmen who might be "handy" with the gloves, or fancy divers and tumblers—great keepers rarely dive because their feet are always moving better than their hands. What should the balance be, a useful batsman and great keeper, or a great keeper and okay batsman? Alec Stewart was very successful behind the stumps, but he was a better batsman when playing only as an opener. Jack Russell, who played at the same time as Stewart, was one of the best (perhaps the best) keepers of modern times, and yet he was kept out of the England team due to the belief that his specialist skills weren't needed and that his batting would fail. When Russell did get to play Test cricket his RI was a very respectable 21.80, which showed that he should have played more for England for the cricket world to enjoy.

The Spinners

The most difficult art to master, imparting spin on the ball to deceive the batsman, is a subtle skill that usually needs the co-operation of the playing surface. Wilfred Rhodes reckoned that the ball only needed a small amount of deviation to get the edge of a bat. Someone who could turn it a yard, and Shane Warne was the best at that, would usually turn it too much and miss the bat. But Warne also had the skill of getting inside the head of the batsman, to get him out that way. Others could bowl balls that turned differently with fast actions that looked the same, such as Abdul Qadir and Muttiah Muralitharan.

The Fast Bowlers

An effective bowler at the highest level will need to have a decent amount of pace. Those rare few who could bowl as fast as humanly possible, such as Harold Larwood, Frank Tyson, Jeff Thomson and Michael Holding, did so for only a brief time in their careers. There must be more in the bowling armoury, such as the ability to cut and swing the ball, to be accurate and canny enough to bowl to the batsman's weakness. Pace bowlers who combined such skills with the gift of pace, such as Malcolm Marshall, Dennis Lillee, Richard Hadlee and Imran Khan, were far more effective.

The World XI

	tests	*runs*	*ri (adj)*	*wkts*	*rwi (adj)*
WG Grace	22	1098	30.50 (41.61)	9	37.87 (57.93)
JB Hobbs	61	5410	53.03 (55.44)		
* DG Bradman	52	6996	87.45		
GA Headley	22	2190	54.75		
WR Hammond	85	7249	51.77	83	50.09
GS Sobers	93	8032	50.20	235	23.02
Imran Khan	88	3807	30.21	362	8.94
† APE Knott	95	4389	29.45		
RJ Hadlee	86	3124	23.31	431	7.75
SF Barnes	27	242	6.20 (11.20)	189	4.34 (5.66)
M Muralitharan	132	1259	7.77	795	6.50

WG Grace (1848-1915) is selected not from his Test performances, but what he did on the cricket field prior to their invention. He was known as WG, the Doctor, the Champion; but just Gilbert to friends and family. Most photographs show him overweight and well past his prime, but in his younger days he was a supreme athlete. Standing 6'2", he dominated most other players. His peak years were 1868-1876 (aged 20-28), when he played 181 first-class games and made 15,629 runs at an RI of 52.27 (adj 72.52). He made 54 centuries in that time with a highest score of 344, the highest score ever seen. This was all on poor pitches. It should also be noted that when he made his fiftieth century, it was the hundredth century from all recorded first-class cricket history. Grace also loved to bowl, and when he wasn't making all those runs in that time period of 1868-1876, he was taking 837 wickets. He was brilliant at making catches and could throw the ball a very long way. In his first-class debut in 1865, playing for *Gentleman of the South* against *Players of the North*, and bowling accurate medium pace, he took 5-44 and 8-40, against the best professionals in the game, and he was sixteen years old. His last game was in 1908, at the age of 59. His first-class career spanned 44 seasons and 870 matches. His final aggregate was 54,211 runs with 124 centuries, and 2,809 wickets. That puts him fifth on the all-time first-class run list, and tenth on the all-time wickets list. Of course, he was a success at Test cricket, but he did not play until the age of 31. By the age of 38, when most modern players would have retired, he had a record of 8 Tests, 469 runs, 39.08 RI (adj

54.08), and an RWI of 33.28 (adj). There really wasn't anything more that one person could have done in the game. The more his career is scrutinised, the more incredible it becomes. To write him off as not a great player is ignorance. There has never been anyone like Grace and it's doubtful we will ever see anyone close to him again.

Jack Hobbs (1882-1963) could have retired from Tests at the age of 46, when his RI peaked at 56.04 (adj 59.03), but he continued to play for England for another year. People who saw Hobbs play said that he was better as a younger man, before World War One, and that his technique was better than anyone else in cricket history. He was certainly the greatest batsman on very bad pitches. No one has ever made more first-class runs (61,760) or scored more centuries (199).

Don Bradman's (1908-2001) astronomical RI is beyond dispute, since his first-class RI was an equally amazing 83.03. His peak was in 1932, by which time he had played 19 Tests and made 2,695 runs at 103.65. It is difficult to comprehend how anyone could average over a hundred every time they batted. Had Bradman not retired at age 39, but rather had carried on until the tour of England 1953 (which is not unreasonable, since the last Test finished eight days before his 45th birthday), his record would have surely decreased, but not enough to put much of a dent in it. Australia played just 25 Tests in that time, and if he performed far below his own standards, and say had a poor RI of 20.00, his career RI would have been 64.96 which would still place him as number one. His fielding and captaincy were also always brilliant.

George Headley (1909-1983) was a stunning mixture of quickness, elegance and power, matched with total fearlessness. Right from his first Test at age 20, he was the best batsmen in the team, and most of the time he had to carry a weak batting line-up. The Australians liked to call him "the black Bradman," but he was a far more exciting player to watch than Bradman. At the age of 30 he had played 19 Tests, made 2,135 runs at 61.00. He didn't play again until after the Second World War, when he was 39. His first-class RI is the third-best ever (again, behind Bradman), at 60.49. When playing for Jamaica, he made 2,848 runs at 73.02. He last represented the West Indies at the age of 45. It is a tragedy that he is the least well known of all the great players.

Wally Hammond (1903-1965) also should have retired before the war, when his RI was 54.19. After the war, aged 45, he made 366 in 13 innings (at 28.15), severely dropping his career RI. He was labelled as a batting successor of Grace, as he played for the same county. A classically correct batsman, Hammond could murder the ball all around the wicket, but particularly through the covers, in a style similar to Viv Richards. On one famous occasion, after a day's play during a county match, Hammond overheard his teammates complaining about the state of the pitch. He told them to follow him back out to the middle, where he said the pitch was not poor and that the ball could be played with a broom handle, which he then proceeded to show them. Hammond also loved to bowl, and had nippy medium pace, and he was a great catcher in the slips. One of his biggest fans was a young Len Hutton, who studied everything about him to try to emulate him.

Garry Sobers (1936) excelled in every sport he tried; a natural and highly gifted athlete, he was a marvel in the field, and able to bowl left-arm bowl pace or wrist spin. But the one thing that Sobers excelled at more than any other was in the way that he batted. His shots were played with a full and flowing arch of the bat, like that of a golfer, with the bat landing flat against his back, and balls that careened to the fence usually did so all along the ground. When he decided to go in the air, he could hit the ball a mile, as proven by his legendary six sixes in one over. On that occasion, the game was heading for a draw and the bowler changed to spin. Sobers hit the first five balls over the fence, but the last one was something special. He actually managed to hit a slow-paced half-volley completely out of the ground. Sobers first played for the West Indies at the age of seventeen, with little success, as his RI as a teenager was a mere 23.46; the rest of his career his RI was 52.96, with 7,680 runs. When he was in his twenties he made 4,565 glorious runs at an amazing 57.78. His bowling RWI at that time was 27.17 from 107 wickets.

Pakistan's **Imran Khan** (1952) could bowl genuinely fast and still be accurate, and he could bat with all the poise and correctness of a top-order player. He was a commanding cricketer with a somewhat regal air, often causing division within the Pakistan team. His stats show that he was the best bowling-all-rounder, as no other player in Test history has an RI over 25.00 and an RWI under 10.00. After retiring from cricket, he became heavily involved with social charities in Pakistan, founded his own political party, and became the Prime Minister of Pakistan.

There has not been a better wicket-keeper than **Allan Knott** (1946). The great BBC commentator Brian Johnston, who closely followed cricket since the 1920s, said that he never saw Knott make a mistake. There was, however, one occasion when Knott dropped a catch, and one of his teammates reacted with, "Now we know you're human." Knott was obsessed with his fitness and liked to constantly exercise on the field of play. He was also very capable with the bat.

Sydney Barnes (1873-1967) is without question the greatest bowler the game has ever seen, and it is almost certain that we will never see his like again. He bowled at good pace and spun the bowl with very powerful fingers, causing it to sharply turn either way off the pitch. The amount of spin achieved by Shane Warne in his prime was reminiscent of Barnes, but Barnes bowled much faster. His first-class debut was in 1894, against WG Grace, which would have been something special, but unfortunately the game was ruined by rain and the two legends never faced each other again. A fiercely stubborn man who hated conforming to the ruling authorities, most of Barnes' early cricket was played in obscurity. It wasn't until he was 28 that he had his break, when he was chosen for his Lancashire teammate's Archie MacLaren's touring team of 1901-02 to South Africa. His first-class record at that time was only 7 games and 13 wickets, but on the tour he took 41 wickets in 6 games. Aside from playing two full first-class seasons for Lancashire (1902 and 1903), most of his top-level cricket was in touring Australia and South Africa, where he was spectacular. The 1913-14 tour of South Africa, Barnes, aged 40, went on a bowling rampage, and took 104 wickets from 12 games. He played 11 first-class games in his fifties, up until the season of 1930, against teams touring England, and took 60 wickets at an RWI of 5.55, with a best bowling performance of 8-41. Even more remarkably, he continued to play English League and club cricket well into his sixties, where he scared every opposition team. Even then, opponents needed to have not two batsmen padded up and ready to go in to bat, but *four.*

Richard Hadlee (1951) is the only genuine fast bowler to ever have an RWI under 8.00. His peak years (1985-86 to 1989-90) were at an age when most fast bowlers retired, in his mid-to-late thirties, and he took 165 wickets in 30 Tests at an RWI of 5.64. What is all the more remarkable is that he had little support from the other New Zealand bowlers or fielders, particularly in the slips. Hadlee had supreme guile and could move the ball either way off the pitch or through the air, seemingly at will, plus retaining the ability to bowl very fast. He was deadly off his perfectly executed short run, in which his footsteps were exactly the same for each delivery. A single-minded professional, Hadlee made a thorough study of opposition batsmen and loved exploiting any weakness. It is doubtful that most New Zealanders had much of an idea of how great he was. Annoyed at the prevalent lack of professionalism in his home country, Hadlee played a season for Tasmania in 1979-80, to learn Australian cricketing ruthlessness, and it worked.

Muttiah Muralitharan (1972) (also spelled as Muralidaran), is the only modern-day bowler, of any type, with a career RWI under 7.00. His fierce competitiveness was hidden beneath great humility. He started as a useful off-break bowler, but when he developed a "doosra" that went the other way, he became world-class. Hated by the Australians due to idiot umpires thinking that he was cheating, which damaged his reputation, many ill-informed people still believe that his bowling action was suspect. It wasn't.

The Second-Best World XI

	tests	*runs*	*ri (adj)*	*wkts*	*rwi (adj)*
BA Richards	4	508	72.57		
* H Sutcliffe	54	4555	54.22		
RG Pollock	23	2256	55.02	4	165.75
ED Weekes	48	4455	55.00		
KC Sangakkara	134	12400	53.21		
GA Faulkner	25	1754	37.31 (42.10)	82	13.93 (16.56)
KR Miller	55	2958	34.00	170	12.86
†JM Blackham	35	800	12.90 (26.93)		
MD Marshall	81	1810	16.91	376	8.40
CV Grimmett	37	557	11.14	216	7.50
WJ O'Reilly	27	410	10.51	144	7.52

South Africa's **Barry Richards** (1945) enjoyed destroying bowlers with a devastating array of shots, especially with the cover drive. Unlike other batsmen who counted where the fielders were stationed, Richards counted the gaps. It is difficult to judge where this great South African batsman fits into the list of great players, but the fact that he never failed at any level, and played until he was 37, indicates that he was undoubtedly one of the very best. He played only four Tests before South Africa was locked out of international cricket. Showing that his performances in the four Tests were no fluke, his innings against various "Invitation XIs" in the 1970s gave him an RI of 77.42. His career first-class RI was also an impressive 49.23.

England's **Herbert Sutcliffe** (1894-1978) was a patient and skilful opening batsman who could also score as quickly as anyone, and he had a great hook shot. A native of Yorkshire, he was always well groomed and mannered. He formed a great batting partnership with Jack Hobbs, and played for England until he was aged 40.

South Africa's **Graeme Pollock** (1944) was one of the greatest left-handed batsmen.

Tall and domineering, with a bat held high as the bowler ran in, he hit the ball with great power, and was confident enough to not worry about getting his feet in the right place. He made a first-class hundred at the age of 16, and a Test hundred at 19. He played for his country until he was 43, and one of his last games was against a Test-strength Australian team, and he made 144.

Everton Weekes (1925-2020) finished playing Tests for West Indies at the age of 33 because of injury. Short, stocky, fast on his feet and always balanced, Weekes hit the ball with tremendous power. Someone once said that being on the receiving end of a Weekes hundred felt like you had been beaten with a stick. He was named after the English football team.

Sri Lankan **Kumar Sangakkara** (1977) was a left-handed genius who never tired of batting. No bowler bettered him, and many times he formed big partnerships with fellow batting genius Mahela Jayawardene. He was also a very accomplished wicket-keeper. An unassuming and humble man, Sangakkara's career was entirely devoid of controversy, and he was never abusive to another player.

South Africa's **Aubrey Faulkner** (1881-1930) was a classical middle-order batsman and accurate leg break and googlie bowler. He was part of the great South African leg spinning quartet, with Reginald Schwarz, Bert Vogler and Gordon White. A tall and solid man, Faulkner suffered from malaria contracted during his time as a soldier in World War One. He retired in 1912, but was asked to strengthen the numbers of a weak South African touring team to England in 1924, at the age of 42 (a game in which they were thrashed). Had it not been for the one Test in which he underperformed, his record would be 38.15 RI (adj 43.15), and 13.07 RWI (adj 14.38), which would make his all-rounder differential 28.77, better than Sobers' 27.18.

Australia's **Keith Miller** (1919-2004) was a gifted cricketer and natural all-rounder; a genuine batsman and a genuine bowler. Tall and strong, he had movie-star looks and demeanour. He was no fan of rules or authority, and did as he pleased on the field. With his carefree attitude, he was known to still be deciding what to bowl as he was running in to deliver it.

Jack Blackham (1854-1932) was the first great wicket-keeper/batsman, and was Australia's first choice keeper for seventeen years. Called "the prince of wicket-keepers," he preferred to stand up to the stumps to the fast bowlers, and he became the standard for all Test keepers to live up to. His batting was also outstanding for his time, and he could bat anywhere in the order.

Malcolm Marshall (1958-1999) was the greatest and deadliest of all the outstanding West Indian fast bowlers. Not a tall man like his contemporaries, Marshall's deliveries would skid instead of bounce, and with his electric pace and ability to produce late swing both ways—it is remarkable that he didn't kill anyone on the cricket field. He loved to bat, and not even a broken hand stopped him from thrashing the ball against a hapless England in 1984.

Clarrie Grimmett (1891-1980) became the world record holder for Test wickets. New Zealand born, he went to Australia after being passed over for national team honours, and became one of the best bowlers ever seen. He did the impossible, by being very accurate with his leg spin, so much so that he reportedly never bowled a wide or a no ball for his entire first-class career. A short man with a low delivery, and always bowling with his cap on, he had many different spinners, and every one accurate. When he realised that his leg spinner produced a finger snap, he learned to snap his left hand fingers to fool the batsman. He played Tests until he was 43, but wanted to play longer because he considered that he was still getting better. He played Australian state cricket until he was 49.

Australia's **Bill O'Reilly** (1905-1992) was one of the most fiery spin bowlers to ever play. Entirely different from Grimmett, they complimented each other well, and it was unfortunate that they did not play more together. A tall man and nicknamed "Tiger", he bowled wrist spin with an action of a pace bowler. His stock leg break could miss off when pitching past leg, and his googly would rear up at the batsman.

They were the best. Now for the worst:

The Worst World XI, 80+ Tests

	team	*tests*	*runs*	*ri*	*wkts*	*rwi*
JG Wright	NZ	82	5334	36.04		
MS Atapattu	SL	90	5502	35.26		
JM Bairstow	Eng	83	4801	32.43		
Mushfiqur Rahim	Ban	80	4932	33.32		
* A Ranatunga	SL	93	5105	32.93	16	227.50
CL Hooper	WI	102	5762	33.30	114	62.85
† MS Dhoni	Ind	90	4876	33.86		
DL Vettori	NZ	112	4523	26.29	361	17.50
WPUJC Vaas	SL	111	3089	19.06	355	16.16
Z Khan	Ind	92	1231	9.69	311	17.47
I Sharma	Ind	105	785	5.52	311	19.58

Eighty Tests are a lot, and you would think that only the best players would ever get to play that many. Most of these players, however, were playing because they both had experience and there was no one else around putting their hand up.

This team is made up of players such as the massively talented but entirely underperforming West Indian **Carl Hooper** (1966), New Zealand's perennially worried **John Wright** (1954), Sri Lanka's, **Marvan Atapattu** (1970), England's batsman and occasional wicket-keeper **Jonny Bairstow** (1989) (who is better off at the 50-over stuff), Bangladesh's batsman and occasional wicket-keeper **Mushfiqur Rahim** (1988), rotund batsman **Arjuna Ranatunga** (1963) and their best fast bowler **Chaminda Vaas** (1974), India's ordinary wicket-keeper, yet dependable batsmen, **MS Dhoni** (1981), decent fast bowler **Zaheer Khan** (1978), and overrated fast bowler **Ishant Sharma** (1988), and New Zealand's Mr Mediocrity himself, left-arm spinner and strange batsman, **Daniel Vettori** (1979).

The Worst World XI, 50+ Tests

	team	*tests*	*runs*	*ri*	*wkts*	*rwi*
RS Mahanama	SL	52	2576	28.94		
GW Flower	Zim	67	3457	28.10	25	147.55
MR Ramprakash	Eng	52	2350	25.54	4	745.31
KR Rutherford	NZ	56	2465	24.89		
Mohammad Ashraful	Ban	61	2737	23.00	21	193.08
TE Bailey	Eng	61	2290	25.16	132	21.02
†JC Buttler	Eng	57	1836	29.07		
* R Illingworth	Eng	61	1836	20.40	122	25.57
JE Emburey	Eng	64	1713	17.84	147	26.90
RAS Lakmal	SL	70	934	8.56	171	25.99
FH Edwards	WI	55	394	4.47	165	22.26

There was a time when only the most outstanding players reached fifty tests. Now even the most amazingly mediocre player can reach that milestone. Several of these players actually captained their teams. Guess they didn't have much else to do.

England's **Trevor Bailey** (1923-2011), an all-rounder who loved to bat without making any runs, **John Emburey** (1952), an off break spinner whose height should have helped him more, who had a face with a permanent sad expression; off break spinner **Ray Illingworth** (1932-2021) who thought he was a bit of an all-rounder, **Mark Ramprakash** (1969) who thought he was great, and perhaps the worst keeper to ever play a Test, **Jos Buttler** (1990), who has an RI of 26.74 when not playing as a specialist batsman.

Sri Lanka's **Roshan Mahanama** (1966) didn't do an awful lot. Zimbabwe's **Grant Flower** (1970) was a regular despite his poor record. New Zealand's tense **Ken Rutherford** (1965). Bangladesh's awful **Mohammad Ashraful** (1984) who was given far too many chances. Sri Lanka's hardy swing bowler **Suranga Lakmal** (1987), and the slinging West Indies fast bowler **Fidel Edwards** (1982).

The Worst World XI, 30+ Tests

	tests	*runs*	*ri*	*wkts*	*rwi*
Javed Omar	40	1720	21.50		
*JM Brearley	39	1442	21.84		
SD Hope	38	1726	23.97		
JM Parker	36	1498	23.77		
Mohammad Ashraful	61	2737	23.00	21	193.08
V Pollard	32	1266	21.45	40	56.74
HDPK Dharmasena	31	868	17.01	69	32.49
†PR Downton	30	785	16.35		
Mohammad Sami	36	487	8.69	85	40.95
Shahadat Hossain	38	521	7.55	72	43.17
DBL Powell	34	391	7.24	79	39.03

There is the Bangladesh opener **Javed Omar** (1976), who started well, with 62 and an unbeaten 85 in his first Test, England's astute captain **Mike Brearley** (1942), and batsman **Mohammad Ashraful**, and fast bowler **Shahadat Hossain** (1986). Sri Lanka's and off spinner **Kumar Dharmasena** (1971) who is better at being an umpire (not really). Current West Indian hopeful **Shai Hope** (1993). New Zealand's **John Parker** (1951), and the spinning all-rounder **Vic Pollard** (1945) who claimed that he was just as good an all-rounder as Richard Hadlee. England's **Paul Downton** (1957) was an average wicket keeper. Plus Pakistan's random fast bowler **Mohammad Sami** (1981) and the West Indies fast bowler **Daren Powell** (1978).

The Worst World XI, 10+ Tests

	tests	*runs*	*ri*	*wkts*	*rwi*
MH Dekker	14	333	15.13		
LSM Miller	13	346	13.84		
J Mubarak	13	385	16.72		
NH Fairbrother	10	219	14.60		
Alok Kapali	17	584	17.17	6	374.17
JT Sparling	11	229	11.45	5	130.80
† CMW Read	15	360	15.65		
ML Nkala	10	187	12.46	11	90.12
EAR de Silva	10	185	11.56	8	242.10
CS Nayudu	11	147	7.73	2	1077.00
Rubel Hossain	27	265	5.63	36	93.82

Ten Tests is more than a trial run, it's when the selectors have decided you are going to succeed and they leave you in the team to prove them right, and … oops.

New Zealand's opener **Lawrie Miller** (1923-1996), and spinning all-rounder **John Sparling** (1938). Sri Lanka's leg spinner **Asoka de Silva** (1956) and batsman **Jehan Mubarak** (1981), who was born in the United States of America. England's **Neil Fairbrother** (1963) and average keeper **Chris Read** (1978). Zimbabwe's opener **Mark Dekker** (1969) and medium pace bowler **Mlueki Nkala** (1981). Bangladesh's wrist spinner all-rounder **Alok Kapali** (1984) and right-arm slinger **Rubel Hossain** (1990). India's leg break and googlie spinner **CS Nayudu** (1914-2002), who never had any success at Test level, but had more than enough chances in a career that lasted a staggering eighteen years.

The World ODI XI (100+ odis)

	team	*odis*	*runs*	*rb*	*rirb*	*wkts*	*rb*	*rwirb*
DA Warner	Aus	128	5455	0.95	41.12			
IVA Richards	WI	187	6721	0.90	36.21	118	0.74	29.42
V Kohli	Ind	260	12311	0.92	45.11	4	1.03	2054.85
† AB de Villiers	SA	228	9577	1.01	44.36			
Shakib Al Hasan	Ban	209	6436	0.82	26.78	266	0.74	17.02
A Flintoff	Eng	141	3394	0.88	24.47	169	0.73	12.52
Kapil Dev	Ind	225	3783	0.95	18.14	253	0.61	14.62
Imran Khan	Pak	175	3709	0.72	17.68	182	0.64	14.31
RJ Hadlee	NZ	115	1751	0.75	13.39	158	0.55	8.40
MA Holding	WI	102	282	0.74	4.96	142	0.55	8.43
Saqlain Mushtaq	Pak	169	711	0.49	3.55	288	0.71	8.85

The Second-Best World ODI XI (100+ odis)

	team	*odis*	*runs*	*rb*	*rirb*	*wkts*	*rb*	*rwirb*
S Dhawan	Ind	149	6284	0.93	40.02			
V Sehwag	Ind	251	8273	1.04	35.11	96	0.87	53.09
HM Amla	SA	181	8113	0.88	40.10			
† Q de Kock	SA	129	5658	0.95	41.66			
GJ Maxwell	Aus	116	3230	1.25	38.08	51	0.94	88.21
SR Watson	Aus	190	5757	0.90	30.65	168	0.82	25.28
Shakib Al Hasan	Ban	221	6755	0.82	26.50	285	0.74	16.67
Shahid Afridi	Pak	398	8064	1.17	25.56	395	0.77	25.02
IT Botham	Eng	116	2113	0.79	15.74	145	0.66	14.93
M Muralitharan	SL	350	674	0.77	3.20	534	0.65	9.57
AA Donald	SA	164	95	0.34	0.80	272	0.69	8.94

The World T20I XI (50+ t20is)

	team	*t20is*	*runs*	*rb*	*rirb*	*wkts*	*rb*	*rwirb*
KL Rahul	Ind	56	1831	1.42	49.99			
E Lewis	WI	50	1423	1.55	45.01			
Babar Azam	Pak	74	2686	1.29	50.20			
V Kohli	Ind	97	3296	1.37	50.73	4	1.35	200.47
† Mohammad Rizwan	Pak	56	1662	1.28	47.27			
GJ Maxwell	Aus	84	1982	1.54	39.63	34	1.24	56.38
SR Watson	Aus	58	1462	1.45	37.84	48	1.27	32.04
Shakib Al Hasan	Ban	96	1908	1.19	23.89	119	1.11	17.61
Umar Gul	Pak	60	165	1.05	6.41	85	1.19	14.24
Saeed Ajmal	Pak	64	91	1.05	4.14	85	1.06	14.00

COUNTRY XIs

The following is the records for each Test nation and the best team selections per decade for each Test nation. In most cases there is the best eleven and second eleven, plus the worst players who have played more than thirty Tests, and the worst who have played more than ten.

ENGLAND

For so long they were the inventors and controllers of the laws of the game, and for years they played with a superior attitude. They were shocked when the Australians beat their best team in 1882 (in which the joke was that English cricket was claimed to have died and the ashes taken to Australia; thus starting the tradition of the two teams playing for the Ashes). Over the years the interest in representing their country faded, and from the 1980s it was seen as a burden by many top players.

Top Test Batsmen for England

(2000+ runs, 35.00+ RI)

		tests	*runs*	*ri (adj)*
1	JB Hobbs	61	5410	53.03 (55.44)
2	H Sutcliffe	54	4555	54.22
3	KF Barrington	82	6806	51.95
4	WR Hammond	85	7249	51.77
5	L Hutton	79	6971	50.51
6	JE Root	117	9889	45.78
7	KP Pietersen	104	8181	45.19
8	DCS Compton	78	5807	44.32
9	ER Dexter	62	4502	44.13
10	AN Cook	161	12472	42.85
11	PBH May	66	4537	42.80
12	M Leyland	41	2764	42.52
13	EH Hendren	51	3525	42.46
14	G Boycott	108	8114	42.04
15	GA Gooch	118	8900	41.39
16	IJL Trott	52	3835	41.23
17	DL Amiss	50	3612	41.04
18	ME Trescothick	76	5825	40.73
19	MC Cowdrey	114	7624	40.55
20	JH Edrich	77	5138	40.45
21	DI Gower	117	8231	40.34
22	TW Graveney	79	4882	39.69
23	AJ Strauss	100	7037	39.53
24	C Washbrook	37	2569	38.92
25	MP Vaughan	82	5719	38.90

26	WJ Edrich	39	2440	38.73
27	AW Greig	58	3599	38.69
28	RA Smith	62	4236	37.82
29	IR Bell	118	7727	37.69
30	GP Thorpe	100	6744	37.67
31	PD Collingwood	68	4259	37.03
32	PE Richardson	34	2061	36.80
33	MA Atherton	115	7728	36.45
34	AJ Stewart	133	8463	36.01
35	BL D'Oliveira	44	2484	35.48
36	FE Woolley	64	3283	33.50 (35.13)

Top Test Bowlers for England

(100+ wkts, -20.00 RWI)

		tests	*wkts*	*ave*	*rwi (adj)*
1	SF Barnes	27	189	16.43	4.34 (5.66)
2	C Blythe	19	100	18.63	6.89 (8.74)
3	FS Trueman	67	307	21.57	8.92
4	JC Laker	46	193	21.24	9.46
5	AV Bedser	51	236	24.89	9.70
6	R Peel	20	101	16.98	5.88 (10.13)
7	JH Wardle	28	102	20.39	10.39
8	MW Tate	39	155	26.16	11.47
9	D Gough	58	229	28.39	11.77
10	ARC Fraser	46	177	27.32	12.19
11	JA Snow	49	202	26.66	12.27
12	H Verity	40	144	24.37	12.35
13	IT Botham	102	383	28.40	12.45
14	JB Statham	70	252	24.84	12.71
15	RGD Willis	90	325	25.20	12.79
16	GP Swann	60	255	29.96	12.80
17	GAR Lock	49	174	25.58	12.93
18	JM Anderson	169	640	26.58	13.04
19	DL Underwood	86	297	25.83	13.13
20	AR Caddick	62	234	29.91	13.42
21	GR Dilley	41	138	29.76	14.01
22	DG Cork	37	131	29.81	14.10
23	SCJ Broad	152	537	27.80	14.49
24	MJ Hoggard	67	248	30.50	15.004
25	GG Arnold	34	115	28.29	15.005
26	CM Old	46	143	28.11	15.92
27	ST Finn	36	125	30.40	16.05
28	SJ Harmison	62	222	31.94	16.25
29	DA Allen	39	122	30.97	16.50
30	MS Panesar	50	167	34.71	17.66
31	PAJ DeFreitas	44	140	33.57	18.22
32	FJ Titmus	53	153	32.22	18.95

Top Test All-Rounders for England

(1000+ runs, 50+ wkts, RI higher than RWI)

		tests	*runs*	*ri (adj)*	*wkts*	*rwi (adj)*	*diff*
1	IT Botham	102	5200	32.29	383	12.45	19.84
2	AW Greig	58	3599	38.69	141	21.23	17.46
3	MW Tate	39	1198	23.03	155	11.47	11.56
4	BA Stokes	79	5061	34.66	174	23.25	11.41
5	A Flintoff	78	3795	29.64	219	20.55	9.09
6	W Rhodes	58	2325	23.72 (27.65)	127	19.10 (22.09)	5.56
7	GP Swann	60	1370	18.02	255	12.80	5.22
8	MM Ali	64	2914	26.25	195	21.05	5.20
9	TE Bailey	61	2290	25.16	132	21.02	4.14
10	CR Woakes	45	1675	22.63	130	20.09	2.54
11	ER Dexter	62	4502	44.13	66	42.33	1.80
12	WR Hammond	85	7249	51.77	83	50.09	1.68
13	SCJ Broad	152	3412	15.23	537	14.49	0.74
14	FJ Titmus	53	1449	19.06	153	18.95	0.11

The Top 10 ODI Batsmen for England

(50+ odis, 1000+ runs)

		odis	*runs*	*ri*	*rb*	*rirb*
1	JM Bairstow	89	3498	43.18	1.05	45.33
2	JJ Roy	98	3658	39.33	1.07	42.08
3	JC Buttler	148	3872	31.47	1.18	37.13
4	JE Root	152	6109	43.02	0.86	36.99
5	AD Hales	70	2419	36.10	0.95	34.29
6	IJL Trott	68	2819	43.36	0.77	33.38
7	BA Stokes	101	2871	33.38	0.95	31.71
8	KP Pietersen	136	4440	35.52	0.86	30.54
9	EJG Morgan	246	7701	33.77	0.91	30.73
10	ME Trescothick	123	4335	35.53	0.85	30.20

The Top 10 ODI Bowlers for England

(50+ odis, 50+ wkts)

		odis	*ib*	*runs*	*wkts*	*rwi*	*rb*	*rwirb*
1	RGD Willis	64	64	1968	80	19.68	0.54	10.62
2	A Flintoff	141	119	4121	169	17.16	0.73	12.52
3	D Gough	159	156	6209	235	17.53	0.73	12.79
4	AD Mullally	50	49	1728	63	21.32	0.64	13.64
5	AR Caddick	54	53	1965	69	21.86	0.66	14.42
6	C White	51	50	1726	65	20.42	0.73	14.90
7	IT Botham	116	115	4139	145	22.63	0.66	14.93
8	WB Rankin	57	55	2212	80	19.00	0.79	15.01
9	GP Swann	79	76	2888	104	20.28	0.75	15.21
10	CC Lewis	53	49	1942	66	21.84	0.73	15.94

The following is the best eleven from all players with at least ten years Test experience.

ENGLAND XI

	years	*tests*	*runs*	*ri (adj)*	*wkts*	*rwi (adj)*
* WG Grace	18	22	1098	30.50 (41.61)	9	37.87 (57.93)
JB Hobbs	22	61	5410	53.03 (55.44)		
KF Barrington	13	82	6806	51.95	29	77.27
WR Hammond	19	85	7249	51.77	83	50.09
FS Jackson	12	20	1415	42.87 (48.33)	24	37.45 (43.07)
G Ulyett	13	23	901	25.02 (40.72)	48	13.77 (24.19)
IT Botham	14	102	5200	32.29	383	12.45
† APE Knott	14	95	4389	29.45		
FS Trueman	13	67	981	11.54	307	8.92
SF Barnes	12	27	242	6.20 (11.20)	189	4.34 (5.66)
JC Laker	11	46	676	10.73	193	9.46

WG Grace peaked at 54.08 (adj) at the age of 38. **Jack Hobbs** peaked at 59.03 (adj) when he was, amazingly, 46 years old. **Wally Hammond** peaked at 54.19 (adj), when he was 39. **Ken Barrington** (1930-1981) can come in at three since he loved to take it slow. At four is **Stanley Jackson** (1870-1947), a masterful all-rounder and one of the best batsmen of his day, and all of his 20 Tests were played in England. Jackson was a soldier in the Boer War, and became a politician and Member of British Parliment with the Conservative Party. The now-forgotten **George Ulyett** (1851-1898) was a powerful batsman and fast roundarm bowler. **Ian Botham** (1955) had an incredible amount of natural ability, but he was also devoid of fear. **Allan Knott**, their great wicket-keeper can bat at eight.

Fred Trueman (1931-2006) was a big-hearted fast bowler and easily England's greatest. He loved to enjoy himself on the field and makes friends with the opposition when off the field. He should have played more Tests for England, except for his habit of running foul of the management. **Sydney Barnes** leads the bowling, of course. Off spinner **Jim Laker** (1922-1986) had a humble nature and an easy smile, but when he bowled he put tremendous rip on the ball. He was most famous for his near-impossible performance in 1956 of 19 wickets in a Test, which remains the most in all first-class cricket.

ENGLAND 2nd XI

	years	*tests*	*runs*	*ri (adj)*	*wkts*	*rwi (adj)*
H Sutcliffe	11	54	4555	54.22		
* L Hutton	17	79	6971	50.51		
CP Mead	16	17	1185	45.57 (48.07)		
DCS Compton	19	78	5807	44.32	25	148.89
ER Dexter	10	62	4502	44.13	66	42.33
FE Woolley	25	64	3283	33.50 (35.13)	83	35.54 (38.00)
R Peel	11	20	427	12.93 (24.60)	101	5.88 (10.13)
MW Tate	11	39	1198	23.03	155	11.47
† AFA Lilley	13	35	903	17.36 (22.36)		
JA Snow	11	49	772	10.87	202	12.27
WE Bowes	14	15	28	2.54	68	9.52

Opening with **Herbert Sutcliffe** is **Len Hutton** (1916-1990) who had exceptional talent. **Phil Mead** (1887-1958) was a very skilful batsman, and is now completely forgotten. It was said that he could get a single at will, and a break from batting never diminished his form. He played for England until he was 41. **Denis Compton** (1918-1997) was the glamour boy for England after World War Two, with flashy shots and the confidence to play them, but he never repeated his prolific scoring in the 1947 season when he made 3,816 first-class runs at a 76.32 RI. **Ted Dexter** (1935-2021) batted with such superiority, confidence and power that he was known as "Lord Ted". **Frank Woolley** (1887-1978) was a tall and elegant left-handed batsman, who played an amazing 978 first-class games. He was also a talented bowler, and took 2,066 wickets with either left-arm seam or spin.

Dick Lilley (1866-1929) was the first keeper to regularly stand back from the stumps to fast bowlers. Left-arm spinner **Bobby Peel** (1857-1941) was also a handy batsman. **Maurice Tate** (1895-1956) began his cricketing life as a batsman but developed into a brilliantly consistent seamer, who gave the impression that he could make the ball gain pace off the pitch. **Bill Bowes** (1908-1987), a tall man with glasses, was England's best fast bowler in the 1930s. **John Snow** (1941) was England's best and most aggressive fast bowler for many years.

ENGLAND 3rd XI

	years	*tests*	*runs*	*ri (adj)*	*wkts*	*rwi (adj)*
A Shrewsbury	11	23	1277	31.92 (45.80)		
AN Cook	12	161	12472	42.85		
J Hardstaff, jr	12	23	1636	43.05		
* PBH May	10	66	4537	42.80		
M Leyland	10	41	2764	42.52		
W Rhodes	30	58	2325	23.72 (27.65)	127	19.10 (22.09)
J Briggs	14	31	809	16.85 (26.95)	97	9.53 (14.39)
†TG Evans	12	91	2438	18.33		
GAR Lock	15	49	742	11.77	174	12.93
JB Statham	14	70	675	7.75	252	12.71
RGD Willis	13	90	840	6.56	325	12.79

Arthur Shrewsbury (1956-1903) was a supremely skilled batsman on poor pitches, and was rated the best in the world when he was in his prime. Opening batsman **Alastair Cook** (1984) may have played with an awkward style, but he was ridiculously successful with it.

Joe Hardstaff, jr (1911-1990) was an elegant right-handed batsman. **Peter May** (1929-1994) was a tall and elegant batsman, but dour and strict as a captain. **Maurice Leyland** (1900-1967), a left-handed batsman, was at his best when his team was in trouble.

Wilfred Rhodes (1877-1973), was an accurate left-arm spinner great at varying the flight, who played 1,110 first-class games and took 4,204 wickets, both the most ever. Possibly his biggest claim to fame was that in his Test career he batted from number eleven to all the way up to opener, as his all-round skills increased.

Johnny Briggs (1862-1902) was a left-arm spinner and useful batsman. **Godfrey Evans** (1920-1999) was a showy but brilliant wicket-keeper with very fast hands, who liked to take a nap during the lunch break. **Tony Lock** (1929-1995) was an attacking left-arm spinner, and an expert fielder at short leg.

Brian Statham (1930-2000) was a consistently accurate fast bowler who didn't like to bowl bouncers, so much that he warned the batsman first. **Bob Willis** (1949-2019) was a tall fast bowler with genuine pace, despite bad knees and a somewhat deathly persona.

ENGLAND Worst XI, 30+ Tests

	tests	*runs*	*ri*	*wkts*	*rwi*
RJ Burns	32	1789	30.32		
*JM Brearley	39	1442	21.84		
JC Buttler	41	2127	29.13		
RES Wyatt	40	1839	28.73	18	71.32
MR Ramprakash	52	2350	25.54	4	745.31
C White	30	1052	21.04	59	28.69
R Illingworth	61	1836	20.40	122	25.57
JE Emburey	64	1712	17.83	148	26.45
†PR Downton	30	785	16.35		
DR Pringle	30	695	13.90	70	26.72
DE Malcolm	40	236	4.06	128	20.86

Current opener with an awkward technique (but lovely hair) **Rory Burns** (1990). **Mike Brearley** was one of the greatest and thoughtful captains to ever play the game, but his batting was not anywhere as good. **Jos Buttler** is better at the limited overs game. **Bob Wyatt** (1901-1995) was something of an all-rounder, and a grim-faced man who was not exactly photogenic. **Mark Ramprakash** looked like he was going to be something special, but wasn't.

Craig White (1969) was an all-rounder who completely failed to live up to his promise. **Paul Downton** was very lucky to have played as many Tests as he did, with ordinary batting and keeping. **Derek Pringle** (1958) was an oddball cricketer; a very big man, he was always in and out of a bad England team. Moderate spinners **Ray Illingworth** and **John Emburey**, and inconsistent fast bowler **Devon Malcolm** (1963) who had genuine pace.

ENGLAND Worst XI, 10+ Tests

	tests	*runs*	*ri (adj)*	*wkts*	*rwi (adj)*
WE Russell	10	362	20.11		
W Larkins	13	493	19.72		
JT Ikin	18	606	19.54	3	432.66
*AW Carr	11	237	18.23		
NH Fairbrother	10	219	14.60		
AO Jones	12	291	13.85 (18.85)	3	59.10 (65.77)
†CMW Read	15	360	15.65		
IDK Salisbury	15	368	14.72	20	92.34
PJW Allott	13	213	11.83	26	37.42
NG Cowans	19	175	6.03	51	27.71
PI Pocock	25	206	5.56	67	28.50

Players who were given time to prove themselves, and didn't. **Eric Russell** (1936) batted with elegance, and **Wayne Larkins** (1953) batted with way too much confidence. **Jack Ikin** (1918-1984) lasted for nine years as an England Test candidate.

Arthur Carr (1893-1962) batted low in the order and, in a team of great players, appeared to be playing as a specialist captain. **Neil Fairbrother** can thank his successful limited-overs performances on being given as many as ten Tests.

Arthur Jones (1872-1914) was an all-rounder who bowled leg break. **Ian Salisbury** (1970) was a rare England leg spinner, and showed why such a craft is so difficult. **Chris Read** was a Test keeper for some reason. The team also includes fast bowler **Norman Cowans** (1961), tall seamer **Paul Allott** (1956), and tall off spinner **Pat Pocock** (1946).

ENGLAND ODI XI (50+ odis)

	odis	*runs*	*rb*	*rirb*	*wkts*	*rb*	*rwirb*
JJ Roy	98	3658	1.07	42.08			
AD Hales	70	2419	0.95	34.29			
*JE Root	146	5922	0.87	37.60	24	0.96	161.32
JM Bairstow	89	3498	1.05	45.33			
†JC Buttler	148	3872	1.18	37.13			
BA Stokes	101	2871	0.95	31.71	74	1.00	47.77
A Flintoff	141	3394	0.88	24.47	169	0.73	12.52
IT Botham	116	2113	0.79	15.74	145	0.66	14.93
GP Swann	79	500	0.90	9.36	104	0.75	15.21
D Gough	159	609	0.64	4.48	235	0.73	12.79
RGD Willis	64	83	0.52	1.96	80	0.54	10.62

ENGLAND T20I XI (20+ t20is)

	t20is	*runs*	*rb*	*rirb*	*wkts*	*rb*	*rwirb*
AD Hales	60	1644	1.36	37.26			
*JE Root	32	893	1.26	37.49	6	1.65	57.32
DJ Malan	36	1239	1.37	48.49			
KP Pietersen	37	1176	1.41	46.05			
†JC Buttler	88	2140	1.41	37.71			
RS Bopara	38	711	1.18	23.96	16	1.20	38.07
LJ Wright	51	759	1.37	23.09	18	1.40	46.20
DJ Willey	32	182	1.32	11.43	38	1.33	25.16
GP Swann	39	104	1.16	7.54	51	1.06	13.29
WB Rankin	26	31	0.96	4.95	28	1.02	17.45
ST Finn	21	14	0.73	3.40	27	1.21	20.31

AUSTRALIA

Australia have had more great cricket players than any other nation.

The Top Test Batsmen for Australia

(2000+ runs, 35.00+ RI)

		tests	*runs*	*ri (adj)*
1	DG Bradman	52	6996	87.45
2	M Labuschagne	26	2390	53.11
3	SPD Smith	85	8010	53.04
4	GS Chappell	87	7110	47.08
5	RT Ponting	167	13278	46.58
6	ML Hayden	102	8437	46.35
7	MEK Hussey	79	6235	45.51
8	DA Warner	94	7753	45.07
9	RN Harvey	79	6149	44.88
10	RM Cowper	27	2061	44.80
11	AR Morris	46	3533	44.72
12	AL Hassett	43	3073	44.53
13	SJ McCabe	39	2748	44.32
14	WH Ponsford	29	2122	44.20
15	MJ Clarke	114	8599	43.87
16	RB Simpson	62	4869	43.86
17	C Hill	49	3412	38.33 (43.33)
18	SM Katich	55	4186	43.15
19	KD Walters	74	5357	42.85
20	JL Langer	104	7674	42.63
21	WM Woodfull	35	2300	42.59
22	WM Lawry	67	5234	42.55
23	UT Khawaja	49	3638	42.30
24	AR Border	156	11174	42.16
25	SR Waugh	168	10927	42.02
26	CJL Rogers	25	2015	41.97
27	CG Macartney	35	2131	38.74 (41.83)
28	DM Jones	52	3631	40.79
29	AC Gilchrist	95	5475	40.55
30	MJ Slater	74	5312	40.54
31	VT Trumper	48	3163	35.53 (40.53)
32	MA Taylor	104	7525	40.45
33	DR Martyn	67	4406	40.42
34	NCL O'Neill	42	2779	40.27
35	W Bardsley	41	2469	37.40 (39.90)
36	IR Redpath	66	4737	39.47
37	GN Yallop	39	2756	39.37
38	IM Chappell	75	5345	39.30
39	DC Boon	107	7422	39.06
40	ME Waugh	128	8029	38.41
41	WW Armstrong	50	2863	34.08 (38.30)
42	CC McDonald	47	3107	37.43
43	KJ Hughes	70	4415	35.60
44	KR Stackpole	43	2807	35.08

The Top Test Bowlers for Australia

(100+ wkts, -20.00 RWI)

		tests	*wkts*	*ave*	*ri (adj)*
1	CV Grimmett	37	216	24.21	7.50
2	WJ O'Reilly	27	144	22.59	7.52
3	CTB Turner	17	101	16.53	4.90 (8.34)
4	PJ Cummins	41	197	21.27	8.52
5	DK Lillee	70	355	23.92	8.89
6	AK Davidson	44	186	20.53	9.05
7	BA Reid	27	113	24.63	9.15
8	GD McGrath	123	560	21.68	9.33
9	SK Warne	144	702	25.53	9.85
10	RJ Harris	27	113	23.52	10.82
11	H Trumble	32	141	21.78	8.80 (10.94)
12	WA Johnston	40	160	23.91	11.20
13	RR Lindwall	61	228	23.03	11.41
14	TM Alderman	41	170	27.15	11.65
15	CJ McDermott	71	291	28.63	12.19
16	SCG MacGill	43	199	29.92	12.47
17	MHN Walker	34	138	27.47	12.54
18	JR Thomson	51	200	28.00	12.60
19	R Benaud	63	248	27.03	12.64
20	MG Johnson	73	313	28.40	12.70
21	KR Miller	55	170	22.97	12.83
22	JR Hazlewood	57	215	27.60	12.89
23	MG Hughes	53	212	28.38	12.98
24	MA Starc	69	282	27.60	13.01
25	GF Lawson	46	180	30.56	13.24
26	GD McKenzie	60	246	29.78	13.67
27	JN Gillespie	71	259	26.13	13.82
28	B Yardley	33	126	31.63	14.55
29	B Lee	75	308	30.70	14.75
30	G Giffen	31	103	27.09	11.30 (15.20)
31	RM Hogg	38	123	28.47	15.27
32	NM Lyon	108	427	32.15	15.35
33	AN Connolly	29	102	29.22	15.75
34	AA Mallett	38	132	29.84	16.05
35	PM Siddle	64	214	30.28	16.97
36	PR Reiffel	35	104	26.96	17.36
37	MA Noble	42	121	25.00	14.66 (17.60)
38	IWG Johnson	45	109	29.19	19.81

The Top Test All-Rounders for Australia

(1000+ runs, 50+ wkts, RI higher than RWI)

		tests	*runs*	*ri (adj)*	*wkts*	*rwi (adj)*	*diff*
1	KR Miller	55	2958	34.00	170	12.83	21.17
2	G Giffen	31	1238	23.35 (34.49)	103	11.30 (15.20)	19.29
3	JM Gregory	24	1146	33.70	85	15.39	18.31
4	MA Noble	42	1997	27.35 (32.35)	121	14.66 (17.60)	14.75
5	AK Davidson	44	1328	21.77	186	9.05	12.72
6	R Benaud	63	2201	22.69	248	12.64	10.05

7	C Kelleway	26	1422	33.85 (36.71)	52	27.38 (29.25)	7.46
8	RR Lindwall	61	1502	17.88	228	11.41	6.47
9	MG Johnson	73	2065	18.94	313	12.70	6.24
10	SK Warne	144	3142	15.94	702	9.85	6.09
11	MA Starc	69	1805	17.87	282	13.01	4.86
12	WW Armstrong	50	2863	34.08 (38.30)	87	30.88 (34.59)	3.71
13	MG Hughes	53	1032	14.74	212	12.98	1.76
14	B Lee	75	1447	16.44	308	14.75	1.69

The Top 10 ODI Batsmen for Australia

(50+ odis, 1000+ runs)

		odis	*runs*	*ri*	*rb*	*rirb*
1	DA Warner	128	5455	43.29	0.95	41.12
2	GJ Maxwell	116	3230	30.47	1.25	38.08
3	AJ Finch	135	5255	40.11	0.88	35.29
4	SPD Smith	128	4378	38.74	0.88	34.09
5	AC Gilchrist	286	9595	34.51	0.96	33.12
6	SE Marsh	71	2747	39.24	0.81	31.78
7	ML Hayden	161	6133	39.56	0.78	30.85
8	SR Watson	190	5757	34.06	0.90	30.65
9	MEK Hussey	185	5442	34.66	0.87	30.15
10	RT Ponting	375	13704	37.54	0.8	30.03

The Top 10 ODI Bowlers for Australia

(50 odis, 50+ wkts)

		odis	*ib*	*runs*	*wkts*	*rwi*	*rb*	*rwirb*
1	DK Lillee	63	63	2145	103	12.73	0.59	7.51
2	GD McGrath	249	247	8354	380	14.28	0.64	9.13
3	CG Rackemann	52	52	1833	82	14.17	0.65	9.21
4	MA Starc	99	99	4379	195	11.39	0.85	9.68
5	TM Alderman	65	65	2056	88	17.25	0.60	10.35
6	B Lee	221	217	8877	380	13.33	0.79	10.53
7	CJ McDermott	138	138	5018	203	16.79	0.67	11.24
8	CJ McKay	59	59	2364	97	14.82	0.79	11.70
9	SK Warne	194	191	7541	293	16.77	0.70	11.73
10	NW Bracken	116	116	4240	174	16.23	0.73	11.84

AUSTRALIA XI

	years	*tests*	*runs*	*ri (adj)*	*wkts*	*rwi (adj)*
ML Hayden	14	102	8437	46.35		
WA Brown	14	22	1592	45.48		
* DG Bradman	19	52	6996	87.45		
SPD Smith	11	85	8010	53.04	18	177.22
GS Chappell	13	87	7110	47.08	47	76.20
G Giffen	14	31	1238	23.35 (34.49)	103	11.30 (15.20)
KR Miller	10	55	2958	34.00	170	12.83
† JM Blackham	17	35	800	12.90 (26.93)		
PJ Cummins	10	41	833	14.36	197	8.52
CV Grimmett	11	37	557	11.14	216	7.50
WJ O'Reilly	14	27	410	10.51	144	7.52

Matthew Hayden (1971) had an unattractive batting technique of belligerent stand-and-deliver power shots, but he forced his way into this best-ever Ausie team by his shear weight of runs. **Bill Brown** (1912-2008) had all the shots but he preferred to take his time. **Don Bradman**, is the captain, of course.

After a slow start to his career, once **Steve Smith** (1989) discovered his own uniquely flamboyant batting style, he dominated every bowler in a way seldolm ever seen in the game.

Greg Chappell (1948) was the best Australian batsman after Bradman, and he knew it; tall and beautifully balance, he played with elegance and power, and was one of the very best at playing the on-drive. **George Giffen** (1859-1927) was a genuine all-rounder, and bowled medium paced spin. **Keith Miller** bats at seven. **Jack Blackham** set the standard for Test wicket-keepers.

Clarrie Grimmett and **Bill O'Reilly** were by far the greatest spinning duo. Current captain **Pat Cummins** (1993) has the best record of any Australian fast bowler.

AUSTRALIA 2nd XI

	years	*tests*	*runs*	*ri (adj)*	*wkts*	*rwi (adj)*
* RB Simpson	20	62	4869	43.86	71	49.99
DA Warner	10	94	7753	45.07	4	319.43
RT Ponting	16	167	13278	46.58		
RN Harvey	15	79	6149	44.88		
AL Hassett	15	43	3073	44.53		
MA Noble	11	42	1997	27.35 (32.35)	121	14.66 (17.60)
† RW Marsh	13	96	3633	24.22		
H Trumble	13	32	851	14.92 (20.71)	141	8.80 (10.94)
SK Warne	15	144	3142	15.94	702	9.85
DK Lillee	12	70	905	10.05	355	8.89
GD McGrath	13	123	639	4.69	560	9.33

Bob Simpson (1936) was a magnificent cricketer, great with the bat or fielding in slips, plus useful leg spin bowling. After retiring early at 32, he made a comeback at the age of 41 during the years of the Kerry Packer Flying Circus (the so-called World Series Cricket, when most of the world's leading players decided to not play for their country), producing an impressive RI of 38.54, which pushed his career RI down from 44.90.

David Warner (1986) is a bullying batsmen who loves to dominate the opposition.

Ricky Ponting (1974) was positive and effective, and always scored quickly.

Neil Harvey (1928) was one of the greatest of all left-handed batsmen. Always capless, he was balanced and aggressive, especially to the spinners (he was known to charge the spinners by as many as five paces). He was also an outstanding baseball infielder, and he used those skills in cricket. **Lindsay Hassett** (1913-1993) made batting look easy, who started out as a great shot maker but by the end of his career preferred to play slowly. **Monty Noble** (1873-1940) was an all-rounder of the highest quality, capable of making big scores, and bowling either medium pace or spin.

Rod Marsh (1947-2022) had the nickname "Iron Gloves" which was first given as a derogatory term, but as he improved it became a name of honour. Without looking anything like an athlete, he was very quick with good footwork.

Hugh Trumble (1867-1938) was a tall man with long fingers and he bowled off-break spin at medium pace, and had a great slower ball, and was a more than useful lower order batsman.

Shane Warne (1969-2022) was a natural showman and effortless self-promoter, and a master of making the ball turn a mile. He had a fierce leg break and brilliant top-spinner, but he was quick to resort to gamesmanship and impatience if wickets did not come his way.

Dennis Lillee (1949) was a dominating personality, and had the perfect run up for a fast bowler; all aggression, balance and power. His fightback to overcome career-ending injuries was heroic. **Glenn McGrath** (1970) was a tall bowler who preferred great accuracy, with off-cut and bounce, over pace.

AUSTRALIA 3rd XI

	years	*tests*	*runs*	*ri (adj)*	*wkts*	*rwi (adj)*
JL Langer	13	104	7674	42.63		
VT Trumper	12	48	3163	35.53 (40.53)	8	74.28 (83.66)
C Hill	15	49	3412	38.33 (43.33)		
MJ Clarke	10	114	8599	43.87	31	80.07
KD Walters	15	74	5357	42.85	49	42.72
CG Macartney	18	35	2131	38.74 (41.83)	45	27.55 (31.33)
†IA Healy	11	119	4356	23.93		
*R Benaud	12	63	2201	22.69	248	12.64
RR Lindwall	13	61	1502	17.88	228	11.41
CJ McDermott	11	71	940	10.43	291	12.19
JR Thomson	12	51	679	9.30	200	12.60

Justin Langer (1970) was caught in the shadow of the dominant Hayden, but his career figures are very impressive. He was a batsman who got on with his job without fuss. **Victor Trumper** (1877-1915) was celebrated as the most exciting batsman ever seen, and the photograph of his leaping down the pitch is the greatest taken of any cricketer. He was a treasured player and when he died at only 37, 20,000 people lined the road to his funeral.

Clem Hill (1877-1845) was rated as one of the best left-handed batsmen of his time. He loved batting at number three and was merciless with anything on his legs. **Michael Clarke** (1981) was an elegant right-hand batsman and lucky left-arm spin bowler, hampered by persistent back problems.

Doug Walters (1945) was an easy-going farm boy who swapped technique for guts and instinct, playing magnificent shots whenever he wanted. His medium pace deliveries had the happy knack of getting a wicket when it was needed. **Charlie Macartney** (1886-1958) was known as "The Governor General" because of his dominance. With very quick hands and great footwork, he played audacious shots only known to him, and he inspired the young Don Bradman. He batted right-handed but bowled left-arm spin.

Ian Healy (1964) was an efficient keeper and useful batsman. **Richie Benaud** (1930-2015) was a batsman who liked to hit the ball hard and in the air, a studied wrist spinner who found dangerous bounce, and thoughtful captain, and then a much-admired television commentator. **Craig McDermott** (1965) was a big and strong fast bowler who played at a time when Australia needed him. **Ray Lindwall** (1921-1996) was a dangerous fast bowler, and the best in Australia for many years, but he preferred batting.

Jeff Thomson (1950) was one of the fastest bowlers ever seen, who looked like he had a javelin and not a cricket ball. He was the first to be measured at bowling 100 miles an hour, but it is likely that he was even faster in his peak years, perhaps up to the incredible heights of 110.

Australia has enjoyed a long history of cricket and the two leading states sides New South Wales and Victoria have had so many good players that they warrant a place here in these lists. The selection criteria are to be born in, and then represent, their state, and to have played at least seven years for their country.

NEW SOUTH WALES XI

	years	*tests*	*runs*	*ri (adj)*	*wkts*	*rwi (adj)*
SG Barnes	9	13	1072	56.42		
DA Warner	10	94	7753	45.07	4	319.43
* DG Bradman	19	52	6996	87.45		
SPD Smith	11	85	8010	53.04	18	177.22
SJ McCabe	8	39	2748	44.32	36	73.81
† AC Gilchrist	8	95	5475	40.55		
JM Gregory	7	24	1146	33.70	85	15.39
AK Davidson	9	44	1328	21.77	186	9.05
CTB Turner	8	17	323	10.09 (21.18)	101	4.90 (8.34)
PJ Cummins	10	41	833	14.36	216	8.52
WJ O'Reilly	14	27	410	10.51	144	7.52

Sid Barnes (1916-1973) was impressive an opener, but was never one to follow the ideas of the authorities, and he should have played a lot more than he did. Left-hander **Dave Warner** is the other opener, **Don Bradman** bats at three, the brilliant **Steve Smith** at four, and at five there is **Stan McCabe** (1920-1968) who was short and stocky and loved attacking fast bowlers. **Adam Gilchrist** (1971) was a moderate keeper but an amazing attacking batsman.

Jack Gregory (1895-1973) was a hard-hitting left-handed batsman and a furious right-arm fast bowler. He never wore batting gloves, or a box. **Alan Davidson** (1929-2021) was a left-arm fast bowler who could make the ball swing late. **Charlie Turner** (1862-1944), known as "Terror Turner", was not tall or fast but he was very aggressive, and he could put a lot of off-break spin on the ball. And the leggy **Bill O'Reilly**.

VICTORIA XI

	years	*tests*	*runs*	*ri (adj)*	*wkts*	*rwi (adj)*
WH Ponsford	9	29	2122	44.20		
*WM Woodfull	8	35	2300	42.59		
RN Harvey	15	79	6149	44.88		
AL Hassett	15	43	3073	44.53		
J Ryder	9	20	1394	43.56	17	71.97
KR Miller	10	55	2958	34.00	170	12.86
†JM Blackham	17	35	800	12.90 (26.93)		
H Trumble	13	32	851	14.92 (20.71)	141	8.80 (10.94)
SK Warne	15	144	3142	15.94	702	9.85
MG Hughes	8	53	1032	14.74	212	12.98
AN Connolly	7	29	260	5.77	102	15.75

Bill Ponsford (1900-1991) loved batting and making big scores, and twice managed scores of over 400 (the first, 429, was in only his third game at the age of 22). He had a first-class career RI of 58.80, which is unbelievable for an opener. He was also a very good baseball player, and liked both sports the same.

Bill Woodfull (1897-1965) played for defence and hardly had any bat backlift. He also had a great first-class career RI of 54.64. He was always a gentleman on the field. **Neil Harvey** bats at three, **Lindsay Hassett** at four. **Jack Ryder** (1889-1977) was an underrated batsman, but he was always positive and loved to drive. **Keith Miller** is at six, **Jack Blackham** is the wicket-keeper, **Hugh Trumble** and **Shane Warne** are the spinners.

Merv Hughes (1961) was only ever serious when running in to bowl, and then he was fearsome, with a big moustache and glare, and found good pace from a long run up. **Alan Connolly** (1939) was a reliable medium pacer.

AUSTRALIA Worst XI, 30+ Tests

	tests	*runs*	*ri (adj)*	*wkts*	*rwi (adj)*
GM Wood	59	3374	30.12		
J Dyson	30	1359	23.43		
GM Ritchie	30	1690	31.88		
AP Sheahan	31	1594	30.07		
*SE Gregory	58	2282	22.82 (28.37)		
KD Mackay	37	1507	28.98	50	36.48
MR Marsh	32	1260	22.90	42	49.67
PR Reiffel	35	955	19.10	104	17.36
IWG Johnson	45	1000	15.15	109	19.81
†ATW Grout	51	890	13.28		
MS Kasprowicz	38	445	8.24	113	21.24

Graeme Wood (1956) was a slow and defensive batsman. **John Dyson** (1954) was lucky to play as much as he did. **Greg Ritchie** (1960), known as "Fat Cat" because of his weight, thought himself to be far better than he was.

Paul Sheahan (1946) batted mostly down the order, but at the end of his career was tried as an opener and at least made a century there. **Syd Gregory** (1870-1929) was a diminutive batsman who made a remarkably high score (for the time) of 201 in 1884, but did little else in a long career, where he somehow remained in the Australian team until he was 42.

Ken Mackay (1925-1982) was ironically known as "Slasher" for his defensive and odd batting style. He batted left-handed and bowled right-arm seam. **Mitchell Marsh** (1991) looks to have the talent, and when he is at the top of his game he looks great, but he has remained inconsistent, and recent injuries are not helping any kind of comeback.

Paul Reiffel (1966), who looked like he had wandered in from a farm, was a durable type of plodding fast bowler. **Ian Johnson** (1917-1998) is the off spinner, **Wally Grout** (1927-1968) is the wicket-keeper with a poor batting record. **Michael Kasprowicz** (1972) was a steady fast bowler, who was good without setting the world on fire.

AUSTRALIA Worst XI, 10+ Tests

	tests	*runs*	*ri*	*wkts*	*rwi*
J Dyson	30	1359	23.43		
MS Harris	14	607	23.34		
* VY Richardson	19	706	23.53		
CS Serjeant	12	522	22.69		
ID Craig	11	358	19.88		
GB Hole	18	789	23.90	3	195.99
HSTL Hendry	11	335	18.61	16	47.50
† GRA Langley	26	374	10.10		
RJ Bright	25	445	11.41	53	30.26
MS Kasprowicz	38	445	8.24	113	21.24
I Meckiff	18	154	7.70	45	23.89

John Dyson was given way too many chances, as has current player **Marcus Harris** (1992). **Victor Richardson** (1894-1969) was an all-round sportsman, but he is better known as the grandfather of the Chappell brothers.

Craig Serjeant (1951) was a tall batsman who favoured the leg side. **Ian Craig** (1935-2014) was a teenage prodigy and played for Australia at 17, and then had captaincy forced on him. After a string of failures, he retired from first-class cricket at the age of 26.

Graeme Hole (1931-1990) was a stylish batsman but only had a highest score of 66, after batting everywhere in the upper batting order. **Hunter Hendry** (1895-1988) was fast bowler known as 'Stork" because of his height. **Gil Langley** (1919-2001) was good with the keeping gloves but not the batting ones.

Ray Bright (1954) was a left-arm spinner who didn't shine with much luck. **Michael Kasprowicz** the fast bowler, and the controversial **Ian Meckiff** (1935) who was a left-arm fast bowler with a bowling action so front-on that many people thought it made him a thrower.

AUSTRALIA ODI XI (50+ odis)

	odis	*runs*	*rb*	*rirb*	*wkts*	*rb*	*rwirb*
DA Warner	128	5455	0.95	41.12			
AJ Finch	135	5255	0.88	35.29	4	0.91	309.33
GS Chappell	74	2331	0.75	24.50	72	0.67	18.15
SPD Smith	128	4378	0.88	34.09	28	0.90	44.56
GJ Maxwell	116	3230	1.25	38.08	51	0.94	88.21
SR Watson	190	5757	0.90	30.65	168	0.82	25.28
†AC Gilchrist	286	9595	0.96	33.12			
SP O'Donnell	87	1242	0.80	15.52	108	0.71	16.42
DK Lillee	63	240	0.80	5.29	103	0.59	7.51
GD McGrath	249	115	0.48	0.82	380	0.64	9.13
CG Rackemann	52	34	0.44	0.82	82	0.65	9.21

AUSTRALIA T20I XI (20+ t20is)

	t20is	*runs*	*rb*	*rirb*	*wkts*	*rb*	*rwirb*
AJ Finch	89	2741	1.44	44.33			
DA Warner	88	2554	1.40	40.62			
DJM Short	23	642	1.18	32.93	3	1.32	199.3
MEK Hussey	38	721	1.36	32.68			
GJ Maxwell	84	1982	1.54	39.63	34	1.24	56.38
SR Watson	58	1462	1.45	37.84	48	1.27	32.04
MR Marsh	36	885	1.25	31.60	15	1.27	34.54
†BJ Haddin	34	402	1.14	15.80			
JP Faulkner	24	159	1.15	10.15	36	1.32	16.71
JR Hazlewood	27	21	1.61	5.63	40	1.25	16.27
SW Tait	21	11	0.73	1.33	28	1.23	19.39

SOUTH AFRICA

South Africa has a proud history of competitive cricketers, and always the best fielders in the world. For many years the careers were sawn off or destroyed by their country's racist government.

The Top Test Batsmen for South Africa

(2000+ runs, 35.00+ RI)

		tests	*runs*	*ri (adj)*
1	RG Pollock	23	2256	55.02
2	AD Nourse	34	2960	47.74
3	JH Kallis	165	13206	47.50
4	AB de Villiers	114	8765	45.89
5	GC Smith	116	9253	45.58
6	EJ Barlow	30	2516	44.14
7	B Mitchell	42	3471	43.38
8	HM Amla	124	9282	43.17
9	G Kirsten	101	7289	41.41
10	HH Gibbs	90	6167	40.04
11	HW Taylor	42	2936	38.63 (40.01)
12	DJ Cullinan	70	4554	39.60
13	DJ McGlew	34	2440	38.12
14	D Elgar	76	4864	36.29
15	F du Plessis	69	4163	35.27
16	AG Prince	66	3665	35.24

The Top Test Bowlers for South Africa

(100+ wkts, -20.00 RWI)

		tests	*wkts*	*ave*	*rwi*
1	AA Donald	72	330	22.25	8.69
2	K Rabada	52	243	22.41	8.76
3	DW Steyn	93	439	22.95	8.93
4	HJ Tayfield	37	170	25.91	9.29
5	NAT Adcock	26	104	21.10	9.33
6	PM Pollock	28	116	24.18	10.83
7	SM Pollock	108	421	23.11	11.08
8	VD Philander	64	224	22.32	11.85
9	M Ntini	101	390	28.82	14.04
10	M Morkel	86	309	27.66	14.32
11	KA Maharaj	42	150	30.67	15.53
12	TL Goddard	41	123	26.22	15.98
13	A Nel	36	123	31.86	17.87
14	PR Adams	45	134	32.87	18.64

The Top Test All-Rounders for South Africa

(1000+ runs, 50+ wkts, RI higher than RWI)

		tests	*runs*	*ri (adj)*	*wkts*	*rwi (adj)*	*diff*
1	GA Faulkner	25	1754	37.31 (42.10)	82	13.93 (16.56)	25.54
2	JH Kallis	165	13206	47.50	291	30.27	17.23

3	TL Goddard	41	2516	32.25	123	15.98	16.27
4	SM Pollock	108	3781	24.23	421	11.08	13.15
5	VD Philander	64	1779	18.92	224	11.85	7.07
6	BM McMillan	38	1968	31.74	75	28.85	2.89
7	DW Steyn	93	1251	10.51	439	8.93	1.58

The Top 10 ODI Batsmen for South Africa

(Qualification: 50+ odis, 1000+ runs)

		odis	*runs*	*ri*	*rb*	*rirb*
1	AB de Villiers	228	9577	43.93	1.01	44.36
2	Q de Kock	129	5658	43.86	0.95	41.66
3	HM Amla	181	8113	45.57	0.88	40.10
4	F du Plessis	143	5507	40.49	0.88	35.63
5	DA Miller	143	3503	28.71	1.01	28.99
6	GC Smith	197	6989	36.02	0.8	28.81
7	HH Gibbs	248	8094	33.72	0.83	27.98
8	JH Kallis	323	11550	37.37	0.73	27.28
9	G Kirsten	185	6798	36.74	0.72	26.45
10	HH Dippenaar	107	3421	36.01	0.67	24.12

The Top 10 ODI Bowlers for South Africa

(Qualification: 50+ odis, 50+ wkts)

		odis	*ib*	*runs*	*wkts*	*rwi*	*rb*	*rwirb*
1	AA Donald	164	162	5926	272	12.97	0.69	8.94
2	SM Pollock	303	297	9631	393	18.51	0.61	11.29
3	CR Matthews	56	55	1975	79	17.40	0.65	11.31
4	Imran Tahir	107	104	4297	173	14.92	0.77	11.48
5	M Ntini	172	170	6501	265	15.73	0.75	11.79
6	LL Tsotsobe	61	60	2347	94	15.93	0.79	12.584
7	M Morkel	117	114	4761	188	15.35	0.82	12.587
8	DW Steyn	125	124	5087	196	16.41	0.81	13.29
9	PS de Villiers	83	82	2636	95	23.94	0.59	14.12
10	K Rabada	85	83	3655	132	17.40	0.83	14.44

SOUTH AFRICA XI

	years	*tests*	*runs*	*ri (adj)*	*wkts*	*rwi (adj)*
BA Richards	(13)	4	508	72.57		
EJ Barlow	8 (13)	30	2516	44.14	40	39.15
RG Pollock	6 (23)	23	2256	55.02		
AD Nourse	16	34	2960	47.74		
JH Kallis	18	165	13206	47.50	291	30.27
†AB de Villiers	13	114	8765	45.89		
GA Faulkner	18	25	1754	37.31 (42.10)	82	13.93 (16.56)
MJ Procter	3 (15)	7	226	22.60	41	5.12
* HJ Tayfield	10	37	862	14.36	170	9.29
DW Steyn	14	93	1251	10.51	439	8.93
AA Donald	9 (15)	72	652	6.93	330	8.69

It would be a pointless effort to name an all-time South African team without Barry Richards, Graeme Pollock and Allan Donald. All three represented their country for over ten years, and in Pollock's case over twenty.

Barry Richards opens with **Eddie Barlow** (1940-2005), who was a solid man with glasses, and was always popular on the cricket field. He also bowled medium pace. **Graeme Pollock** is at three. **Dudley Nourse** (1910-1981) was a correct and powerfully built batsman who could defend or attack with equal skill. He was the son of another prominent Test player Dave Nourse.

Jacques Kallis (1975) played in a quiet orthodox manner and did everything with class. His bowling was little more than medium pace with a bit of swing now and then. **Aubrey Faulkner**, the great all-rounder and leg spinner, is at six. **AB de Villiers** (1984) batted with an inherent genius, and was brilliant everywhere in the field, including keeping wicket.

Mike Procter (1946) was a rare bread; able to bat with orthodox technique, but when he bowled he looked to be off the wrong foot and when he was young he was able to bowl near to 100 miles an hour.

Hugh Tayfield (1929-1994) was the last great South African spinner. Tall and bowling off-break, he was enduringly accurate. He had a lot of stamina, and once bowled 35 consecutive 8-ball overs. He liked to set odd fields to tempt batsmen, and superstitiously kissed his cap before every over.

Dale Steyn (1983) was all elbows and menace, but it was his accuracy and persistence and ability to move the ball late that made him lethal. **Allan Donald** (1966) was tall and strong and very fast and known as "White Lightning".

SOUTH AFRICA 2nd XI

	years	*tests*	*runs*	*ri (adj)*	*wkts*	*rwi (adj)*
A Melville	10	11	894	47.05		
* GC Smith	11	116	9253	45.58	8	511.61
HM Amla	14	124	9282	43.17		
G Kirsten	10	101	7289	41.41		
TL Goddard	14	41	2516	32.25	123	15.98
BM McMillan	5 (11)	38	1968	31.74	75	28.85
† MV Boucher	14	146	5498	26.95		
SM Pollock	12	108	3781	24.23	421	11.08
JM Blanckenberg	10	18	455	15.16 (16.83)	60	12.61 (13.27)
CP Carter	12	10	181	12.06 (14.73)	28	10.62 (11.30)
M Ntini	11	101	699	6.02	390	14.04

Alan Melville (1910-1983) was a successful but underrated elegant batsman who loved playing against aggressive fast bowlers. **Graeme Smith** had a technique that looked like he had a problem with his balance and struggled to move his feet, but somehow he became one of the leading openers in the world. **Hashim Amla** (1983) was a wristy and elegant batsman. **Gary Kirsten** (1967) was a determined fighter.

Brian McMillan (1963) was a big and tall all-rounder who seemed to move slowly but had great athleticism. **Trevor Goddard** (1931-2016) was a tall left-handed batsman who liked to open, and medium pacer who moved the ball either way. He batted and bowled exactly as the coaching book instructed.

Mark Boucher (1976) was always reliable behind the stumps, but his career stats are very similar to another great keeper Billy Wade, who made 511 runs at 26.89.

Shaun Pollock (1973) was a probing medium pacer and useful batsman; just as good a cricketer as his father Peter, but not his uncle Graeme. **Jimmy Blanckenberg** (1892-1955) was an accurate medium pacer. **Claude Carter** (1881-1952) was a left-arm spinner. **Makhaya Ntini** (1977) was a tireless fast bowler who relied more on persistence than express pace.

SOUTH AFRICA Worst XI, 30+ Tests

	tests	*runs*	*ri*	*wkts*	*rwi*
AN Petersen	36	2093	32.70		
AC Hudson	35	2007	31.85		
RA McLean	40	2120	29.04		
JP Duminy	46	2103	28.41	42	51.72
HH Dippenaar	38	1718	27.70		
L Klusener	49	1906	27.62	80	39.80
† DJ Richardson	42	1359	21.23		
N Boje	43	1312	21.61	100	30.70
PL Harris	37	460	9.58	103	23.16
A Nel	36	337	8.02	123	17.87
PR Adams	45	360	6.54	134	18.64

Openers **Alviro Petersen** (1980) and **Andrew Hudson** (1965). Average batsmen **Boeta Dippenaar** (1977) and **Roy McLean** (1930-2007), below-par all-rounder **JP Duminy** (1984). **Lance Klusener** (1971) was an all-rounder better suited to one-dayers. **Dave Richardson** (1959) was one of South Africa's leading keepers, but he had the lowest RI of them all.

Nicky Boje (1973) bowled left-arm spin. **Andre Nel** (1977) was a tall fast bowler with good aggression. **Paul Harris** (1978) was a tall left-arm spinner. **Paul Adams** (1977) bowled wrist spin with a horrible action.

SOUTH AFRICA Worst XI, 10+ Tests

	tests	*runs*	*ri (adj)*	*wkts*	*rwi*
LA Stricker	13	344	14.33 (19.33)		
* HF Wade	10	327	18.16		
CMH Hathorn	12	325	16.25 (21.25)		
JE Cheetham	24	883	20.53		
TB de Bruyn	12	428	18.60		
CB van Ryneveld	19	724	21.93	17	46.43
ARA Murray	10	289	20.64	18	35.05
PNF Mansell	13	355	16.13	11	109.47
† TA Ward	23	459	10.92 (13.19)		
ACB Langton	15	298	12.95	40	26.26
CN McCarthy	15	28	1.16	36	29.12

Openers **Louis Stricker** (1884-1960) and **Herbert Wade** (1905-1980), who managed to captain every Test he played. Batsmen **Maitland Hathorn** (1878-1920), **Jack Cheetham** (1920-1980), and **Theunis de Bruyn** (1992). **Clive van Ryneveld** (1928-2018) was an all-rounder and leg spinner. **Anton Murray** (1922-95) was an attacking batsman and right-arm medium pace bowler.

Percy Mansell (1920-1995) bowled wrist spin and sometimes turned to seam when that (obviously) didn't work. **Tommy Ward** (1887-1936) was a wicket-keeper, who died by electrocution in a gold mine. **Arthur Langton** (1912-1942) and **Cuan McCarthy** (1929-2000) were fast bowlers.

SOUTH AFRICA ODI XI (50+ odis)

	odis	*runs*	*rb*	*rirb*	*wkts*	*rb*	*rwirb*
* GC Smith	197	6989	0.80	28.81	18	0.92	116.10
† Q de Kock	129	5658	0.95	41.66			
HM Amla	181	8113	0.88	40.10			
AB de Villiers	228	9577	1.01	44.36	7	1.05	38.94
JH Kallis	323	11550	0.73	27.28	269	0.80	26.42
F du Plessis	143	5507	0.88	35.63			
L Klusener	171	3576	0.89	23.22	192	0.78	19.95
SM Pollock	303	3519	0.86	14.75	393	0.61	11.29
CR Matthews	56	141	0.69	4.41	79	0.65	11.31
Imran Tahir	107	157	0.69	3.00	173	0.77	11.48
AA Donald	164	95	0.34	0.80	272	0.69	8.94

SOUTH AFRICA T20I XI (20+ t20is)

	t20is	*runs*	*rb*	*rirb*	*wkts*	*rb*	*rwirb*
AK Markram	20	588	1.47	48.01	5	1.24	53.17
† Q de Kock	61	1827	1.35	40.43			
HE van der Dussen	34	933	1.30	39.11			
* F du Plessis	50	1528	1.34	40.95			
JH Kallis	25	666	1.19	34.45	12	1.20	52.71
JP Duminy	81	1934	1.26	32.48	21	1.29	71.82
D Pretorius	22	170	1.61	24.87	23	1.29	21.83
RE van der Merwe	24	174	1.31	15.19	29	1.13	16.85
RJ Peterson	21	124	1.09	11.25	24	1.25	18.58
Imran Tahir	38	19	1.05	4.98	63	1.12	10.15
DW Steyn	47	21	0.80	1.40	64	1.15	15.49

WEST INDIES

This team represents some fifteen countries and dependencies in the Caribbean, all with their different cultures and rivalries. Noted for playing with carefree enjoyment, they went for years with the best team in the world, and looked to have a never-ending supply of great cricketers. The modern team, however, has been a shadow of its former self, and sadly, it is difficult to see it returning to past glory.

The Top Test Batsmen for West Indies

(2000+ runs, 35.00+ RI)

		tests	*runs*	*ri*
1	ED Weekes	48	4455	55.00
2	GA Headley	22	2190	54.75
3	BC Lara	130	11912	51.79
4	CL Walcott	44	3798	51.32
5	GS Sobers	93	8032	50.20
6	IVA Richards	121	8540	46.92
7	SM Nurse	29	2523	46.72
8	RB Kanhai	79	6227	45.45
9	FMM Worrell	51	3860	44.36
10	CH Lloyd	110	7515	42.94
11	S Chanderpaul	164	11867	42.38
12	LG Rowe	30	2047	41.77
13	CC Hunte	44	3245	41.60
14	CG Greenidge	108	7558	40.85
15	RB Richardson	86	5949	40.74
16	AI Kallicharran	66	4399	40.35
17	BF Butcher	44	3104	39.79
18	RC Fredericks	59	4334	39.76
19	CH Gayle	103	7214	39.63
20	JB Stollmeyer	32	2159	38.55
21	RR Sarwan	87	5842	37.93
22	DL Haynes	116	7487	37.06
23	DM Bravo	54	3506	35.77

The Top Test Bowlers for West Indies

(100 wkts, -20.00 RWI)

		tests	*wkts*	*ave*	*rwi*
1	MD Marshall	81	376	20.94	8.40
2	J Garner	58	259	20.97	8.98
3	CEL Ambrose	98	405	20.99	9.27
4	CEH Croft	27	125	23.30	9.69
5	MA Holding	60	249	23.68	10.74
6	CA Walsh	132	519	24.44	11.39
7	AME Roberts	47	202	25.61	11.41
8	IR Bishop	43	161	24.27	11.45
9	WW Hall	48	192	26.38	12.64
10	AL Valentine	36	139	30.32	13.74
11	LR Gibbs	79	309	29.09	13.933
12	S Ramadhin	43	158	28.98	13.939

13	KAJ Roach	71	242	27.18	14.37
14	M Dillon	38	131	33.57	16.91
15	D Bishoo	36	117	37.17	18.74
16	JO Holder	56	142	28.03	19.34
17	ST Gabriel	56	161	31.84	19.38
18	PT Collins	32	106	34.63	19.92

The Top Test All-Rounders for West Indies

(1000+ runs, 50+ wickets, RI higher than RWI)

		tests	*runs*	*ri*	*wkts*	*rwi*	*diff*
1	GS Sobers	93	8032	50.20	235	23.02	27.18
2	MD Marshall	81	1810	16.91	376	8.40	8.51
3	JO Holder	56	2571	25.71	142	19.34	6.37
4	GE Gomez	29	1243	27.02	58	21.73	5.29
5	DJ Bravo	40	2200	30.98	86	28.25	2.73
6	CEL Ambrose	98	1439	9.92	405	9.27	0.65

The Top 10 ODI Batsmen for West Indies

(Qualification: 50+ odis, 1000+ runs)

		odis	*runs*	*ri*	*rb*	*rirb*
1	IVA Richards	187	6721	40.24	0.90	36.21
2	SD Hope	89	3738	44.50	0.74	32.93
3	CH Gayle	301	10480	35.64	0.87	31.00
4	AD Russell	56	1034	22.00	1.30	28.60
5	BC Lara	299	10405	36.00	0.79	28.44
6	E Lewis	57	1847	34.20	0.82	28.04
7	CG Greenidge	128	5134	40.42	0.64	25.86
8	RR Sarwan	181	5804	34.34	0.75	25.75
9	S Chanderpaul	268	8778	34.97	0.70	24.47
10	CH Lloyd	87	1977	28.65	0.81	23.20

The Top 10 ODI Bowlers for West Indies

(Qualification: 50+ odis, 50+ wkts)

		odis	*ib*	*runs*	*wkts*	*rwi*	*rb*	*rwirb*
1	J Garner	98	98	2752	146	12.64	0.51	6.44
2	AME Roberts	56	56	1771	87	13.09	0.56	7.33
3	MA Holding	102	102	3034	142	15.34	0.55	8.43
4	RD King	50	50	1807	76	15.63	0.69	10.78
5	CEL Ambrose	176	175	5429	225	18.75	0.58	10.87
6	BP Patterson	59	58	2206	90	15.79	0.72	11.36
7	SP Narine	65	65	2435	92	18.69	0.68	12.70
8	MD Marshall	136	134	4233	157	23.01	0.58	13.34
9	IR Bishop	84	83	3127	118	18.63	0.72	13.41
10	IDR Bradshaw	62	62	2299	78	23.42	0.72	16.86

WEST INDIES XI

	years	*tests*	*runs*	*ri*	*wkts*	*rwi*
CG Greenidge	16	108	7558	40.85		
RB Kanhai	16	79	6227	45.45		
GA Headley	24	22	2190	54.75		
BC Lara	15	130	11912	51.79		
ED Weekes	10	48	4455	55.00		
* GS Sobers	20	93	8032	50.20	235	23.02
† DL Murray	17	62	1993	20.76		
MD Marshall	12	81	1810	16.91	376	8.40
MA Holding	11	60	910	11.97	249	10.74
CEL Ambrose	12	98	1439	9.92	405	9.27
J Garner	10	58	672	9.88	259	8.98

Gordon Greenidge (1951) played perfect power shots with great gusto, and was more dangerous when he had a leg or foot injury. **Rohan Kanhai** (1935) was a short batsman who played destructive full-blooded shots. He was an occasional wicket-keeper, and played most of his career in the middle order, but opened for a while at the start.

George Headley at three, **Everton Weekes** at five, **Garry Sobers** at six.

Brian Lara (1969) was a left-handed batsman blessed with not only technical brilliance and elegance, but also the rare trait of being desperate to make very big scores. His five highest first-class scores were 501, 400, 375, 277 and 231, and were part of a collection of thirteen double centuries, nine of them made in Tests. His peak year was 1994, when for the English county team Warwickshire he scored 1,276 runs in 9 consecutive innings, with an RI of 159.50. He was also magnificent when batting with tail-end batsmen, and no spin bowler ever troubled him.

Deryck Murray (1943) was the West Indies' best gloveman for many years, and kept with assurance to their many great bowlers. **Malcolm Marshall** leads the fast bowlers. **Michael Holding** (1954) was the fastest bowler in the world at his peak, with an elegant style and a run up that seemed to start at the sight screen. **Curtley Ambrose** (1963) was a tall, gangly, and unrelentingly accurate fast bowler. **Joel Garner** (1952), at 6'8" was known as "Big Bird", was the best of all the very tall fast bowlers. He was much faster than he looked, coupled with nasty bounce.

WEST INDIES 2nd XI

	years	*tests*	*runs*	*ri*	*wkts*	*rwi*
CH Gayle	14	103	7214	39.63	73	60.87
JB Stollmeyer	15	32	2159	38.55	13	69.00
IVA Richards	16	121	8540	46.92	32	197.53
CL Walcott	12	44	3798	51.32	11	74.18
* FMM Worrell	15	51	3860	44.36	69	46.01
S Chanderpaul	21	164	11867	42.38	9	468.74
† D Ramdin	10	74	2898	23.00		
LN Constantine	11	18	635	19.24	58	15.05
WW Hall	10	48	818	12.39	192	12.64
CA Walsh	16	132	936	5.05	519	11.39
AL Valentine	11	36	141	2.76	139	13.74

Chris Gayle (1979) seemed to always moved slowly, with all the time in the world, except when he was thrashing the ball over the fence. He batted left-handed, but his dainty right-arm spin was also effective. **Jeffrey Stollmeyer** (1921-1989) was a tall and elegant batsman, and bowled leg break.

Viv Richards (1952) was devastatingly destructive, with thrilling majestic power and a perfect technique, and he commanded every shot. Had he played with the modern bats of today, he probably would have killed bowlers, fielders and umpires. He fell short of greatness when he became impatient at the end of his career, and never mastered batting against leg spin. As a fielder he was confident anywhere, and he loved bowling something that might have been spin.

Clyde Walcott (1926-2006) was powerful and tall, and from a crouched stance unleashed cuts or hooks, and also loved to drive. He was able to keep wicket, or bowl good in-swing. **Frank Worrell** (1924-1967) was not only a stylish right-handed batsman and useful left-arm bowler of seam or spin, but also a gentleman, and one of the most astute captains to ever walk onto to a cricket field. He was the first black man to captain the West Indies in a time of discrimination, and greatly helped to eradicate such idiotic ideas. He died of leukaemia at 42.

Shivnarine Chanderpaul (1974) was a fighting and intense left-handed batsmen who developed an unusual batting stance. **Denesh Ramdin** (1985) was a wicket-keeper who faced many hurdles, such as being given the captaincy of a mostly disinterested team.

Learie Constantine (1901-1971) was a gifted all-rounder and spectacular to watch; a dangerous fast bowler, and a batsman capable of spontaneous shots. His record should be better than it was, since he had limited opportunity to play Tests. **Wes Hall** (1937) was the greatest fast bowler ever seen for the West Indies until the overload came in the late 1970s. **Courtney Walsh** (1962) was a fast bowler who could bowl for very long spells and never seem to tire. **Alf Valentine** (1930-2004) was a left-arm spinner who formed a great bowling partnership with Sonny Ramadhin (RWI 13.89) in the 1950s.

WEST INDIES Worst XI, 30+ Tests

	tests	*runs*	*ri*	*wkts*	*rwi*
DS Smith	43	1760	23.15		
SC Williams	31	1183	22.75		
SD Hope	38	1726	23.97		
J Blackwood	46	2437	29.01	4	272.25
KLT Arthurton	33	1382	27.64		
RL Chase	43	2009	25.43	79	33.00
* DJG Sammy	38	1323	21.00	84	27.69
†JR Murray	33	918	20.40		
VA Holder	40	682	11.55	109	21.97
DBL Powell	37	407	7.14	85	37.15
FH Edwards	55	394	4.47	165	22.26

Devon Smith (1981) was given way too many chances, and only made one Test hundred, as did **Stuart Williams** (1969). Current batsmen **Shai Hope** shouldn't be struggling for runs as much as he does at Test level, and **J Blackwood** (1991) is capable but too impatient.

Keith Arthurton (1965) was a left-handed batsman who failed to live up to his early promise. **Roston Chase** (1992) is only a useful all-rounder. **Junior Murray** played as wicket-keeper more because of his batting skills. **Darren Sammy** (1983) was a likeable character and a good captain, but his place in the team was always debatable, with his medium pace seam not good enough at international level.

Vanburn Holder (1945) played at a time when West Indies cricket found great fast bowlers scarce. **Daren Powell** was a fast bowler persisted with despite his obvious poor record. **Fidel Edwards** was a short fast bowler with a horrible slinging delivery who was lucky to have played as much as he did.

WEST INDIES Worst XI, 10+ Tests

	tests	*runs*	*ri*	*wkts*	*rwi*
* PV Simmons	26	1002	21.31	4	257.00
JD Campbell	18	752	20.88		
RIC Holder	11	380	22.35		
RS Morton	15	573	21.22		
GC Grant	12	413	18.77		
EAE Baptiste	10	233	21.18	16	41.77
RO Hinds	15	505	20.20	13	113.24
OAC Banks	10	318	19.87	28	34.87
†D Williams	11	242	12.73		
DBL Powell	37	407	7.14	85	37.15
ML Cummins	14	114	5.18	27	34.19

John Campbell (1993) currently opens for West Indies, but plays too negatively and is struggling to find runs. **Phil Simmons** (1963) was a very good one-day player, but not in Tests. **Roland Holder** (1967) was a stylish batsman. **Runako Morton** (1978-2012) was a troubled man who died in a car accident at 33.

Jackie Grant (1907-1978) was given the captaincy of the West Indies in his first Test, and for the whole tour of Australia no less, not because he deserved his place in the team, or that the senior players were not up to the task, but because he was a white man.

Eldine Baptiste (1960) was an all-rounder and fast bowler. **Ryan Hinds** (1981) was an all-rounder and left-arm spinner. **Omari Banks** (1982) was a right-arm spinner. **David Williams** (1963) was a wicket-keeper who tried hard, but at 5'4" was too short to succeed in catching wayward deliveries from tall fast bowlers. Current fast bowler **Miguel Cummins** (1990), and **Daren Powell.**

WEST INDIES ODI XI (50+ odis)

	odis	*runs*	*rb*	*rirb*	*wkts*	*rb*	*rwirb*
CG Greenidge	128	5134	0.64	26.23			
CH Gayle	301	10480	0.87	31.00	167	0.79	33.39
IVA Richards	187	6721	0.90	36.29	118	0.74	29.79
* BC Lara	299	10405	0.79	28.44	4	1.24	23.63
† SD Hope	89	3738	0.74	32.93			
AD Russell	56	1034	1.30	28.60	70	0.97	24.25
KA Pollard	123	2706	0.94	22.50	55	0.94	55.05
DJ Bravo	164	2968	0.82	17.32	199	0.90	20.06
MA Holding	102	282	0.74	5.01	142	0.55	8.43
AME Roberts	56	231	0.64	4.61	87	0.56	7.33
J Garner	98	239	0.66	3.85	146	0.51	6.44

WEST INDIES T20I XI (20+ t20is)

	t20is	*runs*	*rb*	*rirb*	*wkts*	*rb*	*rwirb*
E Lewis	50	1423	1.55	45.01			
CH Gayle	79	1899	1.37	34.68	20	1.15	37.95
† N Pooran	57	1193	1.28	30.54			
MN Samuels	67	1611	1.16	28.74	22	1.29	49.71
R Powell	39	619	1.38	27.54	4	1.46	78.56
LMP Simmons	68	1527	1.20	27.34	6	1.67	16.70
KA Pollard	101	1569	1.35	25.51	42	1.38	58.53
DJ Bravo	91	1255	1.15	19.49	78	1.35	34.77
SP Narine	51	155	1.12	7.53	52	1.00	20.02
KOK Williams	26	19	1.11	3.00	41	1.46	18.16
S Badree	52	43	0.66	1.76	56	1.02	19.95

NEW ZEALAND

New Zealand, the world champions of mediocrity (until recently). Propped with the excuse that their population is both small and rugby-mad, the New Zealand team is usually comprised of players who are in the favour of the selectors because of their personality and not their cricketing skills. Many a time a promising but green young player will be selected and then kept in the team to gain experience, until finally he has so much experience that that is the sole reason for him playing, and the only way out of the team is in his retirement. During the entire career of such a player, he will produce only a handful of good performances, and an appalling record to go with it. Ken Rutherford and Adam Parore were such players, but there were many more. Remarkably however, New Zealand still produced players of true class.

The Top Test Batsmen for New Zealand

(2000+ runs, 35.00+ RI)

		tests	*runs*	*ri*
1	KS Williamson	86	7272	48.48
2	MH Richardson	38	2776	42.70
3	MD Crowe	77	5444	41.55
4	GM Turner	41	2991	40.97
5	TWM Latham	65	4502	39.84
6	AH Jones	39	2922	39.48
7	LRPL Taylor	112	7683	39.19
8	SP Fleming	111	7172	37.94
9	HM Nicholls	46	254	36.66
10	BB McCullum	101	6453	36.66
11	JG Wright	82	5334	36.04
12	B Sutcliffe	42	2727	35.88

The Top Test Bowlers for New Zealand

(100+ wkts -20.00 RWI)

		tests	*wkts*	*ave*	*rwi*
1	RJ Hadlee	86	431	22.29	7.75
2	N Wagner	58	244	26.49	11.92
3	BR Taylor	30	111	26.60	12.70
4	TA Boult	75	301	27.42	13.02
5	TG Southee	85	338	28.19	13.34
6	CL Cairns	62	218	29.40	14.02
7	RO Collinge	35	116	29.25	15.63
8	DK Morrison	48	160	34.68	16.47
9	RC Motz	32	100	31.48	17.31
10	DL Vettori	112	361	34.15	17.50
11	BL Cairns	43	130	32.92	18.23
12	CS Martin	71	233	33.81	18.28
13	EJ Chatfield	43	123	32.17	19.09

The Top Test All-Rounders for New Zealand

(1000+ runs, 50+ wickets, RI higher than RWI)

		tests	*runs*	*ri*	*wkts*	*rwi*	*diff*
1	CL Cairns	62	3320	31.92	218	14.02	17.90
2	RJ Hadlee	86	3124	23.31	431	7.75	15.56
3	DL Vettori	112	4523	26.29	361	17.50	8.79
4	JR Reid	58	3428	31.74	85	28.24	3.50
5	TG Southee	85	1769	14.74	338	13.34	1.40

The Top 10 ODI Batsmen for New Zealand

(Qualification: 50+ odis, 1000+ runs, 20+ RIRB)

		odis	*runs*	*ri*	*rb*	*rirb*
1	KS Williamson	151	6173	42.86	0.81	34.71
2	MJ Guptill	189	7041	37.85	0.87	32.92
3	LRPL Taylor	236	8607	39.12	0.83	32.46
4	BB McCullum	260	6083	26.67	0.96	25.60
5	TWM Latham	105	2995	30.87	0.84	25.93
6	RG Twose	87	2717	33.54	0.75	25.15
7	C Munro	57	1271	23.98	1.04	24.93
8	MD Crowe	143	4704	33.60	0.72	24.19
9	NJ Astle	223	7090	32.67	0.72	23.52
10	GD Elliott	83	1976	28.63	0.81	23.19

The Top 10 ODI Bowlers for New Zealand

(Qualification: 50+ odis, 50+ wkts, -25 RWIRB)

		odis	*ib*	*runs*	*wkts*	*rwi*	*rb*	*rwirb*
1	SE Bond	82	80	3070	147	11.36	0.71	8.06
2	RJ Hadlee	115	112	3407	158	15.28	0.55	8.40
3	C Pringle	64	64	2459	103	14.83	0.74	10.97
4	TA Boult	93	93	4261	169	13.87	0.83	11.51
5	MJ Henry	57	55	2538	103	13.50	0.87	11.74
6	EJ Chatfield	114	112	3618	140	20.67	0.59	12.19
7	KD Mills	170	169	6485	240	19.02	0.78	14.83
8	DK Morrison	96	95	3470	126	20.75	0.75	15.56
9	MC Snedden	93	90	3237	114	22.41	0.71	15.91
10	BL Cairns	78	75	2717	89	25.71	0.67	17.22

NEW ZEALAND XI

	years	*tests*	*runs*	*ri*	*wkts*	*rwi*
* GM Turner	14	41	2991	40.97		
B Sutcliffe	18	42	2727	35.88		
KS Williamson	11	86	7272	48.48	30	89.84
MD Crowe	13	77	5444	41.55	14	121.05
LRPL Taylor	14	112	7683	39.19		
CL Cairns	14	60	3320	31.92	218	14.02
DL Vettori	17	112	4323	26.29	361	17.50
RJ Hadlee	17	86	3124	23.31	431	7.75
† IDS Smith	11	63	1815	20.62		
TA Boult	10	75	704	8.00	301	13.02
J Cowie	12	9	90	6.92	45	6.21

Glenn Turner (1947) was a professionally-minded batsman and determined enough to strongly disagree with administrators, enough to make himself unavailable for Tests from 1977 to 1983. He started his career as a slow scoring defensive and reliable batsman, but by the end he was free scoring and confident.

Bert Sutcliffe (1923-2001) was a brilliant free-scoring batsman who was easily one of the best left-handers ever seen, before suffering a nasty hit on the head from a fast bowler in 1953. Before the accident he had made 1,007 runs at 43.78, but after that 1,720 runs at 32.45. He had made 385 for Otago exactly a year earlier in 1952; the highest ever for a left-hander until Brian Lara came along.

The calm and masterful **Kane Williamson** (1990) is more suited to the longer format of the game, but he can easily adapt to the limited version. **Martin Crowe** (1962-2016) was a gifted and elegant batsman, assured in attack and defence, and a bowler capable of generating good pace. **Ross Taylor** (1984) should have played for his country earlier than he did but he was mistakenly labelled a one-day-only player.

Chris Cairns (1970) was an immensely talented all-rounder, who preferred to think of himself as a fast bowler and not a batsman. His ability to hit the ball with power but with elegance is very rare, but he did not apply himself as he should have. **Richard Hadlee** was New Zealand's greatest and most professional cricketer.

Daniel Vettori (1979) was a good left-arm spinner who relied more on change of pace than actual spin, and over the years not only became a challenging batsman with his own weird style, but he also grew in height by some five inches in his early twenties. He was thrown into the international game too young, at 18, and expected to be the team's main spin bowler.

Ian Smith (1957) was a wicket-keeper faultless in his prime, and when batting loved the cut shot. **Trent Boult** (1989) is an accurate left-arm fast bowler. **Jack Cowie** (1912-1994) was probably the world's best fast bowler in the 1930s. He loved to bowl, and at good pace, he could swing the ball or cut it off the pitch. In his only clash with Don Bradman, in 1937, he had him caught behind for 11.

NEW ZEALAND 2nd XI

	years	*tests*	*runs*	*ri*	*wkts*	*rwi*
JG Wright	15	82	5334	36.04		
*WA Hadlee	13	11	543	28.57		
MP Donnelly	12	7	582	48.50		
SP Fleming	14	111	7172	37.94		
NJ Astle	10	81	4702	34.32	51	77.43
JR Reid	15	58	3428	31.74	85	28.24
†BB McCullum	11	101	6453	36.66		
BL Cairns	11	43	928	14.27	130	18.23
TG Southee	13	79	1728	15.56	314	13.30
RO Collinge	13	35	533	10.66	116	15.62
SL Boock	11	30	207	5.04	74	22.46

John Wright was a battling left-handed batsman who played with too much defensive tension at Test level, but in his later years freed up and became more attacking, which was his natural game. He had an RI of 50.36 (18 Tests, 1,662 runs) in the decade of the 1990s, and the end of his career. **Walter Hadlee** (1915-2006) was a tall bespectacled batsman and a thoughtful captain. Three of his sons played cricket for New Zealand, and after his playing days he worked in cricket administration.

Martin Donnelly (1917-1999) was a short but exciting left-handed batsman who had all the shots and played the ball late. He was based in England and had few chances to represent his country, but when he did he showed that he was one of the world's best batsmen. He also once represented England at rugby.

Stephen Fleming (1973) was a tall and elegant left-handed batsman, and an outstanding fielder in the slips. **Nathan Astle** (1971) started as a good one-day all-rounder, but developed into a fine attacking batsman. **John Reid** (1928-2020) was an attacking batsman who hit the ball very hard, and a bowler capable of bowling seam or spin, and he could also keep wicket.

Brendon McCullum (1981) preferred smashing the ball as hard as he could, to actual proper batting, except for one innings in which he mixed sound defence with his aggression and made 302. His wicket-keeping was good enough but nothing spectacular.

Lance Cairns (1949) was a swing bowler with an unorthodox action, but he made a name for himself with his unusual axeman-like batting coupled with sheer brutal power. Current swing bowler and clean-hitting batsman **Tim Southee** (1988). **Richard Collinge** (1946) was a tall and strong left-arm fast bowler with a long run up and able to swing the ball late. The best of the New Zealand-representative spinners was left-armer **Stephen Boock** (1951).

NEW ZEALAND Worst XI, 30+ Tests

	tests	*runs*	*ri*	*wkts*	*rwi*
BA Edgar	39	1958	28.79		
MJ Horne	35	1788	27.50		
* KR Rutherford	56	2465	24.89		
JJ Crowe	39	1601	24.63		
JM Parker	36	1498	23.77		
V Pollard	32	1266	21.45	40	56.74
† AC Parore	78	2865	22.38		
DN Patel	37	1200	18.18	75	29.71
JEC Franklin	31	808	17.56	82	22.37
JG Bracewell	41	1001	16.68	102	23.52
EJ Chatfield	43	180	3.33	123	19.09

Bruce Edgar (1956) liked to play defensively, **Matt Horne** (1970) tried to play positively. **Ken Rutherford** loved to attack and play a late cut that he always got out to. **Jeff Crowe** (1953) played in Australia where he was spoken of as a Test player, as they do for most players. **John Parker** as a professional batsman in English County cricket, so there is no excuse for his Test failures. True to form for New Zealand administrators, Rutherford, Crowe and Parker all managed to become Test captain.

Vic Pollard the all-rounder. **Adam Parore** (1971) was groomed for the New Zealand keeping role to take over from Ian Smith, but never proved himself worthy of the position.

Dipak Patel (1958) was from Kenya and moved to England when he was 10. He was not good enough to make the poor England teams of the mid-1980s, so he tried for New Zealand in 1986. At first he was an elegant shot maker, but when his technique proved to be poor he somehow retained his place in the team with his inert off-spin.

James Franklin (1980) was given many chances, as a tall left-arm swing bowler and useful tail ender before he was dropped, but two years later was foolishly brought back into the Test team as an apparent all-rounder to bat at six. The result of his comeback was 10 Tests, 303 runs at a 16.83 RI, and 6 wickets at a 267.90 RWI. **John Bracewell** (1958) was a gifted off-break bowler and dangerous batsman, but did not appear to believe in his talent.

Ewen Chatfield (1950) was known as "Charlie" because his peculiar batting style might have been how Chaplin's Tramp might have played. A tall bowler with not much pace, he was famous for being able to drop it on a dime, and bowl for long spells, but he was always content to be a back-up.

NEW ZEALAND Worst XI, 10+ Tests

	tests	*runs*	*ri*	*wkts*	*rwi*
* ME Chapple	14	497	18.40		
LSM Miller	13	346	13.84		
JW Guy	12	440	19.13		
SN McGregor	25	892	18.97		
CZ Harris	23	777	18.50	16	132.53
MJF Shrimpton	10	265	13.94	5	37.92
JT Sparling	11	229	11.45	5	130.80
† KC James	11	52	4.00		
MJ Henry	13	224	14.00	31	41.56
DR O'Sullivan	11	158	7.52	18	56.66
GI Allott	10	27	1.80	19	49.23

Murray Chapple (1930-1985) had a long first-class career but no success at Test level, and opener **Lawrie Miller**. **John Guy** (1934) was promising young left-handed batsman who never took to Tests. **Noel McGregor** (1931-2007) was a positive batsman, quick on his feet, but his only success was 111 against Pakistan (so his other Test innings were made at an RI of 16.97).

Chris Harris (1969) was one of New Zealand's greatest fielders, but his left-handed batting and dainty swing bowling were more suited to the limited-overs game. Leg spinner and all-rounder **Mike Shrimpton** (1940-2015), followed by all-rounder **John Sparling**. **Ken James** (1904-1976) was a very good keeper, and was actually regarded as a good batsman, coming in at 7 or 8 in the order.

David O'Sullivan (1944) was a left-arm spinner much more at home at first-class level. **Geoff Allott** (1971) was a left-arm fast bowler who only had success in one-day games, and current fast bowler **Matt Henry** (1991) who is better suited to the one-dayers.

NEW ZEALAND ODI XI (50+ odis)

	odis	*runs*	*rb*	*rirb*	*wkts*	*rb*	*rwirb*
MJ Guptill	189	7041	0.87	32.92	4	0.89	59.95
†BB McCullum	260	6083	0.96	25.60			
*KS Williamson	151	6173	0.81	34.71	37	0.89	55.34
LRPL Taylor	236	8607	0.83	32.46			
MD Crowe	143	4704	0.72	24.19	29	0.73	38.08
JDS Neesham	66	1320	0.97	22.86	68	1.01	28.95
CL Cairns	215	4950	0.84	21.53	201	0.80	24.28
JDP Oram	160	2434	0.86	18.04	173	0.73	18.95
RJ Hadlee	115	1751	0.75	13.39	158	0.55	8.40
SE Bond	82	292	0.76	5.54	147	0.71	8.06
C Pringle	64	193	0.75	3.52	103	0.74	10.97

NEW ZEALAND T20I XI (20+ t20is)

	t20is	*runs*	*rb*	*rirb*	*wkts*	*rb*	*rwirb*
C Munro	65	1724	1.56	43.36	4	1.57	219.01
MJ Guptill	112	3299	1.36	41.53			
*KS Williamson	74	2021	1.23	34.51	6	1.38	75.43
DP Conway	20	602	1.39	49.21			
†BB McCullum	71	2140	1.36	41.57			
CJ Anderson	31	485	1.38	27.87	14	1.37	72.63
SB Styris	31	578	1.19	23.71	18	1.12	25.31
DL Vettori	34	205	1.07	9.96	38	0.95	16.72
IS Sodhi	66	87	1.04	7.54	83	1.34	22.69
SE Bond	20	21	1.00	2.62	25	1.34	20.14
TA Boult	44	30	0.75	2.04	62	1.35	20.77

INDIA

Once the Indian people saw the English playing cricket, in the form of sailors from the East India Company in 1737, they were never the same. Because of the climate, cricket was traditionally played in the winter, until the recent gluttonous match scheduling began.

The Top Test Batsmen for India

(2000+ runs, 35.00+ RI)

		tests	*runs*	*ri*
1	SR Tendulkar	200	15921	48.39
2	V Sehwag	103	8503	47.76
3	SM Gavaskar	125	10122	47.29
4	V Kohli	101	8043	47.03
5	RS Dravid	163	13265	46.70
6	M Azharuddin	99	6215	42.27
7	VS Hazare	30	2192	42.15
8	CA Pujara	95	6713	41.43
9	NS Sidhu	51	3202	41.05
10	RG Sharma	45	3137	40.74
11	G Gambhir	58	4154	39.94
12	S Dhawan	34	2315	39.91
13	GR Viswanath	91	6080	39.22
14	VVS Laxman	134	8781	39.02
15	M Amarnath	69	4378	38.74
16	PR Umrigar	59	3631	38.62
17	SC Ganguly	113	7212	38.36
18	M Vijay	61	3982	37.92
19	DB Vengsarkar	116	6868	37.12
20	DN Sardesai	30	2001	36.38
21	AM Rahane	82	4931	35.22

The Top Test Bowlers for India

(100 wkts, -20.00 RWI)

		tests	*wkts*	*ave*	*rwi*
1	R Ashwin	86	442	24.13	8.84
2	JJ Bumrah	29	123	21.73	9.89
3	A Kumble	132	619	29.65	11.30
4	RA Jadeja	59	242	24.44	11.31
5	BS Chandrasekhar	58	242	29.74	11.92
6	SP Gupte	36	149	29.55	12.09
7	BS Bedi	67	266	28.71	12.73
8	PP Ojha	24	113	30.26	12.85
9	EAS Prasanna	49	189	30.38	13.82
10	MH Mankad	44	162	32.32	13.96
11	Mohammed Shami	59	214	27.05	14.15
12	Harbhajan Singh	103	417	32.46	14.78
13	DR Doshi	33	114	30.71	14.81
14	Kapil Dev	131	434	29.64	15.50
15	J Srinath	67	236	30.49	15.63
16	IK Pathan	29	100	32.26	17.42
17	Z Khan	92	311	32.94	17.47

18	I Sharma	105	311	32.40	19.58
19	UT Yadav	52	158	30.80	19.88

The Top Test All-rounders for India

(1000+ runs, 50+ wickets, RI higher than RWI)

		tests	*runs*	*ri*	*wkts*	*rwi*	*diff*
1	RA Jadeja	59	2396	27.54	242	11.31	16.23
2	MH Mankad	44	2109	29.29	162	13.96	15.33
3	R Ashwin	86	2931	23.82	442	8.84	14.98
4	Kapil Dev	131	5248	28.52	434	15.50	13.02
5	IK Pathan	29	1105	27.62	100	17.42	10.20
6	A Kumble	132	2506	14.48	619	11.30	3.18
7	SA Durani	29	1202	24.04	75	21.72	2.32
8	M Prabhakar	39	1600	27.58	96	26.42	1.16
9	Harbhajan Singh	103	2224	15.33	417	14.78	0.55

The Top 10 ODI Batsmen for India

(Qualification: 50+ odis, 1000+ runs)

		odis	*runs*	*ri*	*rb*	*rirb*
1	V Kohli	260	12311	49.04	0.92	45.11
2	S Dhawan	149	6284	43.40	0.93	40.02
3	RG Sharma	230	9283	41.62	0.89	37.04
4	V Sehwag	251	8273	33.76	1.04	35.11
5	SR Tendulkar	463	18426	40.76	0.86	35.05
6	HH Pandya	60	1267	28.79	1.17	33.68
7	MS Dhoni	350	10773	36.27	0.87	31.55
8	G Gambhir	147	5238	36.62	0.85	31.12
9	SC Ganguly	311	11363	37.87	0.73	27.64
10	Yuvraj Singh	296	8539	31.50	0.87	27.40

The Top 10 ODI Bowlers for India

(Qualification: 50+ odis, 50+ wkts)

		odis	*ib*	*runs*	*wkts*	*rwi*	*rb*	*rwirb*
1	JJ Bumrah	70	70	2873	113	15.74	0.77	12.11
2	Mohammed Shami	79	78	3793	148	13.50	0.93	12.55
3	YS Chahal	61	60	2854	104	15.83	0.86	13.61
4	Kuldeep Yadav	66	64	3084	109	16.61	0.87	14.45
5	Kapil Dev	225	221	6945	253	23.97	0.61	14.62
6	J Srinath	229	227	8847	315	20.23	0.74	14.97
7	AB Agarkar	191	188	8021	288	18.17	0.84	15.26
8	M Prabhakar	130	127	4534	157	23.35	0.71	16.57
9	S Madan Lal	67	64	2137	73	25.66	0.67	17.19
10	A Kumble	271	265	10412	337	24.29	0.71	17.24

INDIA XI

	years	*tests*	*runs*	*ri*	*wkts*	*rwi*
* SM Gavaskar	16	125	10122	47.29		
V Sehwag	11	103	8503	47.76	40	107.72
RS Dravid	15	163	13265	46.70		
SR Tendulkar	24	200	15921	48.39	46	170.75
V Kohli	11	101	8043	47.03		
† FM Engineer	13	46	2611	30.01		
MH Mankad	12	44	2109	29.29	162	13.96
Kapil Dev	15	131	5248	28.52	434	15.50
R Ashwin	10	86	2931	23.82	442	8.84
A Kumble	18	132	2506	14.48	619	11.30
BS Chandrasekhar	15	58	167	2.08	242	11.92

Sunil Gavaskar (1949) built his game around his perfect defence, and he could bat for long periods. **Virender Sehwag** (1978) thought there was only one was to play: hit the ball to the boundary, no matter if it was new and swinging, or old and spinning. He also bowled a bit of off spin. **Rahul Dravid** (1973) was all class in his shot play, and had beautiful defence. **Virat Kohli** (1988) has great ability and will give back as good as he gets on the field.

Sachin Tendulkar (1973) was as gifted a batsman as anyone could be, but he was more at home in limited-over contests. Put into the Indian team at only 16, he proved worthy of his place, and somehow remained calm amongst overwhelming praise that followed him in everything he did. His peak years were from 1993 to 1996, when from 21 Tests he made 1,826 runs at 62.96.

Farokh Engineer (1938) was a reliable wicket-keeper/batsman, and for much of his career opened the batting. **Vinoo Mankad** (1917-1978) was a class all-rounder, being a genuine batsman who liked to open the batting, and was a leading left-arm spinner.

Kapil Dev (1959) could swing the ball and had an amazing batting eye, capable of easily smashing the ball over the fence. He burst onto the cricket scene at the age of 19, when he opened the bowling for India.

Ravichandran Ashwin (1986) is a brilliant off-break bowler, and currently has the best record of all India's spinners, by a long way. **Anil Kumble** (1970) was an accurate and unflappable leg spinner, who used his height and changes of pace more than turn. **Bhagwath Chandrasekhar** (1945) was a deceptive wrist spinner despite having his right arm deformed from polio. He bowled all kinds of deliveries with a fast arm action.

INDIA 2nd XI

	years	*tests*	*runs*	*ri*	*wkts*	*rwi*
VM Merchant	17	10	859	47.22		
NS Sidhu	15	51	3202	41.05		
CA Pujara	11	95	6713	41.43		
M Azharuddin	15	99	6215	42.27		
M Amarnath	18	69	4377	38.73	32	123.54
* RJ Shastri	10	80	3830	31.65	151	33.90
† PA Patel	15	25	934	24.57		
Harbhajan Singh	17	103	2224	15.33	417	14.78
J Srinath	10	67	1009	10.96	236	15.63
EAS Prasanna	16	49	735	8.75	189	13.82
BS Bedi	12	67	656	6.49	266	12.73

Vijay Merchant (1911-1987) amassed many runs at first-class level, at a 57.56 RI. **Navjot Sidhu** (1963) started as a plodding batsman, but after a time away from the national team returned as something of a swashbuckler. **Cheteshwar Pujara** (1988) is a patient and assured run scorer.

Mohammad Azharuddin (1963) was capable of staggering timing and power with strong wrists, and made three centuries in his first three Tests. **Mohinder Amarnath** (1950) was a batsman who liked to take his time, and could also bowl some kind of dribbly medium pace. **Ravi Shastri** (1962) was a tall right-handed batsman and probing left-arm spinner.

Parthiv Patel (1985) was chosen for India at age of only 17, and then spent eight years on the outer before a surprise, and successful, call-up at age 31.

Harbhajan Singh (1980) was an attacking off spinner who liked to vary his pace more than try for turn. **Javagal Srinath** (1969) had good pace. **Erapalli Prasanna** (1940) bowled off-break with great flight and always a plan. **Bishan Bedi** (1946) bowled subtle and thoughtful left-arm spin, who could flight the ball beautifully and spin a web around a batsman, and he loved the challenge of bowling after being hit for six.

INDIA Worst XI, 30+ Tests

	tests	*runs*	*ri*	*wkts*	*rwi*
K Srikkanth	43	2062	28.63		
AD Gaekwad	40	1985	28.35	2	794.75
Yuvraj Singh	40	1900	30.64	9	236.37
* AL Wadekar	37	2113	29.76		
Yashpal Sharma	37	1606	27.22		
DG Phadkar	31	1229	27.31	62	28.52
GS Ramchand	33	1180	22.26	41	63.25
† KS More	49	1285	20.07		
S Madan Lal	39	1042	16.80	71	35.56
S Venkataraghavan	57	748	9.84	156	22.22
UT Yadav	52	408	6.69	158	19.88

Anshuman Gaekwad (1952) was a blocker, but **Kris Srikkanth** (1959) was a thrasher. **Yuvraj Singh** (1981) was a left-handed thrasher, and son of Punjabi film star Yograj Singh who played one Test for India. **Ajit Wadekar** (1941-2018) captained the Indian team. **Yashpal Sharma** (1954-2021) had "limitations" with his batting.

Dattu Phadkar (1925-1985) was an all-rounder who bowled seam and spin. **Gulabrai Ramchand** (1927-2003) was a bowler who ran faster than he bowled. **Kiran More** (1962) was a moderate keeper.

Madan Lal (1951) was a seamer. **Srinivasaraghavan Venkataraghavan** (1945) not only has a great name, but was a right-arm spinner and later a Test umpire. And current fast bowler **Umesh Yadav** (1987).

INDIA Worst XI, 10+ Tests

	tests	*runs*	*ri*	*wkts*	*rwi*
WV Raman	11	448	23.57	2	225.75
A Chopra	10	437	23.00		
SK Raina	18	768	24.77	13	78.48
AA Baig	10	428	23.77		
DK Gaekwad	11	350	17.50		
ED Solkar	27	1068	22.25	18	145.29
AG Kripal Singh	14	422	21.10	10	87.60
S Madan Lal	39	1042	16.80	71	35.56
AB Agarkar	26	571	14.64	58	37.52
†NS Tamhane	21	225	8.33		
CS Nayudu	11	147	7.73	2	1077.00

Woorkeri Raman (1965) was a left-hander and bit of a spin bowler. **Aakash Chopra** (1977) only had a highest score of 60 in 10 Tests. **Suresh Raina** (1986) was a left-handed batsman and right-arm off break spinner, good in limited-overs cricket but not so much in Tests.

Abbas Ali Baig (1939) made 112 on Test debut against England, and then only 316 more runs at an 18.58 RI. **Datta Gaekwad** (1928) apparently had "sound defence."

Eknath Solkar (1948-2005) was a left-handed all-rounder who could bowl both seam and spin, and was known as the "poor man's Sobers."

Kripal Singh (1933-1987) was an all-rounder and off break spinner, who started Test cricket with an unbeaten 100 in easy circumstances, but failed to do anything of note again. **Ajit Agarkar** (1977) was a short and spindly fast bowler who had good pace, but was better in limited-overs cricket. **Naren Tamhane** (1931-2002) had good keeping skills, but not so much with the bat; even his first-class RI was only 15.19. Plus seamer **Madan Lal** and spinner **CS Nayudu**.

INDIA ODI XI (50+ odis)

	odis	*runs*	*rb*	*rirb*	*wkts*	*rb*	*rwirb*
V Sehwag	241	7995	1.04	35.38	94	0.87	52.23
S Dhawan	149	6284	0.93	40.02			
SR Tendulkar	463	18426	0.86	35.05	154	0.85	66.28
V Kohli	260	12311	0.92	45.11	4	1.03	2054.85
RG Sharma	230	9283	0.89	37.04	8	0.86	262.94
*† MS Dhoni	350	10773	0.87	31.55			
KM Jadhav	73	1389	1.01	26.97	27	0.85	49.93
Kapil Dev	225	3783	0.95	18.14	253	0.61	14.62
Mohammed Shami	79	161	0.82	3.46	148	0.93	12.55
YS Chahal	61	66	0.62	3.41	104	0.86	13.61
JJ Bumrah	70	45	0.51	1.20	113	0.77	12.11

INDIA T20I XI (20+ t20is)

	t20is	*runs*	*rb*	*rirb*	*wkts*	*rb*	*rwirb*
KL Rahul	56	1831	1.42	49.99			
RG Sharma	125	3313	1.39	39.35			
V Kohli	97	3296	1.37	50.73	4	1.35	200.47
SS Iyer	36	809	1.41	35.64			
SK Raina	78	1605	1.34	32.57	13	1.26	88.96
Yuvraj Singh	58	1177	1.36	31.37	28	1.17	23.07
*† MS Dhoni	98	1617	1.26	23.96			
SN Thakur	25	69	1.81	20.81	33	1.52	25.85
IK Pathan	24	172	1.19	14.61	28	1.33	24.09
Kuldeep Yadav	24	43	0.89	12.75	41	1.17	9.67
JJ Bumrah	57	8	0.61	0.81	67	1.08	17.94

PAKISTAN

After splitting from the nation of India in 1947, the new Islamic Republic of Pakistan succeeded in producing many world-class cricketers.

The Top Test Batsmen for Pakistan

(2000+ runs, 35.00+ RI)

		tests	*runs*	*ri*
1	Mohammad Yousuf	90	7530	48.26
2	Younis Khan	118	10099	47.41
3	Javed Miandad	124	8832	46.73
4	Inzamam-ul-Haq	119	8829	44.59
5	Saeed Anwar	55	4052	44.52
6	Zaheer Abbas	78	5062	40.82
7	Hanif Mohammad	55	3915	40.36
8	Azhar Ali	94	7021	40.35
9	Babar Azam	40	2851	40.15
10	Shoaib Mohammad	45	2705	39.77
11	Misbah-ul-Haq	75	5222	39.56
12	Saeed Ahmed	41	2991	38.34
13	Saleem Malik	103	5768	37.45
14	Majid Khan	63	3931	37.08
15	Mushtaq Mohammad	57	3643	36.43
16	Asad Shafiq	77	4660	36.40
17	Asif Iqbal	58	3575	36.11
18	Ijaz Ahmed	60	3315	36.03
19	Mohammad Hafeez	50	3452	35.93
20	Taufeeq Umar	44	2963	35.69
21	Mudassar Nazar	76	4114	35.46

Top Bowlers for Pakistan

(100 wkts, -20.00 RWI)

		tests	*wkts*	*ave*	*rwi*
1	Imran Khan	88	362	22.81	8.94
2	Fazal Mahmood	34	139	24.70	9.41
3	Waqar Younis	87	373	23.56	9.72
4	Mohammad Asif	23	106	24.36	10.11
5	Wasim Akram	104	414	23.62	10.32
6	Saeed Ajmal	35	178	28.10	10.57
7	Yasir Shah	45	235	30.83	10.88
8	Shoaib Akhtar	46	178	25.69	11.83
9	Saqlain Mushtaq	49	208	29.83	12.33
10	Iqbal Qasim	50	171	28.11	14.13
11	Danish Kaneria	61	261	34.79	14.92
12	Abdul Qadir	67	236	32.80	15.42
13	Mushtaq Ahmed	52	185	32.97	15.86
14	Mohammad Amir	36	119	30.46	17.15
15	Sarfraz Nawaz	55	177	32.75	17.57
16	Umar Gul	47	163	34.06	18.80

The Top Test All-rounders for Pakistan

(1000+ runs, 50+ wickets, RI higher than RWI)

		tests	*runs*	*ri*	*wkts*	*rwi*	*diff*
1	Imran Khan	88	3807	30.21	362	8.94	21.27
2	Mushtaq Mohammad	57	3643	36.43	79	25.89	10.55
3	Wasim Akram	104	2898	19.71	414	10.32	9.39
4	Asif Iqbal	58	3575	36.11	53	28.86	7.25

The Top 10 ODI Batsmen for Pakistan

(Qualification: 50+ odis, 1000+ runs)

		odis	*runs*	*ri*	*rb*	*rirb*
1	Babar Azam	86	4261	50.72	0.90	45.64
2	Fakhar Zaman	56	2427	43.33	0.95	41.16
3	Zaheer Abbas	62	2572	42.86	0.84	36.00
4	Saeed Anwar	247	8824	36.16	0.80	28.92
5	Imad Wasim	55	986	24.65	1.10	27.11
6	Salman Butt	78	2725	34.93	0.76	26.54
7	Mohammad Yousuf	288	9720	35.60	0.75	26.70
8	Azhar Ali	53	1845	34.81	0.74	25.75
9	Shahid Afridi	398	8064	21.85	1.17	25.56
10	Misbah-ul-Haq	162	5122	34.37	0.73	25.09

The Top 10 ODI Bowlers for Pakistan

(Qualification: 50+ odis, 50+ wkts)

		odis	*ib*	*runs*	*wkts*	*rwi*	*rb*	*rwirb*
1	Saqlain Mushtaq	169	165	6275	288	12.47	0.71	8.85
2	Saeed Ajmal	113	112	4182	184	13.82	0.69	9.53
3	Wasim Akram	356	351	11812	502	16.44	0.64	10.52
4	Waqar Younis	262	258	9919	416	14.78	0.78	11.52
5	Shoaib Akhtar	163	162	6169	247	16.37	0.79	12.93
6	Abdul Qadir	104	100	3454	132	19.81	0.67	13.27
7	Imran Khan	175	153	4844	182	22.36	0.64	14.31
8	Mudassar Nazar	122	104	3432	111	28.96	0.57	16.50
9	Mohammad Sami	87	85	3567	121	20.70	0.83	17.18
10	Mohammad Amir	61	60	2400	81	21.94	0.79	17.33

PAKISTAN XI

	years	*tests*	*runs*	*ri*	*wkts*	*rwi*
Saeed Anwar	10	55	4052	44.52		
Hanif Mohammad	17	55	3915	40.36		
Younis Khan	17	118	10099	47.41	9	187.89
Javed Miandad	17	124	8832	46.73	17	84.93
Mohammad Yousuf	12	85	7027	46.84		
Mushtaq Mohammad	20	57	3643	36.43	79	25.89
* Imran Khan	20	88	3807	30.21	362	8.94
Wasim Akram	16	102	2898	19.71	414	10.32
† Wasim Bari	16	81	1366	12.19		
Iqbal Qasim	11	50	549	9.63	171	14.13
Waqar Younis	13	87	1010	8.41	373	9.72

Saeed Anwar (1968) was an exciting left-handed batsman, not relying on power but expert timing. **Hanif Mohammad** (1934-2016) was a short batsman capable of very big scores, such as 337 in a Test and 499 at first-class level.

Younis Khan (1977) was a dignified batsman and useful seamer, and somehow escaped deserved accolades. **Javed Miandad** (1957) was a natural batsman with his own technique but always a straight bat, and a cheeky grin to go with it. **Mohammad Yousuf** (1974) was a run machine, and also largely ignored by the world's cricketing media.

Mushtaq Mohammad (1943), a brother of Hanif, was an underrated all-rounder and wrist spinner. He claimed to be the youngest player in first-class cricket history, at 13. **Imran Khan** always carried a sense of superiority about himself. **Wasim Akram** (1966) was a gifted bowler with a very fast left-arm and the ability to both swing and seam it. As his career quickly developed, so too did his batting, until he became a dangerous hitter.

Wasim Bari (1948) was a weak batsman but he more than made up for it with assured glovework, and his footwork was so good that he rarely needed to dive.

Iqbal Qasim (1953) was a quiet and accurate left-arm spinner. **Waqar Younis** (1971) was a fast bowler who sprinted to the crease and let rip with good pace and an ability to swing the ball late into the stumps.

PAKISTAN 2nd XI

	years	*tests*	*runs*	*ri*	*wkts*	*rwi*
Shoaib Mohammad	12	45	2705	39.77	5	176.80
Mudassar Nazar	12	76	114	35.46	66	55.79
* Zaheer Abbas	16	78	5062	40.82		
Inzamam-ul-Haq	15	119	8829	44.59		
Azhar Ali	10	94	7021	40.35		
Asif Iqbal	15	58	3575	36.11	53	28.86
† Moin Khan	13	69	2741	26.35		
Abdul Qadir	12	67	1029	13.36	236	15.42
Mushtaq Ahmed	13	52	656	9.11	185	15.86
Shoaib Akhtar	10	46	544	8.11	178	11.83
Mohsin Kamal	10	9	37	3.36	24	17.12

Shoaib Mohammad (1961), son of Hanif, was best as an innings-builder than any kind of great shot maker. **Mudassar Nazar** (1956) was a stylish batsman and very useful seam bowler. **Zaheer Abbas** (1947) did not look like a great batsman, being stooped and wearing glasses, but he did when he was driving and hooking with flourish and power.

Inzamam-ul-Haq (1970) was a big and tall batsman who never seemed in a rush, especially when fielding, but he could hit the ball with great power. **Azhar Ali** is a correct and consistent batsman. **Asif Iqbal** (1943) was a very good all-rounder who loved to play the cover drive, and who bowled medium pace swing. **Moin Khan** (1971) was a good keeper and batsman.

Abdul Qadir (1955-2019) had the tools and the talent to be the greatest of all wrist spinners; accurate with either leg break or two different googlies, but he proved to be inconsistent, especially against India (27 wickets at a 45.78 RWI, but against every other team, 209 wickets at 12.64).

Mushtaq Ahmed (1970) was a good wrist spinner. **Shoaib Akhtar** (1975) bowled very fast with a somewhat wonky arm. **Mohsin Kamal** (1963) was a good fast bowler but a fringe player for ten years, but given his record, he should have played more.

PAKISTAN Worst XI, 30+ Tests

	tests	*runs*	*ri*	*wkts*	*rwi*
Salman Butt	33	1889	30.46		
Rameez Raja	57	2833	30.13		
* Majid Khan	63	3931	37.08	27	119.82
Ijaz Ahmed	60	3315	36.03	2	115.50
Shoaib Malik	35	1898	31.63	32	63.77
Wasim Raja	57	2821	30.66	51	48.43
Abdul Razzaq	43	1684	22.75	96	26.93
† Saleem Yousuf	32	1055	23.97		
Intikhab Alam	47	1493	19.38	125	22.43
Mohammad Sami	36	487	8.69	85	40.95
Umar Gul	47	577	8.61	163	18.80

Salman Butt (1984) had an average career as a left-handed opener, that got a whole lot worse in 2011 when he went to prison for making money out of cheating. As the captain of Pakistan, he had his fast bowlers deliberately bowl no balls, so the ruining of his name and the end of his cricketing career wasn't even for anything interesting. **Rameez Raja** (1962) was an attractive but inconsistent batsmen.

Majid Khan (1946), a cousin of Imran Kahn, was primarily a batsman who also bowled seam or spin, and he developed into a dependable opener. **Ijaz Ahmed** (1968) was a stylish right-handed batsman who bowled a bit of left-arm seam. **Shoaib Malik** (1982) was a mostly reliable batsman, and off spinner.

Wasim Raja (1952-2006), older brother of Rameez, was a left-handed batsman and wrist spinner. **Abdul Razzaq** (1979) was a lightweight all-rounder and seam bowler more suited to the limited-overs format.

Saleem Yousuf (1959) the wicket-keeper. **Intikhab Alam** (1941) was a wrist spinner and useful lower-order batsman. **Mohammad Sami** (1981) was a fast bowler probably given too many opportunities at Test level. **Umar Gul** (1984) was a good but not great fast bowler.

PAKISTAN Worst XI, 10+ Tests

	tests	*runs*	*ri*	*wkts*	*rwi*
Saleem Elahi	13	436	18.16		
Rizwan-uz-Zaman	11	345	18.15	4	8.62
Asif Mujtaba	25	928	22.63	4	303.00
Mansoor Akhtar	19	655	22.58		
W Mathias	21	783	21.75		
* AH Kardar	23	847	22.89	21	56.23
Maqsood Ahmed	16	507	18.77	3	318.30
† Adnan Akmal	21	591	20.37		
Tahir Naqqash	15	300	15.78	34	32.64
Shujauddin	19	395	12.34	20	50.06
Mohammad Sami	36	487	8.69	85	40.95

Saleem Elahi (1976) played Tests only because of limited-over success. **Rizwan-uz-Zaman** (1961) was chosen for Pakistan in the 1981-82 season, and then made a comeback six years later, and failed both times. **Asif Mujtaba** (1967) looked like an exciting batting prospect when he debuted three days after his 19th birthday, but it was not to be. Batsman **Mansoor Akhtar** (1957) made one century in 19 Tests, but is better known for his part (224) in an opening partnership with Waheed Mirza of 561 runs, for Karachi Whites in 1977. **Wallis Mathias** (1935-1994) was famous for being the first non-Muslim to play for Pakistan, and was a stylish batsman and outstanding slips catcher.

Abdul Kardar (1925-1996) was a left-handed batsman and spin bowler, and fine captain, and he also played for India (under the name Abdul Hafeez), without success. Despite his failings as a player, he was an important figure in the development of cricket in Pakistan.

Maqsood Ahmed (1925-1999) was a carefree batsman who had an unfortunate highest score of 99, and also bowled a bit of seam. **Adnan Akmal** (1985) the keeper. **Tahir Naqqash** (1959) was a seam bowler, with **Mohammad Sami**. And **Shujauddin** (1930-2006) was a left-arm spinner.

PAKISTAN ODI XI (50+ odis)

	odis	*runs*	*rb*	*rirb*	*wkts*	*rb*	*rwirb*
Fakhar Zaman	56	2427	0.95	41.16			
Saeed Anwar	247	8824	0.80	28.92	6	0.78	53.78
Zaheer Abbas	62	2572	0.84	36.00	7	0.79	43.12
Babar Azam	86	4261	0.90	45.64			
Imad Wasim	55	986	1.10	27.11	42	0.81	43.12
Shahid Afridi	398	8064	1.17	25.56	395	0.77	25.02
† Sarfaraz Ahmed	117	2315	0.87	22.12			
* Imran Khan	175	3709	0.72	17.68	182	0.64	14.31
Wasim Akram	356	3717	0.88	11.67	502	0.64	10.52
Saqlain Mushtaq	169	711	0.49	3.55	288	0.71	8.85
Saeed Ajmal	113	324	0.60	2.77	184	0.69	9.53

PAKISTAN T20I XI (20+ t20is)

	t20is	*runs*	*rb*	*rirb*	*wkts*	*rb*	*rwirb*
Ahmed Shehzad	59	1471	1.14	28.42			
Imran Nazir	25	500	1.35	28.12			
* Babar Azam	74	2686	1.29	50.20			
† Mohammad Rizwan	56	1662	1.28	47.27			
Shoaib Malik	124	2435	1.25	27.41	28	1.18	49.76
Mohammad Hafeez	119	2514	1.22	28.38	61	1.10	32.40
Shahid Afridi	98	1405	1.50	23.41	97	1.10	26.49
Shadab Khan	64	275	1.36	14.37	73	1.18	21.12
Imad Wasim	58	339	1.43	13.09	55	1.05	25.55
Umar Gul	60	165	1.05	6.41	85	1.19	14.24
Saeed Ajmal	64	91	1.05	4.14	85	1.06	14.00

SRI LANKA

They were awarded Test status in 1982 despite playing international teams since the 1920s, when they were called Ceylon. The next few years were not easy for their team, as players came and went, and separatists with their bombs threatened to tear their country apart. But the team soon matured and took on the best, proving their rightful place in international cricket by winning the 1996 World Cup.

The Top Test Batsmen for Sri Lanka

(2000+ runs, 35.00+ RI)

		tests	*runs*	*ri*
1	KC Sangakkara	134	12400	53.21
2	DPMD Jayawardene	149	11814	46.88
3	TT Samaraweera	81	5462	41.37
4	PA de Silva	93	6361	40.00
5	FDM Karunaratne	76	5630	38.23
6	AD Mathews	94	6432	38.05
7	TM Dilshan	87	5492	37.87
8	ST Jayasuriya	110	6973	36.89
9	LD Chandimal	64	4217	36.04
10	MS Atapattu	90	5502	35.26
11	AP Gurusinha	41	2452	35.02

The Top Test Bowlers for Sri Lanka

(100+ wickets, -20.00 RWI)

		tests	*wkts*	*ave*	*rwi*
1	M Muralitharan	132	795	22.67	6.50
2	HMRKB Herath	93	433	28.07	11.02
3	WPUJC Vaas	111	355	29.58	16.16
4	MDK Perera	43	161	35.90	17.39
5	SL Malinga	30	101	33.15	19.36

The Top Test All-Rounders for Sri Lanka

(1000+ runs, 50+ wickets, RI higher than RWI)

		tests	*runs*	*ri*	*wkts*	*rwi*	*diff*
1	WPUJC Vaas	111	3089	19.06	355	16.16	2.90
2	M Muralitharan	132	1259	7.77	795	6.50	1.27
3	HMRKB Herath	93	1699	11.79	433	11.02	0.72

The Top 10 ODI Batsmen for Sri Lanka

(Qualification: 50+ odis, 1000+ runs)

		odis	*runs*	*ri*	*rb*	*rirb*
1	N Dickwella	53	1578	31.56	0.93	29.35
2	KC Sangakkara	404	14234	37.45	0.78	29.21
3	TM Dilshan	330	10290	33.96	0.86	29.20
4	ST Jayasuriya	441	13364	31.15	0.91	28.34
5	MDKJ Perera	107	3071	30.10	0.92	27.69

6	AD Mathews	218	5835	31.03	0.83	25.75
7	PA de Silva	308	9284	31.36	0.81	25.40
8	BKG Mendis	82	2297	28.71	0.83	23.59
9	DPMD Jayawardene	448	12650	30.26	0.78	23.60
10	WU Tharanga	235	6951	31.17	0.75	23.37

The Top 10 ODI Bowlers for Sri Lanka

(Qualification: 50+ odis, 50+ wkts)

		odis	*ib*	*runs*	*wkts*	*rwi*	*rb*	*rwirb*
1	M Muralitharan	350	341	12326	534	14.73	0.65	9.57
2	BAW Mendis	87	84	3324	152	12.08	0.80	9.66
3	WPUJC Vaas	322	320	11014	400	22.02	0.69	15.19
4	SL Malinga	226	220	9760	338	18.79	0.89	16.72
5	MF Maharoof	109	105	3789	135	21.82	0.81	17.67
6	DNT Zoysa	95	93	3213	108	25.61	0.75	19.20
7	CPH Ramanayake	62	62	2049	68	27.47	0.71	19.50
8	CRD Fernando	147	141	5648	187	22.71	0.86	19.53
9	HMRKB Herath	71	67	2362	74	28.89	0.72	20.80
10	UDU Chandana	147	136	4818	151	28.73	0.78	22.40

SRI LANKA XI

	years	*tests*	*runs*	*ri*	*wkts*	*rwi*
TM Dilshan	13	87	5492	37.87	39	85.49
ST Jayasuriya	15	110	6973	36.89	98	49.05
KC Sangakkara	15	134	12400	53.21		
* DPMD Jayawardene	17	149	11814	46.88	6	189.41
TT Samaraweera	11	81	5462	41.37	15	107.16
PA de Silva	17	93	6361	40.00	29	83.30
† HP Tillakaratne	14	83	4545	34.69		
WPUJC Vaas	14	111	3089	19.06	355	16.16
HMRKB Herath	19	93	1699	11.79	433	11.02
RAS Lakmal	11	70	934	8.56	171	25.99
M Muralitharan	17	132	1259	7.77	795	6.50

Tillakaratne Dilshan (1976) was a confrontational and aggressive batsman, and occasional off break bowler. **Sanath Jayasuriya** (1969) was a chancy left-handed batsman with strong wrists, and a useful spin bowler, and even better in the limited-over game.

Kumar Sangakkara was Sri Lanka's greatest batsman, followed by **Mahela Jayawardene** (1977), who was a short and classical batsman with great timing and unflappable determination. **Thilan Samaraweera** (1976) was a steady and patient batsman who played in the shadow of Sangakkara and Jayawardene.

Aravinda de Silva (1965) was fearless and sensational when playing the pull, hook, or cut, and he also bowled some off break spin. **Hashan Tillakaratne** (1967) was originally chosen as a specialist batsman, plus an outstanding fielder, but his keeping quickly developed.

Chaminda Vaas was an accurate left-arm swing bowler. **Suranga Lakmal** bowled with heart but lacked pace. **Rangana Herath** (1978) was a short left-arm spinner whose career flourished after the age of 30. **Muttiah Muralitharan** was the most successful slow bowler in history.

SRI LANKA Worst XI, 10+ Tests

	tests	*runs*	*ri*	*wkts*	*rwi*	
RP Arnold	44	1821	26.39	11	54.36	138.37
HDRL Thirimanne	44	2088	24.56			
RS Madugalle	21	1029	26.38			
KDK Vithanage	10	370	23.12			
J Mubarak	13	385	16.73			
HDPK Dharmasena	31	868	17.01	69	32.49	
MF Maharoof	22	556	16.35	25	91.33	
RS Kalpage	11	294	16.33	12	85.99	
EAR de Silva	10	185	11.56	8	241.87	
†RG de Alwis	11	152	8.00			
Nuwan Pradeep	28	137	2.74	70	32.48	

Russel Arnold (1973) was a wiry opener and right-arm spinner, current batsman **Lahiru Thirimanne** (1989), batsmen **Ranjan Madugalle** (1959), **Kithuruwan Vithanage** (1991) and **Jehan Mubarak**.

Kumar Dharmasena played as an all-rounder and off break spinner, but struggled to prove his place. **Farveez Maharoof** (1984) was a medium pace bowler. **Ruwan Kalpage** (1970) was a right-arm spinner and apparently an all-rounder. **Asoka de Silva** was a leg spinner with one of the worst records ever, but was better as an umpire. **Guy de Alwis** (1959-2013) was a specialist keeper but his batting was not good enough for the modern game. Fast bowler **Nuwan Pradeep** (1986) was known as ANPR Fernando when he first played for Sri Lanka.

SRI LANKA ODI XI (50+ odis)

	odis	*runs*	*rb*	*rirb*	*wkts*	*rb*	*rwirb*
TM Dilshan	330	10290	0.86	29.20	106	0.81	70.25
ST Jayasuriya	441	13364	0.91	28.34	320	0.79	33.03
* KC Sangakkara	404	14234	0.78	29.21			
AD Mathews	218	5835	0.83	25.75	120	0.77	33.81
PA de Silva	308	9284	0.81	25.40	106	0.81	46.96
† N Dickwella	53	1578	0.93	29.35			
NLTC Perera	166	2316	1.12	19.79	175	0.97	28.53
MF Maharoof	109	1113	0.86	12.76	135	0.81	17.67
WPUJC Vaas	322	2018	0.72	6.63	400	0.69	15.19
M Muralitharan	350	674	0.77	3.20	534	0.65	9.57
BAW Mendis	87	188	0.71	3.17	152	0.80	9.66

SRI LANKA T20I XI (20+ t20is)

	t20is	*runs*	*rb*	*rirb*	*wkts*	*rb*	*rwirb*
P Nissanka	20	562	1.16	34.30			
ST Jayasuriya	31	629	1.29	27.03	19	1.22	36.97
KC Sangakkara	56	1382	1.19	31.02			
* DPMD Jayawardene	55	1493	1.33	36.09			
† MDKJ Perera	60	1539	1.31	34.16			
MD Gunathilaka	27	542	1.21	25.21	6	1.24	55.68
NLTC Perera	84	1204	1.51	24.56	51	1.55	68.54
BMAJ Mendis	22	207	1.18	16.28	12	1.18	28.55
PWH de Silva	35	345	1.20	14.26	57	1.06	8.43
SL Malinga	84	136	0.84	3.46	107	1.23	19.82
BAW Mendis	39	8	0.47	0.47	66	1.07	9.11

ZIMBABWE

The nation formally known as Rhodesia, enjoyed participating in South African domestic cricket competitions, and provided a few players to their rival's national team. They were awarded Test status in 1992. Recent political problems in their country have resulted in a drastic decline in their cricket.

The Top 10 ODI Batsmen for Zimbabwe

(Qualification: 50+ odis, 1000+ runs)

		odis	*runs*	*ri*	*rb*	*rirb*
1	BRM Taylor	205	6684	32.92	0.76	25.01
2	SC Williams	142	4149	30.28	0.82	24.82
3	Sikandar Raza	111	3086	29.11	0.84	24.45
4	A Flower	213	6786	32.62	0.74	24.13
5	CR Ervine	105	2837	28.94	0.75	21.70
6	GW Flower	221	6571	30.70	0.67	20.56
7	H Masakadza	209	5658	27.20	0.73	19.85
8	ADR Campbell	188	5185	28.17	0.66	18.59
9	DL Houghton	63	1530	25.50	0.70	17.85
10	MW Goodwin	71	1818	25.97	0.68	17.65

The Top 10 ODI Bowlers for Zimbabwe

(Qualification: 50+ odis, 50+ wkts)

		odis	*ib*	*runs*	*wkts*	*rwi*	*rb*	*rwirb*
1	HH Streak	189	185	7129	239	23.08	0.75	17.31
2	AG Cremer	96	95	3597	119	24.12	0.76	18.33
3	TL Chatara	76	76	3205	100	24.35	0.85	20.69
4	EA Brandes	59	59	2266	70	27.28	0.80	21.84
5	PA Strang	95	89	3173	96	30.64	0.72	22.06
6	RW Price	102	99	3575	100	35.39	0.66	23.35
7	GB Brent	70	69	2776	75	34.04	0.81	27.57
8	HK Olonga	50	49	1977	58	28.79	0.96	27.63
9	DT Hondo	56	56	2171	61	32.67	0.91	29.72
10	CB Mpofu	84	83	3581	93	34.36	0.90	30.92

ZIMBABWE XI

	years	*tests*	*runs*	*ri*	*wkts*	*rwi*
GW Flower	11	67	3457	28.10	25	147.55
SV Carlisle	10	37	1615	24.46		
* A Flower	10	63	4794	42.80		
BRM Taylor	17	34	2320	34.11		
H Masakadza	17	38	2223	29.25	16	45.84
ADR Campbell	10	60	2858	26.22		
†T Taibu	10	28	1546	28.62		
HH Streak	11	65	1990	18.59	216	13.28
AG Cremer	12	19	540	14.21	57	21.63
T Panyangara	10	9	201	11.16	31	13.53
RW Price	13	22	261	6.86	80	15.77

Grant Flower (1970) was a regular player, as an opening batsman and occasional left-arm spin bowler, but he never put any consistent performances together to justify playing so many games. **Stuart Carlisle** (1972) was an opener who managed only two centuries.

Andy Flower (1968), brother of Grant, was Zimbabwe's most successful batsman, and one of the best wicket-keeper/batsmen in the history of the game. He was hardnosed and determined at the crease.

Brendan Taylor (1986) is a batsman who can dominate the bowling, and a part-time wicket-keeper. **Hamilton Masakadza** (1983) was a tall and solid right-handed batsman and useful seam bowler. **Alistair Campbell** (1972) was a left-handed batsman who batted far below what he should have. **Tatenda Taibu** (1983) was a promising keeper/batsman who retired early, at age 29.

Heath Streak (1974) was Zimbabwe's best bowler; a big and strong man with hostile pace, swing and accuracy. **Tinashe Panyangara** (1985) was a fast bowler who did well in his limited opportunities. **Graeme Cremer** (1986) is a talented leg spinner who never quite has things go his way. **Ray Price** (1976) was an underrated left-arm spinner.

ZIMBABWE Worst XI, 10+ Tests

	tests	*runs*	*ri*	*wkts*	*rwi*
V Sibanda	14	591	21.10		
MH Dekker	14	333	15.13		
SV Carlisle	37	1615	24.46		
GJ Rennie	23	1023	22.23		
CB Wishart	27	1098	21.96		
†RW Chakabva	22	1061	24.67		
E Chigumbura	14	569	21.07	21	48.19
DT Tiripano	15	508	17.51	26	44.27
ML Nkala	10	187	12.46	11	90.12
BA Murphy	11	123	8.20	18	65.26
AR Whittall	10	114	6.33	7	180.02

Openers **Vusi Sibanda** (1983), who debuted too young, at the age of 19, and left-handed batsman **Mark Dekker**, batsman **Stuart Carlisle**, left-hander **Gavin Rennie** (1976), batsman **Craig Wishart** (1974), and keeper **Regis Chakabva** (1987).

All-rounder **Elton Chigumbura** (1986), medium pace bowlers **Mluleki Nkala** and **Donald Tiripano** (1988), leg spinner **Brian Murphy** (1976), and **Andy Whittall** (1973), an off break spinner with not a lot of success.

ZIMBABWE ODI XI (50+ odis)

	odis	*runs*	*rb*	*rirb*	*wkts*	*rb*	*rwirb*
GW Flower	221	6571	0.67	20.56	104		46.91
†A Flower	213	6786	0.74	24.13			
BRM Taylor	205	6684	0.76	25.01	9	1.02	107.35
SC Williams	142	4149	0.82	24.82	76	0.81	58.83
Sikandar Raza	111	3086	0.84	24.45	63	0.81	46.17
H Masakadza	209	5658	0.73	19.85	39	0.88	80.43
AM Blignaut	54	626	1.06	16.17	50	0.87	38.04
HH Streak	187	2901	0.73	13.48	237	0.75	17.35
EA Brandes	59	404	0.90	8.86	70	0.80	21.84
AG Cremer	96	744	0.62	6.49	119	0.76	18.33
TL Chatara	70	165	0.49	1.79	95	0.84	18.91

ZIMBABWE T20I XI (20+ t20is)

	t20is	*runs*	*rb*	*rirb*	*wkts*	*rb*	*rwirb*
H Masakadza	66	1662	1.17	29.46	2	1.56	396.63
CR Ervine	34	777	1.05	24.71			
MN Waller	32	613	1.38	27.28			
SC Williams	45	927	1.28	26.36	32	1.21	50.09
†BRM Taylor	43	878	1.19	25.14			
W Madhevere	21	448	1.19	25.38	3	1.29	348.41
E Chigumbura	57	893	1.40	22.31	16	1.54	53.91
LM Jongwe	22	158	1.01	9.38	33	1.41	16.59
KM Jarvis	22	55	0.85	3.89	28	1.31	27.61
TL Chatara	30	18	0.66	2.37	34	1.29	28.14
AG Cremer	29	68	0.66	2.35	35	1.48	17.34

BANGLADESH

Bangladesh was East Pakistan until 1971, and at that time they provided players to the Pakistan cricket team. Through the 1970s and 1980s they showed little reason to be given Test status of their own, but nevertheless it was granted in the year 2000. Only in the last few years have they started to produce some good players, so perhaps their future looks promising.

The Top Test Batsmen for Bangladesh

(2000+ runs, 35.00+ RI)

		tests	*runs*	*ri*
1	Tamim Iqbal	65	4848	38.78
2	Mominul Haque	51	3514	36.98
3	Shakib Al Hasan	59	4029	36.96

The Top Test Bowlers for Bangladesh

(100+ wickets, -20.00 RWI)

		tests	*wkts*	*ave*	*rwi*
1	Taijul Islam	36	153	32.01	12.97
2	Shakib Al Hasan	59	215	31.30	14.41
3	Mehidy Hasan Miraz	33	128	34.77	15.21
4	Mohammad Rafique	33	100	40.76	19.56

The Top Test All-Rounders for Bangladesh

(1000+ runs, 50+ wickets, RI higher than RWI)

		tests	*runs*	*ri*	*wkts*	*rwi*	*diff*
1	Shakib Al Hasan	59	4029	36.96	215	14.41	22.55
2	Mehidy Hasan Miraz	33	1072	17.57	128	15.21	2.36

The Top 10 ODI Batsmen for Bangladesh

(Qualification: 50+ odis, 1000+ runs)

		odis	*runs*	*ri*	*rb*	*rirb*
1	Soumya Sarkar	61	1768	30.48	0.97	29.56
2	Liton Das	53	1671	31.52	0.88	27.73
3	Tamim Iqbal	225	7826	35.09	0.78	27.37
4	Shakib Al Hasan	221	6755	32.32	0.82	26.50
5	Mushfiqur Rahim	233	6697	30.72	0.78	23.96
6	Imrul Kayes	78	2434	31.20	0.71	22.15
7	Sabbir Rahman	66	1333	22.59	0.91	20.55
8	Shahriar Nafees	75	2201	29.34	0.69	20.24
9	Nasir Hossain	65	1281	24.63	0.79	19.45
10	Mahmudullah	206	4562	25.48	0.76	19.36

The Top 10 ODI Bowlers for Bangladesh

(Qualification: 50+ odis, 50+ wkts)

		odis	*ib*	*runs*	*wkts*	*rwi*	*rb*	*rwirb*
1	Mustafizur Rahman	74	73	3098	131	13.17	0.85	11.19
2	Shakib Al Hasan	221	218	8401	285	22.54	0.74	16.67
3	Abdur Razzak	153	152	6065	207	21.50	0.76	16.34
4	Mashrafe Mortaza	220	220	8893	270	26.83	0.81	21.73
5	Syed Rasel	52	52	2051	61	28.65	0.77	22.06
6	Mehidy Hasan Miraz	58	57	2183	64	30.37	0.74	22.47
7	Rubel Hossain	104	102	4427	129	27.12	0.94	25.49
8	Mohammad Rafique	125	125	4739	125	37.60	0.73	27.44
9	Shafiul Islam	60	60	2529	70	30.95	0.99	30.64
10	Tapash Baisya	56	56	2452	59	39.43	0.94	37.06

BANGLADESH XI (7+ years)

	years	*tests*	*runs*	*ri*	*wkts*	*rwi*
Tamim Iqbal	11	65	4848	38.78		
Imrul Kayes	10	39	1797	23.64		
Mominul Haque	9	51	3514	36.98	7	337.85
* Shakib Al Hasan	14	59	4029	36.96	215	14.41
† Mushfiqur Rahim	16	80	4932	33.32		
Mahmudullah	10	50	2914	31.00	43	69.88
Mohammad Rafique	7	33	1059	16.80	100	19.54
Mashrafe Mortaza	7	36	797	11.89	78	27.14
Shahadat Hossain	9	38	521	7.55	72	43.17
Nazmul Hossain	7	2	16	4.00	5	23.28
Enamul Haque, jr	9	15	59	2.26	44	23.99

Aggressive and confident left-handed batsman **Tamim Iqbal** (1989) who in his first Test opened the batting at the age 18, and top-scored in both innings. His usual opening partner was the left-handed **Imrul Kayes** (1987).

The current captain is the left-handed batsman **Mominul Haque** (1991). **Shakib Al Hasan** (1987) is a world-class cricketer both as a left-handed batsman and left-arm spinner. **Mushfiqur Rahim** is of more value to his team as a batsman than a wicket-keeper. **Mahmudullah** (1986) played for many years as an all-rounder and off spinner who did very little as a bowler.

Mohammad Rafique (1970) was a left-arm spinner. **Shahadat Hossain** was a fast bowler who should have a much better record. **Nazmul Hossain** (1987) a medium fast bowler who should have played a lot more, with two Tests in seven years. **Enamul Haque, jr** (1986) was a left-arm spinner, and seamer **Mashrafe Mortaza** (1983).

BANGLADESH Worst XI, 10+ Tests

	tests	*runs*	*ri*	*wkts*	*rwi*
Javed Omar	40	1720	21.50		
Hannan Sarkar	17	662	20.06		
Sabbir Rahman	11	481	21.86		
Aminul Islam	13	530	20.38		
Mohammad Mithun	10	333	18.50		
Aftab Ahmed	16	582	18.77	5	85.32
Alok Kapali	17	584	17.17	6	374.17
†Khaled Mashud	44	1409	16.77		
Abdur Razzak	12	245	12.25	23	52.73
Khaled Mahmud	12	266	11.56	13	83.69
Rubel Hossain	27	265	5.63	36	93.82

Right-handed opener **Javed Omar**, and batsmen **Hannan Sarkar** (1982), **Sabbir Rahman** (1991) and **Mohammad Mithun** (1991). **Aminul Islam** (1968) played Tests at the tail end of his career when he was past his prime, but still managed 145 in his first innings. **Aftab Ahmed** (1985) was a right-handed batsman and medium pace bowler, and all-rounder **Alok Kapali**.

Khaled Mashud (1976) was a wicket-keeper and not much of a batsman, left-arm spinner **Abdur Razzak** (1982), seam bowler **Khaled Mahmud** (1971), and fast bowler **Rubel Hossain**.

BANGLADESH ODI XI (50+ odis)

	odis	*runs*	*rb*	*rirb*	*wkts*	*rb*	*rwirb*
Tamim Iqbal	225	7826	0.78	27.37			
Imrul Kayes	78	2434	0.71	22.15			
Soumya Sarkar	61	1768	0.97	29.56	11	0.97	56.12
† Liton Das	53	1671	0.88	27.73			
Shakib Al Hasan	221	6755	0.82	26.50	285	0.74	16.67
Mushfiqur Rahim	224	6344	0.82	23.55			
Nasir Hossain	65	1281	0.79	19.45	24	0.78	57.51
Mehidy Hasan Miraz	58	570	0.75	11.87	64	0.74	22.47
Mashrafe Mortaza	220	1787	0.87	9.83	270	0.76	21.73
Abdur Razzak	153	779	0.76	6.10	207	0.76	16.34
Mustafizur Rahman	74	82	0.54	1.33	131	0.85	11.19

BANGLADESH T20I XI (20+ t20is)

	t20is	*runs*	*rb*	*rirb*	*wkts*	*rb*	*rwirb*
Tamim Iqbal	78	1758	1.16	26.13			
Mohammad Naim	34	809	1.03	24.50			
Sabbir Rahman	44	946	1.20	26.40	6	1.04	16.16
† Liton Das	48	917	1.23	23.99			
Mohammad Ashraful	23	450	1.26	25.64	8	1.52	39.90
Shakib Al Hasan	96	1908	1.19	23.89	119	1.11	17.61
Mahmudullah	115	2002	1.18	22.07	37	1.19	58.91
Mohammad Saifuddin	29	196	1.15	13.24	31	1.37	34.14
Nasum Ahmed	20	35	0.89	3.45	26	1.07	13.16
Abdur Razzak	34	41	0.55	1.27	44	1.14	16.27
Al-Amin Hossain	31	7	0.58	0.67	43	1.18	13.49

DECADE XIs

Since we are still a little way into the decade in 2021 and a limited number of Tests have been played, the teams of the 2020s for this edition are based entirely on opinion of each player's class and experience over their stats.

WORLD 2020s XI

	tests	*runs*	*ri*	*wkts*	*rwi*
RG Sharma	13	996	41.50		
FDM Karunaratne	12	1199	52.13		
* KS Williamson	8	893	68.69	1	116.00
M Labuschagne	13	1205	50.20	1	3859.00
SPD Smith	13	846	40.28	1	120.00
† Q de Kock	10	617	36.29		
RA Jadeja	11	552	20.22	31	14.87
R Ashwin	16	546	20.22	80	7.18
PJ Cummins	12	194	12.93	58	8.15
K Rabada	11	200	10.52	53	8.23
Shaheen Shah Afridi	17	106	5.30	70	10.01

India's dominating batsman **Rohit Sharma** (1987) and spinners **Ravichandran Ashwin** and **Ravindra Jadeja** (1988), Sri Lanka's batsman **Dimuth Karunaratne** (1988), New Zealand's **Kane Williamson**, Australia's run machine **Marnus Labuschagne** (1994), quirky batsman **Steve Smith**, and classy fast bowler **Pat Cummins**, South Africa's keeper and quick-scoring batsman **Quinton de Kock** (1992) and fast bowler **Kagiso Rabada** (1995), and Pakistan's young left-arm fast bowling sensation **Shaheen Shah Afridi** (2000).

WORLD 2020s 2nd XI

	tests	*runs*	*ri*	*wkts*	rwi
D Elgar	16	1198	39.93		
DA Warner	11	665	35.00		
Azhar Ali	17	1136	40.57		
* JE Root	28	2530	48.65	17	94.46
V Kohli	17	841	28.03		
† Mohammad Rizwan	17	857	35.88		
AR Patel	6	197	19.70	39	3.82
KA Jamieson	14	351	19.50	66	7.94
Rashid Khan	1	-	-	11	4.54
B Muzarabani	5	88	9.77	19	9.41
JJ Bumrah	17	156	5.77	61	12.72

Australia's aggressive batsman **David Warner**, South Africa's dependable opener **Dean Elgar** (1987), Pakistan's reliable **Azhar Ali** (1985) and confident batsman/keeper

Mohammad Rizwan (1992), England's elegant **Joe Root** (1990), India's superstar **Virat Kohli** and a brilliant spinner who gets little chances in **Axar Patel** (1994), and the freaky fast bowler **Jasprit Bumrah** (1993), New Zealand's talented tall left-arm seamer **Kyle Jamieson** (1994), Zimbabwe's even taller fast bowler **Blessing Muzarabani** (1996), and Afganistan's brilliant leg-spinner **Rashid Khan** (1998).

WORLD 2010s XI (22+ Tests)

	tests	*runs*	*ri*	*wkts*	*rwi*
DA Warner	83	7088	46.32	4	319.43
* AN Cook	111	8818	43.87		
KC Sangakkara	46	4851	56.40		
SPD Smith	72	7164	55.10	17	178.80
JH Kallis	33	2810	51.09	34	64.66
Shakib Al Hasan	42	3147	39.83	162	14.60
† Q de Kock	44	2683	36.25		
R Ashwin	70	2385	24.84	362	9.17
PJ Cummins	29	639	14.86	139	8.67
DW Steyn	59	808	10.63	267	9.01
K Rabada	41	586	9.76	190	8.90

Australia's **David Warner, Steve Smith** and fast bowler **Pat Cummins**, England's **Alastair Cook**, Sri Lanka's **Kumar Sangakkara**, South Africa's **Jacques Kallis**, Bangladesh's **Shakib Al Hasan**, South Africa's keeper **Quinton de Kock** and fast bowlers **Dale Steyn** and **Kagiso Rabada**, and India's spinner **Ravichandran Ashwin**.

WORLD 2010s 2nd XI (22+ Tests)

	tests	*runs*	*ri*	*wkts*	rwi
CJL Rogers	24	1996	43.39		
* GC Smith	38	2814	42.63		
AB de Villiers	60	5059	51.62		
V Kohli	84	7202	51.07		
Younis Khan	55	4839	47.91	2	487.50
BA Stokes	60	3787	34.42	139	23.83
† BJ Watling	66	3538	34.01		
VD Philander	61	1700	19.31	220	11.39
RJ Harris	27	603	15.46	113	10.85
HMRKB Herath	72	1492	12.75	363	9.67
Saeed Ajmal	30	422	9.81	160	9.44

South Africa's batsmen **Graeme Smith** (1981) and **AB de Villiers**, and seam and swing bowler **Vernon Philander** (1985), Australia's **Chris Rogers** (1977) and impressive fast bowler **Ryan Harris** (1979) who found success late in his career, India's **Virat Kohli**, New Zealand's batsman/wicket-keeper **BJ Watling** (1985), England's all-rounder **Ben Stokes** (1991), Pakistan's batsman **Younis Khan** and right-arm spinner **Saeed Ajmal** (1977), and Sri Lanka's off spinner **Rangana Herath**.

WORLD 2000s XI (22+ Tests)

	tests	*runs*	*ri*	*wkts*	*rwi*
V Sehwag	71	6165	50.95	30	99.12
G Gambhir	27	2553	53.18		
* BC Lara	65	6339	53.72		
Mohammad Yousuf	71	6439	53.21		
RT Ponting	106	9358	51.41		
JH Kallis	100	8547	49.69	204	26.95
† A Flower	24	2214	52.71		
DW Steyn	34	443	10.30	172	8.77
Shoaib Akhtar	33	474	9.67	144	8.79
M Muralitharan	83	773	7.80	560	5.66
GD McGrath	65	355	5.54	294	9.03

India's **Virender Sehwag** and **Gautam Gambhir** (1981), West Indies' **Brian Lara**, Pakistan's **Mohammad Yousuf** and **Shoaib Akhtar**, Australia's **Ricky Ponting** and **Glenn McGrath**, South Africa's **Jacques Kallis** and **Dale Steyn**, Zimbabwe's **Andy Flower**, and Sri Lanka's **Muttiah Muralitharan**.

WORLD 2000s 2nd XI (22+ Tests)

	tests	*runs*	*ri*	*wkts*	*rwi*
ML Hayden	95	8176	48.09		
* GC Smith	78	6439	47.00	8	400.48
KC Sangakkara	88	7549	51.35		
DPMD Jayawardene	95	8187	51.16	5	49.20
Inzamam-ul-Haq	61	5112	50.61		
† AC Gilchrist	90	5035	39.64		
DL Vettori	68	3168	30.75	221	16.32
MG Johnson	30	875	22.43	137	11.87
SK Warne	64	1565	18.63	351	9.04
A Kumble	74	1427	14.56	355	11.62
D Gough	24	341	9.74	94	11.37

Australia's **Matthew Hayden**, **Adam Gilchrist**, rangy left-arm fast bowler **Mitchell Johnson** (1981), and **Shane Warne**, South Africa's **Graeme Smith**, Sri Lanka's **Kumar Sangakkara** and **Mahela Jayawardene**, Pakistan's **Inzamam-ul-Haq**, New Zealand's **Daniel Vettori**, India's **Anil Kumble**, and England's fast bowler **Darren Gough** (1970).

1990s XI

	tests	*runs*	*ri*	*wkts*	*rwi*
GA Gooch	45	4176	50.31	9	121.39
NS Sidhu	38	2517	44.94		
BC Lara	65	5573	49.75		
SR Tendulkar	69	5626	51.61	13	108.86
RS Dravid	34	2698	46.51		
* SR Waugh	89	6213	43.44	47	48.50
SM Pollock	38	1404	25.07	161	8.51
Wasim Akram	62	1956	20.37	289	8.23
† RC Russell	47	1489	20.12		
M Muralitharan	48	481	7.75	227	8.81
AA Donald	59	532	7.09	284	8.07

England's **Graham Gooch** (1953) and **"Jack" Russell** (1963), India's **Navjot Sidhu, Sachin Tendulkar** and **Rahul Dravid**, West Indies' **Brian Lara**, Australia's **Steve Waugh** (1965), South Africa's **Shaun Pollock** and **Allan Donald**, Pakistan's **Wasim Akram**, and Sri Lanka's **Muttiah Muralitharan**.

1990s 2nd XI

	tests	*runs*	*ri*	*wkts*	*rwi*
Saeed Anwar	44	3366	44.88		
MJ Slater	58	4425	42.96		
PA de Silva	62	4448	42.76	23	71.36
SC Ganguly	32	2432	45.03	19	66.10
* MD Crowe	32	2317	42.12		
M Azharuddin	64	3880	41.27		
† IA Healy	102	3949	24.83		
SK Warne	80	1577	13.95	351	10.67
CEL Ambrose	71	1016	9.76	309	8.34
Waqar Younis	58	611	7.83	279	8.31
GD McGrath	58	286	3.97	266	9.62

Pakistan's **Saeed Anwar** and **Waqar Younis**, Australia's **Michael Slater** (1970), **Ian Healy**, **Shane Warne**, and **Glenn McGrath**, Sri Lanka's **Aravinda de Silva**, India's **Sourav Ganguly** (1972), New Zealand's **Martin Crowe**, India's **Mohammad Azharuddin**, and West Indies' **Curtley Ambrose**.

1980s XI

	tests	runs	ri	wkts	rwi
SM Gavaskar	65	4475	42.21		
BA Richards	0				
Javed Miandad	76	5642	51.29		
GS Chappell	33	2712	49.30	13	89.91
RG Pollock	0				
* Imran Khan	54	2430	34.22	256	6.72
† PJL Dujon	64	2885	32.41		
RJ Hadlee	53	2040	25.50	289	6.07
MD Marshall	63	1430	18.10	323	7.39
DK Lillee	35	408	9.06	171	9.00
J Garner	49	486	8.67	210	9.13

India's **Sunil Gavaskar**, South Africa's **Barry Richards** and **Graeme Pollock**, Pakistan's **Javed Miandad** and **Imran Khan**, Australia's **Greg Chappell** and **Dennis Lillee**, West Indies' **Jeff Dujon** (1956), **Malcolm Marshall**, and **Joel Garner**, and New Zealand's **Richard Hadlee**.

1980s 2nd XI

	tests	runs	ri	wkts	rwi
KC Wessels	24	1761	41.92		
Shoaib Mohammad	26	1543	41.70	4	82.00
AR Border	97	7386	45.03	21	92.03
IVA Richards	78	5113	45.65	28	156.69
* CH Lloyd	44	2881	47.22		
IT Botham	75	4051	32.66	258	15.06
Kapil Dev	80	3353	28.41	272	14.55
† Saleem Yousuf	25	878	25.82		
MA Holding	45	685	12.68	184	10.67
Iqbal Qasim	32	421	12.38	131	10.87
TM Alderman	33	163	3.88	136	11.94

Australia's **Kepler Wessels** (1957), **Allan Border** and **Terry Alderman** (1956), Pakistan's **Shoaib Mohammad**, **Saleem Yousuf** and **Iqbal Qasim**, West Indies' **Viv Richards**, **Clive Lloyd** (1944) and **Michael Holding**, England's **Ian Botham**, and India's **Kapil Dev**.

1970s XI

	tests	*runs*	*ri*	*wkts*	*rwi*
BA Richards	4	508	72.57		
SM Gavaskar	60	5647	52.28		
IVA Richards	29	2640	55.00	4	220.31
RG Pollock	4	517	73.85		
Javed Miandad	25	2059	47.88	17	40.39
* GS Sobers	17	1256	44.85	42	23.24
IT Botham	22	1068	35.60	118	6.53
† APE Knott	71	3509	31.33		
DK Lillee	35	497	11.04	184	8.78
JR Thomson	34	433	9.41	152	10.27
AME Roberts	29	290	7.63	140	10.23

South Africa's **Barry Richards** and **Graeme Pollock**, India's **Sunil Gavaskar**, West Indies' **Viv Richards**, **Garry Sobers**, and brutal fast bowler **Andy Roberts** (1951), Pakistan's **Javed Miandad**, England's **Ian Botham**, and **Allan Knott**, and Australia's **Dennis Lillee** and **Jeff Thomson**.

1970s 2nd XI

	tests	*runs*	*ri*	*wkts*	*rwi*
EJ Barlow	4	360	51.42	11	16.98
G Boycott	44	3806	49.42		
* GS Chappell	53	4357	46.35	34	68.26
DI Gower	17	1187	45.65		
IR Redpath	33	2861	44.70		
MJ Procter	4	209	29.85	26	4.17
Kapil Dev	23	893	28.80	87	12.74
† RW Marsh	55	2471	28.07		
MA Holding	15	225	10.22	65	10.95
G Dymock	15	198	7.92	62	10.63
BS Chandrasekhar	42	95	1.66	180	11.35

South Africa's **Eddie Barlow** and **Mike Proctor**, England's stubborn opener **Geoff Boycott** (1940) and the gentle left-hander **David Gower** (1957), Australia's **Greg Chappell**, **Ian Redpath** (1941), **Rod Marsh**, and underrated left-handed fast bowler **Geoff Dymock** (1945), India's **Kapil Dev** and **Bhagwath Chandrasekhar**, and West Indies' **Michael Holding**.

1960s XI

	tests	runs	ri	wkts	rwi
WM Lawry	58	4717	44.92		
* RB Simpson	46	3995	47.55	60	44.42
KF Barrington	75	6397	52.43	24	95.05
RG Pollock	19	1739	51.14	4	147.00
KD Walters	21	1992	58.58	11	71.39
GS Sobers	49	4563	53.05	162	17.73
† DT Lindsay	17	1021	37.81		
AK Davidson	17	540	21.60	94	7.21
FS Trueman	36	580	11.37	179	8.23
K Higgs	15	185	9.73	71	7.88
EAS Prasanna	22	362	9.52	113	9.57

Australia's **Bill Lawry** (1937), **Bob Simpson**, **Doug Walters** and **Alan Davidson**, England's **Ken Barrington**, **Fred Trueman**, and fast bowler **Ken Higgs** (1937-2016), South Africa's **Graeme Pollock** and **Denis Lindsay** (1939-2005), West Indies' **Garry Sobers**, and India's **Erapalli Prasanna**.

1960s 2nd XI

	tests	runs	ri	wkts	rwi
EJ Barlow	26	2156	43.12	29	49.92
* JH Edrich	40	2711	43.03		
RB Kanhai	43	3739	49.19		
TW Graveney	31	2292	48.76		
SM Nurse	29	2523	46.72		
TL Goddard	23	1606	36.50	67	15.97
Asif Iqbal	17	872	30.06	40	16.83
† APE Knott	18	666	25.61		
PM Pollock	24	533	15.67	101	10.98
GD McKenzie	54	886	11.35	238	11.96
LR Gibbs	42	226	3.64	184	11.65

South Africa's **Eddie Barlow**, **Trevor Goddard** and **Peter Pollock** (1941), England's **John Edrich** (1937-2020), **Tom Graveney** (1927-2015) and **Allan Knott**, West Indies' **Rohan Kanhai**, **Seymour Nurse** (1933-2019), and off spinner **Lance Gibbs** (1934), Pakistan's **Asif Iqbal**, and Australia's fast bowler **Graham McKenzie** (1941).

1950s XI

	tests	*runs*	*ri*	*wkts*	*rwi*
* L Hutton	38	3183	48.22		
RB Kanhai	18	1317	41.15		
CL Walcott	33	3129	54.89	10	58.68
ED Weekes	39	3383	49.75		
GS Sobers	27	2213	48.10	31	58.60
MH Mankad	31	1536	32.00	122	12.47
† TG Evans	64	1693	18.20		
HJ Tayfield	30	674	14.04	153	8.18
Fazal Mahmood	26	541	13.87	125	7.60
FH Tyson	17	230	9.58	76	7.08
AV Bedser	28	263	7.30	147	6.88

England's **Len Hutton**, **Godfrey Evans**, blistering fast bowler **Frank Tyson** (1930-2015) and classy medium-fast bowler **Alec Bedser** (1918-2010), West Indies' **Rohan Kanhai**, **Clyde Walcott**, **Everton Weekes** and **Garry Sobers**, India's **Vinoo Mankad**, South Africa's **Hugh Tayfield**, and Pakistan's fast bowler **Fazal Mahmood** (1927-2005).

1950s 2nd XI

	tests	*runs*	*ri*	*wkts*	*rwi*
PE Richardson	25	1623	40.57		
DJ McGlew	24	1825	40.55		
RN Harvey	56	4573	46.19		
* FMM Worrell	29	2397	45.22	47	36.95
PBH May	59	4182	44.96		
TL Goddard	15	852	29.37	47	16.06
† Imtiaz Ahmed	29	1320	27.50		
R Benaud	42	1440	22.85	165	10.74
FS Trueman	31	401	11.79	128	9.82
JC Laker	38	453	9.24	162	8.20
Khan Mohammad	13	100	5.88	54	9.74

England's **Peter Richardson** (1931-2017), **Peter May**, **Fred Trueman** and **Jim Laker**, South Africa's **Jackie McGlew** (1929-1998) and **Trevor Goddard**, Australia's **Neil Harvey** and **Richie Benaud**, West Indies' **Frank Worrell**, and Pakistan's **Imtiaz Ahmed** (1928-2016) and fast bowler **Khan Mohammad** (1928-2009).

1940s XI

	tests	*runs*	*ri*	*wkts*	*rwi*
AR Morris	15	1408	61.20		
SG Barnes	12	998	58.70		
* DG Bradman	15	1903	82.73		
ED Weekes	9	1072	82.46		
DCS Compton	28	2664	55.50	18	119.62
† CL Walcott	9	585	41.78		
KR Miller	17	804	38.28	45	13.32
RR Lindwall	16	442	24.55	65	9.06
J Cowie	6	82	10.25	26	5.94
WA Johnston	10	94	9.40	51	6.74
WJ O'Reilly	1	-	-	8	1.03

Australia's **Arthur Morris** (1922-2015), **Sid Barnes**, **Don Bradman**, **Keith Miller**, **Ray Lindwall**, **Bill O'Reilly**, and **Bill Johnston** (1922-2007), who alternated between spin or fast bowing, West Indies' **Everton Weekes** and **Clyde Walcott**, England's **Denis Compton**, and New Zealand's **Jack Cowie**.

The decade of the 1940s is highly difficult to select since so little international cricket was played.

1940s 2nd XI

	tests	*runs*	*ri*	*wkts*	*rwi*
B Sutcliffe	5	481	60.12		
JB Stollmeyer	6	506	56.22	5	43.20
FMM Worrell	3	294	73.50		
* AD Nourse	11	1193	56.80		
B Mitchell	10	1072	53.60	3	140.76
† WW Wade	6	420	38.18		
DG Phadkar	8	554	36.93	22	13.73
MH Mankad	13	573	23.87	40	18.74
AV Bedser	23	451	12.88	89	15.31
ERH Toshack	12	73	6.63	47	10.29
CN McCarthy	6	6	0.75	23	12.30

New Zealand's **Bert Sutcliffe**, West Indies' **Jeffrey Stollmeyer** and **Frank Worrell**, South Africa's **Dudley Nourse**, **Bruce Mitchell** (1909-1995), **Billy Wade** (1914-2003) and **Cuan McCarthy**, India's **Dattu Phadkar** and **Vinoo Mankad**, England's **Alec Bedser**, and Australia's left-arm medium pacer **Ernie Toshack** (1914-2003).

1930s XI

	tests	*runs*	*ri*	*wkts*	*rwi*
L Hutton	13	1345	64.01		
WH Ponsford	20	1604	50.12		
* DG Bradman	33	4625	94.38		
GA Headley	19	2135	61.00		
WR Hammond	60	5194	53.00	59	51.08
EH Hendren	19	1656	50.18		
† LEG Ames	46	2434	34.28		
CV Grimmett	28	400	11.42	169	6.62
WJ O'Reilly	26	410	10.51	136	8.00
WE Bowes	14	26	2.60	67	8.69
J Cowie	3	8	1.60	19	6.56

England's **Len Hutton, Wally Hammond, Patsy Hendren** (1889-1962), **Les Ames** (1905-1990) and **Bill Bowes**, Australia's **Bill Ponsford, Don Bradman, Clarrie Grimmett** and **Bill O'Reilly**, West Indies' **George Headley**, and New Zealand's **Jack Cowie**.

The decade of the 1930s was probably the strongest decade ever for batsmen, although it was mostly weak in fast bowling reserves. Don Bradman's run-making this decade has never been matched by anyone in the history of the game.

1930s 2nd XI

	tests	*runs*	*ri*	*wkts*	*rwi*
CS Dempster	10	723	48.20		
* WA Brown	16	1324	47.28		
AD Nourse	14	1097	42.19		
E Paynter	20	1540	49.67		
SJ McCabe	39	2748	44.32	36	73.61
† HB Cameron	17	816	27.20		
LN Constantine	15	546	20.22	53	13.73
H Larwood	9	208	17.33	37	9.56
H Verity	40	669	15.20	144	12.35
EA Martindale	10	58	4.14	37	9.97
IAR Peebles	9	36	3.27	40	9.30

New Zealand's **Stewie Dempster** (1903-1974), Australia's **Bill Brown** and **Stan McCabe**, South Africa's **Dudley Nourse** and **Jock Cameron** (1905-1935) who suddenly died of typhoid fever, England's aggressive batsman **Eddie Paynter** (1901-1979), fast bowler **Harold Larwood** (1904-1935), left-arm spinner **Hedley Verity** (1905-1943), and leg spinner **Ian Peebles** (1908-1980), and West Indies' **Learie Constantine** and short but effective fast bowler **Manny Martindale** (1909-1972).

1920s XI

	tests	*runs*	*ri*	*wkts*	*rwi*
JB Hobbs	28	2644	60.09		
H Sutcliffe	32	2960	59.20		
*CG Macartney	14	1252	59.61	11	38.24
WR Hammond	17	1689	58.24	24	46.03
GE Tyldesley	14	990	49.50		
WW Armstrong	10	616	47.38	17	23.03
JM Gregory	24	1146	33.70	85	15.39
†HB Cameron	9	423	28.20		
MW Tate	26	814	24.66	118	9.80
G Geary	11	187	11.68	41	11.29
CV Grimmett	9	157	10.46	47	11.00

England's **Jack Hobbs**, **Herbert Sutcliffe**, **Wally Hammond**, **Ernest Tyldesley** (1889-1962), **Maurice Tate** and fast bowler **George Geary** (1893-1981), Australia's **Charlie Macartney**, **Jack Gregory**, **Clarrie Grimmett**, and **Warwick Armstrong** (1879-1947) the all-rounder who could do anything, and South Africa's keeper **Jock Cameron**.

1910s XI

	tests	*runs*	*ri (adj +5)*	*wkts*	*rwi (adj +5)*
JB Hobbs	21	2031	58.02 (63.02)		
W Bardsley	15	1094	47.56 (52.56)		
VT Trumper	10	930	48.94 (53.94)		
GA Faulkner	16	1471	47.45 (52.75)	56	13.79 (16.20)
G Gunn	5	381	42.33 (47.33)		
*C Hill	10	699	38.83 (43.83)		
FR Foster	11	330	22.00 (27.00)	45	8.86 (10.79)
HV Hordern	7	254	19.53 (24.53)	46	6.60 (8.01)
†H Carter	10	287	15.94 (20.94)		
WJ Whitty	13	152	8.94 (13.94)	65	7.14 (8.90)
SF Barnes	15	75	3.94 (8.94)	122	3.11 (4.22)

England's **Jack Hobbs**, **George Gunn** (1879-1958), **Sydney Barnes**, and right-hand bat and left-arm medium pace bowler **Frank Forster** (1889-1958), Australia's **Warren Bardsley**, **Victor Trumper**, **Clem Hill**, Yorkshire-born wicket-keeper **Sammy Carter** (1878-1948), leg spinner **Herbert "Ranji" Hordern** (1883-1938) who played cricket in the United States of America while studying dentistry, and left-arm fast bowler **Bill Whitty** (1886-1974), and South Africa's **Aubrey Faulkner**.

1900s XI

	tests	runs	ri (adj +5)	wkts	rwi (adj .+5)
RA Duff	22	1317	32.92 (37.92)		
AC MacLaren	19	998	32.19 (37.19)		
C Hill	28	1930	37.11 (42.11)		
* FS Jackson	10	803	47.23 (52.23)	19	15.89 (19.57)
W Bardsley	5	396	39.60 (44.60)		
MA Noble	33	1524	25.83 (30.83)	89	15.51 (18.60)
JB King	0				
† AFA Lilley	28	630	15.00 (20.00)		
H Trumble	13	310	12.40 (17.40)	78	5.50 (6.97)
SF Barnes	12	167	8.35 (13.35)	67	7.10 (8.82)
C Blythe	17	176	6.28 (11.28)	88	7.22 (9.09)

Australia's **Reggie Duff** (1878-1911), **Clem Hill**, **Warren Bardsley**, **Monty Noble**, and **Hugh Trumble**, England's **Archie MacLaren** (1871-1944), **Stanley Jackson**, **Dick Lilley**, **Sydney Barnes**, and left-arm spinner **Colin Blythe** (1879-1917), and the masterful all-rounder **Bart King** (1873-1965) from Philadelphia, U.S.A., who was credited with inventing the art of swing bowling, which he adapted from baseball.

1890s XI

	tests	*runs*	*ri (adj +20, +5)*	*wkts*	*rwi (adj +10, +5)*
AE Stoddart	15	963	34.39 (41.17)		
FA Iredale	14	807	35.08 (40.08)		
KS Ranjitsinhji	12	970	44.09 (49.09)		
C Hill	11	783	41.21 (46.21)		
TW Hayward	15	976	39.35 (44.35)	7	121.78 (133.21)
MA Noble	9	473	33.78 (38.78)	32	12.35 (14.85)
* G Giffen	14	775	29.80 (36.92)	74	8.41 (10.81)
† AFA Lilley	7	273	27.30 (32.30)		
R Peel	11	330	16.50 (23.50)	47	7.88 (10.15)
GA Lohmann	6	53	5.88 (15.33)	28	7.31 (11.36)
T Richardson	14	177	7.37 (12.58)	88	6.87 (9.23)

England's **Andrew Stoddart** (1863-1915), (borrowed from India:) **Kumar Ranjitsinhji** (1872-1933), **Tom Hayward** (1871-1939), **Dick Lilley**, **Bobby Peel**, brilliant medium pacer **George Lohmann** (1865-1901), and the frighteningly quick bowler **Tom Richardson** (1870-1912), Australia's **Frank Iredale** (1867-1926), **Clem Hill**, **Monty Noble** and **George Giffen**.

1880s XI

	tests	*runs*	*ri (adj, +15)*	*wkts*	*rwi (adj, +15)*
*WG Grace	11	542	33.87 (48.87)	7	18.28 (33.28)
A Shrewsbury	18	963	31.06 (46.06)		
WL Murdoch	14	841	33.64 (48.64)		
AG Steel	13	600	30.00 (45.00)	29	14.38 (24.73)
G Ulyett	21	712	22.25 (42.25)	42	11.99 (23.24)
W Bates	15	656	25.23 (40.34)	50	7.55 (14.45)
W Barnes	19	706	23.53 (38.53)	49	8.30 (16.26)
†JM Blackham	23	580	14.50 (29.50)		
CTB Turner	6	107	8.91 (23.91)	50	2.03 (5.03)
R Peel	9	97	7.46 (22.00)	54	4.25 (9.25)
JJ Ferris	6	75	6.25 (21.25)	35	4.18 (8.47)

England's **WG Grace**, **Arthur Shrewsbury**, talented all-rounder **Allan Steel** (1858-1914), **George Ulyett**, **Billy Bates** (1855-1900), **Billy Barnes** (1852-1899) and **Bobby Peel**, Australia's **Billy Murdoch** (1854-1911), **Jack Blackham**, **Charlie Turner** and the dangerous left-arm swing bowler **JJ Ferris** (1867-1900), who joined the British army for the Boer War and died there from typhoid fever.

1870s XI

	tests	*runs*	*ri (adj, +20)*	*wkts*	*rwi (adj, +20)*
WG Grace	0				
H Jupp	2	68	17.00 (37.00)		
AN Hornby	1	6	3.00 (23.00)		
GF Grace	0				
*R Daft	0				
S Cosstick	0				
†JM Blackham	3	60	12.00 (32.00)		
A Shaw	2	13	3.25 (23.25)	8	9.12 (19.12)
FR Spofforth	2	56	18.66 (38.66)	17	3.05 (7.76)
F Morley	0				
J Southerton	2	3	2.33 (22.33)	7	4.36 (10.07)

England's **WG Grace**, **Harry Jupp** (1841-1889), **AN Hornby** (1847-1925), **Fred Grace** (1850-1880), the noble batsman **Richard Daft** (1835-1900), rotund slow bowler **Alfred Shaw** (1842-1907), left-arm fast bowler **Fred Morley** (1850-1884) and lob bowler **James Southerton** (1827-1880), Australia's fine all-rounder **Sam Cosstick** (1836-1896), **Jack Blackham**, and fiery fast bowler **Fred Spofforth** (1853-1926).

The decade of the 1870s was the beginning of Test Cricket, except they didn't know it at the time. Touring teams to Australia were privately organised and funded, and it was not until many years later when the games were recognised as official Tests.

DECADE XIs PER COUNTRY

ENGLAND 2020s XI (5+ Tests, to April 2022)

	tests	*runs*	*ri*	*wkts*	*rwi*
DP Sibley	19	971	28.55		
Z Crawley	20	1086	29.35		
*JE Root	28	2530	48.65	17	94.46
BA Stokes	19	1274	35.38	35	20.85
JM Bairstow	13	771	30.84		
DW Lawrence	11	551	26.23		
CR Woakes	13	530	25.23	38	19.85
†BT Foakes	6	174	14.50		
OE Robinson	9	125	7.81	39	9.27
SCJ Broad	17	254	10.16	61	10.97
JM Anderson	19	81	2.89	63	12.05

Openers **Dom Sibley** (1995) and **Zak Crawley** (1998), batsmen **Joe Root**, **Jonny Bairstow** and **Dan Lawrence** (1997), batsman and medium pacer **Ben Stokes**, keeper **Ben Foakes** (1993), tall swing bowler **Ollie Robinson** (1993), fast bowlers **Stuart Broad** (1986) and **Chris Woakes** (1989), and swing bowler **James Anderson** (1982).

AUSTRALIA 2020s XI (2+ Tests, to April 2022)

	tests	*runs*	*ri*	*wkts*	*rwi*
DA Warner	11	665	35.00		
UT Khawaja	5	751	83.44		
M Labuschagne	13	1205	50.20	1	3859.00
SPD Smith	13	846	40.28	1	120.00
TM Head	10	497	35.50		
C Green	12	619	34.38	16	42.44
†AT Carey	8	362	30.16		
MA Starc	13	312	18.35	42	18.93
* PJ Cummins	12	194	12.93	58	8.15
NM Lyon	13	197	13.13	47	15.23
JR Hazlewood	6	43	5.37	20	13.92

Openers **David Warner** and (after making a surprise comeback) the elegant **Usman Khawaja** (1986), batsmen **Marnus Labuschagne**, **Steve Smith** and **Travis Head** (1993), all-rounder **Cameron Green** (1999), keeper **Alex Carey** (1991), fast bowlers **Pat Cummins**, **Josh Hazlewood** (1991) and **Mitchell Starc** (1990), and off spinner **Nathan Lyon** (1987).

SOUTH AFRICA 2020s XI (3+ Tests, to April 2022)

	tests	*runs*	*ri*	*wkts*	*rwi*
D Elgar	16	1198	39.93		
SJ Erwee	4	240	30.00		
KD Peterson	7	453	34.84		
*F du Plessis	7	364	30.33		
T Bavuma	12	800	36.36		
†Q de Kock	10	617	36.29		
M Jansen	5	118	14.75	28	6.54
KA Maharaj	14	387	17.59	48	14.14
K Rabada	11	200	10.52	53	8.23
A Nortje	9	64	4.26	41	10.51
L Ngidi	8	37	3.36	32	9.29

Openers **Dean Elgar** and **Sarel Erwee** (1989), batsman **Keegan Peterson** (1993), **Faf du Plessis** (1984) and **Temba Bavuma** (1990), keeper **Quinton de Kock**, promising left-arm fast bowler **Marco Jansen** (2000) all-rounder spinner **Keshav Maharaj** (1990), and fast bowlers **Kagiso Rabada**, **Anrich Nortje** (1993) and **Lungi Ngidi** (1996).

WEST INDIES 2020s XI (3+ Tests, to April 2022)

	tests	*runs*	*ri*	*wkts*	*rwi*
KC Brathwaite	18	1247	34.63	7	132.87
JD Campbell	12	454	18.91		
NE Bonner	12	754	35.90	1	656.00
J Blackwood	18	1075	30.71	2	72.00
SSJ Brooks	8	327	21.80		
KR Mayers	11	664	31.61	20	16.11
*JO Holder	16	673	21.70	36	26.51
†JA da Silva	14	640	25.60		
V Permaul	3	47	11.75	13	14.02
KAJ Roach	15	193	8.04	49	15.62
JNT Seales	7	30	2.72	27	11.26

Openers **Kraigg Brathwaite** (1992) and **John Campbell**, batsmen **Nkrumah Bonner** (1989) and **Sharmarh Brooks** (1988), fast-scoring batsman **Jermaine Blackwood**, all-rounder **Kyle Mayers** (1992), tall and talented all-rounder **Jason Holder** (1991) keeper **Joshua da Silva** (1998), left-arm spinner **Veerasammy Permaul** (1989), and fast bowlers **Kemar Roach** (1988) and **Jayden Seales** (2001).

NEW ZEALAND 2020s XI (3+ Tests, to April 2022)

	tests	*runs*	*ri*	*wkts*	*rwi*
TWM Latham	16	948	35.11		
WA Young	9	439	31.35		
* KS Williamson	8	893	68.69		
DP Conway	7	767	63.91		
HM Nicholls	15	833	37.86		
C de Grandhomme	7	346	34.60	6	98.66
† BJ Watling	8	174	15.81		
KA Jamieson	14	351	19.50	66	7.94
TG Southee	14	107	6.68	68	8.94
TA Boult	10	89	11.12	45	10.69
AY Patel	4	31	5.16	21	8.32

Openers **Tom Latham** (1992) and **Will Young** (1992), batsmen **Kane Williamson, Devon Conway** (1991) and **Henry Nicholls** (1991), uncomplicated all-rounder **Colin de Grandhomme** (1986), keeper **BJ Watling**, towering 6'8" all-rounder **Kyle Jamieson**, medium-fast bowler **Tim Southee**, polite left-arm fast bowler **Trent Boult**, and underused left-arm spinner **Ajaz Patel** (1988).

INDIA 2020s XI (4+ Tests, to April 2022)

	tests	*runs*	*ri*	*wkts*	*rwi*
RG Sharma	13	996	41.50		
KL Rahul	7	541	38.64		
CA Pujara	20	973	25.60		
* V Kohli	17	841	28.03		
† RR Pant	19	1166	35.33		
SS Iyer	4	388	55.42		
RA Jadeja	11	552	30.66	31	14.87
SN Thakur	6	245	22.27	26	9.54
R Ashwin	16	546	20.22	80	7.18
AR Patel	6	197	19.70	39	3.82
JJ Bumrah	17	156	5.77	61	12.72

Openers **Rohit Sharma** and **KL Rahul** (1992), batsmen **Cheteshwar Pujara, Virat Kohli** and **Shreyas Iyer** (1994), explosive batsman keeper **Rishabh Pant** (1997), all-rounders **Ravindra Jadeja** and **Shardul Thakur** (1991), outstanding spinners **Ravichandran Ashwin, Axar Patel**, and fast bowler **Jasprit Bumrah**.

PAKISTAN 2020s XI (3+ Tests, to April 2022)

	tests	*runs*	*ri*	*wkts*	*rwi*
Imam-ul-Haq	3	370	61.66		
Abdullah Shafique	5	547	60.77		
Azhar Ali	17	1136	40.57		
* Babar Azam	15	1144	47.66	2	20.00
Fawad Alam	15	736	33.45	2	40.50
† Mohammad Rizwan	17	897	35.88		
Faheem Ashraf	10	498	33.20	13	56.54
Nauman Ali	10	203	18.45	28	22.02
Yasir Shah	8	145	12.08	26	19.56
Hasan Ali	10	157	12.07	43	8.74
Shaheen Shah Afridi	17	106	5.30	70	10.01

Openers **Imam-ul-Haq** (1995) and **Abdullah Shafique** (1999), batsmen **Azhar Ali**, **Babar Azam** (1994) and the aspiring actor **Fawad Alam** (1985), keeper **Mohammad Rizwan**, all-rounder **Faheem Ashraf** (1994), leg spinner **Yasir Shah** (1986), left-arm spinner **Nauman Ali** (1986), tall left-arm fast bowler **Shaheen Shah Afridi** and fast bowler **Hasan Ali** (1994).

SRI LANKA 2020s XI (2+ Tests, to April 2022)

	tests	*runs*	*ri*	*wkts*	*rwi*
* FDM Karunaratne	12	1199	52.13		
HDRL Thirimanne	9	684	40.23		
P Nissanka	7	494	41.16		
AD Mathews	10	728	40.44		
DM de Silva	11	759	44.64	11	103.67
BKG Mendis	6	301	27.36		
† N Dickwella	12	672	33.60		
WRT Mendis	4	100	14.28	26	6.62
RAS Lakmal	11	130	8.12	30	14.64
L Embuldeniya	10	132	8.25	53	10.76
P Jayawickrama	4	12	2.40	25	5.45

Openers **Dimuth Karunaratne** and **Lahiru Thirimanne**, batsmen **Pathum Nissanka** (1998) and **Kusal Mendis** (1995), batsman and medium-pacer **Angelo Mathews** (1987), batsman and spinner **Dhananjaya de Silva** (1991), keeper **Niroshan Dickwella** (1993), left-arm spinners **Lasith Embuldeniya** (1996) and **Praveen Jayawickrama** (1998), off spinner **Ramesh Mendis** (1995) who also went with the name RTM Wanigamuni, and medium-pacer **Suranga Lakmal**.

ZIMBABWE 2020s XI (1+ Test, to April 2022)

	tests	*runs*	*ri*	*wkts*	*rwi*
PS Masvaure	6	291	26.45		
KT Kasuza	7	249	20.75		
CR Ervine	3	267	44.50		
BRM Taylor	6	480	40.00		
* SC Williams	4	481	68.71	4	112.05
Sikandar Raza	5	369	41.00	14	16.14
† RW Chakabva	8	383	25.53		
CT Mumba	1	11	11.00	2	28.00
B Muzarabani	5	88	9.77	19	9.41
R Ngarava	3	31	5.16	5	44.96
VM Nyauchi	6	40	4.00	15	27.71

Openers **Prince Masvaure** (1988) and **Kevin Kasuza** (1993), batsman **Craig Ervine** (1985), batsman and keeper **Brendan Taylor**, batsman and off spinner **Sikandar Raza** (1986), batsman and left-arm spinner **Sean Williams** (1986), keeper **Regis Chakabva**, and fast bowlers **Richard Ngarava** (1997), **Victor Nyauchi** (1992) and **Carl Mumba** (1995), and 6'8" fast bowler **Blessing Muzarabani** (1996) who looks taller.

BANGLADESH 2020s XI (2+ Tests, to April 2022)

	tests	*runs*	*ri*	*wkts*	*rwi*
Tamim Iqbal	7	521	40.07		
Mahmudul Hasan Joy	4	225	32.14		
Najmul Hossain Shanto	13	769	30.76		
* Mominul Haque	13	857	35.70		
Shakib Al Hasan	3	167	41.75	5	31.04
Mushfiqur Rahim	11	722	38.00		
† Liton Das	13	986	44.81		
Mehidy Hasan Miraz	11	434	22.84	38	19.34
Taskin Ahmed	6	119	13.22	18	22.09
Taijul Islam	9	114	7.12	47	9.66
Khaled Ahmed	3	0	0.00	9	19.25

Openers **Tamim Iqbal** and **Mahmudul Hasan Joy** (2000), left-handed batsmen **Najmul Hossain Shanto** (1998) and **Mominul Haque**, all-rounder **Shakib Al Hasan**, batsman/keeper **Mushfiqur Rahim**, keeper **Liton Das** (1994) all-rounder and off-spinner **Mehidy Hasan Miraz** (1997), left-arm spinner **Taijul Islam** (1992), and fast bowlers **Khaled Ahmed** (1992) and **Taskin Ahmed** (1995).

AFGHANISTAN 2020s XI (1+ Test, to April 2022)

	tests	*runs*	*ri*	*wkts*	*rwi*
Ibrahim Zadran	2	208	52.00	1	13.00
Javed Ahmadi	1	8	4.00	1	120.00
Rahmat Shah	2	87	21.75		
Hashmatullah Shahidi	2	215	53.75		
* Asghar Afghan	2	191	63.66		
Nasir Jamal	1	59	29.50		
† Afsar Zazai	2	37	18.50		
Rashid Khan	1	-	-	11	4.54
Sayed Shirzad	1	-	-	3	21.55
Yamin Ahmadzai	1	1	0.50	1	106.00
Zahir Khan	1	0	0.50	2	20.25

Openers **Ibrahim Zadran** (2001) and **Javed Ahmadi** (1992), batsmen **Rahmat Shah** (1993), **Hashmatullah Shahidi** (1994), **Asghar Afghan** (1987) and **Nasir Jamal** (1993), keeper **Afsar Zazai** (1993), leg spinner **Rashid Khan**, left-arm spinner **Zahir Khan** (1998) and fast bowlers **Yamin Ahmadzai** (1992) and **Sayed Shirzad** (1994).

ENGLAND 2010s XI (22+ Tests)

	tests	*runs*	*ri*	*wkts*	*rwi*
AN Cook	111	8818	43.87		
* AJ Strauss	31	1670	32.11		
IJL Trott	49	3560	40.45	5	461.28
JE Root	89	7359	44.87	24	167.63
KP Pietersen	48	3382	41.75	6	260.69
BA Stokes	60	3787	34.42	139	23.83
† MJ Prior	54	2709	32.63		
GP Swann	46	907	15.37	193	13.11
SCJ Broad	111	2354	14.26	403	14.20
ST Finn	36	279	5.93	125	16.05
JM Anderson	106	729	4.79	429	11.35

Openers **Alastair Cook** and **Andrew Strauss** (1977), batsmen **Jonathan Trott** (1981), **Joe Root**, and **Kevin Pietersen** (1980), all-rounder and medium pacer **Ben Stokes**, keeper **Matt Prior** (1982) tall fast bowler **Stuart Broad**, off spinner **Graeme Swann** (1979), tall fast bowler **Steven Finn** (1989), and swing bowler **James Anderson**.

AUSTRALIA 2010s XI (19+ Tests)

	tests	*runs*	*ri*	*wkts*	*rwi*
DA Warner	83	7088	46.32	4	319.43
CJL Rogers	24	1996	43.39		
SPD Smith	72	7164	55.10	17	179.37
* MJ Clarke	59	4717	44.08	12	77.45
AC Voges	20	1485	47.90		
MEK Hussey	33	2597	44.77	5	186.76
† TD Paine	30	1295	26.42		
JL Pattinson	20	415	17.29	81	11.33
RJ Harris	27	603	15.46	113	10.85
PJ Cummins	29	639	14.86	139	8.67
NM Lyon	95	1025	8.40	380	15.37

Openers **David Warner** and **Chris Rogers**, batsmen **Steve Smith**, **Michael Clarke**, **Adam Voges** (1979), and **Michael Hussey** (1975), and keeper **Tim Paine** (1984), fast bowlers **James Pattinson** (1990), **Ryan Harris** and **Pat Cummins**, and off spinner **Nathan Lyon**.

SOUTH AFRICA 2010s XI (17+ Tests)

	tests	*runs*	*ri*	*wkts*	*rwi*
* GC Smith	38	2814	42.63		
AK Markram	17	1358	43.80		
HM Amla	85	6695	45.85		
JH Kallis	33	2810	51.09	34	64.66
AB de Villiers	60	5059	51.62		
F du Plessis	62	3799	35.83		
† Q de Kock	44	2683	36.25		
VD Philander	61	1700	19.31	220	11.39
KA Maharaj	28	566	12.86	102	16.20
DW Steyn	59	806	10.63	267	9.01
K Rabada	41	586	9.76	190	8.90

Openers **Graeme Smith** and **Aiden Markram** (1994), batsman **Hashim Amla**, all-rounder **Jacques Kallis**, batsman/keeper **AB de Villiers**, batsman **Faf du Plessis**, keeper **Quinton de Kock**, accurate swing and seam bowler **Vernon Philander**, fast bowlers **Dale Steyn** and **Kagiso Rabada**, and left-arm spinner **Keshav Maharaj**.

WEST INDIES 2010s XI (11+ Tests)

	tests	*runs*	*ri*	*wkts*	*rwi*
CH Gayle	18	1366	42.68	2	264.00
KC Brathwaite	59	3496	31.21	18	117.04
DM Bravo	54	3506	35.77		
MN Samuels	42	2509	33.01	34	52.48
S Chanderpaul	41	3198	45.68		
RL Chase	32	1695	29.22	59	33.03
JO Holder	40	1898	27.50	106	17.16
*† D Ramdin	35	1479	25.50		
SJ Benn	14	235	12.36	52	15.44
KAJ Roach	51	844	10.55	173	14.14
S Shillingford	16	266	10.23	70	13.32

Openers **Chris Gayle** and **Kraigg Brathwaite**, batsmen **Darren Bravo** (1989), **Marlon Samuels**, **Shivnarine Chanderpaul**, and batsman and dainty spinner **Roston Chase**, tall and talented all-rounder **Jason Holder**, keeper **Danesh Ramdin**, tall left-arm spinner **Sulieman Benn** (1981), right-arm spinner **Shane Shillingford** (1983), and fast bowler **Kemar Roach**.

NEW ZEALAND 2010s XI (15+ Tests)

	tests	*runs*	*ri*	*wkts*	*rwi*
TWM Latham	49	3554	41.32		
MJ Guptill	39	2257	30.09	5	177.48
* KS Williamson	78	6379	46.56	29	88.24
LRPL Taylor	76	5486	41.24	2	42.50
BB McCullum	52	3979	41.88		
† BJ Watling	66	3538	34.01		
C de Grandhomme	21	1044	32.62	42	28.56
DL Vettori	16	752	26.85	49	22.39
TG Southee	65	1535	16.32	255	13.79
N Wagner	46	554	9.23	201	11.34
TA Boult	65	615	7.68	256	13.45

Openers **Tom Latham** and **Martin Guptill** (1986), batsmen **Kane Williamson**, **Ross Taylor** and **Brendon McCullum**, all-rounder **Colin de Grandhomme**, keeper **BJ Watling**, all-rounder **Daniel Vettori**, medium fast bowler **Tim Southee**, scowling bouncer-happy fast bowler **Neil Wagner** (1986), and left-arm fast bowler **Trent Boult**.

INDIA 2010s XI (16+ Tests)

	tests	*runs*	*ri*	*wkts*	*rwi*
V Sehwag	32	2338	41.01	10	186.24
RG Sharma	32	2141	40.39	2	756.00
CA Pujara	75	5740	46.29		
V Kohli	84	7202	51.07		
* SR Tendulkar	38	2951	46.10	2	776.00
† MS Dhoni	50	2700	32.92		
RA Jadeja	48	1844	26.72	211	10.74
R Ashwin	70	2385	24.84	362	9.17
Z Khan	24	327	9.34	91	13.73
Mohammed Shami	47	453	7.55	175	14.08
PP Ojha	22	83	3.32	104	12.86

Openers **Virender Sehwag** and **Rohit Sharma**, batsmen **Cheteshwar Pujara**, **Sachin Tendulkar** and **Virat Kohli**, keeper **MS Dhoni**, useful batsman and outstanding spinner **Ravichandran Ashwin**, left-arm spinners **Ravindra Jadeja**, and **Pragyan Ojha** (1986), and fast bowlers **Zaheer Khan** and **Mohammed Shami** (1990).

PAKISTAN 2010s XI (15+ Tests)

	tests	*runs*	*ri*	*wkts*	*rwi*
Mohammad Hafeez	44	2975	35.41	49	39.05
Taufeeq Umar	19	1234	33.35		
Azhar Ali	77	5885	40.30	8	334.11
Younis Khan	55	4839	47.91	2	487.50
* Misbah-ul-Haq	57	4225	41.83		
Asad Shafiq	73	4528	37.11	2	520.00
† Sarfaraz Ahmed	49	2657	30.89		
Yasir Shah	38	702	12.31	209	10.33
Mohammad Amir	29	598	11.28	101	16.67
Saeed Ajmal	30	422	9.81	160	9.44
Mohammad Abbas	14	63	3.00	66	7.71

Opener and off spinner **Mohammad Hafeez** (1980), opener **Taufeeq Umar** (1981) batsmen **Azhar Ali**, **Younis Khan**, **Misbah-ul-Haq** (1974) and **Asad Shafiq** (1986), keeper **Sarafraz Ahmed** (1987), fast bowler **Mohammad Amir** (1992), leg spinner **Yasir Shah**, off spinner **Saeed Ajmal** and fast bowler **Mohammad Abbas** (1990).

SRI LANKA 2010s XI (15+ Tests)

	tests	*runs*	*ri*	*wkts*	*rwi*
TM Dilshan	27	1801	36.02	26	71.53
FDM Karunaratne	64	4421	35.65	2	409.75
KC Sangakkara	46	4851	56.40		
* DPMD Jayawardene	39	2694	38.48		
LD Chandimal	55	3846	38.46		
AD Mathews	77	5325	38.03	28	130.66
† HAPW Jayawardene	28	1080	25.11		
MDK Perera	41	1208	16.54	156	16.75
HMRKB Herath	72	1492	12.75	363	9.67
KTGD Prasad	21	410	11.71	62	19.95
CBRLS Kumara	19	49	1.81	60	19.89

Openers **Tillakaratne Dilshan** and **Dimuth Karunaratne**, batsmen **Kumar Sangakkara**, **Mahela Jayawardene**, and **Dinesh Chandimal** (1989), batsman and medium pacer **Angelo Mathews**, keeper **Prasanna Jayawardene** (1979), off spinner **Dilruwan Perera** (1982), spinner **Rangana Herath**, and right-arm medium-fast bowler **Dhammika Prasad** (1983), and fast bowler **Lahiru Kumara** (1997).

ZIMBABWE 2010s XI (5+ Tests)

	tests	*runs*	*ri*	*wkts*	*rwi*
H Masakadza	23	1438	31.26	14	45.91
TMK Mawoyo	11	615	27.95		
* BRM Taylor	18	1418	39.38		
Sikandar Raza	12	818	34.08	20	44.50
PJ Moor	8	533	33.31		
SC Williams	10	553	27.21	17	42.73
† RW Chakabva	14	678	24.21		
AG Cremer	13	450	17.30	44	20.74
SW Masakadza	5	88	9.77	16	18.10
T Panyangara	6	73	6.08	23	11.95
KM Jarvis	12	126	5.72	46	12.59

Openers **Tino Mawoyo** (1986) and **Hamilton Masakadza**, batsmen and keepers **Brendan Taylor** and **Peter Moor** (1991), batsman and off spinner **Sikandar Raza**, batsman and left-arm spinner **Sean Williams**, keeper **Regis Chakabva**, leg spinner **Graeme Cremer**, and fast bowlers **Shingi Masakadza** (1986), **Tinashe Panyangara** and **Kyle Jarvis** (1989).

BANGLADESH 2010s XI (10+ Tests)

	tests	*runs*	*ri*	*wkts*	*rwi*
Tamim Iqbal	46	3719	41.32		
Soumya Sarkar	15	818	29.21	3	342.39
Mominul Haque	38	2657	37.42	4	634.50
* Shakib Al Hasan	42	3147	39.83	162	14.60
Mushfiqur Rahim	53	3531	36.03		
Nasir Hossain	19	1044	32.62	8	172.65
† Liton Das	18	744	24.00		
Sohag Gazi	10	325	20.31	38	19.92
Mehidy Hasan	22	638	15.19	90	13.61
Taijul Islam	27	374	8.31	106	14.53
Mustafizur Rahman	13	56	2.94	28	26.37

Openers **Tamim Iqbal** and **Soumya Sarkar** (1993), left-handed batsman **Mominul Haque**, all-rounder **Shakib Al Hasan**, batsman/keeper **Mushfiqur Rahim**, keeper **Liton Das** (1994) all-rounder **Nasir Hossain** (1991), off spinner **Sohag Gazi** (1991), left-arm spinner **Taijul Islam**, off spinner **Mehidy Hasan Miraz**, and left-arm fast bowler **Mustafizur Rahman** (1995).

IRELAND 2010s XI

	tests	*runs*	*ri*	*wkts*	*rwi*
* WTS Porterfield	3	58	9.66		
PR Stirling	3	104	17.33		
EC Joyce	1	47	23.50		
† NJ O'Brien	1	18	9.00		
A Balbirnie	3	146	24.33		
KJ O'Brien	3	258	43.00		
AR White	0				
GH Dockrell	1	64	32.00	2	60.50
DT Johnson	0				
WB Rankin	2	30	7.50	7	18.19
TJ Murtagh	3	109	18.16	13	7.55

Openers **William Portfield** (1984), **Paul Stirling** (1990), and **Ed Joyce** (1978), wicket-keeper-batsman **Niall O'Brien** (1981), batsman **Andy Balbirnie** (1990), all-rounders **Kevin O'Brien** (1984) and **Andrew White** (1980), left-arm spinner **George Dockrell** (1992), Australian fast bowler **Trent Johnson** (1974), tall fast bowler **Boyd Rankin** (1984) who also played for England, and medium-pacer **Tim Murtagh** (1981).

AFGHANISTAN 2010s XI

	tests	*runs*	*ri*	*wkts*	*rwi*
Noor Ali Zadran	0				
Mohammad Shahzad	2	69	17.25		
Rahmat Shah	4	298	37.25		
Nawroz Mangal	0				
* Asghar Afghan	4	249	35.57		
Mohammad Nabi	3	33	5.50	8	19.84
† Ikram Alikhil	1	7	7.00		
Samiullah Shinwari	0				
Rashid Khan	4	106	15.14	23	6.41
Yamin Ahmadzai	4	31	4.42	10	14.77
Dalwat Zadran	0				

Openers **Noor Ali Zadran** (1988) and **Mohammad Shahzad** (1988), batsmen **Rahmat Shah**, **Nawroz Mangal** (1984), and **Asghar Afghan**, all-rounder **Mohammad Nabi** (1985), keeper **Ikram Alikhil** (2000), leg spinners **Samiullah Shinwari** (1987) and **Rashid Khan**, and fast bowlers **Yamin Ahmadzai** and **Dalwat Zadran** (1988).

ENGLAND 2000s XI

	tests	*runs*	*ri*	*wkts*	*rwi*
AJ Strauss	69	5367	42.59		
ME Trescothick	76	5825	40.73		
* MP Vaughan	80	5631	39.37	6	441.75
KP Pietersen	56	4799	47.99	4	1050.00
GP Thorpe	43	3145	42.50		
PD Collingwood	55	3732	38.87	15	194.03
† MJ Prior	25	1390	34.75		
A Flintoff	73	3645	30.37	213	19.48
GP Swann	14	463	27.23	62	11.85
DG Cork	10	230	16.42	33	12.29
D Gough	24	341	9.74	94	11.37

Openers **Andrew Strauss** and **Marcus Trescothick** (1975), batsmen **Michael Vaughan** (1974), **Kevin Pietersen**, **Graham Thorpe** (1969) and **Paul Collingwood** (1976), keeper **Matt Prior**, all-rounder and fast bowler **Andrew Flintoff** (1977), off spinner **Graeme Swann**, and fast bowlers **Dominc Cork** (1971) and **Darren Gough**.

AUSTRALIA 2000s XI

	tests	*runs*	*ri*	*wkts*	*rwi*
ML Hayden	95	8176	48.09		
JL Langer	75	5972	45.24		
RT Ponting	106	9358	51.41		
MEK Hussey	44	3638	47.86	2	231.75
MJ Clarke	55	3882	43.61	19	81.55
* SR Waugh	44	2825	44.84	3	694.14
† AC Gilchrist	90	5035	39.64		
MG Johnson	30	875	22.43	137	11.87
SK Warne	64	1565	18.63	351	9.04
SR Clark	24	248	9.53	94	12.18
GD McGrath	65	355	5.54	294	9.03

Openers **Matthew Hayden** and **Justin Langer**, batsmen **Ricky Ponting**, **Michael Hussey**, **Michael Clarke** and **Steve Waugh**, free scoring batsman/keeper **Adam Gilchrist**, fast bowler **Mitchell Johnson**, leg spinner **Shane Warne**, medium pace bowlers **Stuart Clark** (1975) and **Glenn McGrath**.

SOUTH AFRICA 2000s XI

	tests	*runs*	*ri*	*wkts*	*rwi*
* GC Smith	78	6439	47.00	8	400.48
G Kirsten	45	3497	46.01		
HH Gibbs	73	4950	41.91		
JH Kallis	100	8547	49.69	204	26.95
DJ Cullinan	17	1200	42.85		
AB de Villiers	54	3706	39.84	2	99.00
† MV Boucher	103	4007	26.71		
SM Pollock	70	2377	23.77	260	12.85
DW Steyn	34	443	10.30	172	8.77
M Ntini	97	690	6.21	380	13.71
AA Donald	13	120	6.31	46	12.97

Openers **Graeme Smith** and **Gary Kirsten**, batsman **Herschelle Gibbs** (1974), all-rounder **Jacques Kallis**, batsmen **Daryll Cullinan** (1967) and **AB de Villiers**, keeper **Mark Boucher**, fast bowlers **Shaun Pollock**, **Dale Steyn**, **Makhaya Ntini** and **Allan Donald**.

WEST INDIES 2000s XI

	tests	*runs*	*ri*	*wkts*	*rwi*
CH Gayle	85	5848	38.98	71	56.89
D Ganga	44	2085	26.06		
RR Sarwan	83	5759	39.44	23	123.10
* BC Lara	65	6339	53.72		
S Chanderpaul	86	6435	43.47	2	660.00
DJ Bravo	34	2009	31.88	81	24.48
† RD Jacobs	54	2071	22.75		
CEL Ambrose	10	142	8.87	36	8.83
M Dillon	31	465	8.45	110	16.61
CA Walsh	20	102	3.18	93	7.63
JJC Lawson	13	52	2.47	51	14.52

Openers **Chris Gayle** and **Daren Ganga** (1979), batsmen **Ramnaresh Sarwan** (1980), **Brian Lara, Shivnarine Chanderpaul**, all-rounder **Dwayne Bravo** (1983), keeper **Ridley Jacobs** (1967), and fast bowlers **Curtley Ambrose, Mervyn Dillon** (1974), **Courtney Walsh** and **Jermaine Lawson** (1982).

NEW ZEALAND 2000s XI

	tests	*runs*	*ri*	*wkts*	*rwi*
MH Richardson	38	2776	42.70		
L Vincent	23	1332	33.30		
LRPL Taylor	22	1644	41.10		
JD Ryder	11	898	44.90	4	172.25
* SP Fleming	63	4188	39.88		
CL Cairns	18	1265	42.16	68	14.37
† BB McCullum	49	2474	30.54		
DL Vettori	68	3168	30.75	221	16.32
DR Tuffey	24	349	10.57	74	17.47
SE Bond	18	168	8.40	87	8.12
SB O'Connor	9	64	5.81	29	14.43

Openers **Mark Richardson** (1971) and **Lou Vincent** (1978), batsmen **Ross Taylor, Jesse Ryder** (1984) and **Stephen Fleming** (1973), all-rounder and fast bowler **Chris Cairns**, batsman/keeper **Brendon McCullum**, all-rounder **Daniel Vettori**, fast bowlers **Daryl Tuffey** (1978) and **Shane Bond** (1975), and left-arm fast bowler **Shayne O'Connor** (1973).

INDIA 2000s XI

	tests	runs	ri	wkts	rwi
V Sehwag	71	6165	50.95	30	99.12
G Gambhir	27	2553	53.18		
RS Dravid	102	8535	48.22		
* SR Tendulkar	89	7129	47.52	31	164.12
VVS Laxman	92	6291	41.94	2	73.75
SC Ganguly	81	4780	35.67	13	380.07
† MS Dhoni	40	2176	35.09		
A Kumble	74	1427	14.56	355	11.62
Harbhajan Singh	72	1493	14.93	322	12.42
S Sreesanth	16	225	9.78	58	16.71
J Srinath	24	238	7.93	74	17.66

Openers **Virender Sehwag** and **Gautam Gambhir**, batsmen **Rahul Dravid**, **Sachin Tendulkar**, **VVS Laxman** and **Sourav Ganguly**, keeper **MS Dhoni**, spinners **Anil Kumble** and **Harbhajan Singh**, and fast bowlers **Sreesanth** (1983) and **Javagal Srinath**.

Tendulkar's RI drop from the previous decade (51.61 in 1990s) mirrors Viv Richards' RI drop in the 1980s (45.65) from the 1970s (55.00).

PAKISTAN 2000s XI

	tests	runs	ri	wkts	rwi
Saeed Anwar	11	686	42.87		
Imran Farhat	31	1944	32.94	3	287.20
Younis Khan	63	5260	46.96	7	125.25
Mohammad Yousuf	71	6439	53.21		
* Inzamam-ul-Haq	61	5112	50.61		
Shahid Afridi	20	1329	37.97	36	34.43
† Kamran Akmal	47	2525	31.56		
Saqlain Mushtaq	25	525	13.12	101	13.31
Shoaib Akhtar	33	474	9.67	144	8.79
Shabbir Ahmed	10	88	5.86	51	8.57
Mohammad Asif	15	75	3.12	73	9.14

Openers **Saeed Anwar** and **Imran Farhat** (1982), batsmen **Younis Khan**, **Mohammad Yousuf** and **Inzamam-ul-Haq**, fast scoring all-rounder and leg spinner **Shahid Afridi** (1980), keeper **Kamran Akmal** (1982), off spinner **Saqlain Mushtaq** (1976), fast bowlers **Shoaib Akhtar**, **Shabbir Ahmed** (1976) and **Mohammad Asif** (1982).

SRI LANKA 2000s XI

	tests	*runs*	*ri*	*wkts*	*rwi*
ST Jayasuriya	66	4222	37.03	69	39.74
MS Atapattu	61	4055	38.61		
KC Sangakkara	88	7549	51.35		
* DPMD Jayawardene	95	8187	51.16	5	49.20
TT Samaraweera	57	3938	43.75	14	110.85
TM Dilshan	57	3482	38.26	13	103.11
† HAPW Jayawardene	30	1044	26.10		
WPUJC Vaas	77	2409	20.94	247	16.94
M Muralitharan	83	773	7.80	560	5.66
BAW Mendis	10	64	5.81	44	11.39
SL Malinga	28	192	5.64	91	20.42

Openers **Sanath Jayasuriya** and **Marvan Atapattu**, batsman **Kumar Sangakkara**, **Mahela Jayawardene**, **Thilan Samaraweera** and **Tillakaratne Dilshan**, keeper **Prasanna Jayawardene**, left-arm swing bowler **Chaminda Vaas**, the great spinner **Muttiah Muralitharan**, tricky right-arm spinner **Ajantha Mendis** (1985) and right-arm sling bowler **Lasith Malinga** (1983).

ZIMBABWE 2000s XI

	tests	*runs*	*ri*	*wkts*	*rwi*
GW Flower	29	1227	23.15	19	86.89
DD Ebrahim	29	1225	22.27		
* A Flower	24	2214	52.71		
GJ Whittall	15	839	29.96	9	51.87
ADR Campbell	21	1085	27.82		
H Masakadza	15	785	26.16	2	39.00
† T Taibu	24	1273	27.67		
AM Blignaut	19	886	24.61	53	20.97
HH Streak	38	1454	22.71	105	16.42
RW Price	17	218	7.78	69	13.91
BT Watambwa	6	11	1.37	14	22.49

Openers **Grant Flower** and **Dion Ebrahim** (1980), batsman and wicket-keeper **Andy Flower**, batsman and seamer **Guy Whittall** (1972), batsmen **Alistair Campbell** and **Hamilton Masakadza**, keeper **Tatenda Taibu**, left-handed batsman and right-arm fast bowler **Andy Blignaut** (1978), fast bowler **Heath Streak**, spinner **Ray Price**, and fast-medium bowler **Brighton Watambwa** (1977).

BANGLADESH 2000s XI

	tests	*runs*	*ri*	*wkts*	*rwi*
Tamim Iqbal	12	608	27.63		
Nafees Iqbal	11	518	23.54		
Habibul Bashar	50	3026	30.56		
Shahriar Nafees	15	810	27.00		
Rajin Saleh	24	1141	24.80	2	1072.00
* Shakib Al Hasan	14	715	27.50	48	12.32
† Mushfiqur Rahim	16	679	23.41		
Mohammad Rafique	33	1059	16.80	100	19.54
Mashrafe Mortaza	36	797	11.89	78	27.14
Shahadat Hossain	23	231	5.37	53	28.85
Enamul Haque, jr	14	53	2.20	41	22.96

Openers **Tamim Iqbal** and **Nafees Iqbal** (1985), batsmen **Habibul Bashar**, **Shahriar Nafees** (1985), who was a left-handed batsman who started in Tests at the age of 19 but then had a contract fallout with the authorities, and **Rajin Saleh** (1983), all-rounder **Shakib Al Hasan**, keeper **Mushfiqur Rahim**, spinner **Mohammad Rafique**, seamer **Mashrafe Mortaza**, fast bowler **Shahadat Hossain**, and spinner **Enamul Haque, jr**.

ENGLAND 1990s XI

	tests	*runs*	*ri*	*wkts*	*rwi*
GA Gooch	45	4176	50.31	9	121.39
* MA Atherton	91	6217	37.00		
RA Smith	54	3538	36.85		
AJ Stewart	93	6407	37.91		
AJ Lamb	22	1558	39.94		
GA Hick	54	3005	31.96	22	145.31
† RC Russell	47	1489	20.12		
D Gough	34	514	10.07	135	12.05
DW Headley	15	186	7.15	60	10.67
ARC Fraser	43	341	5.50	168	11.83
PCR Tufnell	40	144	2.61	119	20.59

Openers **Graham Gooch** and **Michael Atherton** (1968), batsmen **Robin Smith** (1963), **Alec Stewart** (1963), **Allan Lamb** (1954), batsmen and part-time off spinner **Graeme Hick**, brilliant keeper **Jack Russell**, fast bowlers **Darren Gough** and **Dean Headley** (1970), swing bowler **Angus Fraser** (1965), and left-arm spinner **Phil Tufnell** (1966).

AUSTRALIA 1990s XI

	tests	*runs*	*ri*	*wkts*	*rwi*
* MA Taylor	93	6306	37.98		
MJ Slater	58	4425	42.96		
DC Boon	62	4303	39.84		
ME Waugh	99	6371	38.84	50	83.32
RT Ponting	33	2092	40.23		
SR Waugh	89	6213	43.44	47	48.50
† IA Healy	102	3949	24.83		
SK Warne	80	1577	13.95	351	10.67
JN Gillespie	14	233	10.59	50	10.63
SCG MacGill	12	164	9.11	59	8.30
GD McGrath	58	286	3.97	266	9.62

Openers **Mark Taylor** (1964) and **Michael Slater**, batsmen **David Boon** (1960), **Mark Waugh** (1965), **Ricky Ponting** and **Steve Waugh**, keeper **Ian Healy**, spinner **Shane Warne**, fast bowlers **Jason Gillespie** (1975), leg spinner **Stuart MacGill** (1971), and medium pacer **Glenn McGrath**.

SOUTH AFRICA 1990s XI

	tests	*runs*	*ri*	*wkts*	*rwi*
G Kirsten	56	3792	37.92		
KC Wessels	16	1027	35.41		
* WJ Cronje	64	3689	34.80	37	68.36
DJ Cullinan	53	3354	38.55		
JH Kallis	32	1849	36.25	53	25.22
JN Rhodes	48	2321	31.79		
SM Pollock	38	1404	25.07	161	8.51
† DJ Richardson	42	1359	21.23		
PS de Villiers	18	359	13.80	85	9.49
AA Donald	59	532	7.09	284	8.07
PR Adams	28	139	4.48	86	16.26

Openers **Gary Kirsten** and **Kepler Wessels**, who previously played 24 Tests for Australia, batsmen **Hansie Cronje** (1969-2002), who was involved in match fixing scams before dying in a plane crash at the age of 32, and **Daryll Cullinan**, all-rounder **Jacques Kallis**, batsman and great fielder **Jonty Rhodes** (1969), useful batsman and fast/swing bowler **Shaun Pollock**, keeper **Dave Richardson**, fast bowlers **Fanie de Villiers** (1964) and **Allan Donald**, and leg spinner **Paul Adams**.

WEST INDIES 1990s XI

	tests	*runs*	*ri*	*wkts*	*rwi*
DL Haynes	31	2147	38.33		
SL Campbell	36	2184	34.66		
* RB Richardson	41	2629	37.55		
BC Lara	65	5573	49.75		
JC Adams	39	2326	36.92	19	95.96
CL Hooper	64	3514	31.94	86	46.85
† JR Murray	31	917	21.83		
MD Marshall	15	372	16.17	50	12.71
IR Bishop	39	577	9.94	145	11.61
CEL Ambrose	71	1016	9.76	309	8.34
CA Walsh	78	557	5.06	304	12.21

Openers **Desmond Haynes** (1956) and **Sherwin Campbell** (1970), batsmen **Richie Richardson** (1962), **Brian Lara** and **Jimmy Adams** (1968), all-rounder **Carl Hooper**, keeper **Junior Murray** (1968), and the great fast bowlers **Malcolm Marshall**, **Ian Bishop** (1967), **Curtley Ambrose** and **Courtney Walsh**.

NEW ZEALAND 1990s XI

	tests	*runs*	*ri*	*wkts*	*rwi*
* JG Wright	18	1662	50.36		
MJ Horne	24	1453	32.28		
AH Jones	29	2171	39.47		
MD Crowe	32	2317	42.12		
CD McMillan	19	1256	39.35	8	96.50
SP Fleming	48	2984	35.52		
CL Cairns	43	2026	28.13	150	13.48
† AC Parore	58	2249	22.94		
DJ Nash	30	642	14.93	92	14.78
DL Vettori	28	603	14.35	91	17.93
SB Doull	30	501	10.89	97	13.63

Openers **John Wright** and **Matt Horne**, batsmen **Andrew Jones** (1959), **Martin Crowe**, **Craig McMillan** (1976) and **Stephen Fleming**, all-rounder **Chris Cairns**, keeper **Adam Parore**, medium-fast bowler **Dion Nash** (1971), left-arm spinner **Daniel Vettori**, and swing bowler **Simon Doull** (1969).

INDIA 1990s XI

	tests	*runs*	*ri*	*wkts*	*rwi*
NS Sidhu	38	2517	44.94		
RJ Shastri	11	794	46.70	10	98.08
RS Dravid	34	2698	46.51		
SR Tendulkar	69	5626	51.61	13	108.86
VG Kambli	17	1084	51.61		
SC Ganguly	32	2432	45.03	19	66.10
* Kapil Dev	28	1002	28.62	75	22.78
† KS More	21	587	22.57		
A Kumble	58	1079	14.38	264	10.84
J Srinath	43	771	12.43	162	14.72
SLV Raju	27	236	7.15	92	15.86

Opener **Navjot Sidhu** and all-rounder **Ravi Shastri**, batsmen **Rahul Dravid**, **Sachin Tendulkar**, **Vinod Kambli** (1972) and **Sourav Ganguly**, all-rounder and swing bowler **Kapil Dev**, keeper **Kiran More**, spinner **Anil Kumble**, fast bowler **Javagal Srinath**, and left-arm spinner **Venkatapathy Raju** (1969).

PAKISTAN 1990s XI

	tests	*runs*	*ri*	*wkts*	*rwi*
Saeed Anwar	44	3366	44.88		
Aamer Sohail	45	2777	35.15	20	102.12
Shoaib Mohammad	19	1162	37.48		
Saleem Malik	47	3126	40.59		
Ijaz Ahmed	44	2815	39.64		
Inzamam-ul-Haq	58	3717	38.31		
† Moin Khan	50	2049	26.61		
Wasim Akram	62	1956	20.37	289	8.23
Saqlain Mushtaq	24	402	10.57	107	11.43
Mushtaq Ahmed	43	606	9.61	172	12.71
Waqar Younis	58	611	7.83	279	8.31

Openers **Saeed Anwar**, **Aamer Sohail** (1966) and **Shoaib Mohammad**, batsmen **Saleem Malik** (1963), **Ijaz Ahmed** and **Inzamam-ul-Haq**, keeper **Moin Khan**, brilliant left-arm fast bowler **Wasim Akram**, spinner **Saqlain Mushtaq**, leg spinner **Mushtaq Ahmed**, and devastating fast bowler **Waqar Younis**.

SRI LANKA 1990s XI

	tests	*runs*	*ri*	*wkts*	*rwi*
ST Jayasuriya	44	2751	37.17	29	75.08
RP Arnold	12	635	33.42		
AP Gurusinha	32	2038	37.05	13	99.38
PA de Silva	62	4448	42.76	23	71.36
DPMD Jayawardene	15	933	42.40		
† HP Tillakaratne	55	2966	33.32		
HDPK Dharmasena	20	660	18.85	50	24.98
WPUCJ Vaas	34	680	14.46	108	14.38
M Muralitharan	48	481	7.75	227	8.81
KR Pushpakumara	19	100	4.00	52	22.14
KPJ Warnaweera	9	36	3.60	31	14.49

Openers **Sanath Jayasuriya** and **Russel Arnold**, batsmen **Asanka Gurusinha** (1966), **Aravinda de Silva, Mahela Jayawardene, Hasan Tillakaratne**, spinner **Kumar Dharmasena**, left-armer **Chaminda Vaas**, spinner **Muttiah Muralitharan**, and fast bowlers **Ravindra Pushpakumara** (1975) and **Jayananda Warnaweera** (1960).

ZIMBABWE 1990s XI

	tests	*runs*	*ri*	*wkts*	*rwi*
GW Flower	38	2230	31.85	6	422.91
NC Johnson	9	426	26.62	7	35.14
† A Flower	39	2580	36.85		
DL Houghton	22	1464	40.66		
MW Goodwin	15	1086	37.44		
ADR Campbell	39	1773	25.32		
GJ Whittall	31	1368	25.33	42	39.64
PA Strang	20	747	21.97	57	21.41
HH Streak	27	936	21.76	111	10.61
DH Brain	9	115	8.84	30	15.25
M Mbangwa	11	20	1.05	28	15.42

Openers **Grant Flower** and **Neil Johnson** (1970), wicket-keeper/batsman **Andy Flower**, batsman (and keeper early in his career) **David Houghton** (1957), batsmen **Murray Goodwin** (1972) and **Alistair Campbell**, all-rounder **Guy Whittall**, leg spinner **Paul Strang** (1970), **Heath Streak**, left-arm fast bowler **David Brain** (1964) and right-arm fast bowler **Pommie Mbangwa** (1976).

BANGLADESH 1990s XI

Shahriah Hossain
Javed Omar
Al Shahriar
* Akram Khan
Aminul Islam
Minhajul Abedin
† Khaled Mashud
Enamul Haque
Mohammad Rafique
Hasibul Hossain
Shafiuddin Ahmed

Openers **Shahriah Hossain** (1976) and **Javed Omar**, all-rounder and leg spinner **Al Shahriar** (1978), batsmen **Akram Khan** (1968), **Aminul Islam** (1968) and **Minhajul Abedin** (1965), keeper **Khaled Mashud** (1976), left-arm spinner **Enamul Haque** (1966), left-arm spinner **Mohammad Rafique**, and fast bowlers **Hasibul Hossain** (1977) and **Shafiuddin Ahmed** (1973).

ENGLAND 1980s XI

	tests	*runs*	*ri*	*wkts*	*rwi*
GA Gooch	56	3970	37.80		
BC Broad	25	1661	37.75		
* DI Gower	89	6196	39.46		
DW Randall	21	1370	38.05		
MW Gatting	66	3859	33.85		
IT Botham	75	4051	32.66	258	15.06
† RW Taylor	34	652	11.85		
NA Foster	28	410	9.53	88	16.61
GR Dilley	40	467	8.33	135	13.85
NGB Cook	15	179	6.88	52	15.61
RGD Willis	39	399	6.87	143	12.59

Openers **Graham Gooch** and **Chris Broad** (1957), elegant lefty batsmen **David Gower**, the happy-go-lucky **Derek Randall** (1951), who was also a great fieldsman, the moody and portly **Mike Gatting** (1957), the natural all-rounder **Ian Botham**, consistent keeper **Bob Taylor** (1941) who played until he was 41, fast bowlers **Neil Foster** (1962) and **Graham Dilley** (1959-2011), left-arm spinner **Nick Cook** (1956), and fast bowler **Bob Willis**.

AUSTRALIA 1980s XI

	tests	*runs*	*ri*	*wkts*	*rwi*
MA Taylor	11	1219	60.95		
KC Wessels	24	1761	41.92		
GS Chappell	33	2712	49.30	13	89.9
* AR Border	97	7386	45.03	21	92.03
DM Jones	30	2370	44.71		
SR Waugh	35	1889	34.98	42	50.64
† WB Phillips	27	1485	30.93		
B Yardley	19	402	14.35	89	10.61
DK Lillee	35	408	9.06	171	9.00
TM Alderman	33	163	3.88	136	11.94
BA Reid	18	75	3.40	62	12.89

Openers **Mark Taylor** and **Kepler Wessels**, batsmen **Greg Chappell**, **Allan Border** and **Dean Jones** (1961-2020), all-rounder and medium pacer **Steve Waugh**, keeper **Wayne Phillips** (1958), off spinner **Bruce Yardley** (1947-2019), fast bowler **Dennis Lillee**, swing bowler **Terry Alderman**, and tall left-arm fast bowler **Bruce Reid** (1963).

SOUTH AFRICA 1980s XI

BA Richards
SJ Cook
PN Kirsten
RG Pollock
HR Fotheringham
* CEB Rice
BM McMillan
† RV Jennings
AJ Kourie
VAP van der Bijl
AA Donald

Openers **Barry Richards** and **Jimmy Cook** (1953), batsmen **Peter Kirsten** (1955), **Graeme Pollock** and **Henry Fotheringham** (1953), all-rounders and fast-medium bowlers **Clive Rice** (1949-2015) and **Brian McMillan**, keeper **Ray Jennings** (1954), left-arm spinner **Alan Kourie** (1951), 6'7" fast bowler **Vintcent van der Bijl** (1948) and the very quick **Allan Donald**.

WEST INDIES 1980s XI

	tests	*runs*	*ri*	*wkts*	*rwi*
CG Greenidge	75	5094	41.41		
DL Haynes	81	5074	36.50		
RB Richardson	45	3320	43.68		
IVA Richards	78	5113	45.65	28	156.69
HA Gomes	49	2490	34.58	14	178.05
* CH Lloyd	44	2881	47.22		
† PJL Dujon	64	2885	32.41		
MD Marshall	63	1430	18.10	323	7.39
MA Holding	45	685	12.68	184	10.67
J Garner	49	486	8.67	210	9.13
CEH Croft	18	96	3.84	73	11.43

The great opening combination of **Gordon Greenidge** and **Desmond Haynes**, batsmen **Richie Richardson**, **Viv Richards**, **Larry Gomes** (1953) and brutal left-handed batsman **Clive Lloyd** (who preferred to bat down the order, where he made more runs than the more flashy and impatient Richards), keeper **Jeff Dujon**, and the seriously dangerous-to-your-health fast bowlers **Malcolm Marshall**, **Michael Holding**, **Joel Garner**, and the surly **Colin Croft** (1953).

NEW ZEALAND 1980s XI

	tests	*runs*	*ri*	*wkts*	*rwi*
* JG Wright	56	3271	32.71		
BA Edgar	33	1662	29.15		
JF Reid	18	1277	44.03		
MD Crowe	45	3127	41.41	13	111.33
MJ Greatbatch	7	693	53.30		
JV Coney	45	2303	31.54	24	65.27
RJ Hadlee	53	2040	25.50	289	6.07
† IDS Smith	49	1376	19.65		
BL Cairns	29	581	14.52	101	15.71
SL Boock	21	178	6.84	57	21.62
EJ Chatfield	39	149	3.17	115	17.33

Openers **John Wright** and **Bruce Edgar**, batsmen **John Reid** (1956-2020), **Martin Crowe**, **Mark Greatbatch** (1963) and **Jeremy Coney** (1952), great fast bowler **Richard Hadlee**, keeper **Ian Smith**, swing bowler and massive hitter **Lance Cairns**, left-arm spinner **Stephen Boock**, and accurate medium-fast bowler **Ewen Chatfield**.

INDIA 1980s XI

	tests	*runs*	*ri*	*wkts*	*rwi*
* SM Gavaskar	65	4475	42.21		
SV Manjrekar	9	784	52.26		
M Azharuddin	34	2224	43.60		
DB Vengsarkar	71	4501	40.18		
M Amarnath	43	2912	42.82	9	222.33
RJ Shastri	69	3036	29.19	141	30.54
Kapil Dev	80	3353	28.41	272	14.55
† SMH Kirmani	49	1399	20.88		
C Sharma	23	396	14.14	61	22.66
DR Doshi	23	86	2.96	74	16.71
ND Hirwani	7	26	2.88	42	6.41

Openers **Sunil Gavaskar** and **Sanjay Manjrekar** (1965), batsmen **Mohammad Azharuddin**, **Dilip Vengsarkar** (1956) and **Mohinder Amarnath** (1950), all-rounders **Ravi Shastri** and **Kapil Dev**, keeper **Syed Kirmani**, fast bowler **Chetan Sharma** (1966), left-arm spinner **Dilip Doshi** (1947) and leg spinner **Narendra Hirwani** (1968) who took an amazing 16 wickets in his first Test.

PAKISTAN 1980s XI

	tests	*runs*	*ri*	*wkts*	*rwi*
Shoaib Mohammad	26	1543	41.70	4	82.00
Mudassar Nazar	61	3328	36.97	56	53.94
Zaheer Abbas	41	2460	42.41		
Javed Miandad	76	5642	51.29		
Qasim Umar	26	1502	34.93		
Saleem Malik	56	2642	34.31	5	52.52
* Imran Khan	54	2430	34.22	256	6.72
† Saleem Yousuf	25	878	25.82		
Abdul Qadir	57	914	13.84	216	14.06
Wasim Akram	29	468	13.76	94	14.68
Iqbal Qasim	32	421	12.38	131	10.87

Opener **Shoaib Mohammad**, opener and medium pace bowler **Mudassar Nazar**, batsmen **Zaheer Abbas**, **Javed Miandad**, **Qasim Umar** (1957) and **Saleem Malik**, all-rounder and fast bowler **Imran Khan**, keeper **Saleem Yousuf**, wonderful wrist spinner **Abdul Qadir**, left-arm fast bowler **Wasim Akram**, and underrated spinner **Iqbal Qasim**.

SRI LANKA 1980s XI

	tests	*runs*	*ri*	*wkts*	*rwi*
S Wettimuny	23	1221	28.39		
†SAR Silva	9	353	22.06		
A Ranatunga	26	1621	35.23	11	164.87
*LRD Mendis	24	1329	30.90		
RL Dias	20	1285	35.69		
PA de Silva	17	974	31.31	3	59.54
RS Madugalle	21	1029	26.38		
DS de Silva	12	406	18.45	37	18.69
ALF de Mel	17	326	11.64	59	16.90
RJ Ratnayake	15	277	11.08	49	15.58
VB John	6	53	5.30	28	7.04

Openers **Sidath Wettimuny** (1956) and the wicket-keeper **Amal Silva** (1960), batsmen **Arjuna Ranatunga**, **Duleep Mendis** (1952), **Roy Dias** (1952), **Aravinda de Silva** and **Ranjan Madugalle**, world-class leg spinner **Somachandra de Silva** (1942), and fast bowlers **Ashantha de Mel** (1959), **Rumesh Ratnayake** (1964) and **Vinothen John** (1960).

After waiting so long to make the jump into Tests, most of their top cricketers chose to go the rebel route, and tour the apartheid South Africa. They were then banned from Sri Lankan cricket for the rest of their lives (which was later revoked).

ZIMBABWE 1980s XI

JG Heron
KJ Arnott
GA Hick
†DL Houghton
AJ Pycroft
*DAG Fletcher
KM Curran
IP Butchart
PEW Rawson
EA Brandes
AJ Traicos

Openers **Jack Heron** (1948) and **Kevin Arnott** (1961), a batsman who defected to England in **Graeme Hick** (1966), dependable batsman/keeper **David Houghton**, batsman **Andy Pycroft** (1956) who was a mainstay of the team and had a first-class RI of 33.90, left-handed batsman and medium pacer **Duncan Fletcher** (1948), all-rounder **Kevin Curran** (1959-2012), medium pacer **Iain Butchart** (1960), fast bowlers **Peter Rawson** (1957) and **Eddo Brandes** (1963), and tall off spinner **John Traicos** (1947), of Greek descent and born in Egypt, represented South Africa in 1970 when he was 22, and such was his longevity in the game that he played for Zimbabwe until the age of 45.

BANGLADESH 1980s XI

Raqibul Hasan
Faruk Ahmed
* Gazi Ashraf
Minhajul Abedin
Athar Ali Khan
Jahangir Shah
† Shafiq-ul-Haque
Golam Faruq
DR Chowdhury
Golam Nousher
Samiur Rahman

Openers **Raqibul Hasan** (1953) and **Faruk Ahmed** (1966), batsmen **Gazi Ashraf** (1960), **Minhajul Abedin** and **Athar Ali Khan** (1962), all-rounder and fast-medium bowler **Jahangir Shah** (1949), keeper **Shafiq-ul-Haque** (1946), right-arm fast-medium bowler **Golam Faruq** (1962), left-arm fast-medium bowler **Dipu Chowdhury** (1955), left-arm medium pacer **Golam Nousher** (1964), and right-arm medium pacer **Samiur Rahman** (1953).

ENGLAND 1970s XI

	tests	*runs*	*ri*	*wkts*	*rwi*
G Boycott	44	3806	49.42		
DL Amiss	45	3487	43.58		
JH Edrich	37	2427	37.92		
DI Gower	17	1187	45.65		
* AW Greig	58	3599	38.69	141	21.23
IT Botham	22	1068	35.60	118	6.53
† APE Knott	71	3509	31.33		
JA Snow	24	499	13.13	103	11.54
DL Underwood	59	661	7.96	202	14.50
RGD Willis	51	441	6.30	182	12.93
M Hendrick	25	98	3.50	78	13.06

Openers **Geoff Boycott** and **Dennis Amiss** (1943), batsmen **John Edrich** and **David Gower**, tall all-rounder **Tony Greig** (1946-2012), all-rounder **Ian Botham**, keeper **Allan Knott**, fast bowlers **John Snow**, **Bob Willis**, and **Mike Hendrick** (1948), and medium pace left-arm spinner **Derek Underwood** (1945).

AUSTRALIA 1970s XI

	tests	*runs*	*ri*	*wkts*	*rwi*
KR Stackpole	26	1868	37.36	5	247.20
RB McCosker	23	1545	36.78		
* IM Chappell	45	3512	41.80	9	125.12
GS Chappell	53	4357	46.35	34	68.26
IR Redpath	33	2861	44.70		
KD Walters	47	2968	36.19	38	30.78
† RW Marsh	55	2471	28.07		
DK Lillee	35	497	11.04	184	8.78
JR Thomson	34	433	9.41	152	10.27
AA Mallett	28	294	8.16	91	16.67
G Dymock	15	198	7.92	62	10.63

Openers **Keith Stackpole** (1940) and **Rick McCosker** (1946), batsmen **Ian Chappell** (1943), **Greg Chappell**, and **Ian Redpath**, batsman and useful medium pacer **Doug Walters**, keeper **Rod Marsh**, fast bowlers **Dennis Lillee**, **Jeff Thomson**, **Geoff Dymock**, and off spinner **Ashley Mallett** (1945-2021).

SOUTH AFRICA 1970s XI

	tests	*runs*	*ri*	*wkts*	*rwi*
BA Richards	4	508	72.57		
EJ Barlow	4	360	51.42	11	16.98
HM Ackerman	0				
RG Pollock	4	517	73.85		
† BL Irvine	4	353	50.42		
CEB Rice	0				
MJ Procter	4	209	29.85	26	4.17
DL Hobson	0				
PD Swart	0				
PM Pollock	4	74	10.57	15	9.17
VAP van der Bijl	0				

Opener **Barry Richards** and all-rounder **Eddie Barlow**, batsmen **Hylton Ackerman** (1947-2009), **Graeme Pollock**, left-handed batsman and keeper **Lee Irvine** (1944), all-rounders **Clive Rice** and **Mike Procter**, leg spinner **Denys Hobson** (1951), medium pacer **Peter Swart** (1946-2000), and fast bowlers **Peter Pollock** and **Vintcent van der Bijl**.

Richards' RI against the international "invitation" teams in the 1970s was 77.42, from 542 runs.

WEST INDIES 1970s XI

	tests	*runs*	*ri*	*wkts*	*rwi*
CG Greenidge	21	1732	43.30		
RC Fredericks	49	3809	42.32	7	480.86
IVA Richards	29	2640	55.00	4	220.31
AI Kallicharran	53	3956	44.44		
LG Rowe	26	1785	43.35		
* GS Sobers	17	1256	44.85	42	23.24
† DL Murray	43	1553	23.89		
KD Boyce	21	657	21.90	60	19.50
MA Holding	15	225	10.22	65	10.95
AME Roberts	29	290	7.63	140	10.23
LR Gibbs	29	151	4.19	100	18.09

Openers **Gordon Greenidge** and **Roy Fredericks** (1942-2000), batsmen **Viv Richards**, **Alvin Kallicharran** (1949) and the gifted **Lawrence Rowe** (1949), and **Garry Sobers** at the end of his great career, keeper **Deryck Murray**, useful batsman and fast bowler **Keith Boyce** (1943-1996), fiery fast bowlers **Michael Holding** and **Andy Roberts**, and off spinner **Lance Gibbs**.

NEW ZEALAND 1970s XI

	tests	*runs*	*ri*	*wkts*	*rwi*
GM Turner	30	2370	45.57		
JM Parker	30	1316	25.30		
* BE Congdon	32	1935	34.55	48	36.30
GP Howarth	17	1040	32.50		
MG Burgess	33	1815	30.76		
JFM Morrison	14	610	25.41		
† KJ Wadsworth	24	886	24.61		
RJ Hadlee	26	844	17.95	107	13.23
BR Taylor	10	186	14.30	49	9.66
DR Hadlee	18	323	11.13	44	28.09
HJ Howarth	21	248	8.85	50	31.60

Openers **Glenn Turner** and **John Parker**, batsmen **Bevan Congdon** (1938-2018), **Geoff Howarth** (1951), **Mark Burgess** (1944) and **John Morrison** (1947), keeper **Ken Wadsworth** (1946-1976) who died of cancer aged 29, fast bowlers **Richard Hadlee** (who had not yet become a great bowler), **Bruce Taylor** (1943-2021) and **Dayle Hadlee** (1948), and left-arm spinner **Hedley Howarth** (1943-2008).

INDIA 1970s XI

	tests	*runs*	*ri*	*wkts*	*rwi*
SM Gavaskar	60	5647	52.28		
CPS Chauhan	29	1501	31.93		
M Amarnath	25	1450	33.72	21	100.57
* GR Viswanath	62	4611	42.69		
DB Vengsarkar	34	1997	35.66		
ED Solkar	22	877	22.48	15	144.00
Kapil Dev	23	893	28.80	87	12.74
† SMH Kirmani	39	1360	23.85		
EAS Prasanna	27	373	8.10	76	21.37
BS Bedi	48	452	6.55	196	12.76
BS Chandrasekhar	42	95	1.66	180	11.35

Openers **Sunil Gavaskar** and **Chetan Chauhan** (1947-2020), batsmen **Mohinder Amarnath, Gundappa Viswanath** (1949), **Dilip Vengsarkar**, all-rounders **Eknath Solkar** and **Kapil Dev**, keeper **Syed Kirmani**, and spin bowlers **Erapalli Prasanna**, **Bishan Bedi** and **Bhagwath Chandrasekhar**.

PAKISTAN 1970s XI

	tests	*runs*	*ri*	*wkts*	*rwi*
Majid Khan	38	2884	41.79	15	113.08
Sadiq Mohammad	33	2271	38.49		
Zaheer Abbas	36	2563	40.04		
Javed Miandad	25	2059	47.88	17	40.39
* Mushtaq Mohammad	35	2449	40.14	65	22.84
Asif Iqbal	39	2644	40.06	13	83.06
Intikhab Alam	21	739	22.39	76	14.65
Imran Khan	25	832	19.80	98	14.63
Sarfraz Nawaz	33	626	13.31	120	14.71
† Wasim Bari	45	892	13.11		
Sikander Bakht	17	105	4.77	57	14.05

Openers **Majid Khan** and, brother of Hanif and Mushtaq, **Sadiq Mohammad** (1945), batsmen **Zaheer Abbas** and **Javed Miandad**, spinning all-rounders **Mushtaq Mohammad** and **Intikhab Alam**, useful all-rounder **Asif Iqbal**, fast bowling all-rounder **Imran Khan**, fast bowler **Sarfraz Nawaz** (1948) who was one of the pioneers of so-called "reverse swing" (which is the art—for want of a better word—of making an old ball move in the air differently than a new ball), keeper **Wasim Bari**, and fast bowler **Sikander Bakht** (1957).

SRI LANKA 1970s XI

SRD Wettimuny
* B Warnapura
APB Tennekoon
LRD Mendis
PD Heyn
RL Dias
† ER Fernando
HSM Pieris
DS de Silva
ARM Opatha
GRA de Silva

Openers **Sunil Wettimuny** (1949) and **Bandula Warnapura** (1953), batsmen **Anura Tennekoon** (1946), **Duleep Mendis**, **David Heyn** (1945) and **Roy Dias**, keeper **Ranjit Fernando** (1944), fast bowler **Mevan Pieris** (1946), spinner **Somachandra de Silva**, medium pacer **Tony Opatha** (1947-2020), and left-arm spinner **Ajit de Silva** (1952).

ENGLAND 1960s XI

	tests	*runs*	*ri*	*wkts*	*rwi*
JH Edrich	40	2711	43.03		
G Pullar	25	1732	38.48		
KF Barrington	75	6397	52.43	24	95.05
TW Graveney	31	2292	48.76		
* ER Dexter	55	4232	46.00	60	44.32
MC Cowdrey	65	4788	43.52		
† APE Knott	18	666	25.61		
FJ Titmus	47	1272	19.87	145	17.21
FS Trueman	36	580	11.37	179	8.23
K Higgs	15	185	9.73	71	7.88
JB Statham	23	246	8.20	93	12.25

Openers **John Edrich** and **Geoff Pullar** (1935-2014), batsmen **Ken Barrington** and **Tom Graveney**, batsman and useful medium pacer **Ted Dexter**, batsmen **Colin Cowdrey** (1932-2000), keeper **Allan Knott**, off spinner **Fred Titmus** (1932-2011), fast bowlers **Fred Trueman**, **Ken Higgs** (1937-2016) and **Brian Statham**.

AUSTRALIA 1960s XI

	tests	*runs*	*ri*	*wkts*	*rwi*
WM Lawry	58	4717	44.92		
RB Simpson	46	3995	47.55	60	44.42
RM Cowper	27	2061	44.80	36	31.63
NC O'Neill	32	2219	41.86		
KD Walters	21	1992	58.58	11	71.39
PJP Burge	30	1931	38.62		
* R Benaud	21	761	22.38	83	16.77
AK Davidson	17	540	21.60	94	7.21
† BN Jarman	18	399	14.25		
GD McKenzie	54	886	11.35	238	11.96
NJN Hawke	27	365	9.86	91	16.15

Openers **Bill Lawry** and **Bob Simpson**, batsmen **Bob Cowper** (1940), **Norm O'Neill** (1937-2008), **Doug Walters** and **Peter Burge** (1932-2001), all-rounder and leg spinner **Richie Benaud**, left-arm swing bowler **Alan Davidson**, keeper **Barry Jarman** (1936-2020), and fast bowlers **Graham McKenzie** and **Neil Hawke** (1939-2000).

SOUTH AFRICA 1960s XI

	tests	*runs*	*ri*	*wkts*	*rwi*
EJ Barlow	26	2156	43.12	29	49.92
TL Goddard	23	1606	36.50	67	15.97
RG Pollock	19	1739	51.14	4	147.00
KC Bland	21	1669	42.79		
† DT Lindsay	17	1021	37.81		
RA McLean	12	700	31.81		
* PL van der Merwe	15	533	23.17		
PM Pollock	24	533	15.67	101	10.98
AH McKinnon	8	107	8.23	26	20.52
JT Partridge	11	73	6.08	44	14.18
NAT Adcock	7	66	6.00	35	7.79

Opening batsmen and all-rounders **Eddie Barlow** and **Trevor Goddard**, great left-handed batsman **Graeme Pollock**, batsman and great fielder **Colin Bland** (1938-2018), batsman/keeper **Denis Lindsay**, batsmen **Roy McLean** (1930-2007) and **Peter van der Merwe**, fast bowler **Peter Pollock**, left-arm spinner **Atholl McKinnon** (1932-1983), medium pacer **Joe Partridge** (1932-1988), and fast bowler **Neil Adcock** (1931-2013).

WEST INDIES 1960s XI

	tests	*runs*	*ri*	*wkts*	*rwi*
CC Hunte	33	2386	40.44		
MC Carew	13	863	34.52	8	85.31
RB Kanhai	43	3739	49.19		
SM Nurse	29	2523	46.72		
* FMM Worrell	19	1169	38.96	21	53.58
GS Sobers	49	4563	53.05	162	17.73
BF Butcher	36	2485	38.23	5	14.60
† FCM Alexander	10	592	32.88		
WW Hall	40	764	13.40	146	15.14
CC Griffith	28	530	12.61	94	15.18
LR Gibbs	42	226	3.64	184	11.65

Openers **Conrad Hunte** (1932-1999) and **Joey Carew** (1937-2011), batsmen **Rohan Kanhai** and **Seymour Nurse**, batsmen and useful bowlers **Frank Worrell** and **Basil Butcher** (1933-2019), supreme all-rounder **Garry Sobers**, keeper **Gerry Alexander** (1928-2011), fast bowlers **Wes Hall** and **Charlie Griffith** (1938), and off spinner **Lance Gibbs**.

NEW ZEALAND 1960s XI

	tests	*runs*	*ri*	*wkts*	*rwi*
GT Dowling	35	2163	31.34		
GM Turner	9	550	30.55		
BF Hastings	11	620	29.52		
* JR Reid	24	1768	38.43	38	25.15
BW Sinclair	21	1148	28.70		
BE Congdon	29	1513	26.08	11	58.72
BR Taylor	20	712	19.24	62	15.14
† AE Dick	17	370	12.33		
RC Motz	32	612	10.92	100	17.31
HJ Howarth	9	43	3.07	36	10.54
FJ Cameron	19	116	3.86	62	16.83

Openers **Graham Dowling** (1937) and **Glenn Turner**, batsmen **Brian Hastings** (1940), **John Reid**, **Barry Sinclair** (1936) and **Bevan Congdon**, fast bowler **Bruce Taylor**, keeper **Artie Dick** (1936), fast bowler **Dick Motz** (1940-2007), spinner **Hedley Howarth**, and medium pacer **Frank Cameron** (1932).

INDIA 1960s XI

	tests	*runs*	*ri*	*wkts*	*rwi*
NJ Contractor	15	790	32.91		
ML Jaisimha	35	2004	31.31		
PR Umrigar	15	1081	47.00	17	42.47
VL Manjrekar	23	1526	40.15		
MAK Pataudi	39	2552	35.94		
†FM Engineer	30	1607	28.19		
S Abid Abli	8	423	26.43	14	26.57
SA Durani	23	935	23.37	71	18.85
S Venkataraghavan	14	254	11.04	47	13.38
EAS Prasanna	22	362	9.52	113	9.57
BS Bedi	19	204	6.37	70	12.47

Openers **Nari Contractor** (1934) and **ML Jaisimha** (1939-1999), batsmen **Polly Umrigar** (1926-2006), **Vijay Manjrekar** (1931-1983) and the remarkable one-eyed batsman the **Nawab of Pataudi** (1941 2011), keeper **Farokh Engineer**, batsman and medium pace bowler **Syed Abid Abli** (1941), left-arm spinner **Salim Durani** (1934), spinners **Srinivasaraghavan Venkataraghavan**, **Erapalli Prasanna** and **Bishan Bedi**.

PAKISTAN 1960s XI

	tests	*runs*	*ri*	*wkts*	*rwi*
Hanif Mohammad	28	1978	40.36		
†Imtiaz Ahmed	12	759	31.62		
Saeed Ahmed	27	1792	35.13	20	54.16
Mushtaq Mohammad	21	1176	31.78	14	35.07
Javed Burki	25	1341	27.93		
Asif Iqbal	17	872	30.06	40	16.83
Nasim-ul-Ghani	18	562	18.12	18	76.73
Intikhab Alam	25	748	17.80	46	39.49
Mohammad Farooq	7	85	9.44	21	17.00
Haseeb Ahsan	7	50	6.25	19	17.32
Pervez Sajjad	11	67	5.15	48	8.40

Opener **Hanif Mohammad** and opener/keeper **Imtiaz Ahmed**, batsmen and off spinner **Saeed Ahmed** (1937), batsman and leg spinner **Mushtaq Mohammad**, batsman **Javed Burki** (1938), batsman and medium pacer **Asif Iqbal**, batsman and left-arm spinner and medium pace bowler **Nasim-ul-Ghani** (1941), spinner **Intikhab Alam**, fast bowler **Mohammad Farooq** (1938), off spinner **Haseeb Ahsan** (1939-2013), and left-arm spinner **Pervez Sajjad** (1942).

CEYLON 1960s XI

ACM Lafir
TCT Edward
APB Tennekoon
MH Tissera
CC Inman
PD Heyn
CI Gunasekera
† HIK Fernando
SR Wimalaratne
MAH Fuard
D Sahabandu

Openers **Abdul Latif** (1939) and **Trevelyan Edward** (1938-1995), batsmen **Anura Tennekoon**, **Michael Tissera** (1939), **Clive Inman** (1936) and **David Heyn**, batsman and leg spinner **Ievers Gunasekera** (1920-2010), keeper **Herbert Fernando** (1933), medium pace bowler **Sarath Wimalaratne** (1942), off spinner **Abu Fuard** (1936-2012) and left-arm spinner **Dayananda Sahabandu** (1940).

ENGLAND 1950s XI

	tests	*runs*	*ri*	*wkts*	*rwi*
* L Hutton	38	3183	48.22		
PE Richardson	5	1623	40.57		
MC Cowdrey	39	2440	40.00		
PBH May	59	4182	44.96		
DCS Compton	42	2675	37.67	5	348.68
TE Bailey	57	2071	24.08	116	21.29
† TG Evans	64	1693	18.20		
FS Trueman	31	401	11.79	128	9.82
FH Tyson	17	230	9.58	76	7.08
JC Laker	38	453	9.24	162	8.20
AV Bedser	28	263	7.30	147	6.88

Openers **Len Hutton** and **Peter Richardson**, batsmen **Colin Cowdrey**, **Peter May** and **Denis Compton**, all-rounder **Trevor Bailey**, keeper **Godfrey Evans**, fast bowlers **Fred Trueman** and **Frank Tyson**, off spinner **Jim Laker**, and medium-fast bowler **Alec Bedser**.

AUSTRALIA 1950s XI

	tests	*runs*	*ri*	*wkts*	*rwi*
AR Morris	30	2059	38.12		
CC McDonald	36	2590	40.46		
* AL Hassett	22	1712	43.89		
RN Harvey	56	4573	46.19		
NC O'Neill	10	560	35.50		
KR Miller	37	2080	32.50	122	12.37
R Benaud	42	1440	22.85	165	10.74
AK Davidson	27	788	21.88	92	10.91
† ATW Grout	14	352	20.70		
RR Lindwall	42	1041	16.52	152	12.28
LF Kline	10	40	3.63	29	9.87

Openers **Arthur Morris** and **Colin McDonald** (1928-2021), batsmen **Lindsay Hassett**, **Neil Harvey** and **Norm O'Neill**, all-rounders **Keith Miller** and **Richie Benaud**, left-arm swing bowler **Alan Davidson**, keeper **Wally Grout**, fast bowler **Ray Lindwall** and left-arm wrist spinner **Lindsay Kline** (1934-2015).

SOUTH AFRICA 1950s XI

	tests	*runs*	*ri*	*wkts*	*rwi*
DJ McGlew	24	1825	40.55		
TL Goddard	15	852	29.37	47	16.06
WR Endean	28	1630	31.34		
† JHB Waite	31	1518	26.63		
JE Cheetham	21	788	21.29		
KJ Funston	18	325	25.00		
RA McLean	28	1420	27.84		
JC Watkins	13	532	23.13	26	24.52
* HJ Tayfield	30	674	14.04	153	8.18
PS Heine	13	178	7.73	56	10.61
NAT Adcock	19	80	2.85	69	10.11

Openers **Jackie McGlew** and **Trevor Goddard**, batsman **Russell Endean** (1924-2003), batsman/keeper **John Waite** (1930-2011), batsmen **Jack Cheetham** (1920-1980), **Ken Funston** (1925-2005) and **Roy McLean**, attacking all-rounder and medium pacer **John Watkins** (1923-2021), off spinner **Hugh Tayfield**, and fast bowlers **Peter Heine** (1928-2005) and **Neil Adcock**.

WEST INDIES 1950s XI

	tests	*runs*	*ri*	*wkts*	*rwi*
CC Hunte	11	859	45.21		
RB Kanhai	18	1317	41.15		
* FMM Worrell	29	2397	45.22	47	36.95
ED Weekes	39	3383	49.75		
CL Walcott	33	3129	54.89	10	58.68
GS Sobers	27	2213	48.10	31	58.60
OG Smith	26	1331	31.69	48	26.09
† FCM Alexander	15	369	18.45		
S Ramadhin	37	299	5.98	138	13.48
R Gilchrist	13	60	4.28	57	10.76
AL Valentine	29	102	2.61	123	11.78

Openers **Conrad Hunte** and **Rohan Kanhai**, the "Three Ws": **Frank Worrell**, **Everton Weekes**, and **Clyde Walcott** who had a career record of 2,910 runs at 58.20 RI when not playing as wicket-keeper, great all-rounder **Garry Sobers**, hard hitting batsman and useful spin bowler **Collie Smith** (1933-1959), keeper **Gerry Alexander**, spin duo of right-armer **Sonny Ramadhin** (1929-2022) and left-armer **Alf Valentine**, and the aggressive and angry fast bowler **Roy Gilchrist** (1934-2001).

Collie Smith was considered by many to be as good a cricketer as Sobers. Smith died after a car accident en route to London for a charity match at the age of 26, in which Sobers had been the driver.

NEW ZEALAND 1950s XI

	tests	*runs*	*ri*	*wkts*	*rwi*
B Sutcliffe	29	1854	34.33		
VJ Scott	4	244	34.85		
RO Rabone	8	414	29.57	12	19.24
* JR Reid	32	1487	25.63	47	29.85
JEF Beck	8	394	26.26		
JW Guy	10	422	22.21		
AR MacGibbon	26	814	17.69	70	16.30
† FLH Mooney	11	244	13.55		
AM Moir	17	327	10.90	28	34.36
HB Cave	15	185	7.11	30	21.15
JA Hayes	15	73	3.31	30	25.68

Openers **Bert Sutcliffe** and **Verdun Scott** (1916-1980), batsmen **Geoff Rabone** (1921-2006), **John Reid**, **John Beck** (1934-2000) and **John Guy**, fast bowler **Tony MacGibbon** (1924-2010), keeper **Frank Mooney** (1921-2004), leg spinner **Alex Moir** (1919-2000), and fast bowlers **Harry Cave** (1922-1989) and **John Hayes** (1927-2007).

The promise of New Zealand's team, seen in the 1940s, evaporated into a vapour that was this collection of no-hopers. Of all the Test nations, they seemed to take the longest to recover from the effects of WWII, but that may be a convenient excuse for what was a prevalent amateurish attitude, some of which still remains today. They weren't helped by captain John Reid's terrible lack of form, and even Bert Sutcliffe became a shadow of his younger self. It is possible that they were convinced that they were second-rate because Australia refused to allow their first-eleven to play against them.

INDIA 1950s XI

	tests	*runs*	*ri*	*wkts*	*rwi*
MH Mankad	31	1536	32.00	122	12.47
Pankaj Roy	39	2280	31.66		
PR Umrigar	43	2520	36.00	18	71.84
VS Hazare	17	1097	40.62	9	123.44
VL Manjrekar	32	1682	31.14		
NJ Contractor	16	821	29.32		
GS Ramchand	30	1124	23.41	41	54.02
DG Phadkar	23	675	22.50	40	38.47
† PG Joshi	11	155	8.15		
Ghulam Ahmed	19	161	6.19	60	14.55
SP Gupte	31	182	4.66	134	11.30

Opener and spinner **Vinoo Mankad**, opener **Pankaj Roy** (1928-2001), batsmen **Polly Umrigar**, **Vijay Hazare** (1915-2004), **Vijay Manjrekar** and **Nari Contractor**, all-rounders who bowled medium pace: **Gulabrai Ramchand** (1927-2003) and **Dattu Phadkar** (1925-1985), keeper **Nana Joshi** (1926-1987), off spinner **Ghulam Ahmed** (1922-1998) and leg spinner **Subhash Gupte** (1929-2002).

PAKISTAN 1950s XI

	tests	*runs*	*ri*	*wkts*	*rwi*
Hanif Mohammad	27	1937	40.35		
Alimuddin	19	708	20.82		
Waqar Hasan	21	1071	30.60		
Saeed Ahmed	11	1041	49.57		
† Imtiaz Ahmed	29	1320	27.50		
AH Kardar	23	847	22.89	21	56.23
Wazir Mohammad	20	801	24.27		
Zulfiqar Ahmed	9	200	20.00	20	9.15
Fazal Mahmood	26	541	13.87	125	7.60
Nasim-ul-Ghani	10	116	6.82	34	12.91
Khan Mohammad	13	100	5.88	54	9.74

Openers **Hanif Mohammad** and **Alimuddin** (1930-2012), batsmen **Waqar Hasan** (1932-2020), **Saeed Ahmed** and **Wazir Mohammad** (1929), batsman/keeper **Imtiaz Ahmed**, all-rounder and left-arm spinner **Abdul Kardar** (1925-1996), off spinner **Zulfiqar Ahmed** (1926-2008), and fast bowlers **Fazal Mahmood**, **Nasim-ul-Ghani** and **Khan Mohammad** (1928-2009).

CEYLON 1950s XI

CH Gunasekera
ACM Lafir
FC de Saram
S Jayasinghe
CI Gunasekera
VG Prins
S Coomaraswamy
G Goonesena
† HIK Fernando
B Wijesinha
FM Francke

Openers **Channa Gunasekera** (1931-2008) and **Abdul Lafir**, batsmen **Derrick de Saram** (1912-1983), **Stanley Jayasinghe** (1931) and **Vernon Prins** (1924-2003), all-rounders **Ievers Gunasekera**, **Sathyendra Coomaraswamy** (1919-1988) and **Gamini Goonesena** (1931-2011), keeper **Herbert Fernando**, medium pace bowler **Bertie Wijesinha** (1920-2017), and Australian born-and-raised leg spinner **Malcolm Francke** (1939).

ENGLAND 1940s XI

	tests	*runs*	*ri*	*wkts*	*rwi*
* L Hutton	28	2443	47.90		
C Washbrook	25	1962	42.65		
WJ Edrich	20	1699	51.48		
DCS Compton	28	2664	55.50	18	119.62
JDB Robertson	6	571	47.58		
NWD Yardley	16	697	25.81	20	27.58
† TG Evans	27	746	18.65		
JC Laker	8	223	15.92	31	16.15
AV Bedser	23	451	12.88	89	15.31
DVP Wright	17	97	5.38	58	20.62
R Pollard	4	13	4.33	15	11.66

Openers **Len Hutton** and **Cyril Washbrook** (1914-1999), batsmen **Bill Edrich** (1916-1986), **Denis Compton** and **Jack Robertson** (1917-1996), all-rounder and medium-pacer **Norman Yardley** (1915-1989), keeper **Godfrey Evans**, off spinner **Jim Laker**, fast-medium bowler **Alec Bedser**, leg spinner **Doug Wright** (1914-1998), and fast bowler **Dick Pollard** (1912-1985).

AUSTRALIA 1940s XI

	tests	*runs*	*ri*	*wkts*	*rwi*
AR Morris	15	1408	61.20		
SG Barnes	12	998	58.70		
* DG Bradman	15	1903	82.73		
AL Hassett	16	1105	52.61		
SJE Loxton	5	325	65.00	6	64.33
KR Miller	17	804	38.28	45	13.32
RR Lindwall	16	442	24.55	65	9.06
† D Tallon	15	340	21.25		
WA Johnston	10	94	9.40	51	6.74
WJ O'Reilly	1	0	-	8	1.03
ERH Toshack	12	73	6.63	47	10.29

Openers **Arthur Morris** and **Sid Barnes**, batsmen **Don Bradman**, **Lindsay Hassett** and **Sam Loxton** (1921-2011), all-rounders **Keith Miller** and **Ray Lindwall**, keeper **Don Tallon** (1916-1984), fast and spin bowler **Bill Johnston**, great leg spinner **Bill O'Reilly**, and left-arm medium pacer **Ernie Toshack** (1914-2003).

SOUTH AFRICA 1940s XI

	tests	*runs*	*ri*	*wkts*	*rwi*
A Melville	6	608	50.66		
EAB Rowan	5	411	41.10		
B Mitchell	10	1072	53.60	3	140.76
* AD Nourse	11	1193	56.80		
† WW Wade	6	420	38.18		
KG Viljoen	7	335	25.76		
OC Dawson	9	293	19.53	10	57.80
AMB Rowan	10	185	13.21	36	19.21
NBF Mann	11	194	11.41	34	19.45
L Tuckett	9	131	9.35	19	46.14
CN McCarthy	6	6	0.75	23	12.30

Openers **Alan Melville** and **Eric Rowan** (1909-1993), batsmen **Bruce Mitchell** and **Dudley Nourse**, batsman/keeper **Billy Wade**, batsmen **Ken Viljoen** (1910-1974), medium pacer **Ossie Dawson** (1919-2008), off spinner and brother of Eric, **Athol Rowan** (1921-1998), left-arm spinner **Tufty Mann** (1920-1952) who died at age 31 after a medical operation, and fast bowlers **Lindsay Tuckett** (1919-2016) and **Cuan McCarthy**.

WEST INDIES 1940s XI

	tests	*runs*	*ri*	*wkts*	*rwi*
JB Stollmeyer	6	506	56.22	5	43.20
AF Rae	5	374	53.42		
* GA Headley	2	38	12.66		
ED Weekes	9	1072	82.46		
FMM Worrell	3	294	73.50		
† CL Walcott	9	585	41.78		
GE Gomez	9	488	37.53	17	20.13
EAV Williams	3	112	22.40	9	16.14
W Ferguson	7	148	18.50	33	12.98
J Trim	3	21	7.00	13	8.23
PEW Jones	6	38	5.42	21	15.29

Openers **Jeffrey Stollmeyer** and **Allan Rae** (1922-2005), batsman **George Headley**, **Everton Weekes**, **Frank Worrell**, and batsman/keeper **Clyde Walcott**, all-rounder **Gerry Gomez** (1919-1996), fast bowler **Foffie Williams** (1914-1997), leg spinner **Wilf Ferguson** (1917-1961), fast bowler **John Trim** (1915-1960), and the genuinely quick bowler **Prior Jones** (1917-1991).

West Indies played only 9 Tests in the 1940s. Headley is included because his first-class RI for the 1940s was 44.35. Like many players, the war robbed him of his best years.

NEW ZEALAND 1940s XI

	tests	*runs*	*ri*	*wkts*	*rwi*
B Sutcliffe	5	481	60.12		
* WA Hadlee	6	318	31.80		
JR Reid	2	173	43.25		
MP Donnelly	4	462	77.00		
FB Smith	3	191	47.75		
GO Rabone	4	148	24.66	4	102.18
† FLH Mooney	3	99	24.75		
TB Burtt	5	155	22.14	17	15.08
J Cowie	6	82	10.25	26	5.94
GF Cresswell	1	12	6.00	6	4.66
C Burke	1	4	2.00	2	7.50

Openers **Bert Sutcliffe** and **Walter Hadlee**, batsmen **John Reid**, **Martin Donnelly**, **Brun Smith** (1922-1997) and **Geoff Rabone**, keeper **Frank Mooney**, left-arm spinner **Tom Burtt** (1915-1988), fast bowler **Jack Cowie**, medium pacer **Fen Cresswell** (1915-1966) and leg spinner **Ces Burke** (1914-1987) who took exactly 200 first-class wickets at a very good average of 25.99.

New Zealand had an outstanding team at this time, building on the work from the 1930s, but they had little opportunity to play anyone.

INDIA 1940s XI

	tests	*runs*	*ri*	*wkts*	*rwi*
VM Merchant	3	245	49.00		
S Mushtaq Ali	5	346	38.44		
VS Hazare	13	1095	43.80	11	121.97
RS Modi	8	697	46.47		
HR Adhikari	10	410	22.77		
L Amarnath	13	503	20.12	29	19.37
DG Phadkar	8	554	36.93	22	13.73
MH Mankad	13	573	23.87	40	18.74
†PK Sen	8	92	8.36		
Ghulam Ahmed	3	31	6.20	8	28.20
CR Rangachari	4	8	1.33	9	24.34

Openers **Vijay Merchant** and **Mushtaq Ali** (1914-2005), batsmen **Vijay Hazare**, **Rusi Modi** (1924-1996) and **Hemu Adhikari** (1919-2003), all-rounder and medium pace bowlers **Lala Amarnath** (1911-2000) and **Dattu Phadkar** (1925-1985), and batsman and spinner **Vinoo Mankad**, keeper **Khokhan Sen** (1926-1970), off spinner **Ghulam Ahmed** and fast bowler **Commandur Rangachari** (1916-1993).

CEYLON 1940s XI

M Rodrigo
M Makkin Salih
FC de Saram
M Sathasivam
SS Jayawickreme
CI Gunasekera
S Coomaraswamy
RL de Kretser
AH Gooneratne
LE de Zoysa
†B Navaratne

Openers **Mahesha Rodrigo** (1927-2011) and **Makkin Salih** (1923-2003), batsmen **Derrick de Saram** and **Mahadevan Sathasivam** (1915-1977), all-rounder and medium pace bowler **Sargo Jayawickreme** (1911-1983), all-rounders **Ievers Gunasekera** and **Sathyendra Coomaraswamy**, off spinner **Robert de Krester** (1919), leg spinners **Alexander Gooneratne** (dates unknown) and **Lucien de Zoysa** (1917-1995), and keeper **Benedict Navaratne** (1916-1979).

ENGLAND 1930s XI

	tests	*runs*	*ri*	*wkts*	*rwi*
L Hutton	13	1345	64.01		
H Sutcliffe	22	1595	46.91		
KS Duleepsinhji	11	982	57.76		
* WR Hammond	60	5194	53.00	59	51.08
EH Hendren	19	1656	50.18		
E Paynter	20	1540	49.67		
† LEG Ames	46	2434	34.28		
H Larwood	9	208	17.33	37	9.56
H Verity	40	669	15.20	144	12.35
IAR Peebles	9	36	3.27	40	9.30
WE Bowes	14	26	2.60	67	8.69

Openers **Len Hutton** and **Herbert Sutcliffe**, batsmen **Kumar Duleepsinhji** (1905-1959) the nephew of Kumar Ranjitsinhji, **Wally Hammond**, **Patsy Hendren** and **Eddie Paynter**, keeper **Les Ames**, lighting-fast bowler **Harold Larwood**, left-arm spinner **Hedley Verity**, leg spinner **Ian Peebles**, and fast bowler **Bill Bowes**.

AUSTRALIA 1930s XI

	tests	*runs*	*ri*	*wkts*	*rwi*
WH Ponsford	20	1604	50.12		
WA Brown	16	1324	47.28		
* DG Bradman	33	4625	94.38		
SJ McCabe	39	2748	44.32	36	73.61
JHW Fingleton	18	1189	41.00		
AG Fairfax	9	345	31.36	19	23.97
† WAS Oldfield	34	728	15.48		
CV Grimmett	28	400	11.42	169	6.62
WJ O'Reilly	26	410	10.51	136	8.00
EL McCormick	12	54	3.85	36	17.48
H Ironmonger	12	37	2.17	68	5.31

Openers **Bill Ponsford** and **Bill Brown**, batsmen **Don Bradman**, **Stan McCabe**, **Jack Fingleton** (1908-1981) and **Alan Fairfax** (1906-1955), keeper **Bert Oldfield** (1894-1976), leg spinners **Clarrie Grimmett** and **Bill O'Reilly**, fast bowler **Ernie McCormick** (1906-1991) and left-arm spinner **Bert Ironmonger** (1882-1971) who debuted in Tests at the age of 45 and continued for four years.

SOUTH AFRICA 1930s XI

	tests	*runs*	*ri*	*wkts*	*rwi*
B Mitchell	27	2148	42.11	22	58.06
IJ Siedle	14	921	34.11		
EAB Rowan	12	727	31.60		
AD Nourse	14	1097	42.19		
* HW Taylor	10	622	34.55		
KG Viljoen	20	1030	27.83		
† HB Cameron	17	816	27.20		
ACB Langton	15	298	12.95	40	26.26
Q McMillan	11	239	12.57	33	17.53
CL Vincent	16	284	11.83	48	17.07
NA Quinn	8	44	3.38	22	17.45

Openers **Bruce Mitchell** and **Jack Siedle** (1903-1982), batsmen **Eric Rowan**, **Dudley Nourse**, **Herbie Taylor** (1889-1973) and **Ken Viljoen**, keeper **Jock Cameron**, fast-medium bowler **Chud Langton** (1912-1942), leg spinner **Quintin McMillan** (1904-1948), left-arm spinner **Cyril Vincent** (1902-1968), and left-arm fast bowler **Neville Quinn** (1908-1934) who died suddenly at only 26.

WEST INDIES 1930s XI

	tests	*runs*	*ri*	*wkts*	*rwi*
CA Roach	13	821	31.57		
JB Stollmeyer	3	133	26.60		
GA Headley	19	2135	61.00		
JED Sealy	11	478	25.15	3	62.66
RS Grant	7	220	20.00	11	32.09
LN Constantine	15	546	20.22	53	13.73
† IM Barrow	11	276	14.52		
OC Scott	6	97	10.77	20	18.49
HC Griffith	10	83	4.88	33	13.67
GN Francis	7	53	4.41	17	17.67
EA Martindale	10	58	4.14	37	9.97

Openers **Clifford Roach** (1904-1988) and **Jeffrey Stollmeyer**, batsmen **George Headley** and **Derek Sealy** (1912-1982) who was just 17 when he first played his first Test, all-rounders **Rolph Grant** (1909-1977) and **Learie Constantine**, keeper **Ivan Barrow** (1911-1979), leg spinner **Tommy Scott** (1892-1961), and fast bowlers **Herman Griffith** (1893-1980), **George Francis** (1897-1942) and **Manny Martindale**.

NEW ZEALAND 1930s XI

	tests	*runs*	*ri*	*wkts*	*rwi*
CS Dempster	10	723	48.20		
HG Vivian	7	421	42.10	17	21.90
GL Weir	11	416	26.00	7	34.11
RC Blunt	9	330	25.38	12	45.88
*TC Lowry	7	223	27.87		
ML Page	14	492	24.60	5	110.88
FT Badcock	7	137	15.22	16	21.44
WE Merritt	6	73	9.12	12	38.55
†EWT Tindill	3	58	9.66		
GR Dickinson	3	31	6.20	8	22.96
J Cowie	3	8	1.60	19	6.56

Openers **Stewie Dempster** and **Giff Vivian** (1912-1983), batsman **Lindsay Weir** (1908-2003), all-rounder and leg spinner **Roger Blunt** (1900-1966), batsman **Tom Lowry** (1898-1976), **Curly Page** (1902-1987), an all-rounder in most sports he played, fast bowler **Ted Badcock** (1897-1982), leg spinner **Bill Merritt** (1908-1977), keeper **Eric Tindill** (1910-2010) who lived to the age of 99, and fast bowlers **George Dickinson** (1903-1978) and **Jack Cowie**.

INDIA 1930s XI

	tests	*runs*	*ri*	*wkts*	*rwi*
VM Merchant	6	460	38.33		
S Mushtaq Ali	5	244	24.40		
L Amarnath	3	203	33.83	4	28.25
CK Nayudu	7	350	25.00	9	47.64
S Wazir Ali	7	237	16.92		
†Dilawar Hussain	3	254	42.33		
S Nazir Ali	2	30	7.50	4	5.18
M Jahangir Khan	4	39	5.57	4	95.62
L Amar Singh	7	292	20.85	28	14.22
Mohammad Nissar	6	55	5.00	25	12.44
RJD Jamshedji	1	5	2.50	3	15.21

Openers **Vijay Merchant** and **Mushtaq Ali**, batsmen **Lala Amarnath**, **CK Nayudu** (1895-1967) and **Syed Wazir Ali** (1903-1950), keeper **Dilawar Hussain** (1907-1967), all-rounders and fast bowlers **Nazir Ali** (1906-1975) and **Jahangir Khan** (1910-1988), fast bowlers **Amar Singh** (1910-1940), who died of typhoid fever at age 29, and **Mohammad Nissar** (1910-1963), and left-arm spinner **Rustomji Jamshedji** (1892-1976).

India played only 7 tests in the 1930s, and players such as Jahangir Khan were much better than what they produced on the cricket field in their limited opportunities.

CEYLON 1930s XI

MK Albert
WL Mendis
AMH Kelaart
FC de Saram
EGS Kelaart
SS Jayawickreme
BD Gunasekera
† VC Schokman
HE Poulier
BS Perera
LE Bakelman

Openers **Mohotti Albert** (1895-1944) and **Louis Mendis**, batsmen **Mervyn Kelaart** (1908-1968), **Derrick de Saram**, **Edward Kelaart** (1900-1989) and **Sargo Jayawickreme**, leg spinner **Barney Gunasekera** (?-1984), keeper **Vernon Schokman** (1905-1991), bowlers **Hilton Poulier** (1909-1979) and **Bertram Perera** (1906-1974), and left-arm spinner **Ladislaus Bakelman** (1900-1965).

ENGLAND 1920s XI

	tests	*runs*	*ri*	*wkts*	*rwi*
JB Hobbs	28	2644	60.09		
H Sutcliffe	32	2960	59.20		
GE Tyldesley	14	990	49.50		
WR Hammond	17	1689	58.24	24	46.03
FE Woolley	33	2003	40.06	31	72.92
EH Hendren	32	1869	37.38		
MW Tate	26	814	24.66	118	9.80
VWC Jupp	8	208	16.00	28	11.00
G Geary	11	187	11.68	41	11.29
AP Freeman	12	154	9.62	66	8.62
† H Strudwick	17	139	5.56		

Openers **Jack Hobbs** and **Herbert Sutcliffe**, batsmen **Ernest Tyldesley** and **Patsy Hendren**, all-rounders **Wally Hammond** and **Frank Woolley**, useful batsman and outstanding seamer **Maurice Tate**, off spinner **Vallance Jupp** (1891-1960), fast bowler **George Geary**, leg spinner **Tich Freeman** (1888-1965), and keeper **Herbert Strudwick** (1880-1970).

AUSTRALIA 1920s XI

	tests	*runs*	*ri*	*wkts*	*rwi*
HL Collins	19	1352	43.61		
WM Woodfull	10	797	49.81		
CG Macartney	14	1252	59.61	11	38.24
J Ryder	20	1394	43.56		
* WW Armstrong	10	616	47.38	17	23.03
C Kelleway	11	590	32.77	29	19.13
JM Gregory	24	1146	33.70	85	15.39
† WAS Oldfield	20	699	21.18		
CV Grimmett	9	157	10.46	47	11.00
EA McDonald	11	116	9.66	43	16.24
AA Mailey	21	222	7.65	99	11.64

Openers **Herbie Collins** (1888-1959) and **Bill Woodfull**, batsmen and medium pacer **Charlie Macartney**, batsmen **Jack Ryder**, all-rounders **Warwick Armstrong**, **Charlie Kelleway** (1886-1944) and **Jack Gregory**, keeper **Bill Oldfield**, leg spinners **Clarrie Grimmett** and **Arthur Mailey** (1886-1967), and fast bowler **Ted McDonald** (1891-1937).

U.S.A. 1920s XI

JM Crosman
CM Graham
CC Morris
SW Mifflin
W Graham
WP O'Neill
GW Cupitt
TM Logan
† CH Winter
EM Mann
R Waad

Jim Crosman, **Mervyn Graham**, **Christopher Morris** (1882-1971) who was one of America's greatest cricketers and supporters of the game, **Samuel Mifflin** (1880-1959), all-rounder and left-arm spinner **Willard Graham**, left-arm medium pace bowler **William O'Neill** (1880-1966), **GW Cupitt**, **TM Logan**, keeper **Charles Winter** (1890-1969), **EM Mann**, and fast bowler **Rudolph Waad** (1886-1926).

The 1920s were the last years of competitive American cricket. Most of these players represented the Philadelphians club.

SOUTH AFRICA 1920s XI

	tests	*runs*	*ri*	*wkts*	*rwi*
HW Taylor	21	1612	43.56		
RH Catterall	20	1378	38.27		
MJ Susskind	5	268	33.50		
AW Nourse	13	722	31.39	5	211.20
DPB Morkel	10	514	30.23	16	36.44
HG Deane	15	598	24.91		
†HB Cameron	9	423	28.20		
JM Blanckenberg	13	351	17.55	41	14.86
CL Vincent	9	242	17.28	36	12.24
EP Nupen	13	306	12.75	28	40.46
AE Hall	6	11	1.57	36	6.79

Openers **Herbie Taylor** and **Bob Catterall** (1900-1961), batsmen **Fred Susskind** (1891-1957) and **Dave Nourse** (1879-1948), all-rounder **Denys Morkel** (1906-1980), batsman **Nummy Deane** (1885-1939), keeper **Jock Cameron**, medium pacer **Jimmy Blanckenberg**, spinner **Cyril Vincent**, fast bowler **Buster Nupen** (1902-1977) and left-arm fast bowler **Alf Hall** (1896-1964).

WEST INDIES 1920s XI

	tests	*runs*	*ri*	*wkts*	*rwi*
*G Challenor	3	101	16.33		
PH Tarilton	0				
GA Headley	0				
WH St Hill	2	54	13.50		
ELG Hoad	1	17	8.50		
FR Martin	3	175	29.16		
†RK Nunes	3	87	14.50		
CR Browne	2	84	21.00	2	62.50
LN Constantine	3	89	14.83	5	31.44
VS Pascall	0				
HC Griffith	3	8	1.33	11	6.19

Openers **George Challenor** (1888-1947) and **Percy Tarilton** (1885-1953), batsmen **George Headley**, **Wilton St Hill** (1893-1957) and **Teddy Hoad** (1896-1986), all-rounder and left-arm spinner **Freddie Martin** (1893-1967), keeper **Karl Nunes** (1894-1958), medium pacer **Snuffy Browne** (1890-1964), fast bowler **Learie Constantine**, left-arm spinner **Victor Pascall** (1886-1930) who was the uncle of Learie, and fast bowler **Herman Griffith**.

The brilliant Headley debuted at age 18, and batted number four for Jamaica. In his second game, batting at three, he made 211. In 1929, aged just 19, playing for a West Indies XI, again at three, he made 143. His success changed his life, and the proposed dentist career in America.

NEW ZEALAND 1920s XI

	team
JS Hiddleston	Wellington
RVD Worker	Canterbury, Otago, Wellington
RC Blunt	Canterbury, Otago
HHL Kortlang	Wellington
CCR Dacre	Auckland
SG Smith	Auckland
HM McGirr	Wellington
FT Badcock	Wellington
† KC James	Wellington
GR Dickinson	Otago
DJ McBeath	Canterbury, Southland, Otago

Openers **Syd Hiddleston** (1890-1940) and **Rupert Worker** (1896-1989), all-rounder **Roger Blunt**, Australian batsman **Harry Kortlang** (1880-1961) who also played in the U.S.A., batsmen and left-arm spinners **Ces Dacre** (1899-1975), and **Sydney Smith** (1881-1963) from Trinidad, batsman and medium pace bowler **Herb McGirr** (1891-1964), fast bowler **Ted Badcock**, keeper **Ken James**, fast bowler **George Dickinson**, and left-arm medium pacer **Dan McBeath** (1897-1963).

INDIA 1920s XI

	team
Ferozuddin	Muslims
† Dilawar Hussain	Muslims
S Wazir Ali	Muslims
CK Nayudu	Hindus
P Vithal	Hindus
S Nazir Ali	Muslims
Abdus Salaam	Muslims
JN Mehta	Hindus
CR Ganapathy	Madras
MH Rana	Hindus
RJD Jamshedji	Parsees

Opener **Ferozuddin** (unknown age), batsman/keeper **Dilawar Hussain**, batsmen **Syed Wazir Ali**, **CK Nayudu** and **Panvekhar Vithal** (1884-1971), all-rounders **Nazir Ali** and **Abdus Salaam** (unknown age), bowler **Jagan Mehta** (unknown age), medium pace bowler **CR Ganapathy** (1886-1954), bowler **MH Rana** (unknown age), and spinner **Rustomji Jamshedji**.

ENGLAND 1910s XI

	tests	*runs*	*ri (adj +5)*	*wkts*	*rwi (adj +5)*
JB Hobbs	21	2031	58.02 (63.02)		
W Rhodes	21	1235	35.28 (40.28)	11	97.72 (109.09)
G Gunn	5	381	42.33 (47.33)		
CP Mead	9	483	37.15 (42.15)		
FE Woolley	21	929	29.96 (34.96)	39	20.38 (24.86)
GJ Thompson	5	267	29.66 (34.66)	23	11.69 (13.87)
JWHT Douglas	11	410	25.62 (30.62)	25	18.05 (21.85)
FR Foster	11	330	22.00 (27.00)	45	8.86 (10.79)
† H Strudwick	11	91	5.35 (10.35)		
SF Barnes	15	75	3.94 (8.94)	122	3.11 (4.22)
C Blythe	2	7	2.33 (7.33)	12	4.66 (6.33)

Opener **Jack Hobbs** and all-rounder **Wilfred Rhodes**, batsmen **George Gunn** and **Phil Mead**, all-rounders **Frank Woolley**, **George Thompson** (1877-1943), **Johnny Douglas** (1882-1930) and **Frank Foster**, keeper **Herbert Strudwick**, fast spin bowler **Sydney Barnes** and left-arm spinner **Colin Blythe**.

AUSTRALIA 1910s XI

	tests	*runs*	*ri (adj +5)*	*wkts*	*rwi (adj +5)*
W Bardsley	15	1094	47.56 (52.56)		
C Kelleway	15	832	34.66 (39.66)	23	39.82 (45.04)
* C Hill	10	699	38.83 (43.83)		
VT Trumper	10	930	48.94 (53.94)		
WW Armstrong	10	734	40.77 (45.77)	20	39.94 (44.69)
CG Macartney	11	458	30.53 (35.53)	8	73.12 (81.25)
HV Hordern	7	254	19.53 (24.53)	46	6.60 (8.01)
† H Carter	10	287	15.94 (20.94)		
A Cotter	9	192	12.00 (17.00)	34	17.36 (19.86)
WJ Whitty	13	152	8.94 (13.94)	65	7.14 (8.90)
GR Hazlitt	7	33	4.12 (9.12)	23	9.92 (12.09)

Opener **Warren Bardsley**, all-rounder **Charlie Kelleway**, batsmen **Clem Hill** and **Victor Trumper**, all-rounders **Warwick Armstrong**, **Charlie Macartney**, and leg spinner **Ranji Hordern**, keeper **Sammy Carter**, fast bowler **Tibby Cotter** (1884-1917), last arm fast bowler **Bill Whitty**, and off spinner **Gerry Hazlitt** (1888-1915).

U.S.A. 1910s XI

JB King
HA Furness
HHL Kortlang
CC Morris
W Graham
LR Miller
WP O'Neill
PH Clark
†JH Scattergood
EM Mann
R Waad

Bart King, the great all-rounder, batsmen **Harold Furness** (1887-1975), Australian **Harry Kortlang, Christopher Morris** and **Willard Graham**, left-arm spinner **Leslie Miller** (1883-1951) from New York, **William O'Neill**, useful batsman and fast bowler **Percy Clark** (1873-1965), keeper **Joseph Scattergood** (1877-1953), and bowlers **EM Mann** and **Rudolph Waad**.

SOUTH AFRICA 1910s XI

	tests	*runs*	*ri (adj +5)*	*wkts*	*rwi (adj +5)*
HW Taylor	11	702	33.42 (38.42)	4	53.81 (62.56)
JW Zulch	13	792	30.46 (35.46)		
AW Nourse	21	981	23.92 (28.92)	25	44.83 (50.83)
GA Faulkner	16	1471	47.45 (52.75)	56	13.79 (16.20)
GC White	9	420	24.70 (29.70)	3	127.99 (141.33)
SJ Snooke	15	633	21.82 (26.82)	4	176.31 (192.56)
RO Schwarz	12	292	12.16 (17.16)	28	18.66 (21.52)
AEE Vogler	7	156	12.00 (17.00)	40	7.79 (9.41)
JM Blanckenberg	5	104	10.40 (15.40)	19	8.29 (10.13)
SJ Pegler	11	303	14.42 (19.42)	38	13.36 (15.73)
†TA Ward	10	143	7.52 (12.52)		

Openers **Herbie Taylor** and **Billy Zulch** (1886-1924), batsman **Dave Nourse**, all-rounder **Aubrey Faulkner**, batsman **Gordon White** (1882-1918), all-rounder and medium pacer **Tip Snooke** (1881-1966), medium pacer and leg spinner **Reggie Schwarz** (1875-1918), brilliant bowler of fast leg break **Bert Vogler** (1876-1946), medium pacer **Jimmy Blanckenberg**, medium pace bowler with leg break **Sid Pegler** (1888-1972), and keeper **Tommy Ward** (1887-1936).

WEST INDIES 1910s XI

	team
ERD Moulder	British Guiana
PH Tarilton	Barbados
G Challenor	Barbados
LS Constantine	Trinidad
HW Ince	Barbados
†R Challenor	Barbados
WO Gibbs	Barbados
JCS Rogers	Trinidad
OH Layne	British Guiana
G John	Trinidad
SM Worme	Barbados

Openers **Edwin Moulder** (1875-1942) and **Percy Tarilton**, batsmen **George Challenor**, **Lebrun Constantine** (1874-1942), father of Learie, and **Harry Ince** (1893-1978), batsman/keeper **Robert Challenor** (1884-1977), all-rounder and medium pacer **Will Gibbs** (1885-1949), all-rounder **Joseph Rogers** (?-1946), medium pacer **Oliver Layne** (1876-1932), fast-medium bowler **George John** (1883-1944), and fast bowler **Stanley Worme** (1887-1942).

NEW ZEALAND 1910s XI

	team
LG Hemus	Auckland
HB Whitta	Canterbury
FA Midlane	Wellington, Auckland
HB Lusk	Wellington, Auckland, Canterbury
JS Hiddleston	Wellington
SG Smith	Auckland
WR Patrick	Canterbury, Otago
D Reese	Canterbury
†JW Condliffe	Otago, Wellington
AWS Brice	Wellington
JH Bennett	Canterbury

Openers **Lancelot Hemus** (1881-1933) and **Henry Whitta** (1883-1944), batsmen **Frederick Midlane** (1883-1976), **Harold Lusk** (1877-1961) and **Syd Hiddleston**, all-rounder **Sydney Smith**, all-rounder and off spinner **Bill Patrick** (1885-1946), all-rounder and off spinner **Dan Reese** (1879-1953) who was New Zealand's leading cricketer of this time, keeper **James Condliffe** (1888-1945), and medium pace bowlers **William Brice** (1880-1959) and **Jospeh Bennett** (1881-1947).

Clarrie Grimmett played three unremarkable seasons in New Zealand, 1911-12 to 1913-14, aged 21 to 23. He went to Australia soon after not being selected for New Zealand's tour there—a leg spinner named Sandman was chosen instead. Grimmett went on to play more Tests, and claim more Test wickets than anyone else before him.

INDIA 1910s XI

	team
JG Greig	Europeans
HD Kanga	Parsees
DB Deodhar	Hindus
P Vithal	Hindus
FA Tarrant	Europeans
JS Warden	Parsees
HL Simms	Europeans
† HF Mulla	Parsees
BP Baloo	Hindus
SM Joshi	Hindus
MB Vatcha	Parsees

Openers **John Greig** (1871-1958), who was born in India and had a career RI of 33.55, and **Hormasji Kanga** (1880-1945), **Dinkar Deodhar** (1892-1993) who lived to the age of 101, **Panvekhar Vithal**, Australian **Frank Tarrant** (1880-1951), all-rounder and left-arm spinner **Jehangir Warden** (1885-1928), Australian all-rounder and fast bowler **Harry Simms** (1888-1942), keeper **Hormasji Mulla** (1885-?), great left-arm spinner **Palwankar Baloo** (1876-1955) who was accurate and able to spin it both ways, and bowlers **SM Joshi** and **MB Vatcha**.

ENGLAND 1900s XI

	tests	*runs*	*ri (adj +5)*	*wkts*	*rwi (adj +5)*
AC MacLaren	19	998	32.19 (37.19)		
JB Hobbs	7	434	31.00 (36.00)		
JT Tyldesley	27	1452	30.89 (35.89)		
* FS Jackson	10	803	47.23 (52.23)	19	15.89 (19.57)
CB Fry	13	714	32.45 (37.45)		
TW Hayward	20	1023	28.41 (33.41)	5	13.56 (16.56)
W Rhodes	23	712	18.73 (23.73)	81	11.25 (13.78)
† AFA Lilley	28	630	15.00 (20.00)		
EG Arnold	10	160	10.66 (15.66)	31	15.57 (18.63)
SF Barnes	12	167	8.35 (13.35)	67	7.10 (8.82)
C Blythe	17	176	6.28 (11.28)	88	7.22 (9.09)

Openers **Archie MacLaren** and **Jack Hobbs**, batsman **Johnny Tyldesley** (1873-1930), all-rounder **Stanley Jackson**, batsman **CB Fry** (1872-1956), all-rounders **Tom Hayward** and **Wilfred Rhodes**, keeper **Dick Lilley**, fast bowler **Ted Arnold** (1876-1942), great bowler **Sydney Barnes**, and left-arm spinner **Colin Blythe**.

AUSTRALIA 1900s XI

	tests	*runs*	*ri (adj +5)*	*wkts*	*rwi (adj +5)*
VT Trumper	33	1953	32.01 (37.01)		
RA Duff	22	1317	32.92 (37.92)		
* C Hill	28	1930	37.11 (42.11)		
W Bardsley	5	396	39.60 (44.60)		
VS Ransford	10	641	33.73 (38.73)		
WW Armstrong	30	1513	28.54 (33.54)	50	29.98 (34.48)
MA Noble	33	1524	25.83 (30.83)	89	15.51 (18.60)
† H Carter	10	368	20.44 (25.44)		
A Cotter	12	265	12.61 (17.61)	55	9.49 (11.40)
H Trumble	13	310	12.40 (17.40)	78	5.50 (6.97)
JV Saunders	14	39	1.69 (6.69)	79	7.76 (9.47)

Openers **Victor Trumper** and **Reggie Duff**, batsmen **Clem Hill**, **Warren Bardsley** and **Vernon Ransford** (1885-1958), all-rounders **Warwick Armstrong** and **Monty Noble**, keeper **Sammy Carter**, fast bowler **Tibby Cotter**, medium pace off break bowler **Hugh Trumble**, and left-arm spinner **Jack Saunders** (1876-1927).

U.S.A. 1900s XI

CC Morris
JL Evans
RH Patton
AM Wood
PN LeRoy
JB King
JA Lester
PH Clark
EM Cregar
† TC Jordan
HV Hordern

Christopher Morris, **John Evans**, **Richard Patton** (1881-1928), **Arthur Wood** (1861-1947) from England, **Philip LeRoy** (1880-1953), **Bart King**, all-rounder and slow bowler **John Lester** (1871-1969), **Percy Clark**, medium-slow bowler **Edward Cregar** (1868-1916), keeper **Thomas Jordan** (1877-1925), and Australia's leg spinner **Ranji Hordern**.

SOUTH AFRICA 1900s XI

	tests	*runs*	*ri (adj +5)*	*wkts*	*rwi (adj +5)*
LJ Tancred	9	363	21.35 (26.35)		
† PW Sherwell	8	247	20.58 (25.58)		
CMH Hathorn	11	314	17.44 (22.44)		
AW Nourse	11	531	27.94 (32.94)	11	22.18 (29.00)
GC White	8	452	32.28 (37.28)	6	26.16 (31.16)
JH Sinclair	11	513	27.00 (32.00)	34	16.81 (19.75)
GA Faulkner	8	246	17.57 (22.57)	26	10.86 (13.75)
SJ Snooke	8	321	26.75 (31.75)	25	6.03 (8.03)
CB Llewellyn	3	113	18.83 (23.83)	25	4.30 (5.50)
AEE Vogler	8	184	14.15 (19.15)	24	12.91 (16.03)
RO Schwarz	8	82	7.45 (12.45)	27	10.32 (13.10)

Opener **Louis Tancred** (1876-1934), batsman/keeper **Percy Sherwell** (1880-1948), batsman **Maitland Hathorn** (1878-1920), **Dave Nourse** and **Gordon White**, all-rounders **Jimmy Sinclair** (1876-1913) and **Aubrey Faulkner**, medium pacer **Tip Snooke**, left-arm spinner **Charlie Llewellyn** (1876-1964), fast spinner **Bert Vogler**, and medium pacer **Reggie Schwarz**.

WEST INDIES 1900s XI

	team
ERD Moulder	British Guiana
G Challenor	Barbados
† LS Constantine	Trinidad
* PA Goodman	Barbados
AEA Harragin	Trinidad
MBG Austin	British Guiana
OH Layne	Barbados
SG Smith	Trinidad
AB Cumberbatch	Trinidad
JM Lucas	Trinidad
J Woods	British Guiana, Trinidad

Openers **Edwin Moulder** and **George Challenor**, batsman/keeper **Lebrun Constantine**, batsmen **Percy Goodman** (1874-1935), **Alfred Harragin** (1877-1941) and **Malcolm Austin** (1880-1958) all-rounder **Oliver Layne**, all-rounder **Sydney Smith** before he went to live in New Zealand, and fast bowlers **Archie Cumberbatch** (1879-?), **Joseph Lucas** (1879-1973), and **Joseph "Float" Woods** (1872-?)

NEW ZEALAND 1900s XI

	team
HC Hickson	Wellington
LG Hemus	Auckland
JD Lawrence	Canterbury
CG Wilson	Otago
D Reese	Canterbury
KH Tucker	Wellington
ST Callaway	Canterbury
†AB Williams	Otago, Wellington
AD Downes	Otago
EF Upham	Wellington
JH Bennett	Canterbury

Openers **Henry Hickson** (1878-1948) and **Lancelot Hemus**, batsmen **James Lawrence** (1867-1946), and **Gillie Wilson** (1969-1952) from Australia, all-rounder **Dan Reese**, all-rounder and leg spinner **Kinder Tucker** (1875-1939), all-rounder and medium pacer **Sydney Callaway** (1868-1923) (from Sydney) who played 3 Tests for Australia, keeper **Arnold Williams** (1870-1929) from Wales, off spinner **Alexander Downes** (1868-1950), medium pace bowlers **Ernest Upham** (1873-1935) and **Joseph Bennett**.

INDIA 1900s XI

	team
JG Greig	Europeans
HD Kanga	Parsees
HE Cheetham	Europeans
RP Meherhomji	Parsees
KM Mistry	Parsees
DC Daruwala	Parsees
†DD Kanga	Parsees
BP Baloo	Hindus
JS Warden	Parsees
KB Mistry	Parsees
MD Bulsara	Parsees

Openers **John Greig** and **Hormasji Kanga**, batsmen **HE Cheetham** (details unknown), **Rustomji Meherhomji** (1877-1943), **Kekhashru Mistry** (1874-1959) and **DC Daruwala** (details unknown), keeper **Dinshaw Kanga** (1869-?), spinner **Palwankar Baloo**, spinner **Jehangir Warden**, bowler **KB Mistry** (details unknown), and medium-fast bowler **Maneksha Bulsara** (1877-?).

ENGLAND 1890s XI

	tests	*runs*	*ri (+10, +5)*	*wkts*	*rwi (+10, +5)*
* WG Grace	11	556	27.80 (35.80)	2	162.00 (192.00)
AE Stoddart	15	963	34.39 (41.17)		
KS Ranjitsinhji	12	970	44.09 (49.09)		
TW Hayward	15	976	39.35 (44.35)	9	121.78 (133.21)
FS Jackson	10	612	38.25 (44.18)	5	202.28 (215.28)
AC MacLaren	16	933	31.10 (36.10)		
† AFA Lilley	7	273	27.30 (32.30)		
R Peel	11	330	16.50 (23.50)	47	7.88 (10.15)
J Briggs	17	452	16.74 (23.03)	63	12.52 (16.15)
GA Lohmann	6	53	5.88 (15.33)	28	7.31 (11.36)
T Richardson	14	177	7.37 (12.58)	88	6.87 (9.23)

Openers **WG Grace** and **Andrew Stoddart**, batsman **Kumar Ranjitsinhji**, all-rounders **Tom Hayward** and **Stanley Jackson**, batsman **Archie MacLaren**, keeper **Dick Lilley**, spinners **Bobby Peel** and **Johnny Briggs**, medium pace bowler **George Lohmann** (1865-1901) and fast bowler **Tom Richardson**.

The exciting and elegant batsman Ranjitsinhji from India was known as "Smith" by English people who couldn't pronounce his name. He loved to play off the back foot and may have been the inventor of the leg glance.

AUSTRALIA 1890s XI

	tests	*runs*	*ri (+10, +5)*	*wkts*	*rwi (+10, +5)*
FA Iredale	14	807	35.08 (40.08)		
J Darling	18	1139	34.51 (39.51)		
C Hill	11	783	41.21 (46.21)		
CE McLeod	7	477	39.75 (44.75)	13	24.43 (27.89)
W Bruce	10	582	32.33 (40.38)	6	64.16 (79.93)
MA Noble	9	473	33.78 (38.78)	32	12.35 (14.85)
G Giffen	14	775	29.80 (36.92)	74	8.41 (10.81)
GHS Trott	21	884	24.55 (31.63)	29	33.08 (38.91)
* JJ Kelly	13	337	16.85 (26.85)		
CTB Turner	11	216	10.80 (19.55)	51	8.92 (12.15)
E Jones	14	100	5.00 (10.00)	56	12.10 (14.33)

Openers **Frank Iredale** and **Joe Darling** (1870-1946), batsman **Clem Hill**, all-rounders **Charlie McLeod** (1869-1918), **William Bruce** (1864-1925), **Monty Noble**, **George Giffen** and **Harry Trott** (1866-1917), keeper **James Kelly** (1867-1938), great medium pacer **Charlie Turner**, and fast bowler **Ernie Jones** (1869-1943).

U.S.A. 1890s XI

* GS Patterson
RD Brown
AM Wood
WW Noble
EW Clark
† FW Ralston
FH Bohlen
JB King
HP Baily
HC Coates
EM Cregar

The great all-rounder **George Patterson** (1868-1943), **Reynolds Brown** (1869-1956) was a batsman with a middle name of Driver, **Arthur Wood**, **William Noble** (1864-1919), all-rounder and fast bowler **Edward Clark** (1857-1946), keeper **Francis Ralston** (1867-1920), all-rounder and fast-medium bowler **Francis Bohlen** (1868-1942), **Bart King**, off spinner **Henry Baily** (1868-1945), **Crawford Coates** (1866-1944) and **Edward Cregar**.

"The WG Grace of American cricket," George Patterson played in America's Halifax Cup competition when he was 23 days short of turning 13, when he represented Chestnut Hill versus Belmont in Philadelphia in 1881. Two years later, at only 14, he opened the batting for Germantown. When he was 19 he opened both the batting and the bowling for U.S.A., in their annual game against Canada.

SOUTH AFRICA 1890s XI

	'Tests'	*runs*	*ri (+10, +5)*	*wkts*	*rwi (+10, +5)*
TW Routledge	4	72	9.00 (15.25)		
F Hearne	4	121	15.12 (21.37)	2	10.00 (12.50)
RM Poore	3	76	12.66 (17.66)	1	4.00 (9.00)
* WH Milton	1	37	18.50 (28.50)		
JH Sinclair	5	303	30.30 (35.30)	17	6.88 (7.51)
M Bisset	2	72	18.00 (23.00)		
† EA Halliwell	5	113	11.30 (17.30)		
CB Llewellyn	2	66	16.50 (21.50)	5	23.40 (25.20)
J Middleton	4	51	6.37 (11.37)	23	3.38 (4.04)
JT Willoughby	2	8	2.00 (7.00)	6	13.25 (14.50)
GA Rowe	4	22	2.75 (7.25)	14	11.41 (12.33)

Openers **Tommy Routledge** (1867-1927) from England, and **Frank Hearne** (1858-1949) from England, tall batsmen **Robert Poore** (1866-1938), born in Ireland, and **William Milton** (1854-1930) from England, all-rounder **Jimmy Sinclair**, batsman **Murray Bisset** (1876-1931), keeper **Barberton Halliwell** (1964-1919) from England, spinner **Charlie Llewellyn**, left-arm spinner **Bonnor Middleton** (1865-1913), from England, fast bowler **Jospeh Willoughby** (1874-1952) from England, and left-arm spinner **George Rowe** (1874-1950).

The above stats are for the so-called "Tests" played against the touring English teams. One player that should have been in consideration, but was left out of the South African touring party on grounds of his skin being different to the white guys, was the outstanding fast bowler Krom Hendricks, called "the Spofforth of South Africa."

WEST INDIES 1890s XI

	team
GBY Cox	Barbados
CH King	Demerara/British Guiana
WE Goodman	Barbados, Demerara/British Guiana
HBG Austin	Barbados
PA Goodman	Barbados
EF Wright	Demerara/British Guiana
CE Goodman	Barbados
OW Weber	Demerara/British Guiana
†LS Constantine	Trinidad
AB Cumberbatch	Trinidad
J Woods	Trinidad

Opener **Gustavus Cox** (1870-1958) and opener/fast bowler **Clement King** (1874-?), batsmen **Walter Goodman** (1872-1910), **Harold Austin** (1877-1943) and **Percy Goodman**, all-rounders **Edward Wright** (1858-1904) from England, **Clifford Goodman** (1869-1911) and **Oscar Weber** (1871-?), keeper **Lebrun Constantine**, and fast bowlers **Archie Cumberbatch** and **Float Woods**.

West Indies cricket came of age in the 1890s, helped by a tour to North America in 1886, but it still remained a sport dominated by the white man. In 1892 the Intercolonial Challenge Cup was established. With more support from England, they could have gained Test status within the next decade. There was plenty of talent to choose from, including the four (white) Goodman brothers from Barbados; Percy, Clifford, Walter, and Gerald. Clifford was a tall man and an outstanding fast bowler, but the best bowlers were the black men Woods and the young Cumberbatch.

NEW ZEALAND 1890s XI

	team
LA Cuff	Canterbury, Auckland
JC Lawton	Otago
HS de Maus	Canterbury
AR Holdship	Wellington
HB Lusk	Auckland, Hawke's Bay
F Wilding	Canterbury
AD Downes	Otago
R Neill	Auckland
†E Wright	Auckland, Wellington
EF Upham	Wellington
FL Ashbolt	Wellington

Openers **Leonard Cuff** (1866-1954) and **Joseph Lawton** (1857-1934) from England, all-rounder and spin bowler **Herbert de Maus** (1871-1932), from Fiji, batsmen **Alfred Holdship** (1867-1923) and **Hugh Lusk** (1866-1944), all-rounder and left-arm spinner

Frederick Wilding (1852-1945) from Wales, off spinner **Alexander Downes**, leg spinner **Robert Neill** (1864-1930) from Scotland, keeper **Ernest Wright** (1867-1940), medium pacer **Ernest Upham**, and off spinner **Frank Ashbolt** (1876-1940).

INDIA 1890s XI

	team
JG Greig	Europeans
JE Trask	Europeans
MR Jardine	Europeans
RM Poore	Europeans
DC Daruwala	Parsees
KM Mistry	Parsees
NC Bapasola	Parsees
†DD Kanga	Parsees
EB Raikes	Europeans
RL Sinclair	Europeans
DN Writer	Parsees

Openers **John Greig**, **John Trask** (1861-1896), batsmen **Malcolm Jardine** (1869-1947), South African **Robert Poore** (1866-1938), **DC Daruwala**, **Kekhashru Mistry**, and **Nasarvanji Bapasola** (1867-1923), keeper **Dinshaw Kanga**, and bowlers **Ernest Raikes** (1863-1931), **Reginald Sinclair** (1874-1928), and **Dinshaw Writer** (1865-?).

This Indian team selection is primarily based on the highest level of cricket, the Bombay Quadrangular tournament (with teams based on religious groups: the Parsees, the Hindus, and the Muslims), plus the Europeans (mostly Englishmen), a team featuring many good players, including the outstanding John Greig, who was born in India. Malcolm Jardine, the father of the famous Douglas, was also born in India. In the 1922-23 season a similar tournament started in Lahore, featuring a team of Sikhs instead of Parsees.

ENGLAND 1880s XI

	tests	*runs*	*ri (adj, +15)*	*wkts*	*rwi (adj, +15)*
WG Grace	11	542	33.87 (48.87)	7	18.28 (33.28)
A Shrewsbury	18	963	31.06 (46.06)		
R Abel	5	270	38.57 (53.57)		
AG Steel	13	600	30.00 (45.00)	29	14.38 (24.73)
G Ulyett	21	712	22.25 (42.25)	42	11.99 (23.24)
W Bates	15	656	25.23 (40.34)	50	7.55 (14.45)
W Barnes	19	706	23.53 (38.53)	49	8.30 (16.26)
J Briggs	14	357	17.00 (32.00)	34	4.35 (10.97)
†A Lyttelton	4	94	13.42 (28.42)		
GA Lohmann	9	150	11.53 (26.53)	49	3.92 (9.43)
R Peel	9	97	7.46 (22.00)	54	4.25 (9.25)

Openers **WG Grace** and **Arthur Shrewsbury**, batsman **Bobby Abel** (1857-1936), all-rounders **Allan Steel**, **George Ulyett**, **Billy Bates**, **Billy Barnes** and **Johnny Briggs**, keeper **Alfred Lyttelton** (1857-1913), medium pacer **George Lohmann**, and spinner **Bobby Peel**.

AUSTRALIA 1880s XI

	tests	*runs*	*ri (adj, +15)*	*wkts*	*rwi (adj, +15)*
PS McDonnell	19	950	27.94 (42.94)		
AC Bannerman	27	1035	21.12 (36.12)		
WL Murdoch	14	841	33.64 (48.64)		
HJH Scott	8	359	25.64 (40.64)		
TP Horan	13	429	17.87 (32.87)	11	9.45 (20.36)
G Giffen	17	463	17.14 (32.14)	29	20.26 (29.57)
†JM Blackham	23	580	14.50 (29.50)		
GE Palmer	16	296	11.84 (26.84)	78	8.27 (14.04)
CTB Turner	6	107	8.91 (23.91)	50	2.03 (5.03)
JJ Ferris	6	75	6.25 (21.25)	35	4.18 (8.47)
FR Spofforth	16	161	6.19 (21.19)	77	6.62 (11.68)

Openers **Percy McDonnell** (1860-1896) and **Alec Bannerman** (1854-1924), batsmen **Billy Murdoch** and **Tup Scott** (1858-1910), all-rounders **Tom Horan** (1854-1916) and **George Giffen**, keeper **Jack Blackham**, off spinner **Joey Palmer** (1859-1910), medium pacer **Charlie Turner**, left-arm swing bowler **JJ Ferris** and fast bowler **Fred Spofforth**.

U.S.A. 1880s XI

GS Patterson
†WC Morgan
RS Newhall
H Tyers
S Law
EW Clark
*G Wright
CA Newhall
AM Wood
H MacNutt
WC Lowry

George Patterson, **William Morgan** (1865-1931), **Robert Newhall** (1852-1910), **Henry Tyers** (1857-1921), **Sutherland Law** (1853-1898), **Edward Clark**, **George Wright** (1947-1937), **Charles Newhall** (1847-1927), **Arthur Wood**, **Howard MacNutt** (1859-1926) and left-arm spinner **William Lowry** (1860-1919).

At this time American cricket was stronger than any other country outside of England and Australia, including South Africa. The Halifax Cup started in 1880 and continued until 1926. Arthur Wood played until 1909, aged 48.

George Wright was a pioneer baseball player and a member of the Baseball Hall of Fame since 1937, but he also excelled at cricket. He represented U.S.A. at the age of 15, against Canada. His father Samuel's St George's Cricket Club was based in New Jersey, but before that had been in Manhattan. George's older brother Harry was a prominent bowler for St George's, and is also in the Baseball Hall of Fame.

The Newhall family of Philadelphia, Pennsylvania, consisted of four brothers and four uncles who played first-class cricket, and they were able to field a team entirely of themselves.

SOUTH AFRICA 1880s XI

A Rose-Innes
AB Tancred
P Hutchinson
CH Vintcent
AE Ochse
WH Milton
* OR Dunell
† FW Smith
NH Theunissen
WH Ashley
GA Kempis

Openers **Albert Rose-Innes** (1868-1946) and **Bernard Tancred** (1865-1911), batsmen **Philip Hutchinson** (1862-1925) from England, **Charles Vintcent** (1866-1943), **Arthur Ochse** (1870-1918), **William Milton** (1854-1930) from England, and **Owen Dunell** (1856-1929), keeper **Fred Smith** (1861-1914), fast bowler **Nicolaas Theunissen** (1867-1929), left-arm medium pacers **Gobo Ashley** (1862-1930) and **Gus Kempis** (1865-1890).

NEW ZEALAND 1880s XI

	teams
JP Firth	Nelson, Wellington
G Watson	Canterbury
GC Heenan	Wellington
RV Blacklock	Wellington
F Wilding	Canterbury
FH Cooke	Otago, Nelson
† JN Fowke	Canterbury
DEL Dunlop	Canterbury
WP McGirr	Wellington
TG Eden	Nelson
C Frith	Canterbury, Otago

Opener and fast bowler **Joseph Firth** (1859-1931), left-handed batsman **George Watson** (1855-1884) who was born in India and made 367 runs for Canterbury at 40.77 RI but died at the age of 29, batsman **George Heenan** (1855-1913) from Ireland, batsman **Robert Blacklock** (1865-1897) from Australia, **Frederick Wilding**, left-arm spinner **Frank Cooke** (1862-1933) from Australia, keeper **John Fowke** (1859-1938) from Wales, leg spinner **David Dunlop** (1855-1900), bowlers **William McGirr** (1859-1934) and **Thomas Eden** (1855-1914), and medium-pace off break spinner **Charles Frith** (1854-1919) from England.

Had they played during the modern era, Joseph Firth and Charles Frith would have been a nightmare for commentators. There was also a good left-arm spinner named Billy Firth playing at this time, who was close to making this team selection.

ENGLAND 1870s XI

	tests	*runs*	*ri (adj)*	*wkts*	*rwi (adj)*
WG Grace	0				
H Jupp	2	68	17.00 (37.00)		
AN Hornby	1	6	3.00 (23.00)		
GF Grace	0				
R Daft	0				
F Penn	0				
†A Lyttelton	0				
T Emmett	3	97	16.16 (36.16)	7	6.36 (14.93)
A Shaw	2	13	3.25 (23.25)	8	9.12 (19.12)
F Morley	0				
J Southerton	2	3	2.33 (22.33)	7	4.36 (10.07)

Openers **WG Grace** and **Harry Jupp**, who once refused to be out LBW to the first ball of the match and said, "they have come to see me bat, not you umpire," batsmen **AN Hornby**, **Fred Grace**, **Richard Daft** and **Frank Penn** (1851-1916), keeper **Alfred Lyttelton**, left-arm roundarm fast bowler **Tom Emmett** (1841-1904), slow bowler **Alfred Shaw**, left-arm fast bowler **Fred Morley**, and lob bowler **James Southerton**.

AUSTRALIA 1870s XI

	tests	*runs*	*ri (adj)*	*wkts*	*rwi (adj)*
C Bannerman	3	239	39.83 (59.83)		
NFD Thomson	2	67	16.75 (36.75)		
*DW Gregory	3	60	12.00 (32.00)		
TJD Kelly	2	64	21.33 (41.33)		
WL Murdoch	2	19	4.75 (24.75)		
E Evans	0				
S Cosstick	0				
WE Midwinter	2	65	16.25 (36.35)	8	9.75 (19.75)
†JM Blackham	3	60	12.00 (32.00)		
FR Spofforth	2	56	18.66 (38.66)	17	3.05 (7.76)
FE Allan	1	5	5.00 (25.00)	4	10.00 (20.00)

Openers **Charles Bannerman** (1851-1930) and **Nat Thomson** (1839-1896), batsmen **Dave Gregory** (1845-1919), **Thomas Kelly** (1844-1893) and **Billy Murdoch**, all-rounders **Edwin Evans** (1849-1921), **Sam Cosstick** and **Billy Midwinter** (1851-1890), keeper **Jack Blackham**, fast bowler **Fred Spofforth**, and left-arm medium pace bowler **Frank Allan** (1849-1917).

NEW ZEALAND 1870s XI

	team
AM Ollivier	Canterbury
IJ Salmon	Wellington
KJ Knapp	Nelson
CC Corfe	Canterbury
GH Paramor	Otago
LE Reade	Canterbury, Otago
†E Fowler	Canterbury
WF Downes	Otago
TS Sweet	Auckland, Canterbury
TG Eden	Nelson
ETA Fuller	Canterbury

Opener **Arthur Ollivier** (1851-1897) from England, all-rounder **Isaac Salmon** (1853-1932) from Australia, batsmen **Kempster Knapp** (1850-1879), and **Charles Corfe** (1847-1935) from England, all-rounders **George Paramor** (1846-1925) from England, and **Lawrence Reade** (1846-1910) from India, keeper **Edwin Fowler** (1840-1909) from England via Australia, bowler **William Downes** (1843-1896) from England, fast bowler **Thomas Sweet** (1851-?) from England, bowler **Thomas Eden**, and fast bowler **Edwin Fuller** (1850-1917) from Australia.

ENGLAND 1860s XI

WG Grace
H Jupp
R Daft
T Hayward
RP Carpenter
RD Walker
†EW Pooley
GF Tarrant
J Jackson
G Wootton
J Southerton

Openers **WG Grace** and **Harry Jupp**, batsmen **Richard Daft**, **Thomas Hayward** (1835-1876) the uncle of Tom Hayward, and **Bob Carpenter** (1830-1901), all-rounder and slow bowler **Russell Walker** (1842-1922), keeper **Ted Pooley** (1842-1907), fast bowlers **George Tarrant** (1838-1870), **John Jackson** (1833-1901) and **George Wootton** (1834-1924), and lob bowler **James Southerton**.

AUSTRALIA 1860s XI

RW Wardill
NFD Thomson
†GWH Gibson
W Caffyn
GHB Gilbert
EJ Gregory
JM Bryant
TW Wills
S Cosstick
J Conway
C Lawrence

Openers **Richard Wardill** (1840-1873) and **Nat Thomson**, batsman/keeper **George Gibson** (1828-1910) who was born in Jamaica, batsmen **William Caffyn** (1828-1919), **George Gilbert** (1853-1924) who was a cousin of WG Grace, all-rounders **Ned Gregory** (1839-1896), **James Bryant** (1826-1881), **Tom Wills** (1835-1880) and **Sam Cosstick**, fast bowler **John Conway** (1836-1896), and roundarmer **Charles Lawrence** (1828-1916).

ENGLAND 1850s XI

J Caesar
HH Stephenson
W Caffyn
†T Lockyer
*G Parr
John Lillywhite
VE Walker
J Wisden
J Grundy
E Willsher
J Jackson

Openers **Julius Caesar** (1830-1878) and **HH Stephenson** (1833-1896), batsman **William Caffyn**, batsman/keeper **Thomas Lockyer** (1826-1869), batsmen **George Parr** (1826-1891), all-rounder who bowled both fast and slow **John Lillywhite** (1826-1874), all-rounder **Edward Walker** (1837-2006), short fast bowler **John Wisden** (1826-1884) who first published his annual report of first-class cricket in 1864, fast bowlers **James Grundy** (1824-1873), **Edgar Willsher** (1828-1885) who had only one lung, and **John Jackson**.

"Julius Caesar" was his actual birth name; a son of Benjamin Caesar who was also a notable player. Julius' mother's maiden name happened to be Bowler.

AUSTRALIA 1850s XI

JM Bryant
G Howell
JLB Tabart
TF Hamilton
†H Hilliard
TW Wills
WJ Hammersley
G Elliott
GHB Gilbert
OH Lewis
EW Ward

Openers **James Bryant** and **George Howell** (1822-1890), batsmen **John Tabart** (1827-1894) and **Thomas Hamilton** (1821-1905), batsman/keeper **Harry Hilliard** (1826-1914), all-rounders **Tom Wills** and **William Hammersley** (1826-1886), roundarm fast bowler **Gideon Elliott** (1826-1869), **George Gilbert**, underhand fast bowler **Oswald Lewis** (1833-1895), left-roundarm fast bowler **Edward Ward** (1823-1890) who was born in India and died in France.

Tom Wills and his cousin Henry Harrison are credited with inventing Australian Rules football, as a game to keep cricketers fit in the off-season. William Hammersley was one of the seven co-signers of the rules, in 1859. Wills also coached the Aboriginal Cricket team, famous for being the first team to tour England, in 1868.

ENGLAND 1840s XI

F Pilch
N Felix
CG Taylor
†T Box
G Parr
A Mynn
HW Fellows
J Wisden
J Dean
WR Hillyer
FW Lillywhite

Fuller Pilch (1803-1870) was singled out as "the greatest batsman ever known until the appearance of WG Grace," and played from 1820 until 1854. His technique in going forward to the ball was known as the Pilch Poke, and it was instrumental in developing batting skills for future players. This was all the more remarkable since it was during the "roundarm period" when bowlers became more commanding.

Nicholas Wanostrocht (1804-1876) preferred to be known by his nickname **Felix**. An interesting character, he wrote the book *Felix on the Bat* in 1845. A man ahead of his time, he invented rubber batting gloves, and a bowling machine he called the Catapulta.

Charles Taylor (1817-1869) was an all-rounder who bowled slow roundarm.

Thomas Box (1808-1876) was the first of the great wicket-keepers, and batsmen **George Parr**.

Alfred Mynn (1807-1861) was a dynamic all-rounder and giant of the game. Known as the Lion of Kent, he was a formidable opponent, being big and strong. He bowled very fast off only six paces, and always attacked when batting.

Harvey Fellows (1826-1907) bowled very fast roundarm, and fast bowler **John Wisden** who managed to take ten wickets in an innings and every one of them bowled. **Jemmy Dean** (1816-1881) was a short and stout man who could bowl fast, be good in the field, or keep wicket. **William Hillyer** (1813-1861) was a masterful medium-pace bowler. With a simple action, he could make the ball rip off the pitch or make it leg cut, but his most lethal delivery was a shooter that bowled many batsmen.

William Lillywhite (1792-1854) dominated bowling for many years despite being only 5'4", with a roundarm style that was illegal for most of his career. His prominence in the game not only saw that he avoided being penalised, but he helped legitimise roundarm, and then over-arm. He was the father of John Lillywhite and uncle of James.

Other leading players of this decade were Thomas Anson, Edward Bushby, William Clarke, James Cobbett, Francis Fenner, and politician Frederick Hervey-Bathurst.

In the 1840s the North America cricketers were ahead of their time, with the first annual U.S.A. vs. Canada game played in 1844, before a crowd of 5,000 and heavy betting. In 1846 it was halted due to an argument, and the rivalry was not resumed until 1856.

ENGLAND 1830s XI

J Broadbridge
J Cobbett
†EG Wenman
F Pilch
A Mynn
T Marsden
CG Taylor
†T Box
S Redgate
WR Hillyer
FW Lillywhite

Jem Broadbridge (1895-1843) was a great all-rounder and leading proponent of roundarm bowling; **James Cobbett** (1804-1842) was, in his prime, was known as "the finest all-rounder of his day." **Ned Wenman** (1803-1879), from Kent, was an outstanding wicket-keeper, but he could also bowl slow underhand. Great batsman **Fuller Pilch**, all-rounder **Alfred Mynn**.

Thomas Marsden (1803-1843) was a Yorkshire left-handed all-rounder who could bowl either fast underhand or slow spin with roundarm. All-rounder **Charles Taylor** (1816-1869). Keeper **Thomas Box**.

Sam Redgate (1810-1851) was a Nottinghamshire fast bowler who was so fearsome that he is credited as the reason for the introduction of batting pads. When Mynn was severely hit by a Redgate delivery, the damage was so bad that his leg almost needed to be amputated.

Medium pacer **William Hillyer**, and slow bowler **William Lillywhite**.

The decade of the 1830s saw the lingering Roundarm Controversy show signs of being resolved. The fierce argument over the correct position of the arm at delivery had plagued a generation of players. A new cricket law was introduced in 1835 that stated that the hand should go no higher than the shoulder during delivery. Some bowlers responded by bowling even higher, and it was not until 1845 that the matter was entirely dropped, when a new law said that bowlers may bowl as high as they wished.

ENGLAND 1820s XI

†J Saunders
T Marsden
W Ward
T Beagley
J Broadbridge
†EH Budd
F Beauclerk
FW Lillywhite
W Mathews
TC Howard
W Ashby

James Saunders (1802-1832) was a fast scoring and apparently "showy" batsman, who loved the square cut. When fielding, he would prefer to be the wicket-keeper rather than bowl. A butcher by trade, he died young of consumption, before he reached his best cricketing years.

All-rounder **Thomas Marsden**.

William Ward (1787-1849) was a notable financial contributor to the game, as well as an outstanding player. In 1825 he helped prevent Lord's from becoming a housing estate, with a donated sum of £5000 (today £500,000). On the field, he was a dominant batsman, and his score of 278 in 1820 was the highest ever recorded until WG Grace came along, some 56 years later.

Thomas Beagley (1789-1858) was a batsman from Hampshire, all-rounder **Jem Broadbridge**, **EH Budd** (1786-1875) was a hard-hitting batsman and great athlete.

Frederick Beauclerk (1773-1850) was the most formidable batsman of his time, plus a useful bowler, but he was a harsh man with a fiery temper, who played by his own rules, without scruples. He was an opponent of roundarm bowling, probably because it interfered with his batting. He was a member of the House of Lords, and in his later years liked to boast about how much money he won through cricket match-fixing. The man was so disliked that when he died The Times did not publish an obituary.

Bowlers **William Lillywhite**, **William Mathews** (1793-1858) who played mostly for Surrey. **Thomas Howard** (1781-1864) was a professional bowler from Hampshire. **William Ashby** (1786-1847) was a slow bowler from Kent.

This decade saw the height of the Roundarm Controversy. In 1816 a cricket law had been introduced that emphatically stated that the ball must be lower than the elbow during delivery, which was known as underhand. In 1822 the bowler John Willes, who had been trying to pioneer the use of roundarm, was no-balled in a game at Lord's. His famous reaction was to throw the ball down, march off the field, get on his horse, and never play there again. But there were other supporters of roundarm, notably William Lillywhite and Jem Broadbridge, and in 1827 a series of three Roundarm Trial matches were played, with Sussex taking on All England. After the second match, the majority of the All England team signed a declaration (that was not followed through on) that they would not play the third, as they judged the bowling to be unfair. The only resulting change was that a law was passed in 1828 permitting the hand to be level with the elbow, but that did not stop it being controversial. Bowlers such as Lillywhite and Broadbridge continued to bowl as they pleased, and they got away with it.

ENGLAND 1810s XI

	m	*runs*	*ri*	*wkts*	*team*
R Robinson	19	664	17.94	18	England
John Sherman	16	376	14.46	11	Surrey, England
W Lambert	26	1600	35.55	93	Surrey, England
EH Budd	28	1215	24.30	75	MCC, England
W Beldham	27	1022	20.44	11	Surrey, England
G Osbaldeston	27	952	18.66	45	MCC
F Beauclerk	29	984	18.22	67	MCC, England
T Beagley	9	312	19.50	1	Hampshire
W Ward	27	768	15.36	22	Hampshire, Surrey
TC Howard	37	909	13.56	167	Hampshire
J Wells	12	237	9.87	37	Surrey

The above stats are only for recorded games. The wickets taken do not include those from catches, only bowled and LBW. Many of the players could also keep wicket.

Robert Robinson (1765-1822) may be the most underrated player in all of cricket history. In this decade he played most of his cricket aged in his late forties and early fifties, and yet remained a leading player. He batted left-handed and hit the ball hard, particularly the cut. What is remarkable is that he lost two fingers on his right hand when he was a boy, and he used a modified batting handle. He was also credited as being the first to try playing with batting pads, but unfortunately they were made of wood, and he was ridiculed.

John Sherman (1788-1861) was a batsman from Surrey.

William Lambert (1779-1851) was recognised as the best batsman in England, and he was also the best all-round cricketer in the game. Amongst allegations of match-fixing, he fell foul of Beauclerk in 1817, and was thereafter banned from ever again playing at Lord's.

Hard hitting batsman and great fielder **EH Budd**.

William "Silver Billy" Beldham (1766-1862) was one of the greatest cricketers to ever play the game, and he heavily influenced and development of batting technique. He was a very hard hitter, with natural flare that thrilled the crowds, but he was also a good bowler, and he always wanted to played the game fair. In this decade he was at the end of his illustrious career. The earliest known photograph of a cricketer was of Beldham, in 1851.

George Osbaldeston (1786-1766) was an outstanding athlete and leading all-rounder, **Frederick Beauclerk** the formidable person and batsman and bowler, batsman **Thomas**

Beagley, batsman **William Ward**, bowler **Thomas Howard**.

John Wells (1760-1835) was a notable fast bowler, but by the 1810s he was at the end of his playing days.

ENGLAND 1800s XI

	m	*runs*	*ri*	*wkts*	*team*
R Robinson	40	1478	19.44	4	Surrey
T Walker	40	1000	12.98	39	Surrey
W Lambert	38	1414	20.49	94	Surrey
F Beauclerk	45	2582	30.73	133	MCC
W Beldham	40	1267	17.59	36	Surrey
EH Budd	11	384	19.20	11	England
TA Smith, jr	26	758	15.79	4	Surrey, Hampshire
J Hammond	37	998	15.35	28	England
John Bennett	36	877	13.08	42	Hampshire
TC Howard	31	453	7.81	89	Hampshire
J Wells	34	384	6.09	123	Surrey

Openers **Robert Robinson** and **Tom Walker** (1762-1831) who was known as "Old Everlasting" due to his impressive defence and ability to play long innings. Not only did Walker never get himself out, but he would also "refuse to bleed" when hit on the knuckles.

Batsmen **William Lambert**, **Frederick Beauclerk** who had a monster decade, **Silver Billy Beldham** and **EH Budd**, and another hard-hitting batsman **Thomas Smith, jr** (1776-1858).

John Hammond (1769-1844) was an all-rounder and notable slow underhand bowler. **John Bennett** (1777-1857) was a fast bowler and "free hitter," plus bowlers **Thomas Howard** and **John Wells**.

In this decade the Marylebone Cricket Club (MCC), based at Lord's in London, took formal control of the game, and the quality of play dramatically increased.

ENGLAND 1790s XI

T Walker
H Walker
W Beldham
W Fennex
R Robinson
F Beauclerk
J Hammond
T Lord
J Wells
T Boxall
D Harris

Tom Walker and his younger brother and left-handed batsman **Harry Walker** (1760-1805). Batsman **Silver Billy Beldham**.

William Fennex (1763-1838) was an all-rounder and one of the first to play off the front foot. Batsman **Robert Robinson**, all-rounders **Frederick Beauclerk** and **John**

Hammond. **Thomas Lord** (1755-1832) was a professional bowler, and later became the owner of the famous cricket ground named after him. Fast bowler **John Wells**. **Thomas Boxall** was a bowler, and wrote a book called Rules and Instructions for Playing at the Game of Cricket.

David Harris (1755-1803) was the most feared fast bowler of his time, and was noted for beginning his bowling with the ball raised over his forehead. Suffering from gout near the end of his playing days, he fielded from a chair.

ENGLAND 1780s XI

	club, county
J Small, sr	Hambeldon, Hampshire
T Walker	Hambeldon, Hampshire
W Bullen	Kent
T Taylor	Hampshire
W Beldham	Hambeldon, Hampshire
R Clifford	Kent
N Mann	Hambeldon, Hampshire
W Fennex	Berkshire, Middlesex
†T Sueter	Hambeldon, Hampshire
E Stevens	Surrey
D Harris	Hampshire

John Small (1737-1826) was the first batsman to revolutionise batting into an art form. A bat maker by trade, his study of batsmanship and straight-bat play gained him such skill that he made scores that were viewed as incredible. At a time when an entire game lasted just one afternoon, here was a player with the ambition to bat all day, and he was good enough to succeed. He remained outstanding into his fifties, and his last recorded innings was in 1798 at the age of 61.

Opener **Tom Walker**, all-rounder **William Bullen**, outstanding all-rounder and fielder **Tom Taylor** (1753-1806), **Silver Billy Beldham**, all-rounder and slow bowler **Robert Clifford** (1752-1811).

Noah Mann (1756-1789) was a good all-rounder with the ability to swing the ball, and was an amazing athlete who could pick a handkerchief off the ground from horseback.

All-rounder **William Fennex**.

Tom Sueter (1750-1827) was a wicket-keeper and capable batsman. He was a carpenter by trade, and a singer in a church choir.

Edward "Lumpy" Stevens (1735-1819) was a professional cricketer and England's leading bowler throughout his long career. He was doubtless given his nickname for his knack of finding the lumpiest ground to set the stumps on, as was the rule of the day. At this time the wickets consisted of only two stumps, and after he put the ball through John Small's stumps three times in one innings without dismissing him, the third stump was introduced. He is the earliest cricketer to have a surviving portrait.

Fast bowler **David Harris**.

ENGLAND 1770s XI

	club, county
J Small, sr	Hambeldon, Hampshire
J Miller	Kent
W Palmer	Surrey
J Minshull	Kent
W Bullen	Kent
T Taylor	Hampshire
R Nyren	Hambeldon, Hampshire
†T Sueter	Hambeldon, Hampshire
E Stevens	Surrey
T Brett	Hambeldon, Hampshire
D Harris	Hampshire

Openers **John Small** and outstanding batsman **Joseph Miller**.

William Palmer (1736-1790) was a leading batsman. **John Minshull** (1741-1793) was not an attractive batsman, but he had a very confident manner. All-rounders **William Bullen** and **Tom Taylor**.

Richard Nyren (1734-1797) was an all-rounder and leader of the famous Hambledon club. Wicket-keeper **Tom Sueter**, and professional bowler **Lumpy Stevens**.

Thomas Brett (1747-1809) was a fast and accurate bowler, as was **David Harris**.

ENGLAND 1760s XI

	club, county
J Small, sr	Hambeldon, Hampshire
J Miller	Kent
W Palmer	Surrey
T Pattenden	Kent
S Harding	Chertsey, Surrey
†W Yalden	Chertsey, Surrey
R Nyren	Hambeldon, Hampshire
S Colchin	Kent
W Hogsflesh	Hambeldon, Hampshire
E Stevens	Surrey
J Frame	Dartford, Kent

Openers **John Small** and **Joseph Miller**, batsmen **William Palmer** and **Thomas Pattenden** (1742-1791), all-rounder **Stephen Harding**, wicket-keeper/batsman **William Yalden** (1740-1824), all-rounder **Richard Nyren**, bowler **Samuel Colchin**, bowler with a "high delivery" **William Hogsflesh**, and bowler **Lumpy Stevens**.

John Frame (1733-1796) was the best bowler of the time, and was described as being "an unusually stout man." Frame started playing as far back as 1749.

In this decade the village team from Hambeldon in Hampshire was good enough to take on the great club Dartford.

ENGLAND 1750s XI

	club, county
T Faulkner	Addington, Surrey
Durling	Addington, Sussex
Bennett	London
Bennett	London
J Edmeads	Chertsey, Surrey
R Eures	Bexley, Kent
S Harding	Chertsey, Surrey
Joe Harris	Addington, Surrey
John Harris	Addington, Surrey
T Brandon	Dartford, Kent
J Frame	Dartford, Kent

Tom Faulkner (1719-1785) was known as "Long Tom" for his height. He was very athletic, not only as a leading single wicket player, but also as a leading wrestler and prize fighting boxer, well into his fifties.

John Edmeads was a noted batsman and fielder, and a farmer. **Robert Eures** was a batsman, **Stephen Harding** an all-rounder, and the great bowler **John Frame**.

Joe Harris and **John Harris** were brothers. **Thomas Brandon** was a batsman and shopkeeper. The first names are unknown for **Durling**, **Bennett**, and **Bennett**.

Cricket at this time was severely hit by the Seven Years War (1755-64), a conflict between Great Britain and France that tore Europe apart.

ENGLAND 1740s XI

	club, county
T Waymark	Berkshire
R Newland	Slindon, Sussex
R Colchin	Bromley, Kent
V Romney	Sevenoaks
J Cutbush	Maidstone, Kent
S Dingate	Richmond, Sussex
W Hodsoll	Dartford, Kent
Joe Harris	Addington, Surrey
John Harris	Addington, Surrey
†J Bell	Dartford, Kent
Ridgeway	Sussex

The romantic images of early cricket, played and a saintly pace by polite and perhaps effeminate men, as something to do on a sunny afternoon, could not be further from the truth. The game was played tough, by tough men, and they were driven to win by huge amounts of money, and watched by crowds of eager gamblers. The 1740s were a boom time for cricket's popularity, thanks to the amount of heavy gambling. Crowds reached over 5,000 per game. In 1743 a three-a-side game featuring some of the best players of the day was watched by 10,000. Single-wicket games were also popular, with very high stakes; probably because the result was usually quickly found.

Thomas Waymark (aged 35 in 1740) was a legend in the game with "extraordinary agility and dexterity," and was still good enough to play a part in the All-England teams in the mid-1740s.

Richard Newland (1713-1778) was the first known outstanding left-handed player. He was the best of three prominent cricketing brothers, who were also uncles of Hambledon's Richard Nyren.

The 1740s were the peak years for **Robert Colchin** (1713-1750), known as "Long Robin" because of his height. Colchin was a formidable competitor. A natural athlete, he was a star player at single-wicket. He was also something of a party animal, and was associated with London's criminal element. The famous game of Kent versus All England featured Colchin and Edward Aburrow, who was a smuggler who went by the alias "Cuddy". His son was known as "Curry", and since "Cuddy" was used in scorecards, his smuggling career could not have been much of a secret. Since these games were played for great stakes, and at least two leading players had criminal connections, it is not unlikely that some form of match-fixing had begun to influence the players. When Colchin died mysteriously in 1750, in only his thirty-seventh year, it is tempting to wonder if it was due to cricket corruption.

Val Romney (1718-1773) was a specialist batsman, and called a "mighty player." He was employed as the head gardener by the 1st Duke of Dorset. **John Cutbush** was a clockmaker and was probably at the end of his playing days in the 1740s.

Stephen Dingate was a barber, and would have been playing since the 1720s. He was employed by the cricket-loving Charles Lennox, 2nd Duke of Richmond, who was a notable player himself.

The brothers **Joe Harris** and **John Harris**. **John Bell** (1718-1774) was a leading wicket-keeper, and his trade was probably shoemaking. Sussex's **Ridgeway**'s first name and any other details are unknown.

William Hodsoll (1718-1776) was a tanner by trade, but on the cricket field he was a feared underhand fast bowler. The earliest known cricket poem, by James Love in 1745, had this to say about Hodsoll:

Four times from Hodsoll's arm it skims the Grass;
Then Mills succeeds. The Seekers-out change Place.
Observe, cries Hodsoll, to the wondering Throng,
Be Judges now, whose Arms are better strung!
He said—then poised, and rising as he threw,
Swift from his Arm the fatal Missive flew.
Nor with more Force the Death conveying Ball,
Springs from the Cannon to the battered Wall;
Nor swifter yet the pointed Arrows go,
Launched from the Vigour of the Parthian Bow.
It whizzed alone, with unimagined Force,
And bore down all, resistless in its Course.
To such impetuous Might compelled to yield
The Bail, and mangled Stumps bestrew the Field.

ENGLAND 1730s XI

	club, county
T Waymark	Richmond, Sussex
R Colchin	Bromley, Kent
T Coleman	London
S Dingate	Richmond, Sussex
E Chapman	Chertsey
J Cutbush	Maidstone, Kent
R Lascoe	Bromley, Kent
Ridgeway	Sussex
T Peake	Dartford, Kent
W Sawyer	Richmond, Sussex
† Kipps	Kent

Most leading cricketers of this time were single-wicket players, indicating that they were capable all-rounders, led by **Thomas Waymark** in his peak years.

Robert Colchin the tall all-rounder. **Tim Coleman** was the leading player for the London club; and **Stephen Dingate**, **John Cutbush**, and **Ridgeway**.

Edmund Chapman was "accounted one of the most dextrous cricket players in England," and was probably a leading player as far back as 1715.

Robert Lascoe (1715-1781) had a trade in making horse collars. Little else is known about **Tom Peake** (1720-1767). **William Sawyer** (1712-1761) was an innkeeper at Richmond.

Kipps (nothing else unknown) was possibly at the end of a long career, and was the first wicket-keeper to be singled out as outstanding. He might have brought a significant change to that fielding position, as did all the leading players throughout the game's history.

Another leading player of this time was John Bowra, one of "three very good gamesters." Squire Land (1714-1791) would have been playing in the late 1730s, and captained the early Hambledon team before he took more interest on fox hunting.

The game's first known great player, William Bedle (1679-1768), was well past his prime by the 1730s, but was possibly still playing.

Cricket Before 1730

Cricket's origins are unknown, but the best players can still be acknowledged. There is no doubt that each era produced its own unique players, and while it now seems fashionable to look down upon the old players because of the style and technique, or their funny clothes, they were still outstanding for their day, and would have been outstanding during any era of the game.

It is generally assumed that the game first developed in southern England amongst shepherds, since the word wicket comes from wicket gate. It can also be assumed that the word cricket was derived from wicket, since the game was once called cricket-a-wicket. What is reasonably certain is that up until the 1600s cricket was a game mostly played by children. It also seems to have been played exclusively in the English counties of Kent, Surrey and Sussex, known as the Weald. This area had Flemish settlers from Flanders, and it is possible that they developed cricket from earlier games.

Cricket drastically changed in about the year 1610, when the adults began to play, with high wagers placed on it. With larger purses came increased interest, and probably because of the stakes, games could turn violent. Hitting the ball twice was allowed, and the tactic could actually be used to thwart off attempted catches. Several people were killed trying to take catches too close to a batsman, which indicates that the game was played with the utmost seriousness for money.

As the years passed, more stakes were placed on games, until the Puritans game along and put a stop to it. The Puritans of the late sixteenth and early seventeenth century ordered that cricket was "profane" and illegal to be played during compulsory church attendance on Sundays. It is possible that they disliked the gambling side more than the actual ball hitting.

From 1660, when the monarchy was restored under Charles II, and the restrictions of the Puritans were lifted, cricket resumed its rise in popularity. Prior to that time it was probably a social game with unwritten rules and limited to southern England, but after the social freedoms returned, the widespread gambling quickly led to competitive teams, massive stakes, and increasingly bigger crowds. By 1697 public interest was so high that a "great match," in Sussex, was reported in the press for the first time, and the stakes were fifty guineas (over £9000 today). This is assumed to be the first known first-class game, but it is doubtful that it was the first high profile game.

The stakes were high, the crowds substantial, and the teams had eleven per side; not really too different from today.

In the early 1700s cricket clubs were formed, and by 1720 the London, Dartford and Croydon clubs became the most famous. They would have featured the best players of the day, all financially rewarded, since they were determined to win. In 1725 cricket reporting in newspapers became more common, but scorecards did not exist until the 1740s, but even then there was scant mention of the results for even the most important games. It is probable that the only reason the newspaper scorecards began to list players' scores was because there were bets placed on the highest scorers. Soon after, the manner of dismissal was listed, again for reasons of betting. Unfortunately for the bowlers, in those days a wicket only counted to them if the batsmen was out bowled or lbw, as catches or stumpings were credited to the fielders.

Throughout the seventeenth century, and well into the eighteenth, the game's most outstanding players were employed by wealthy lord-of-the-manor types. They would be such things as gardeners or horsegrooms, to ensure that they would only play for his lordship's team. Such a patron was Charles Lennox, 1st Duke of Richmond, whose team defeated an Arundel XI in 1702, which was one of the earliest known results. His successor, the 2nd Duke of Richmond (Charles Lennox) followed his father and became a famous patron with his own teams, playing the teams of his keen rival Sir William Gage, from the 1720s.

The earliest known professional cricketer was William Bedle, but it is possible that there were others before him. Bedle became a wealthy farmer and grazier in Dartford, and he would have played for Dartford under the patronage of Edwin Stead (1701-1735). Such was his fame, Bedle's death was widely mourned when he died at the ripe old age of 88. For this to have happened, in an age of no photography or any sort of statistical recordings of his efforts, Bedle must have been so great a player, and made so much money for his patrons, that he remained a vivid part of England's sporting culture many decades after he stopped playing. Compare this to the highly honoured cricketing ability of Thomas Waymark, who played only a generation ahead of Bedle. In his prime, Waymark was easily the best player in England, but there was no record of what became of him after his retirement from the game, not even how or when he died.

These men, and others whose names have been lost to us, were the first professional cricketers; stars on the field, but when not playing they were allowed to work on the rich-men's roses, or look after the horses and clean out the stables.

CALENDAR XIs

Teams based on birthdays, with the qualification of representing their country for at least seven years.

JANUARY XI

day		*team*	*tests*	*runs*	*ri (adj)*	*wkts*	*rwi (adj)*
19	* AR Morris	Aus	46	3533	44.72		
8	B Mitchell	SA	42	3471	43.38	27	73.82
11	RS Dravid	Ind	163	13265	46.70		
25	CA Pujara	Ind	85	6244	43.97		
17	CL Walcott	WI	44	3798	51.32	11	74.18
28	MA Noble	Aus	42	1997	27.35 (32.35)	121	14.66 (17.60)
6	Kapil Dev	Ind	131	5248	28.52	434	15.50
8	JH Wardle	Eng	28	653	15.92	102	10.39
30	HJ Tayfield	SA	37	862	14.36	170	9.29
29	AME Roberts	WI	47	762	12.29	202	11.41
28	† H Strudwick	Eng	28	230	5.47 (7.50)		

Openers **Arthur Morris** and **Bruce Mitchell**, batsmen **Rahul Dravid**, **Clyde Walcott** and **Cheteshwar Pujara**, all-rounders **Monty Noble** and **Kapil Dev**, left-arm spinner **Johnny Wardle** (1923-1985), off spinner **Hugh Tayfield**, fast bowler **Andy Roberts**, and keeper **Bert Strudwick**.

JANUARY 2nd XI

day		*team*	*tests*	*runs*	*ri (adj)*	*wkts*	*rwi (adj)*
8	Shoaib Mohammad	Pak	45	2705	39.77	5	176.80
19	MG Vandort	SL	20	1144	34.66		
25	CA Pujara	Ind	95	6713	41.43		
12	RB Richardson	WI	86	5949	40.74		
28	Asad Shafiq	Pak	77	4660	36.40	3	327.65
9	JC Adams	WI	54	3012	33.46	27	109.95
5	† Imtiaz Ahmed	Pak	41	2079	28.87		
27	DL Vettori	NZ	112	4523	26.29	361	17.50
30	MA Starc	Aus	69	1805	17.87	282	13.01
15	RJ Sidebottom	Eng	23	313	10.09	79	12.86
8	JR Hazlewood	Aus	57	445	6.35	215	12.89

Openers **Shoaib Mohammad** and **Michael Vandort** (1980), swashbuckler batsman **Richie Richardson**, batsmen **Cheteshwar Pujara**, **Asad Shafiq** and **Jimmy Adams**, keeper **Imtiaz Ahmed**, all-rounder **Daniel Vettori**, left-handed fast bowler **Mitchell Starc**, and fast bowlers **Ryan Sidebottom** (1978) and **Josh Hazlewood**.

FEBRUARY XI

day		*team*	*tests*	*runs*	*ri (adj)*	*wkts*	*rwi (adj)*
1	GC Smith	SA	116	9253	45.58	8	511.61
3	* RB Simpson	Aus	62	4869	43.86	71	49.99
27	RG Pollock	SA	23	2256	55.02		
26	ED Weekes	WI	48	4455	55.00		
5	GE Tyldesley	Eng	14	990	49.50		
17	† AB de Villiers	SA	114	8765	45.89		
12	R Peel	Eng	20	427	12.93 (24.60)	101	5.88 (10.13)
6	FS Trueman	Eng	67	981	11.54	307	8.92
9	JC Laker	Eng	46	676	10.73	193	9.46
18	Fazal Mahmood	Pak	34	620	10.33	139	9.41
9	GD McGrath	Aus	123	639	4.69	560	9.33

One of the strongest months, despite the being shortest. Openers **Graeme Smith** and **Bob Simpson**, left-handed batting genius **Graeme Pollock**, powerful hitter **Everton Weekes**, and **Ernest Tyldesley**, batsman/keeper **AB de Villiers**, left-arm spinner **Bobby Peel**, fast bowler **Fred Trueman**, right-arm spin bowling genius **Jim Laker**, fast bowler **Fazal Mahmood**, and mister consistency, medium pacer **Glenn McGrath**.

FEBRUARY 2nd XI

day		*team*	*tests*	*runs*	*ri (adj)*	*wkts*	*rwi (adj)*
11	* WM Lawry	Aus	67	5234	42.55		
21	MJ Slater	Aus	74	5312	40.54		
19	Azhar Ali	Pak	94	7021	40.35	8	358.99
5	EH Hendren	Eng	51	3525	42.46		
8	M Azharuddin	Ind	99	6215	42.27		
26	† MJ Prior	Eng	75	4099	33.32		
1	SJ Snooke	SA	26	1008	21.91 (26.36)	35	16.61 (20.05)
16	MA Holding	WI	60	910	11.97	249	10.74
24	JK Lever	Eng	21	306	9.87	73	13.90
7	Taijul Islam	Ban	36	488	8.00	153	12.97
26	WA Johnston	Aus	40	273	5.57	160	11.20

Openers **Bill Lawry** and **Michael Slater**, batsmen **Azhar Ali**, **Patsy Hendren**, and **Mohammad Azharuddin**, keeper **Matt Prior**, useful batsman and medium pace bowler **Tip Snooke**, left-arm spinner **Taijul Islam**, fast bowler **Michael Holding**, swing bowler **John Lever** (1949), and left-arm bowler **Bill Johnston**.

MARCH XI

day		*team*	*tests*	*runs*	*ri (adj)*	*wkts*	*rwi (adj)*
11	AE Stoddart	Eng	16	996	33.20 (40.53)		
2	* AJ Strauss	Eng	100	7037	39.53		
7	IVA Richards	WI	121	8540	46.92	32	197.53
9	CP Mead	Eng	17	1185	45.57 (48.07)		
3	Inzamam-ul-Haq	Pak	119	8829	44.59		
24	Shakib Al Hasan	Ban	59	4029	36.96	215	14.41
27	G Giffen	Aus	31	1238	23.35 (34.49)	103	11.30 (15.20)
15	† H Carter	Aus	28	873	18.57 (22.40)		
19	HMRKB Herath	SL	93	1699	11.79	433	11.02
30	J Cowie	NZ	9	90	6.92	45	6.21
8	NAT Adcock	SA	26	146	3.74	104	9.33

A surprisingly weak month, but they do have their share of great players. Openers **Andrew Stoddart** and **Andrew Strauss**, batsmen **Viv Richards**, **Phil Mead** and **Inzamam-ul-Haq**, all-rounders **Shakib Al Hasan** and **George Giffen**, keeper **Sammy Carter**, and stocky left-arm spinner **Rangana Herath**, and fast bowlers **Jack Cowie** and **Neil Adcock**.

MARCH 2nd XI

day		*team*	*tests*	*runs*	*ri (adj)*	*wkts*	*rwi (adj)*
26	WJ Edrich	Eng	39	2440	38.73	41	51.36
20	Tamim Iqbal	Ban	65	4848	38.78		
18	* C Hill	Aus	49	3412	38.33 (43.33)		
31	HM Amla	SA	124	9282	43.17		
24	DM Jones	Aus	52	3631	40.79		
28	PR Umrigar	Ind	59	3631	38.62	35	60.11
13	† D Ramdin	WI	74	2898	23.00		
25	WH Lockwood	Eng	12	231	14.43 (22.56)	43	8.60 (11.96)
16	HH Streak	Zim	65	1990	18.59	216	13.28
27	VWC Jupp	Eng	8	208	16.00	28	11.00
13	N Wagner	NZ	58	775	10.47	244	11.94

Openers **Tamim Iqbal** and **Bill Edrich**, batsmen **Clem Hill**, **Hashim Amla**, **Dean Jones**, and **Polly Umrigar**, keeper **Denesh Ramdin**, fast bowlers **Bill Lockwood** (1868-1932), **Heath Streak**, and **Neil Wagner**, and off spinner **Vallance Jupp**.

APRIL XI

day		*team*	*tests*	*runs*	*ri (adj)*	*wkts*	*rwi (adj)*
11	A Shrewsbury	Eng	23	1277	31.92 (45.80)		
7	DL Amiss	Eng	50	3612	41.04		
24	SR Tendulkar	Ind	200	15921	48.39	46	170.75
2	MJ Clarke	Aus	114	8599	43.87	31	80.07
28	* A Flower	Zim	63	4794	42.80		
12	MH Mankad	Ind	44	2109	29.29	162	13.96
9	† APE Knott	Eng	95	4389	29.45		
18	MD Marshall	WI	81	1810	16.91	376	8.40
23	CP Carter	SA	10	181	12.06 (14.73)	28	10.62 (11.30)
19	SF Barnes	Eng	27	242	6.20 (11.20)	189	4.34 (5.66)
17	M Muralitharan	SL	132	1295	7.77	795	6.50

Openers **Arthur Shrewsbury** and **Dennis Amiss**, batsmen **Sachin Tendulkar**, **Michael Clarke** and **Andy Flower**, spinner and all-rounder **Vinoo Mankad**, keeper **Alan Knott**, fast bowler **Malcolm Marshall**, left-arm spinner **Claude Carter**, fast-medium pacer/spinner **Sydney Barnes**, and spinner **Muttiah Muralitharan**.

What would it be like to face the aggressive brilliance of Barnes or the guile of Muralitharan from one end, and the white-hot lethal and swinging pace of Marshall from the other? Probably not many batsmen would be around long enough to find out.

APRIL 2nd XI

day		*team*	*tests*	*runs*	*ri (adj)*	*wkts*	*rwi (adj)*
30	RG Sharma	Ind	45	3137	40.74	2	896.00
6	Mudassar Nazar	Pak	76	4114	35.46	66	55.79
1	DI Gower	Eng	117	8231	40.34		
1	* SP Fleming	NZ	111	7172	37.94		
11	IR Bell	Eng	118	7727	37.69		
25	C Kelleway	Aus	26	1422	33.85 (36.71)	52	27.38 (29.25)
8	† AJ Stewart	Eng	133	8463	36.01		
19	JN Gillespie	Aus	71	1218	13.09	259	13.82
2	RO Collinge	NZ	35	533	10.66	116	15.63
14	CJ McDermott	Aus	71	939	10.43	290	12.28
28	AL Valentine	WI	36	141	2.76	139	13.74

Opener **Rohit Sharma**, opener and useful seam bowler **Mudassar Nazar**, elegant batsmen **David Gower** and **Stephen Fleming**, mister happiness **Ian Bell** (1982), mister no-nonsense **Alec Stewart**, fast bowler and all-rounder **Charles Kelleway**, fast bowlers **Jason Gillespie**, **Richard Collinge** and **Craig McDermott**, and left-arm spinner and **Alf Valentine**.

MAY XI

day		*team*	*tests*	*runs*	*ri (adj)*	*wkts*	*rwi (adj)*
19	A Melville	SA	11	894	47.05		
9	CC Hunte	WI	44	3245	41.60		
30	GA Headley	WI	22	2190	54.75 (61.00)		
2	BC Lara	WI	130	11912	51.79		
27	*DPMD Jayawardene	SL	149	11814	46.88	6	189.41
27	W Barnes	Eng	21	725	21.96 (36.51)	51	8.53 (16.66)
11	†JM Blackham	Aus	35	800	12.90 (26.93)		
30	MW Tate	Eng	39	1198	23.03	155	11.47
12	H Trumble	Aus	32	851	14.92 (20.71)	141	8.80 (10.94)
8	PJ Cummins	Aus	41	833	14.36	197	8.52
30	C Blythe	Eng	19	183	5.90 (10.90)	100	6.89 (8.74)

Openers **Alan Melville** and **Conrad Hunte**, batsmen **George Headley**, **Brian Lara** and **Mahela Jayawardene**, gifted all-rounder **Billy Barnes**, keeper **Jack Blackham**, baby-faced fast bowler **Maurice Tate**, fast bowler **Pat Cummins**, off spinner **Hugh Trumble**, and left-arm spinner **Colin Blythe**.

Is it too much to imagine watching the glory of a batting partnership between Headley and Lara? One right, one left, and both of raw talent, supreme flowing elegance, perfect timing and surprising power. This team lacks a little in the pace bowling, but Blythe and Trumble would be a great spin-twin partnership.

MAY 2nd XI

day		*team*	*tests*	*runs*	*ri (adj)*	*wkts*	*rwi (adj)*
1	CG Greenidge	WI	108	7558	40.85		
26	GM Turner	NZ	41	2991	40.97		
27	MEK Hussey	Aus	79	6235	45.51	7	199.81
23	DCS Compton	Eng	78	5807	44.32	25	148.89
15	*ER Dexter	Eng	62	4502	44.13	66	42.33
27	FE Woolley	Eng	64	3283	33.50 (35.13)	83	35.54 (38.00)
22	†Sarfaraz Ahmed	Pak	49	2657	30.89		
3	JL Pattinson	Aus	21	417	16.68	81	12.35
18	H Verity	Eng	40	669	15.20	144	12.35
3	JT Hearne	Eng	11	86	5.05 (10.05)	48	8.82 (10.80)
17	BS Chandrasekhar	Ind	58	167	2.08	242	11.92

Openers **Gordon Greenidge** and **Glenn Turner**, batsmen **Michael Hussey**, **Denis Compton** and **Ted Dexter**, tall and elegant all-rounder **Frank Woolley**, keeper **Sarfaraz Ahmed**, left-arm spinner **Hedley Verity**, fast bowler **James Pattinson**, seam bowler **Jack Hearne** (1867-1944).and leg spinner **Bhagwath Chandrasekhar**.

JUNE XI

day		*team*	*tests*	*runs*	*ri (adj)*	*wkts*	*rwi (adj)*
23	L Hutton	Eng	79	6971	50.51		
5	SG Barnes	Aus	13	1072	56.42		
19	*WR Hammond	Eng	85	7249	51.77 (54.19)	83	50.09
2	SPD Smith	Aus	85	8010	53.04	18	177.22
12	Javed Miandad	Pak	124	8832	46.73	17	84.93
13	CL Cairns	NZ	60	3320	31.92	218	14.02
23	†N Dickwella	SL	47	2529	30.10		
2	GA Lohmann	Eng	15	203	9.22 (21.95)	77	5.06 (10.12)
14	AK Davidson	Aus	44	1328	21.77	186	9.05
3	Wasim Akram	Pak	102	2898	19.71	414	10.09
27	DW Steyn	SA	93	1251	10.51	439	8.93

Openers **Len Hutton** and **Sid Barnes**, batsmen **Wally Hammond**, **Javed Miandad** and **Steve Smith**, all-rounder **Chris Cairns**, keeper **Niroshan Dickwella**, medium pacer **George Lohmann**, swing bowler **Alan Davidson**, and fast bowlers **Wasim Akram** and **Dale Steyn**.

A powerful all-round team, but it lacks a spinner. They would have the freak medium-pace of Lohmann, who was also good with the bat, but what a pairing of the devastating ability of Davidson and Wasim Akram; both left-armers who swung the ball at pace.

JUNE 2nd XI

day		*team*	*tests*	*runs*	*ri (adj)*	*wkts*	*rwi (adj)*
21	JH Edrich	Eng	77	5138	40.45		
30	ST Jayasuriya	SL	110	6973	36.89	98	49.05
13	G Gunn	Eng	15	1120	38.62 (42.24)		
27	*CG Macartney	Aus	35	2131	38.74 (41.83)	45	27.55 (31.33)
27	KP Pietersen	Eng	104	8181	45.19	10	513.88
4	BA Stokes	Eng	79	5061	34.66	174	23.25
18	†WW Wade	SA	11	511	26.89		
24	VD Philander	SA	64	1779	18.92	224	11.85
30	PM Pollock	SA	28	607	14.80	116	10.83
8	DL Underwood	Eng	86	937	8.07	297	13.13
12	TM Alderman	Aus	41	203	3.83	170	11.65

Openers **John Edrich** and **Sanath Jayasuriya**, batsmen **George Gunn**, the domineering **Charlie Macartney**, the restless **Kevin Pietersen**, all-rounder **Ben Stokes**, keeper **Billy Wade**, fast bowler **Peter Pollock**, medium pacer **Vernon Philander**, swing bowler **Terry Alderman**, and the brilliant spinner **Derek Underwood**.

JULY XI

day		*team*	*tests*	*runs*	*ri (adj)*	*wkts*	*rwi (adj)*
18	*WG Grace	Eng	22	1098	30.50 (41.61)	9	37.87 (57.93)
21	BA Richards	SA	4	508	72.57		
16	SJ McCabe	Aus	39	2748	44.32	36	73.81
28	GS Sobers	WI	93	8032	50.20	235	23.02
3	J Hardstaff, jr	Eng	23	1636	43.05		
20	M Leyland	Eng	41	2764	42.52	6	438.75
14	†HP Tillakaratne	SL	83	4545	34.69		
3	RJ Hadlee	NZ	86	3124	23.31	431	7.75
4	AV Bedser	Eng	51	714	10.056	236	9.70
18	DK Lillee	Aus	70	905	10.055	355	8.89
25	WE Bowes	Eng	15	28	2.54	68	9.52

Openers **WG Grace** and **Barry Richards**, batsmen **Stan McCabe**, **Garry Sobers**, **Joe Hardstaff jr** and **Maurice Leyland**, keeper **Hashan Tillakaratne**, fast bowlers **Richard Hadlee**, **Alec Bedser**, **Dennis Lillee** and **Bill Bowes**.

One of the strongest teams, it's hard to see how they could be beaten, although they lack a specialist spin bowler. Oddly enough, Bedser and Lillee had almost identical batting figures.

JULY 2nd XI

day		*team*	*tests*	*runs*	*ri*	*wkts*	*rwi*
10	SM Gavaskar	Ind	125	10122	47.29		
31	WA Brown	Aus	22	1592	45.48		
24	Zaheer Abbas	Pak	78	5062	40.82	3	205.33
27	* AR Border	Aus	156	11174	42.16	39	98.25
20	EAB Rowan	SA	26	1965	39.30		
10	RH Catterall	SA	24	1555	36.16	7	29.75
7	† MS Dhoni	Ind	90	4876	33.86		
16	SM Pollock	SA	108	3781	24.23	421	11.08
12	BR Taylor	NZ	30	898	17.96	111	12.70
5	GAR Lock	Eng	49	742	11.77	174	12.93
30	JM Anderson	Eng	169	1262	5.28	640	13.04

Openers **Sunil Gavaskar** and **Bill Brown**, batsmen **Allan Border**, **Zaheer Abbas** and **Eric Rowan**, medium pace all-rounder **Bob Catterall**, keeper **MS Dhoni**, fast bowlers **Shaun Pollock** and **Bruce Taylor**, left-arm spinner **Tony Lock**, and swing bowler **James Anderson**.

AUGUST XI

day		*team*	*tests*	*runs*	*ri (adj)*	*wkts*	*rwi (adj)*
12	EJ Barlow	SA	30	2516	44.14	40	39.15
21	SM Katich	Aus	55	4186	43.15	21	35.98
27	DG Bradman	Aus	52	6996	87.45		
8	KS Williamson	NZ	86	7272	48.48	30	89.84
27	Mohammad Yousuf	Pak	90	7530	48.26		
1	* FMM Worrell	WI	51	3860	44.36	69	46.01
14	JM Gregory	Aus	24	1146	33.70	85	15.39
15	† RC Russell	Eng	54	1897	21.80		
6	Iqbal Qasim	Pak	50	549	9.63	171	14.13
16	JR Thomson	Aus	51	679	9.30	200	12.60
13	Shoaib Akhtar	Pak	46	544	8.11	178	11.83

Openers **Eddie Barlow** and **Simon Katich** (1975), batsmen **Don Bradman**, current Kiwi batsman **Kane Williamson, Mohammad Yousuf**, and **Frank Worrell**, all-rounder **Jack Gregory**, the princely wicket-keeper **Jack Russell**, left-arm spinner **Iqbal Qasim**, and ultra-fast bowlers **Jeff Thomson** and **Shoaib Akhtar**.

AUGUST 2nd XI

day		*team*	*tests*	*runs*	*ri (adj)*	*wkts*	*rwi (adj)*
22	* WM Woodfull	Aus	35	2300	42.59		
31	CJL Rogers	Aus	25	2015	41.97		
7	GS Chappell	Aus	87	7110	47.08	47	76.20
8	J Ryder	Aus	20	1394	43.56	17	71.97
28	AL Hassett	Aus	43	3073	44.53		
5	GHS Trott	Eng	24	921	21.92 (30.14)	29	35.13 (41.17)
1	TL Goddard	SA	41	2516	32.25	123	15.98
18	† TG Evans	Eng	91	2438	18.33		
7	DG Cork	Eng	37	864	15.42	131	14.10
30	Pervez Sajjad	Pak	19	123	6.15	59	14.17
8	ARC Fraser	Eng	46	388	5.79	177	12.19

Opener **Bill Woodfull**, and **Chris Rogers** the opener lucky enough to make a successful comeback, **Jack Ryder** who was a batsmen unlucky to be often left out, batsmen **Greg Chappell** and **Lindsay Hassett**, all-rounders **Harry Trott** and **Trevor Goddard**, keeper **Godfrey Evans**, medium pacers **Dominic Cork** (1971) and **Angus Fraser**, and left-arm spinner **Pervez Sajjad**.

SEPTEMBER XI

day		*years*	*tests*	*runs*	*ri (adj)*	*wkts*	*rwi (adj)*
6	Saeed Anwar	Pak	55	4052	44.52		
21	CH Gayle	WI	103	7214	39.63	73	60.87
22	* MD Crowe	NZ	77	5444	41.55	14	120.70
21	TT Samaraweera	SL	81	5462	41.37	15	107.16
24	AG Steel	Eng	13	600	30.00 (45.00)	29	14.38 (24.73)
27	† BB McCullum	NZ	101	6453	36.66		
17	R Ashwin	Ind	86	2931	23.82	442	8.84
15	MJ Procter	SA	7	226	22.60	41	5.12
9	FR Spofforth	Aus	18	217	7.48 (23.00)	94	5.87 (10.94)
13	SK Warne	Aus	144	3142	15.94	702	9.85
21	CEL Ambrose	WI	98	1439	9.92	405	9.27

Quick-scoring openers **Saeed Anwar** and **Chris Gayle**, batsmen **Martin Crowe** and **Thilan Samaraweera**, all-rounders **Allan Steel** and **Mike Procter**, impatient thrasher/keeper **Brendon McCullum**, brilliant spinners **Ravichandran Ashwin** and **Shane Warne**, and dangerous fast bowlers **Fred Spofforth** and **Curtley Ambrose**.

SEPTEMBER 2nd XI

day		*team*	*tests*	*runs*	*ri*	*wkts*	*rwi*
14	KC Wessels	Aus,SA	40	2788	39.26		
14	Aamer Sohail	Pak	47	2823	34.01	25	78.88
3	BF Butcher	WI	44	3104	39.79	5	21.60
26	* IM Chappell	Aus	75	5345	39.30	20	197.40
29	Mominul Haque	Ban	51	3514	36.87	7	337.85
25	WJ Cronje	SA	68	3714	33.45	43	58.50
16	† DJ Richardson	SA	42	1359	21.23		
12	WW Hall	WI	48	818	12.39	192	12.64
18	D Gough	Eng	58	855	9.94	229	11.77
25	BS Bedi	Ind	67	656	6.49	266	12.73
29	LR Gibbs	WI	79	488	4.47	309	13.93

Openers **Kepler Wessels** and **Aamer Sohail**, batsmen **Basil Butcher**, **Ian Chappell**, **Hansie Cronje**, and **Mominul Haque**, keeper **Dave Richardson**, fast bowlers **Wes Hall** and **Darren Gough**, left-arm spinner **Bishan Bedi** and hostile off spinner **Lance Gibbs**.

OCTOBER XI

day		*team*	*tests*	*runs*	*ri (adj)*	*wkts*	*rwi (adj)*
20	V Sehwag	Ind	103	8503	47.76	40	107.72
12	VM Merchant	Ind	10	859	47.22		
27	KC Sangakkara	SL	134	12400	53.21		
16	JH Kallis	SA	165	13206	47.50	291	30.27
17	MP Donnelly	NZ	7	582	48.50		
21	G Ulyett	Eng	23	901	25.02 (40.72)	48	13.77 (24.19)
23	† BJ Haddin	Aus	66	3266	29.16		
6	* R Benaud	Aus	63	2201	22.69	248	12.64
3	RR Lindwall	Aus	61	1502	17.88	228	11.41
17	A Kumble	Ind	132	2506	14.48	619	11.30
20	AA Donald	SA	72	652	6.93	330	8.69

Openers **Virender Sehwag** and **Vijay Merchant**, batsmen **Kumar Sangakkara** and **Martin Donnelly**, all-rounders **Jacques Kallis** and **George Ulyett**, keeper **Brad Haddin** (1977), leg-spinners **Richie Benaud** and **Anil Kumble**, and fast bowlers **Ray Lindwall** and **Allan Donald**.

OCTOBER 2nd XI

day		*team*	*tests*	*runs*	*ri (adj)*	*wkts*	*rwi (adj)*
29	ML Hayden	Aus	102	8437	46.35		
27	DA Warner	Aus	94	7753	45.07	4	319.43
8	RN Harvey	Aus	79	6149	44.88		
18	* WL Murdoch	Aus	18	896	27.15 (42.15)		
21	DR Martyn	Aus	67	4406	40.42		
17	PA de Silva	SL	93	6361	40.00	29	83.30
29	W Rhodes	Eng	58	2325	23.72 (27.65)	127	19.10 (22.09)
21	† JM Parks	Eng	46	1962	28.85		
3	J Briggs	Eng	31	809	16.85 (26.95)	97	9.53 (14.39)
24	IR Bishop	WI	43	632	10.03	161	11.45
30	CA Walsh	WI	132	936	5.05	519	11.39

Openers **Matthew Hayden** and **David Warner**, batsmen **Neil Harvey**, **Billy Murdoch**, **Damien Martyn** (1971) and **Aravinda de Silva**, stalwart all-rounder **Wilfred Rhodes**, keeper **Jim Parks** (1931), left-arm spinner **Johnny Briggs**, and fast bowlers **Ian Bishop** and **Courtney Walsh**.

NOVEMBER XI

day		*team*	*tests*	*runs*	*ri (adj)*	*wkts*	*rwi (adj)*
24	H Sutcliffe	Eng	54	4555	54.22		
10	SM Nurse	WI	29	2523	46.72		
24	KF Barrington	Eng	82	6806	51.95	29	77.27
5	V Kohli	Ind	101	8043	47.03		
21	* FS Jackson	Eng	20	1415	42.87 (48.33)	24	37.45 (43.07)
28	KR Miller	Aus	55	2958	34.00	170	12.86
14	† AC Gilchrist	Aus	95	5475	40.55		
24	IT Botham	Eng	102	5200	32.29	383	12.45
25	Imran Khan	Pak	88	3807	30.21	362	8.94
16	CTB Turner	Aus	17	323	10.09 (21.18)	101	4.90 (8.34)
16	Waqar Younis	Pak	87	1010	8.41	373	9.72

Openers **Herbert Sutcliffe** and **Seymour Nurse**, batsmen **Ken Barrington** and **Virat Kohli**, all-rounders **Stanley Jackson**, **Keith Miller**, **Ian Botham** and **Imran Khan**, batsmen/keeper **Adam Gilchrist**, medium pacer **Charlie Turner**, and fast bowler **Waqar Younis**.

The month of the great all-rounders, with, unbelievably, Botham and Imran Khan batting well down the order. Their only weakness is a lack of a specialist spinner, with Fred Titmus (18.95 RWI) the only notable one for this month, and he too was noted as a useful batsman.

NOVEMBER 2nd XI

day		*team*	*tests*	*runs*	*ri (adj)*	*wkts*	*rwi (adj)*
21	JL Langer	Aus	104	7674	42.63		
23	G Kirsten	SA	101	7289	41.41		
2	VT Trumper	Aus	48	3163	35.53 (40.53)	8	74.28 (83.66)
5	E Paynter	Eng	20	1540	49.67		
12	* AD Nourse	SA	34	2960	47.74		
22	Mushtaq Mohammad	Pak	57	3643	36.43	79	25.89
4	† RW Marsh	Aus	96	3633	24.22		
2	MG Johnson	Aus	73	2065	18.94	313	12.70
8	B Lee	Aus	75	1447	16.44	308	14.75
23	MG Hughes	Aus	53	1032	14.74	212	12.98
21	AR Caddick	Eng	62	861	9.06	234	13.42

Openers **Justin Langer** and **Gary Kirsten**, batsmen **Victor Trumper**, **Eddie Paynter**, and **Dudley Nourse**, all-rounder and this team's only spinner **Mushtaq Mohammad**, keeper **Rod Marsh**, fast bowlers **Mitchell Johnson**, **Brett Lee** (1976), **Merv Hughes** and **Andrew Caddick** (1968).

DECEMBER XI

day		*team*	*tests*	*runs*	*ri (adj)*	*wkts*	*rwi (adj)*
16	JB Hobbs	Eng	61	5410	53.03 (55.44)		
25	* AN Cook	Eng	161	12472	42.85		
19	RT Ponting	Aus	167	13278	46.58	5	397.44
30	JE Root	Eng	117	9889	45.78	45	113.14
21	KD Walters	Aus	74	5357	42.85	49	42.72
17	GA Faulkner	SA	25	1754	37.31 (42.10)	82	13.93 (16.56)
3	†LEG Ames	Eng	47	2434	33.80		
7	GF Lawson	Aus	46	894	13.14	180	13.24
25	CV Grimmett	Aus	37	557	11.14	216	7.50
20	WJ O'Reilly	Aus	27	410	10.51	144	7.52
16	J Garner	WI	10	672	9.88	259	8.82

Openers **Jack Hobbs** and **Alastair Cook**, batsmen **Ricky Ponting**, **Joe Root** and **Doug Walters**, all-rounder **Aubrey Faulkner**, keeper **Les Ames**, fast bowlers **Geoff Lawson** (1957) and **Joel Garner**, and great leg spinners **Clarrie Grimmett** and **Bill O'Reilly**.

DECEMBER 2nd XI

day		*team*	*tests*	*runs*	*ri (adj)*	*wkts*	*rwi (adj)*
21	Hanif Mohammad	Pak	55	3915	40.36		
6	W Bardsley	Aus	41	2469	37.40 (39.90)		
31	* PBH May	Eng	66	4537	42.80		
26	RB Kanhai	WI	79	6227	45.45		
7	W Flowers	Eng	8	254	18.14 (32.42)	14	19.63 (33.22)
22	BM McMillan	SA	38	1968	31.74	75	28.85
3	†MV Boucher	SA	146	5498	26.95		
6	RA Jadeja	Ind	59	2396	27.54	242	11.31
31	JM Blanckenberg	SA	18	455	15.16 (16.83)	60	12.61 (13.27)
29	Saqlain Mushtaq	Pak	49	927	11.88	208	12.33
11	SP Gupte	Ind	36	183	4.35	149	12.09

Openers **Hanif Mohammad** and **Warren Bardsley**, batsmen **Peter May** and **Rohan Kanhai**, spin bowler and all-rounder **Wilf Flowers** (1856-1926), batsmen and fast bowler **Brian McMillan**, keeper **Mark Boucher**, medium pace bowler **Jimmy Blanckenberg**, left-arm spinner **Ravindra Jadeja**, off spinner **Saqlain Mushtaq**, and little ripping leg spinner **Subhash Gupte**.

ALPHABET XIs

In the 1805 season many of the best players had surnames beginning with the letter B, such as Beldham, Budd, and Beauclerk, and they formed a team to take on the rest of England. The team became a tradition until the 1830s. Continuing with that tradition, the following are team selections from about the 1870s through until today. (There will be no team of Xs, unless China ever becomes interested in the game.) What team is the strongest?

The As XI

	tests	*runs*	*ri (adj)*	*wkts*	*rwi (adj)*
DL Amiss	50	3612	41.04		
R Abel	11	555	29.21 (37.63)		
HM Amla	124	9282	43.17		
M Azharuddin	99	6215	42.27		
*WW Armstrong	50	2863	34.08 (38.30)	87	30.88 (34.59)
Asif Iqbal	58	3575	36.11	53	28.86
†LEG Ames	47	2434	33.80		
R Ashwin	86	2931	23.82	442	8.84
L Amar Singh	7	292	20.85	28	14.22
CEL Ambrose	98	1439	9.92	405	9.27
NAT Adcock	26	146	3.74	104	9.33

Openers **Dennis Amiss** and **Bobby Abel**, batsmen **Mohammad Azharuddin**, and **Hashim Amla**, all-rounders **Warwick Armstrong** and **Asif Iqbal**, keeper **Les Ames**, spinner **Ravichandran Ashwin**, and fast bowlers **Curtley Ambrose**, **Amar Singh**, and **Neil Adcock**.

The Bs XI

	tests	*runs*	*ri (adj)*	*wkts*	*rwi (adj)*
SG Barnes	13	1072	56.59		
EJ Barlow	30	2516	44.14	40	39.15
*DG Bradman	52	6996	87.45		
KF Barrington	82	6806	51.95	29	77.27
KC Bland	21	1669	42.79		
W Barnes	21	725	21.96 (36.51)	51	8.53 (16.66)
IT Botham	102	5200	32.29	383	12.45
†JM Blackham	35	800	12.90 (26.93)		
SF Barnes	27	242	6.20 (11.20)	189	4.34 (5.66)
C Blythe	19	183	5.90 (10.90)	100	6.89 (8.74)
AV Bedser	51	714	10.05	236	9.70

Openers **Sid Barnes** and **Eddie Barlow**, batsmen **Don Bradman**, **Ken Barrington**, and **Colin Bland**, all-rounders **Billy Barnes** and **Ian Botham**, keeper **Jack Blackham**, spinner **Colin Blythe**, fast bowler **Alec Bedser**, and **Sydney Barnes**, the greatest of all bowlers.

The Bs 2nd XI

	tests	*runs*	*ri (adj)*	*wkts*	*rwi (adj)*
WA Brown	22	1592	45.48		
G Boycott	108	8114	42.04		
* AR Border	158	11176	42.17	39	99.25
Babar Azam	40	2851	40.15		
W Bates	15	656	25.34 (40.34)	50	7.55 (14.45)
RG Barlow	17	591	19.70 (34.70)	34	17.24 (28.71)
† MV Boucher	146	5498	26.95		
J Briggs	31	809	16.85 (26.95)	97	7.41 (11.09)
IR Bishop	43	632	10.03	161	11.46
BS Bedi	67	656	6.49	266	12.73
JJ Bumrah	29	174	3.95	123	9.89

Openers **Bill Brown** and **Geoff Boycott**, batsmen **Allan Border** and **Babar Azam**, all-rounders **Billy Bates** and **Dick Barlow** (1851-1919), keeper **Mark Boucher**, spinners **Johnny Briggs** and **Bishan Bedi**, and fast bowlers **Ian Bishop** and **Jasprit Bumrah**.

The Cs XI

	tests	*runs*	*ri (adj)*	*wkts*	*rwi (adj)*
HL Collins	19	1352	43.61		
* AN Cook	161	12472	42.85		
GS Chappell	87	7110	47.08		
RM Cowper	27	2061	44.80		
DCA Compton	78	5807	44.32	25	148.89
CL Cairns	62	3320	31.92	218	14.02
† HB Cameron	26	1239	27.53		
PJ Cummins	41	833	14.36	197	8.52
J Cowie	9	90	6.92	45	6.21
CEH Croft	27	158	4.27	125	9.69
BS Chandrasekhar	58	167	2.08	242	11.92

Openers **Herbie Collins** and **Alastair Cook**, batsmen **Greg Chappell**, **Bob Cowper**, and **Denis Compton**, all-rounder **Chris Cairns**, keeper **Jock Cameron**, spinner **Bhagwath Chandrasekhar**, and fast bowlers **Jack Cowie**, **Colin Croft**, and **Pat Cummins**.

The Cs 2nd XI

	tests	*runs*	*ri (adj)*	*wkts*	*rwi (adj)*
RH Catterall	24	1555	36.16	7	29.75
SC Cook	11	632	33.26		
MJ Clarke	114	8599	43.87	31	80.07
S Chanderpaul	164	11867	42.38	9	468.74
MD Crowe	77	5444	41.55	14	121.05
* IM Chappell	75	5345	39.30	20	197.40
LN Constantine	18	634	19.24	58	15.05
† H Carter	28	873	18.57		
CP Carter	10	181	12.06 (14.73)	28	10.62 (11.30)
SR Clark	24	248	9.53	94	12.18
A Cotter	21	457	12.35	89	12.22

Openers **Bob Catterall** and **Stephen Cook** (1982), batsmen **Michael Clarke, Shivnarine Chanderpaul, Martin Crowe**, and **Ian Chappell**, all-rounder **Learie Constantine**, keeper **Sammy Carter**, spinner **Claude Carter**, and fast bowlers **Stuart Clark** and **Tibby Cotter**.

The Ds XI

	tests	*runs*	*ri (adj)*	*wkts*	*rwi (adj)*
CS Dempster	10	723	48.20		
S Dhawan	34	2315	39.91		
RS Dravid	163	13265	46.70		
KS Duleepsinhji	12	995	52.36		
AB de Villiers	114	8765	45.89		
* ER Dexter	62	4502	44.13	66	42.33
† Q de Kock	54	3300	36.26		
AK Davidson	44	1328	21.77	186	9.05
PS de Villiers	18	359	13.80	85	9.49
G Dymock	21	236	7.35	78	12.16
AA Donald	72	652	6.93	330	8.69

Openers **Stewie Dempster** and **Shikhar Dhawan** (1985), batsmen **Rahul Dravid, Kumar Duleepsinhji, AB de Villiers**, and **Ted Dexter**, keeper **Quinton de Kock**, and fast bowlers **Allan Donald, Alan Davidson, Fanie de Villiers**, and **Geoff Dymock**.

The Es XI

	tests	*runs*	*ri (adj)*	*wkts*	*rwi (adj)*
JH Edrich	77	5138	40.45		
D Elgar	76	4864	36.29	15	134.58
* WJ Edrich	39	2440	38.73		
R Edwards	20	1171	36.59		
WR Endean	28	1630	31.34		
T Emmett	7	160	12.30 (37.30)	9	31.55 (50.44)
† TG Evans	91	2438	18.33		
MA Ealham	8	210	16.15	17	16.88
S Elworthy	4	72	14.40	13	21.01
RM Ellison	11	202	12.62	35	17.10
L Embuldeniya	15	183	7.95	70	12.91

Openers **John Edrich** and **Dean Elgar**, batsmen **Bill Edrich**, **Ross Edwards** (1942), and **Russell Endean**, all-rounder **Tom Emmett**, keeper **Godfrey Evans**, spinner **Lasith Embuldeniya**, and fast bowlers **Steve Elworthy** (1965), **Richard Ellison** (1959) and **Mark Ealham** (1969).

The Fs XI

	tests	*runs*	*ri (adj)*	*wkts*	*rwi (adj)*
RC Fredericks	59	4334	39.76		
G Fowler	21	1307	35.32		
JHW Fingleton	18	1189	41.00		
GA Faulkner	25	1754	37.31 (42.10)	82	13.93 (16.56)
† A Flower	63	4764	42.80		
* SP Fleming	111	7172	37.94		
AG Fairfax	10	410	34.16	21	26.32
FR Foster	11	330	22.00 (27.00)	45	8.86 (10.79)
Fazal Mahmood	34	620	10.33	139	9.41
AP Freeman	12	154	9.62	66	8.62
K Farnes	15	58	3.41	60	12.89

Openers **Roy Fredericks** and **Graeme Fowler** (1957), batsmen **Jack Fingleton**, and **Stephen Fleming**, all-rounders **Aubrey Faulkner**, **Alan Fairfax** and **Frank Forster**, batsman/keeper **Andy Flower**, spinner **Tich Freeman**, and fast bowlers **Fazal Mahmood** and **Ken Farnes** (1911-1941).

The Gs XI

	tests	*runs*	*ri (adj)*	*wkts*	*rwi (adj)*
*WG Grace	22	1098	30.50 (41.61)	9	37.87 (57.93)
SM Gavaskar	125	10122	47.29		
G Gunn	15	1120	38.62 (42.24)		
DI Gower	117	8231	40.34		
HH Gibbs	84	5919	39.99		
G Giffen	31	1238	23.35 (34.49)	103	11.30 (15.20)
†AC Gilchrist	95	5475	40.55		
JM Gregory	24	1146	33.70	85	15.39
CV Grimmett	37	557	11.14	216	7.50
J Garner	58	672	9.88	259	8.82
HC Griffith	13	91	3.95	44	11.55

Openers **WG Grace** and **Sunil Gavaskar**, batsmen **George Gunn**, **David Gower**, and **Herschelle Gibbs**, all-rounders **George Giffen** and **Jack Gregory**, keeper **Adam Gilchrist**, spinner **Clarrie Grimmett**, and fast bowlers **Joel Garner** and **Herman Griffith**.

The Gs 2nd XI

	tests	*runs*	*ri (adj)*	*wkts*	*rwi (adj)*
GA Gooch	118	8900	41.39		
CG Greenidge	108	7558	40.85		
*TW Graveney	79	4882	39.69		
AP Gurusinha	39	2374	35.43	19	63.11
SC Ganguly	86	5075	35.99	26	162.33
AW Greig	58	3599	38.69	141	21.23
TL Goddard	41	2516	32.25	123	15.98
†ATW Grout	51	890	13.28		
CC Griffith	28	530	12.61	94	15.18
D Gough	58	855	9.94	229	11.77
SP Gupte	36	183	4.35	149	12.09

Openers **Graham Gooch** and **Gordon Greenidge**, batsmen **Tom Graveney**, **Asanka Gurusinha**, and **Sourav Ganguly**, all-rounders **Tony Greig** and **Trevor Goddard**, keeper **Wally Grout**, spinner **Subhash Gupte**, and fast bowlers **Darren Gough** and **Charlie Griffith**.

The Hs XI

	tests	*runs*	*ri (adj)*	*wkts*	*rwi (adj)*
JB Hobbs	61	5410	53.03		
L Hutton	79	6971	50.51		
GA Headley	22	2190	54.75		
*WR Hammond	85	7249	51.77	83	50.09
RN Harvey	79	6149	44.88		
MEK Hussey	79	6235	45.51		
HV Hordern	7	254	19.53 (24.53)	46	6.60 (8.01)
†IA Healy	119	4356	23.93		
RJ Hadlee	86	3124	23.31	431	7.75
RJ Harris	27	603	15.46	113	10.82
MA Holding	60	910	11.97	249	10.74

Openers **Jack Hobbs** and **Len Hutton**, batsmen **George Headley**, **Wally Hammond**, **Neil Harvey**, and **Michael Hussey**, keeper **Ian Healy**, all-rounder and spinner **Ranji Hordern**, and fast bowlers **Richard Hadlee**, **Michael Holding**, and **Ryan Harris**.

The Hs 2nd XI

	tests	*runs*	*ri (adj)*	*wkts*	*rwi (adj)*
ML Hayden	102	8437	46.35		
CC Hunte	44	3245	41.60		
*C Hill	49	3412	38.33 (43.33)		
J Hardstaff, jr	23	1636	43.05		
EH Hendren	51	3525	42.46		
TW Hayward	32	1810	32.32 (37.32)	12	63.58
†BJ Haddin	66	3266	29.16		
WW Hall	48	818	12.39	192	12.64
JT Hearne	11	86	5.05 (10.05)	48	8.82 (10.80)
DW Headley	15	186	7.15	60	10.67
ND Hirwani	17	54	2.45	66	12.76

Openers **Matthew Hayden** and **Conrad Hunte**, batsmen **Clem Hill**, **Joe Hardstaff, jr**, **Patsy Hendren**, and **Tom Hayward**, keeper **Brad Haddin**, spinner **Narendra Hirwani**, and fast bowlers **Wes Hall**, **Jack Hearne**, and **Dean Headley**.

The Is XI

	tests	*runs*	*ri (adj)*	*wkts*	*rwi (adj)*
FA Iredale	14	1657	35.08 (40.08)		
Imran Farhat	40	2400	31.16		
Ijaz Ahmed	60	3315	36.03		
Inzamam-ul-Haq	113	8813	44.34		
SS Iyer	4	388	55.41		
† BL Irvine	4	353	50.42		
* Imran Khan	88	3807	30.21	362	8.94
Intikhab Alam	47	1493	19.38	125	22.43
Iqbal Qasim	50	549	9.63	171	14.13
DEJ Ironside	3	37	9.25	15	6.10
H Ironmonger	14	42	2.00	74	6.55

Openers **Frank Iredale** and **Imran Farhat**, batsmen **Ijaz Ahmed**, **Inzamam-ul-Haq**, and **Shreyas Iyer**, all-rounder **Imran Khan**, batsman/keeper **Lee Irvine**, spinners **Iqbal Qasim**, **Intikhab Alam**, and **Bert Ironmonger**, and seam bowler **David Ironside** (1925-2005).

The Js XI

	tests	*runs*	*ri (adj)*	*wkts*	*rwi (adj)*
ST Jayasuriya	110	6973	36.89	98	49.05
DR Jardine	22	1296	39.27		
Javed Miandad	124	8832	46.73	17	84.93
DPMD Jayawardene	149	11814	46.88		
* FS Jackson	20	1415	42.87 (48.33)	24	37.45 (43.07)
DM Jones	52	3631	40.79		
RA Jadeja	59	2396	27.54	242	11.31
† HAPW Jayawardene	58	2124	25.59		
KA Jamieson	14	351	19.50	66	7.94
MG Johnson	73	2065	18.94	313	12.70
WA Johnston	40	273	5.57	160	11.20

Openers **Sanath Jayasuriya** and **Douglas Jardine** (1900-1958), batsmen **Javed Miandad**, **Mahela Jayawardene**, and **Dean Jones**, all-rounder **Stanley Jackson**, keeper **Prasanna Jayawardene**, spinner **Ravindra Jadeja**, and fast bowlers **Mitchell Johnson**, **Kyle Jamieson** and **Bill Johnston**.

The Ks XI

	tests	*runs*	*ri (adj)*	*wkts*	*rwi (adj)*
RB Kanhai	79	6227	45.45		
G Kirsten	99	6979	40.10		
SM Katich	55	4186	43.15	21	35.98
JH Kallis	165	13206	47.50	291	30.27
* V Kohli	101	8043	47.03		
C Kelleway	26	1422	33.85 (36.71)	52	27.38 (29.25)
† APE Knott	95	4389	29.45		
Kapil Dev	131	5248	28.52	434	15.50
A Kumble	132	2506	14.48	619	11.30
Khan Mohammad	13	100	5.88	54	9.74
LF Kline	13	58	3.62	34	14.76

Openers **Rohan Kanhai** and **Gary Kirsten**, batsmen **Simon Katich**, **Virat Kohli**, all-rounders **Jacques Kallis**, **Charlie Kelleway**, and **Kapil Dev**, keeper **Allan Knott**, spinners **Anil Kumble** and **Lindsay Kline**, and fast bowler **Khan Mohammad**.

The Ls XI

	tests	*runs*	*ri (adj)*	*wkts*	*rwi (adj)*
WM Lawry	67	5234	42.55		
JL Langer	104	7674	42.63		
BC Lara	130	11912	51.79		
M Labuschagne	26	2390	53.11	13	137.30
* CH Lloyd	110	7515	42.94		
† DT Lindsay	19	1130	36.45		
WH Lockwood	12	231	14.43 (22.56)	43	8.59 (11.61)
GA Lohmann	15	203	9.22 (21.95)	77	5.06 (10.12)
RR Lindwall	61	1502	17.88	228	11.41
JC Laker	46	676	10.73	193	9.46
DK Lillee	70	905	10.05	355	8.89

Openers **Bill Lawry** and **Justin Langer**, batsmen **Brian Lara**, **Clive Lloyd**, and **Marnus Labuschagne**, all-rounder **George Lohmann**, keeper **Denis Lindsay**, spinner **Jim Laker**, and fast bowlers **Dennis Lillee**, **Ray Lindwall**, and **Bill Lockwood**.

The Ls 2nd XI

	tests	*runs*	*ri (adj)*	*wkts*	*rwi (adj)*
TWM Latham	65	4502	39.84		
BM Laird	21	1341	33.52		
DS Lehmann	27	1798	42.80	15	45.76
* M Leyland	41	2764	42.52	6	438.75
VVS Laxman	76	4689	37.21		
JJ Lyons	14	731	27.07 (36.33)	6	38.74 (52.24)
CB Llewellyn	13	478	19.91 (24.91)	43	11.93 (14.02)
† AFA Lilley	35	903	17.36 (22.36)		
H Larwood	21	485	17.32	78	13.08
GF Lawson	46	894	13.14	180	13.07
GAR Lock	49	742	11.77	174	12.93

Openers **Tom Latham** and **Bruce Laird** (1950), batsmen **Darren Lehmann** (1970), **Maurice Leyland**, **VVS Laxman**, and **Jack Lyons** (1863-1927), all-rounder **Charlie Llewellyn**, keeper **Dick Lilley**, spinner **Tony Lock**, and fast bowlers **Harold Larwood** and **Geoff Lawson**.

The Ms XI

	tests	*runs*	*ri (adj)*	*wkts*	*rwi (adj)*
A Melville	11	894	47.05		
VM Merchant	10	859	47.22		
* CP Mead	17	1185	45.47 (48.07)		
Mohammad Yousuf	90	7530	48.26		
SJ McCabe	39	2748	44.32		
KR Miller	55	2958	34.00	170	12.86
MH Mankad	44	2109	29.29	162	13.96
† RW Marsh	96	3633	24.22		
MD Marshall	81	1810	16.91	376	8.40
M Muralitharan	132	1259	7.77	795	6.50
GD McGrath	123	639	4.69	560	9.33

Openers **Alan Melville** and **Vijay Merchant**, batsmen **Phil Mead**, **Mohammad Yousuf**, and **Stan McCabe**, all-rounders **Keith Miller** and **Vinoo Mankad**, keeper **Rod Marsh**, spinner **Muttiah Muralitharan**, and fast bowlers **Malcolm Marshall** and **Glenn McGrath**.

The Ms 2nd XI

	tests	*runs*	*ri (adj)*	*wkts*	*rwi (adj)*
AR Morris	46	3533	44.72		
AK Markram	24	1760	40.00		
B Mitchell	42	3471	43.38	27	73.82
* CG Macartney	35	2131	38.74 (41.83)	45	27.55 (31.33)
PBH May	66	4537	42.80		
Mushtaq Mohammad	57	3643	36.43	79	25.89
† DL Murray	62	1993	20.76		
AA Mailey	21	222	7.65	99	11.64
EA Martindale	10	58	4.14	37	9.97
Mohammad Asif	23	141	3.71	106	10.11
Mohammad Abbas	25	110	3.05	90	11.25

Openers **Arthur Morris** and **Aiden Markram**, batsmen **Bruce Mitchell**, **Charlie Macartney**, and **Peter May**, all-rounder **Mushtaq Mohammad**, keeper **Deryck Murray**, spinner **Arthur Mailey**, and fast bowlers **Manny Martindale**, **Mohammad Abbas**, and **Mohammad Asif**.

The Ns XI

	tests	*runs*	*ri (adj)*	*wkts*	*rwi (adj)*
SM Nurse	29	2523	46.72		
Nazar Mohammad	5	277	34.62		
* AD Nourse	34	2960	47.74		
HM Nicholls	46	2544	36.86		
AW Nourse	45	2234	26.91 (30.53)	41	52.64 (58.75)
MA Noble	42	1997	27.35 (32.35)	121	14.66 (17.60)
RG Nadkarni	41	1414	21.10	88	21.47
† PM Nevill	17	468	20.34		
DJ Nash	32	729	16.20	93	16.23
M Ntini	101	699	6.02	390	14.04
L Ngidi	13	52	2.60	47	10.98

Openers **Seymour Nurse** and **Nazar Mohammad** (1921-1996), batsmen **Dudley Nourse**, **Henry Nicholls** and **Dave Nourse**, all-rounders **Monty Noble** and **Bapu Nadkarni** (1933-2020), keeper **Peter Nevill** (1985), and fast bowlers **Makhaya Ntini**, **Lungi Ngidi** and **Dion Nash**.

The Ps XI

	tests	*runs*	*ri (adj)*	*wkts*	*rwi (adj)*
WH Ponsford	29	2122	44.20		
G Pullar	28	1974	40.28		
RT Ponting	167	13278	46.58	5	397.44
RG Pollock	23	2256	55.02		
E Paynter	20	1540	49.67		
MJ Procter	7	226	22.60	41	5.12
†MJ Prior	79	4099	33.32		
GE Palmer	16	296	11.84 (26.84)	78	8.27 (14.04)
*SM Pollock	108	3781	24.23	421	11.08
R Peel	20	427	12.93 (24.60)	101	5.88 (10.13)
PM Pollock	28	607	14.80	116	10.83

Openers **Bill Ponsford** and **Geoff Pullar**, batsmen **Ricky Ponting**, **Graeme Pollock**, and **Eddie Paynter**, all-rounders **Mike Procter** and **Joey Palmer**, keeper **Matt Prior**, spinner **Bobby Peel**, and fast bowlers **Peter Pollock** and **Shaun Pollock**.

The Rs XI

	tests	*runs*	*ri (adj)*	*wkts*	*rwi (adj)*
BA Richards	4	508	72.57		
CAG Russell	10	910	50.55		
IVA Richards	121	8540	46.92	32	197.53
JE Root	117	9889	45.78	45	113.14
J Ryder	20	1394	43.56	17	71.97
*CEB Rice	0				
†RC Russell	54	1897	22.05		
T Richardson	14	177	7.37 (12.58)	88	6.87 (9.23)
K Rabada	52	786	9.94	243	8.76
S Ramadhin	43	361	6.22	158	13.93
BA Reid	27	93	2.73	113	9.15

Openers **Barry Richards** and **"Jack" Russell** (1887-1961), batsmen **Viv Richards**, **Joe Root**, and **Jack Ryder**, all-rounder **Clive Rice**, keeper **"Jack" Russell**, spinner **Sonny Ramadhin**, and fast bowlers **Tom Richardson**, **Bruce Reid** and **Kagiso Rabada**.

The Rs 2nd XI

	tests	*runs*	*ri (adj)*	*wkts*	*rwi (adj)*
MH Richardson	38	2776	42.70		
CJL Rogers	25	2015	41.97		
KS Ranjitsinhji	15	989	38.03 (43.03)		
LG Rowe	30	2047	41.77		
RB Richardson	86	5949	40.74		
* JR Reid	58	3428	31.74	85	28.24
W Rhodes	58	2345	23.72 (27.65)	127	19.10 (22.09)
† D Ramdin	74	2898	23.00		
AME Roberts	47	762	12.29	202	11.28
KAJ Roach	71	1083	9.50	242	14.37
CG Rackemann	12	53	3.78	39	14.95

Openers **Mark Richardson** and **Chris Rogers**, batsmen **Kumar Ranjitsinhji**, **Lawrence Rowe**, and **Richie Richardson**, all-rounders **John Reid** and **Wilfred Rhodes**, keeper **Denesh Ramdin**, and fast bowlers **Andy Roberts**, **Carl Rackemann** (1960) and **Kemar Roach**.

The Ss XI

	tests	*runs*	*ri (adj)*	*wkts*	*rwi (adj)*
H Sutcliffe	54	4555	54.22		
V Sehwag	103	8503	47.76	40	107.72
KC Sangakkara	134	12400	53.21		
SPD Smith	85	8010	53.04	18	177.22
* GS Sobers	93	8032	50.20	235	23.02
Shakib Al Hasan	59	4029	36.96	215	14.41
† AJ Stewart	133	8463	36.01		
FR Spofforth	18	217	7.48 (23.00)	94	5.87 (10.94)
DW Steyn	93	1251	10.51	439	8.93
Shaheen Shah Afridi	24	145	4.67	95	10.55
JV Saunders	14	39	1.69 (6.69)	79	7.76 (9.47)

Openers **Herbert Sutcliffe** and **Virender Sehwag**, batsmen **Kumar Sangakkara**, and **Steve Smith**, all-rounders **Garry Sobers** and **Shakib Al Hasan**, keeper **Alec Stewart**, spinner **Jack Saunders**, and fast bowlers **Dale Steyn**, **Fred Spofforth** and **Shaheen Shah Afridi**.

The Ss 2nd XI

	tests	*runs*	*ri (adj)*	*wkts*	*rwi (adj)*
A Shrewsbury	23	1277	31.92 (45.80)		
* GC Smith	116	9253	45.58	8	511.61
AG Steel	13	600	30.00 (45.00)	29	14.38 (24.73)
R Subba Row	13	984	44.72		
TT Samaraweera	81	5462	41.37	15	107.16
BA Stokes	79	5061	34.66	174	23.25
† Sarfaraz Ahmed	49	2657	30.89		
Saqlain Mushtaq	46	891	12.04	199	12.19
SR Clark	24	248	9.53	94	12.18
Shoaib Akhtar	46	544	8.11	178	11.83
Saeed Ajmal	35	451	8.50	178	10.57

Openers **Arthur Shrewsbury** and **Graeme Smith**, batsmen **Raman Subba Row** (1932) and **Thilan Samaraweera**, all-rounders **Allan Steel** and **Ben Stokes**, keeper **Sarfaraz Ahmed**, spinners **Saeed Ajmal** and **Saqlain Mushtaq**, and fast bowlers **Stuart Clark** and **Shoaib Akhtar**.

The Ts XI

	tests	*runs*	*ri (adj)*	*wkts*	*rwi (adj)*
GM Turner	41	2991	40.97		
VT Trumper	48	3163	35.53 (40.53)	8	74.28 (83.66)
IJL Trott	52	3835	41.23	5	528.00
SR Tendulkar	200	15921	48.39	46	170.75
GE Tyldesley	14	990	49.50		
* HW Taylor	42	2936	38.63 (40.01)	5	68.64 (77.44)
† HP Tillakaratne	83	4545	34.69		
CTB Turner	17	323	10.09 (21.18)	101	4.90 (8.34)
HJ Tayfield	37	862	14.36	170	9.29
FS Trueman	67	981	11.54	307	8.92
FH Tyson	17	230	9.58	76	7.08

Openers **Glenn Turner** and **Victor Trumper**, batsmen **Jonathan Trott**, **Sachin Tendulkar**, **Ernest Tyldesley**, and **Herbie Taylor**, keeper **Hashan Tillakaratne**, spinner **Hugh Tayfield**, and fast bowlers **Fred Trueman**, **Charlie Turner**, and **Frank Tyson**.

The Vs XI

	tests	*runs*	*ri (adj)*	*wkts*	*rwi (adj)*
PGV van der Bijl	5	460	51.11		
HG Vivian	7	421	42.10	17	21.90
GR Viswanath	91	6080	39.22		
BH Valentine	7	454	50.44		
* MP Vaughan	60	4223	38.74		
DB Vengsarkar	116	6868	37.12		
† K Verreynne	8	343	26.38		
WPUCJ Vaas	102	2786	18.20	330	15.92
AEE Vogler	15	340	13.07 (18.07)	64	9.94 (12.13)
H Verity	40	669	15.20	144	12.35
W Voce	27	308	8.10	98	14.50

Openers **Pieter van der Bijl** (1907-1973) and **Giff Vivian**, batsmen **Gundappa Viswanath**, **Bryan Valentine** (1908-1983), **Michael Vaughan**, and **Dilip Vengsarkar**, keeper **Kyle Verreynne** (1997), spinners **Hedley Verity** and **Bert Vogler**, and fast bowlers **Chaminda Vaas** and **Bill Voce** (1909-1984).

The Ws XI

	tests	*runs*	*ri (adj)*	*wkts*	*rwi (adj)*
DA Warner	94	7753	45.07	4	319.43
WM Woodfull	35	2300	42.59		
* FMM Worrell	51	3860	44.36	69	46.01
ED Weekes	48	4455	55.00		
† CL Walcott	44	3798	51.32		
KD Walters	74	5357	42.85	49	42.72
Wasim Akram	104	2898	19.71	414	10.32
SK Warne	144	3142	15.94	702	9.85
JH Wardle	28	653	15.92	102	10.39
WJ Whitty	14	161	8.47 (13.47)	65	8.12 (10.04)
Waqar Younis	87	1010	8.41	373	9.72

Openers **David Warner** and **Bill Woodfull**, batsmen **Frank Worrell**, **Everton Weekes**, and **Doug Walters**, keeper/batsman **Clyde Walcott**, spinners **Shane Warne** and **Johnny Wardle**, and fast bowlers **Wasim Akram**, **Waqar Younis**, and **Bill Whitty**.

The Ws 2nd XI

	tests	*runs*	*ri (adj)*	*wkts*	*rwi (adj)*
CF Walters	11	784	43.55		
C Washbrook	37	2569	38.92		
KS Williamson	83	7115	49.40	30	86.29
ME Waugh	128	8029	38.41	59	89.29
* SR Waugh	166	10671	41.36	92	60.57
FE Woolley	64	3283	33.50 (35.13)	83	35.54 (38.00)
† BJ Watling	73	3773	33.09		
MHN Walker	34	586	13.62	138	12.54
N Wagner	58	775	10.47	244	11.94
RGD Willis	90	840	6.56	325	12.79
CA Walsh	132	936	5.05	519	11.34

Openers **Cyril Walters** (1905-1992) and **Cyril Washbrook**, batsmen **Kane Williamson**, **Mark Waugh** and his twin **Steve Waugh**, all-rounder **Frank Woolley**, keeper **BJ Watling**, and fast bowlers **Courtney Walsh**, **Bob Willis**, **Max Walker** (1948-2016), and **Neil Wagner**.

The Ys XI

	tests	*runs*	*ri (adj)*	*wkts*	*rwi (adj)*
Yasir Hameed	25	1491	30.42		
BA Young	35	2034	29.91		
* Younis Khan	118	10099	47.41	9	187.89
GN Yallop	39	2756	39.37		
Yuvraj Singh	40	1900	30.64	9	236.37
NWD Yardley	20	812	23.88	21	32.05
B Yardley	33	978	18.11	125	14.67
† RA Young	5	169	16.90		
Yasir Shah	46	847	12.27	235	11.24
NS Yadav	35	404	10.10	102	20.99
UT Yadav	52	408	6.68	158	19.88

Openers **Yasir Hameed** (1978) and **Bryan Young** (1964), batsmen **Younis Khan**, **Graham Yallop** (1952), and **Yuvraj Singh**, all-rounders **Norman Yardley**, keeper **Reece Young** (1979), spinners **Bruce Yardley**, **Yasir Shah** and **Shivlal Yadav** (1957), and fast bowler **Umesh Yadav**.

INDIVIDUAL TEST STATS

All 3059 players in order of appearance. These are the basic stats only, for the purpose of showing RI and RWI. The "n/a" denotes matches approved by I.C.C. that obviously should not be given Test status, and the "adj" is a player's adjusted stats.

ENGLAND

	M	I	R	RI	IB	R	W	A	RWI
1876-77									
H Jupp	2	4	68	17.00					
J Selby	6	12	256	21.33					
HRJ Charlwood	2	4	63	15.75					
G Ulyett	25	39	949	-	35	1020	50		
n/a	2	3	48	-	3	28	2		
adj	23	36	901	25.02	32	992	48	20.66	13.77
A Greenwood	2	4	77	19.45					
T Armitage	2	3	33	11.00	1	15	0		
A Shaw	7	12	111	9.25	10	285	12	23.75	19.79
T Emmett	7	13	160	12.30	9	284	9	31.55	31.55
A Hill	2	4	101	25.25	4	130	7	18.57	10.61
James Lillywhite, jr	2	3	16	5.33	4	126	8	15.75	7.87
J Southerton	2	3	7	2.33	2	107	7	15.28	4.36
1878-79									
AP Lucas	5	9	157	17.44	2	54	0		
AJ Webbe	1	2	4	2.00					
AN Hornby	3	6	21	3.50	1	0	1	0.00	0.00
GRC Harris	4	6	145	24.16	2	29	0		
VPFA Royle	1	2	21	10.50	1	6	0		
FA MacKinnon	1	2	5	2.50					
CA Absolom	1	2	58	29.00					
L Hone	1	2	13	6.50					
SS Schultz	1	2	20	10.00	2	26	1	26.00	52.00
1880									
EM Grace	1	2	36	18.00					
WG Grace	22	36	1098	30.50	13	236	9	26.22	37.87
W Barnes	21	33	725	21.96	28	793	51	15.54	8.53
F Penn	1	2	50	25.00	1	2	0		
AG Steel	13	20	600	30.00	20	605	29	20.86	14.38
A Lyttelton	4	7	94	13.42	1	19	4	4.75	1.18
GF Grace	1	2	0	0.00					
F Morley	4	6	6	1.00	8	296	16	18.50	9.25
1881-82									
RG Barlow	17	30	591	19.70	26	767	34	22.55	17.24
W Bates	15	26	656	25.23	23	821	50	16.42	7.55
A Shrewsbury	23	40	1277	31.92	1	2	0		
WE Midwinter [Aus]	4	7	95	13.57	5	272	10	27.20	13.60
WH Scotton	15	25	510	20.40	1	20	0		
R Pilling	8	13	91	7.00					
E Peate	9	14	70	5.00	15	683	31	22.03	10.65
1882									
CT Studd	5	9	160	17.77	7	98	3	32.66	76.20
JM Read	17	29	461	-					
n/a	2	3	16	-					
adj	15	26	445	17.11					

1882-83									
IFW Bligh	4	7	62	8.85					
CFH Leslie	4	7	106	15.14	3	44	4	11.00	8.25
WW Read	18	27	720	26.66	2	63	0		
EFS Tylecote	6	9	152	16.88					
GB Studd	4	7	31	4.42					
GF Vernon	1	2	14	7.00					
1884									
TC O'Brien	5	8	59	-					
n/a	2	3	33	-					
adj	3	5	26	5.20					
S Christopherson	1	1	17	17.00	2	69	1	69.00	138.00
1884-85									
W Flowers	8	14	254	18.14	13	296	14	21.14	19.63
J Briggs	33	50	815	-	49	2095	118		
n/a	2	2	6	-	4	101	21		
adj	31	48	809	16.85	45	1994	97	20.55	9.53
W Attewell	10	15	150	10.00	18	626	28	22.35	14.36
R Peel	20	33	427	12.93	35	1715	101	16.98	5.98
J Hunter	5	7	93	13.28					
1886									
GA Lohmann	18	26	213	-	36	1205	112		
n/a	3	4	10	-	6	203	35		
adj	15	22	203	9.22	30	1002	77	13.01	5.06
1886-87									
W Gunn	11	20	392	19.60					
M Sherwin	3	6	30	5.00					
R Wood	1	2	6	3.00					
1887-88									
AE Stoddart	16	30	996	33.20	6	94	2	47.00	141.00
W Newham	1	2	26	13.00					
1888									
R Abel	13	22	744	-					
n/a	2	3	189	-					
adj	11	19	555	29.21					
J Shuter	1	1	28	28.00					
FH Sugg	2	2	55	27.50					
H Wood	4	4	204	-					
n/a	2	2	62	-					
adj	2	2	142	71.00					
1888-89									
F Hearne	2	2	47	-					
n/a	2	2	47	-					
adj	0	-	-	-					
MP Bowden	2	2	25	-					
n/a	2	2	25	-					
adj	0	-	-	-					
CA Smith	1	1	3	-	2	61	7		
n/a	1	1	3	-	2	61	7		
adj	0	-	-	-	-	-	-		
BAF Grieve	2	3	40	-					
n/a	2	3	40	-					
adj	0	-	-	-					
CJ Coventry	2	2	13	-					
n/a	2	2	13	-					
adj	0	-	-	-					
AJ Fothergill	2	2	32	-	4	90	8		
n/a	2	2	32	-	4	90	8		
adj	0	-	-	-	-	-	-		

JEP McMaster	1	1	0	-					
n/a	1	1	0	-					
adj	0	-	-	-					
1890									
G MacGregor	8	11	96	12.00					
J Cranston	1	2	31	15.50					
JW Sharpe	3	6	44	7.33	6	305	11	27.72	15.12
F Martin	2	2	14	7.00	3	141	14	10.07	2.15
1891-92									
G Bean	3	5	92	18.40					
H Philipson	5	8	63	7.87					
W Chatterton	1	1	48	-					
n/a	1	1	48	-					
adj	0	-	-	-					
A Hearne n	1	1	9	-					
n/a	1	1	9	-					
adj	0	-	-	-					
WL Murdoch [Aus]	1	1	12	-					
n/a	1	1	12	-					
adj	0	-	-	-					
GG Hearne	1	1	0	-					
n/a	1	1	0	-					
adj	0	-	-	-					
VA Barton	1	1	23	-					
n/a	1	1	23	-					
adj	0	-	-	-					
AD Pougher	1	1	17	-	1	26	3		
n/a	1	1	17	-	1	26	3		
adj	0	-	-	-	-	-	-		
JJ Ferris [Aus]	1	1	16	-	2	91	13		
n/a	1	1	16	-	2	91	13		
adj	0	-	-	-	-	-	-		
JT Hearne	12	18	126	-	20	1082	49		
n/a	1	1	40	-	1	12	1		
adj	11	17	86	5.05	19	1070	48	22.29	8.82
1893									
FS Jackson	20	33	1415	42.87	27	799	24	33.29	37.45
E Wainwright	5	9	132	14.66	3	73	0		
WH Lockwood	12	16	231	14.43	18	883	43	20.53	8.59
AW Mold	3	3	0	0.00	5	234	7	33.42	23.87
A Ward	7	13	487	37.46					
W Brockwell	7	12	202	16.83	9	309	5	61.80	111.24
T Richardson	14	24	177	7.37	24	2220	88	25.22	6.87
1894-95									
AC MacLaren	35	61	1931	31.65					
JT Brown	8	16	470	29.37	1	22	0		
FGJ Ford	5	9	168	18.66	6	129	1	129.00	774.00
LH Gay	1	2	37	18.50					
1895-96									
TW Hayward	35	60	1999	-	22	514	14		
n/a	3	4	189	-	3	92	2		
adj	32	56	1810	32.32	19	422	12	35.16	55.67
CB Fry	26	41	1223	-	1	3	0		
n/a	2	3	122	-	0	-	-		
adj	24	38	1101	28.97	1	3	0		
AJL Hill	3	4	251	-	1	8	4		
n/a	3	4	251	-	1	8	4		
adj	0	-	-	-	-	-	-		

SMJ Woods [Aus]	3	4	122	-	3	129	5		
n/a	3	4	122	-	3	129	5		
adj	0	-	-	-	-	-	-		
HR Bromley-Davenport									
	4	6	128	-	4	98	4		
n/a	4	6	128	-	4	98	4		
adj	0	-	-	-	-	-	-		
MB Hawke	5	8	55	-					
n/a	5	8	55	-					
adj	0	-	-	-					
CW Wright	3	4	125	-					
n/a	3	4	125	-					
adj	0	-	-	-					
AM Miller	1	2	24	-					
n/a	1	2	24	-					
adj	0	-	-	-					
HR Butt	3	4	22	-					
n/a	3	4	22	-					
adj	0	-	-	-					
C Heseltine	2	2	18	-	3	84	5		
n/a	2	2	18		3	84	5		
adj	0	-	-	-	-	-	-		
EJ Tyler	1	1	0	-	2	65	4		
n/a	1	1	0	-	2	65	4		
adj	0	-	-	-	-	-	-		
1896									
AFA Lilley	35	52	903	17.36	1	23	1	23.00	23.00
KS Ranjitsinhji	15	26	989	38.03	4	39	1	39.00	156.00
EG Wynyard	3	6	72	12.00	2	17	0		
1897-98									
JR Mason	5	10	129	12.90	7	149	2	74.50	260.75
W Storer	6	11	215	19.54	4	108	2	54.00	108.00
NF Druce	5	9	252	28.00					
GH Hirst	24	38	790	20.78	44	1770	59	30.00	22.37
1898-99									
F Mitchell [SA]	2	4	88	-					
n/a	2	4	88	-					
adj	0	-	-	-					
PF Warner	15	28	622	-					
n/a	2	4	207	-					
adj	13	24	415	17.29					
JT Tyldesley	31	55	1661	-					
n/a	2	4	159	-					
adj	29	51	1502	29.45					
CEM Wilson	2	4	42	-					
n/a	2	4	42	-					
adj	0	-	-	-					
WR Cuttell	2	4	65	-	3	73	6		
n/a	2	4	65	-	3	73	6		
adj	0	-	-	-	-	-	-	-	
AE Trott [Aus]	2	4	23	-	4	198	17	-	
n/a	2	4	23	-	4	198	17	-	
adj	0	-	-	-	-	-	-	-	
FW Milligan	2	4	58	-	2	29	0	-	
n/a	2	4	58	-	2	29	0	-	
adj	0	-	-	-	-	-	-	-	
JH Board	6	12	108	-					
n/a	2	4	52	-					
adj	4	8	56	7.00					

S Haigh	11	18	113	-	16	622	24		
n/a	2	4	28	-	4	220	14		
adj	9	14	85	6.07	12	402	10	40.20	48.24
AG Archer	1	2	31	-					
n/a	1	2	31	-					
adj	0	-	-	-					
1899									
W Rhodes	58	98	2325	23.72	90	3425	127	26.96	19.10
CL Townsend	2	3	51	17.00	3	75	3	25.00	25.00
GL Jessop	18	26	569	21.88	14	354	10	35.40	49.56
W Mead	1	2	7	3.50	1	91	1	91.00	91.00
WG Quaife	7	13	228	17.53	1	6	0		
HI Young	2	2	43	21.50	4	262	12	21.83	7.27
WM Bradley	2	2	23	11.50	4	233	6	38.83	25.88
AO Jones	12	21	291	13.85	4	133	3	44.33	59.10
1901-02									
LC Braund	23	41	987	24.07	38	1810	47	38.51	31.13
JR Gunn	6	10	85	8.50	9	387	18	21.50	10.75
SF Barnes	27	39	242	6.20	50	3106	189	16.43	4.34
C Blythe	19	31	183	5.90	37	1863	100	18.63	6.89
CP McGahey	2	4	38	9.50					
1902									
LCH Palairet	2	4	49	12.25					
FW Tate	1	2	9	4.50	2	51	2	25.50	25.50
1903-04									
EG Arnold	10	15	160	10.66	19	788	31	25.41	15.57
RE Foster	8	14	602	43.00					
BJT Bosanquet	7	14	147	10.50	11	604	25	24.16	10.63
AE Relf	13	21	416	19.80	21	624	25	24.96	20.96
AE Knight	3	6	81	13.50					
A Fielder	6	12	78	6.50	10	711	26	27.34	10.51
1905									
D Denton	11	22	424	19.27					
A Warren	1	1	7	7.00	2	113	6	18.83	6.27
RH Spooner	10	15	481	32.06					
W Brearley	4	5	21	4.20	7	359	17	21.11	8.69
1905-06									
FL Fane	14	27	682	25.25					
EG Hayes	5	9	86	9.55	3	52	1	52.00	156.00
JN Crawford	12	23	469	20.39	23	1150	39	29.48	17.38
WS Lees	5	9	66	7.33	9	467	26	17.96	6.21
LJ Moon	4	8	182	22.75					
JC Hartley	2	4	15	3.75	3	115	1	115.00	345.00
1907									
NA Knox	2	4	24	6.00	3	105	3	35.00	35.00
1907-08									
RA Young	2	4	27	6.75					
G Gunn	15	29	1120	38.62	1	8	0		
KL Hutchings	7	12	341	28.41	4	81	1	81.00	324.00
J Hardstaff, sr	5	10	311	31.10					
JB Hobbs	61	102	5410	53.03	11	165	1	165.00	1815.00
J Humphries	3	6	44	7.33					
1909									
GJ Thompson	6	10	273	27.30	11	638	23	27.73	13.26
JH King	1	2	64	32.00	1	99	1	99.00	99.00
J Sharp	3	6	188	31.33	4	111	3	37.00	49.33
FE Woolley	64	98	3283	33.50	87	2815	83	33.91	35.54
DW Carr	1	1	0	0.00	2	282	7	40.28	11.50
1909-10									
MC Bird	10	16	280	17.50	12	120	8	15.00	22.50

CP Buckenham	4	7	43	6.14	8	593	21	28.23	10.75
HDG Levenson-Gower	3	6	95	15.83					
GHT Simpson-Hayward	5	8	105	13.12	10	420	23	18.26	7.93
H Strudwick	28	42	230	5.47					
NC Tufnell	1	1	14	14.00					
1911-12									
SP Kinneir	1	2	52	26.00					
CP Mead	17	26	1185	45.57					
JW Hearne	24	36	806	22.38	31	1462	30	48.73	50.35
FR Foster	11	15	330	22.00	19	926	45	20.57	8.86
JWHT Douglas	23	35	962	27.48	37	1486	45	33.02	27.14
EJ Smith	11	14	113	8.07					
JW Hitch	7	10	103	10.30	9	325	7	46.42	59.68
J Vine	2	3	46	15.33					
1912									
H Dean	3	4	10	2.50	5	153	11	13.90	6.31
1913-14									
LH Tennyson	9	12	345	28.75	1	1	0		
MW Booth	2	2	46	23.00	3	130	7	18.57	7.95
1920-21									
CAG Russell	10	18	910	50.55					
EH Hendren	51	83	3525	42.46	2	31	1	31.00	62.00
CH Parkin	10	16	160	10.00	16	1128	32	35.25	17.62
A Waddington	2	4	16	4.00	3	119	1	119.00	357.00
JWH Makepeace	4	8	279	34.87					
H Howell	5	8	15	1.87	7	559	7	79.85	79.85
PGH Fender	13	21	380	18.09	22	1185	29	40.86	30.99
A Dolphin	1	2	1	0.50					
ER Wilson	1	2	10	5.00	2	36	3	12.00	7.99
1921									
DJ Knight	2	4	54	13.50					
P Holmes	7	14	357	25.50					
GE Tyldesley	14	20	990	49.50	1	2	0		
VWC Jupp	8	13	208	16.00	14	616	28	22.00	11.00
TL Richmond	1	2	6	3.00	2	86	2	43.00	43.00
AE Dipper	1	2	51	25.50					
AJ Evans	1	2	18	9.00					
NE Haig	5	9	126	14.00	10	448	13	34.46	26.50
FJ Durston	1	2	8	4.00	2	136	5	27.20	10.88
HTW Hardinge	1	2	30	15.00					
A Ducat	1	2	5	2.50					
G Brown	7	12	299	24.91					
JC White	15	22	239	10.86	27	1581	49	32.26	17.77
C Hallows	2	2	42	21.00					
CWL Parker	1	1	3	3.00	1	32	2	16.00	8.00
A Sandham	14	23	879	38.21					
1922-23									
FT Mann	5	9	281	31.22					
AW Carr	11	13	237	18.23					
GTS Stevens	10	17	263	15.47	17	648	20	32.40	27.54
AS Kennedy	5	8	93	11.62	9	599	31	19.32	5.60
AER Gilligan	11	16	209	13.06	20	1046	36	29.05	16.13
GG Macaulay	8	10	112	11.20	13	662	24	27.58	14.93
GB Street	1	2	11	5.50					
1924									
H Sutcliffe	54	84	4555	54.22					
R Kilner	9	8	233	29.12	12	734	24	30.58	15.29

MW Tate	39	52	1198	23.03	68	4055	155	26.16	11.47
GEC Wood	3	2	7	3.50					
APF Chapman	26	36	925	25.69	2	20	0		
RK Tyldesley	7	7	47	6.71	11	619	19	32.57	18.85
JCW MacBryan	1	-	-	-					
G Geary	14	20	249	12.45	22	1353	46	29.41	14.06
G Duckworth	24	28	234	8.35					
1924-25									
AP Freeman	12	16	154	9.62	22	1707	66	25.86	8.62
WW Whysall	4	7	209	29.85	1	9	0		
1926									
CF Root	3	-	-	-	3	194	8	24.25	9.09
H Larwood	21	28	485	17.32	36	2212	78	28.35	13.08
1927-28									
WR Hammond	85	140	7249	51.77	110	3138	83	37.80	50.09
RES Wyatt	40	64	1839	28.73	36	642	18	35.66	71.32
GB Legge	5	7	299	42.71	1	34	0		
WE Astill	9	15	190	12.66	18	856	25	34.24	24.65
RT Stanyforth	4	6	13	2.16					
IAR Peebles	13	17	98	5.76	20	1391	45	30.91	13.73
SJ Staples	3	5	65	13.00	6	435	15	29.00	11.60
EW Dawson	5	9	175	19.44					
H Elliott	4	5	61	12.20					
1928									
DR Jardine	22	33	1296	39.27	1	10	0		
H Smith	1	1	7	7.00					
M Leyland	41	65	2764	42.52	27	585	6	97.50	438.75
1929									
ET Killick	2	4	81	20.25					
KS Duleepsinhji	12	19	995	52.36	1	7	0		
J O'Connor	4	7	153	21.85	4	72	1	72.00	288.00
RWV Robins	19	27	612	22.66	34	1758	64	27.46	14.58
EH Bowley	5	7	252	36.00	4	116	0		
F Barratt	5	4	28	7.00	7	235	5	47.00	65.80
LEG Ames	47	72	2434	33.80					
EW Clark	8	9	36	4.00	15	899	32	28.09	13.16
1929-30									
AHH Gilligan	4	4	71	17.75					
MS Nichols	14	19	355	18.68	24	1152	41	28.09	16.44
TS Worthington	9	11	321	29.18	11	316	8	39.50	54.31
MJL Turnbull	9	13	224	17.23					
WL Cornford	4	4	36	9.00					
MJC Allom	5	3	14	4.66	8	265	14	18.92	10.81
FSG Calthorpe	4	7	129	18.42	4	91	1	91.00	364.00
W Voce	27	38	308	8.10	51	2733	98	27.88	14.50
LF Townsend	4	6	97	16.16	8	205	6	34.16	45.54
1930									
GOB Allen	25	33	750	22.72	45	2379	81	29.37	16.31
TWJ Goddard	8	5	13	2.60	13	588	22	26.72	15.78
1930-31									
HW Lee	1	2	19	9.50					
W Farrimond	4	7	116	16.57					
1931									
AH Bakewell	6	9	409	45.44	1	8	0		
J Arnold	1	2	34	17.00					
FR Brown	22	30	734	24.46	31	1398	45	31.06	21.39
H Verity	40	44	669	15.20	73	3510	144	24.37	12.35
E Paynter	20	31	1540	49.67					
1932									
WE Bowes	15	11	28	2.54	29	1519	68	22.33	9.52

1932-33									
IAK Pataudi [Ind]	3	5	144	28.80					
TB Mitchell	5	6	20	3.33	8	498	8	62.25	62.25
1933									
CF Walters	11	18	784	43.55					
J Langridge	8	9	242	26.88	13	413	19	21.73	14.86
CJ Barnett	20	35	1098	31.37	8	93	0		
CS Marriott	1	1	0	0.00	2	96	11	8.72	1.58
1933-34									
A Mitchell	6	10	298	29.80	1	4	0		
BH Valentine	7	9	454	50.44					
WHV Levett	1	2	7	3.50					
1934									
K Farnes	15	17	58	3.41	27	1719	60	28.65	12.89
JL Hopwood	2	3	12	4.00	3	155	0		
WW Keeton	2	4	57	14.25					
1934-35									
CIJ Smith	5	10	102	10.20	9	393	15	26.20	15.72
J Iddon	5	7	170	24.28	2	27	0		
ERT Holmes	5	9	114	12.66	4	76	2	38.00	76.00
GAE Paine	4	7	97	13.85	7	467	17	27.47	11.31
WE Hollies	13	15	37	2.46	22	1332	44	30.27	15.13
DCH Townsend	3	6	77	12.83	1	9	0		
1935									
NS Mitchell-Innes	1	1	5	5.00					
W Barber	2	4	83	20.75	1	0	1	0.00	0.00
D Smith	2	4	128	32.00					
J Hardstaff, jr	23	38	1636	43.05					
JM Sims	4	4	16	4.00	8	480	11	43.63	31.73
JC Clay	1	-	-	-	2	75	0		
HD Read	1	-	-	-	2	200	6	33.33	11.10
1936									
H Gimblett	3	5	129	25.80					
AE Fagg	5	8	150	18.75					
LB Fishlock	4	5	47	9.40					
AR Gover	4	1	2	2.00	7	359	8	44.87	39.26
1937									
JH Parks	1	2	29	14.50	2	36	3	12.00	7.99
L Hutton	79	138	6971	50.51	14	232	3	77.33	360.87
AW Wellard	2	4	47	11.75	4	237	7	33.85	19.34
C Washbrook	37	66	2569	38.92	2	33	1	33.00	66.00
DCS Compton	78	131	5807	44.32	66	1410	25	56.40	148.89
ADG Matthews	1	1	2	2.00	2	65	2	32.50	32.50
1938									
WJ Edrich	39	63	2440	38.73	51	1693	41	41.29	51.36
RA Sinfield	1	1	6	6.00	2	123	2	61.50	61.50
DVP Wright	34	39	289	7.41	59	4224	108	39.11	21.36
WFF Price	1	2	6	3.00					
A Wood	4	5	80	16.00					
1938-39									
PA Gibb	8	13	581	44.69					
NWD Yardley	20	34	812	23.88	20	707	21	33.66	32.05
LL Wilkinson	3	2	3	1.50	5	271	7	38.71	27.64
RTD Perks	2	2	3	1.50	3	355	11	32.27	8.80
1939									
WH Copson	3	1	6	6.00	6	297	15	19.80	7.92
N Oldfield	1	2	99	49.50					
1946									
JT Ikin	18	31	606	19.54	11	354	3	118.00	432.66

TF Smailes	1	1	25	25.00	2	62	3	20.66	13.77
AV Bedser	51	71	714	10.05	92	5876	236	24.89	9.70
R Pollard	4	3	13	4.33	7	378	15	25.20	11.75
TPB Smith	4	5	33	6.60	5	319	3	106.33	177.21
TG Evans	91	133	2438	18.33					
1947									
HE Dollery	4	7	72	10.28					
C Cook	1	2	4	2.00	2	127	0		
JW Martin	1	2	26	13.00	2	129	1	129.00	258.00
GH Pope	1	1	8	8.00	2	85	1	85.00	170.00
K Cranston	8	14	209	14.92	13	461	18	25.61	18.49
C Gladwin	8	11	170	15.45	15	571	15	38.06	38.06
JA Young	8	10	28	2.80	14	757	17	44.52	36.66
HJ Butler	2	2	15	7.50	4	215	12	17.91	5.96
JDB Robertson	11	21	881	41.95	5	58	2	29.00	72.50
R Howorth	5	10	145	14.50	10	635	19	33.42	17.58
1947-48									
W Place	3	6	144	24.00					
D Brookes	1	2	17	8.50					
GA Smithson	2	3	70	23.33					
JC Laker	46	63	676	10.73	86	4101	193	21.24	9.46
MF Tremlett	3	5	20	4.00	5	226	4	56.50	70.62
SC Griffith	3	5	157	31.40					
JH Wardle	28	41	653	15.92	52	2080	102	20.39	10.39
1948									
A Coxon	1	2	19	9.50	2	172	3	57.33	38.21
GM Emmett	1	2	10	5.00					
JF Crapp	7	13	319	24.53					
JG Dewes	5	10	121	12.10					
AJ Watkins	15	24	810	33.75	20	554	11	50.36	91.56
1948-49									
RT Simpson	27	45	1401	31.13	3	22	2	11.00	16.50
FG Mann	7	12	376	31.33					
RO Jenkins	9	12	198	16.50	18	1098	32	34.31	19.29
1949									
A Wharton	1	2	20	10.00					
TE Bailey	61	91	2290	25.16	95	3856	132	29.21	21.02
DB Close	22	37	887	23.97	23	532	18	29.55	37.75
HL Jackson	2	2	15	7.50	4	155	7	22.14	12.65
1950									
GHG Doggart	2	4	76	19.00					
R Berry	2	4	6	1.50	4	228	9	25.33	11.25
WGA Parkhouse	7	13	373	28.69					
DJ Insole	9	17	408	24.00					
D Shackleton	7	13	113	8.69	13	768	18	42.66	30.80
DS Sheppard	22	33	1172	35.51					
AJW McIntyre	3	6	19	3.16					
MJ Hilton	4	6	37	6.16	6	477	14	34.07	14.60
1950-51									
JJ Warr	2	4	4	1.00	3	281	1	281.00	843.00
R Tattersall	16	17	50	2.94	29	1513	58	26.08	13.04
JB Statham	70	87	675	7.75	129	6261	252	24.84	12.71
1951									
W Watson	23	37	879	23.75					
TW Graveney	79	123	4882	39.69	9	167	1	167.00	1503.00
FA Lowson	7	13	245	18.84					
PBH May	66	106	4537	42.80					
DV Brennan	2	2	16	8.00					
1951-52									
D Kenyon	8	15	192	12.80					

DB Carr	2	4	135	33.75	2	140	2	70.00	70.00
RT Spooner	7	14	354	25.28					
ND Howard	4	6	86	14.33					
F Ridgway	5	6	49	8.16	7	379	7	54.14	54.14
E Leadbeater	2	2	40	20.00	4	218	2	109.00	218.00
CJ Poole	3	5	161	32.20	1	9	0		
1952									
FS Trueman	67	85	981	11.54	127	6625	307	21.57	8.92
GAR Lock	49	63	742	11.77	88	4451	174	25.58	12.93
1953-54									
AE Moss	9	7	61	8.71	16	626	21	29.80	22.70
CH Palmer	1	2	22	11.00	1	15	0		
1954									
R Appleyard	9	9	51	5.66	17	554	31	17.87	9.79
JM Parks	46	68	1962	28.85	2	51	1	51.00	102.00
JE McConnon	2	3	18	6.00	3	74	4	18.50	13.87
FH Tyson	17	24	230	9.58	29	1411	76	18.56	7.08
PJ Loader	13	19	76	4.00	26	878	39	22.51	15.00
1954-55									
MC Cowdrey	114	188	7624	40.55	10	104	0		
KV Andrew	2	4	29	7.25					
1955									
KF Barrington	82	131	6806	51.95	50	1300	29	44.82	77.27
FJ Titmus	53	76	1449	19.06	90	4931	153	32.22	18.95
1956									
PE Richardson	34	56	2061	36.80	3	48	3	16.00	16.00
ASM Oakman	2	2	14	7.00	1	21	0		
1957									
DV Smith	3	4	25	6.25	4	97	1	97.00	388.00
DW Richardson	1	1	33	33.00					
1958									
MJK Smith	50	78	2278	29.20	5	128	1	128.00	640.00
CA Milton	6	9	204	22.66	1	12	0		
R Subba Row	13	22	984	44.72	1	2	0		
ER Dexter	62	102	4502	44.13	80	2306	66	34.93	42.33
R Illingworth	61	90	1836	20.40	100	3807	122	31.20	25.57
1958-59									
R Swetman	11	17	254	14.94					
JB Mortimore	9	12	243	20.25	15	733	13	56.38	65.05
1959									
K Taylor	3	5	57	11.40	1	6	0		
MJ Horton	2	2	60	30.00	3	59	2	29.50	44.25
T Greenhough	4	4	4	1.00	8	357	16	22.31	11.15
G Pullar	28	49	1974	40.28	3	37	1	37.00	111.00
HJ Rhodes	2	1	0	0.00	4	244	9	27.11	12.04
1959-60									
DA Allen	39	51	918	18.00	65	3779	122	30.97	16.50
1960									
RW Barber	28	45	1495	33.22	42	1806	42	43.00	43.00
PM Walker	3	4	128	32.00	3	34	0		
DEV Padgett	2	4	51	12.75	1	8	0		
1961									
JT Murray	21	28	506	18.07					
JA Flavell	4	6	31	5.16	6	367	7	52.42	44.93
1961-62									
WE Russell	10	18	362	20.11	2	44	0		
DW White	2	2	0	0.00	3	119	4	29.75	22.31
A Brown	2	1	3	3.00	4	150	3	50.00	66.66
DR Smith	5	5	38	7.60	8	359	6	59.83	79.77
BR Knight	29	38	812	21.36	54	2223	70	31.75	24.49

PH Parfitt	37	52	1882	36.19	22	574	12	47.83	87.68
G Millman	6	7	60	8.57					
1962------------									
MJ Stewart	8	12	385	32.08					
LJ Coldwell	7	7	9	1.28	12	610	22	27.72	15.11
JDF Larter	10	7	16	2.28	20	941	37	25.43	13.74
1962-63------------									
AC Smith	6	7	118	16.85					
1963------------									
JH Edrich	77	127	5138	40.45	2	23	0		
PJ Sharpe	12	21	786	37.42					
JB Bolus	7	12	496	41.34	1	16	0		
1963-64------------									
D Wilson	6	7	75	10.71	12	466	11	42.36	46.21
JG Binks	2	4	91	22.75					
JSE Price	15	15	66	4.40	27	1401	40	35.02	23.63
IJ Jones	15	17	38	2.23	27	1769	44	40.20	24.66
1964------------									
G Boycott	108	193	8114	42.04	20	382	7	54.57	155.91
N Gifford	15	20	179	8.95	21	1026	33	31.09	19.78
TW Cartwright	5	7	26	3.71	7	544	15	36.26	16.92
FE Rumsey	5	5	30	6.00	9	461	17	27.11	14.35
1964-65------------									
NI Thomson	5	4	69	17.25	10	568	9	63.11	70.12
KE Palmer	1	1	10	10.00	2	189	1	189.00	378.00
1965------------									
JA Snow	49	71	772	10.87	93	5387	202	26.66	12.27
DJ Brown	26	34	342	10.05	46	2237	79	28.31	16.48
K Higgs	15	19	185	9.73	27	1473	71	20.74	7.88
1966------------									
C Milburn	9	16	654	40.87					
BL D'Oliveira	44	70	2484	35.48	66	1859	47	39.55	55.53
DL Underwood	86	116	937	8.07	151	7674	297	25.83	13.13
DL Amiss	50	88	3612	41.04					
1967------------									
RNS Hobbs	7	8	34	4.25	11	481	12	40.08	36.73
APE Knott	95	149	4389	29.45					
GG Arnold	34	46	421	9.15	61	3254	115	28.29	15.00
1967-68------------									
PI Pocock	25	37	206	5.56	43	2976	67	44.41	28.50
1968------------									
RM Prideaux	3	6	102	17.00	1	12	0		
KWR Fletcher	59	96	3272	34.08	13	193	2	96.50	627.25
1968-69------------									
RMH Cottam	4	5	27	5.40	8	327	14	23.35	13.34
1969------------									
JH Hampshire	8	16	403	25.18					
A Ward	5	6	40	6.66	9	453	14	32.35	20.79
MH Denness	28	45	1667	37.04					
1970-71------------									
BW Luckhurst	21	41	1298	31.65	4	32	1	32.00	128.00
K Shuttleworth	5	6	46	7.66	9	427	12	35.58	26.68
P Lever	17	18	350	19.44	31	1509	41	36.80	27.82
RGD Willis	90	128	840	6.56	165	8190	325	25.20	12.79
RW Taylor	57	83	1156	13.92	1	6	0		
1971------------									
RA Hutton	5	8	219	27.37	8	257	9	28.55	25.37
JA Jameson	4	8	214	26.75	1	17	1	17.00	17.00
1972------------									
AW Greig	58	93	3599	38.69	93	4541	141	32.20	21.23

B Wood	12	21	454	21.61	5	50	0		
1972-73									
AR Lewis	9	16	457	28.56					
CM Old	46	66	845	12.80	81	4020	143	28.11	15.92
GRJ Roope	21	32	860	26.87	6	76	0		
J Birkenshaw	5	7	148	21.14	9	469	13	36.07	24.97
1973									
FC Hayes	9	17	244	14.35					
1974									
M Hendrick	30	35	128	3.65	54	2248	87	25.83	16.03
D Lloyd	9	15	552	36.80	2	17	0		
1975									
GA Gooch	118	215	8900	41.39	66	1069	23	46.47	133.34
DS Steele	8	16	673	42.06	4	39	2	19.50	39.00
RA Woolmer	19	34	1059	31.14	13	299	4	74.75	242.93
PH Edmonds	51	65	875	13.46	84	4273	125	34.18	22.96
1976									
JM Brearley	39	66	1442	21.84					
MWW Selvey	3	5	15	3.00	5	343	6	57.16	47.63
JC Balderstone	2	4	39	9.75	1	80	1	80.00	80.00
P Willey	26	50	1184	23.68	20	456	7	65.14	186.11
G Miller	34	51	1213	23.78	50	1859	60	30.98	25.81
1976-77									
GD Barlow	3	5	17	3.40					
JK Lever	21	31	306	9.87	38	1951	73	26.72	13.90
DW Randall	47	79	2470	31.26	2	3	0		
RW Tolchard	4	7	129	18.42					
1977									
IT Botham	102	161	5200	32.29	168	10878	383	28.40	12.45
1977-78									
BC Rose	9	16	358	22.37					
GA Cope	3	3	40	13.33	5	277	8	34.62	21.63
MW Gatting	79	138	4409	31.94	32	317	4	79.25	634.00
CT Radley	8	10	481	48.10					
1978									
DI Gower	117	204	8231	40.34	5	20	1	20.00	100.00
JE Emburey	64	96	1713	17.84	103	5646	147	38.40	26.90
1979									
AR Butcher	1	2	34	17.00	1	9	0		
DL Bairstow	4	7	125	17.85					
1979-80									
GR Dilley	41	58	521	8.98	65	4107	138	29.76	14.01
W Larkins	13	25	493	19.72					
GB Stevenson	2	2	28	14.00	3	183	5	36.60	21.96
1980									
CJ Tavare	31	56	1755	31.33	2	11	0		
CWJ Athey	23	41	919	22.41					
1980-81									
PR Downton	30	48	785	16.35					
RO Butcher	3	5	71	14.20					
RD Jackman	4	6	42	7.00	7	445	14	31.78	15.89
1981									
PJW Allott	13	18	213	11.83	22	1084	26	41.69	35.27
PWG Parker	1	2	13	6.50					
1981-82									
G Cook	7	13	203	15.61	3	27	0		
1982									
AJ Lamb	79	139	4656	33.49	6	23	1	23.00	138.00
DR Pringle	30	50	695	13.90	52	2518	70	35.97	26.72
IA Greig	2	4	26	6.50	3	114	4	28.50	21.37

EE Hemmings	16	21	383	18.23	28	1825	43	42.44	27.63
G Fowler	21	37	1307	35.32	3	11	0		
VJ Marks	6	10	249	24.90	10	484	11	44.00	39.99
1982-83									
NG Cowans	19	29	175	6.03	36	2003	51	39.27	27.71
1983									
CL Smith	8	14	392	28.00	4	39	3	13.00	17.33
NA Foster	29	45	446	9.91	47	2891	88	32.85	17.54
NGB Cook	15	26	179	6.88	25	1689	52	32.48	15.61
1983-84									
ACS Pigott	1	2	12	6.00	1	75	2	37.50	18.75
1984									
TA Lloyd	1	1	10	10.00					
BC Broad	25	44	1661	37.75	1	4	0		
VP Terry	2	3	16	5.33					
RM Ellison	11	16	202	12.62	20	1048	35	29.94	17.10
JP Agnew	3	4	10	2.50	6	373	4	93.25	139.87
1984-85									
RT Robinson	29	49	1601	32.67	1	0	0		
CS Cowdrey	6	8	101	12.62	9	309	4	77.25	173.81
1985									
A Sidebottom	1	1	2	2.00	1	65	1	65.00	65.00
LB Taylor	2	1	1	1.00	4	178	4	44.50	44.50
1985-86									
DM Smith	2	4	80	20.00					
JGThomas	5	10	83	8.30	8	504	10	50.40	40.32
WN Slack	3	6	81	13.50					
1986									
BN French	16	21	308	14.66					
MR Benson	1	2	51	25.50					
NV Radford	3	4	21	5.25	5	351	4	87.75	109.68
MD Moxon	10	17	455	26.76	2	30	0		
GC Small	17	24	263	10.95	31	1871	55	34.01	19.16
1986-87									
CJ Richards	8	13	285	21.92					
PAJ DeFreitas	44	68	934	13.73	76	4700	140	33.57	18.22
JJ Whitaker	1	1	11	11.00					
1987									
NH Fairbrother	10	15	219	14.60	1	9	0		
DJ Capel	15	25	374	14.96	23	1064	21	50.66	55.48
PW Jarvis	9	15	132	8.80	16	965	21	45.95	35.00
1988									
JH Childs	2	4	2	0.50	3	183	3	61.00	61.00
TS Curtis	5	9	140	15.55	1	7	0		
RA Smith	62	112	4236	37.82	1	6	0		
RJ Bailey	4	8	119	14.87					
MP Maynard	4	8	87	10.87					
KJ Barnett	4	7	207	29.57	1	32	0		
RC Russell	54	86	1897	22.05					
PJ Newport	3	5	110	22.00	6	417	10	41.70	25.02
DV Lawrence	5	6	60	10.00	10	676	18	37.55	20.86
1989									
ARC Fraser	46	67	388	5.79	79	4836	177	27.32	12.19
MA Atherton	115	212	7728	36.45	14	302	2	151.00	1057.00
DE Malcolm	40	58	236	4.06	72	4748	128	37.09	20.86
JP Stephenson	1	2	36	18.00					
AP Igglesden	3	5	6	1.20	5	329	6	54.83	45.69
1989-90									
AJ Stewart	133	235	8463	36.01	2	13	0		
N Hussain	96	171	5764	33.70	1	15	0		

1990								
CC Lewis	30	51	1105	21.66	55	3490	93	37.52	22.18
JE Morris	3	5	71	14.20					
NF Williams	1	1	38	38.00	1	148	2	74.00	37.00
1990-91									
PCR Tufnell	42	59	153	2.59	70	4560	121	37.68	21.79
1991									
GA Hick	65	114	3383	29.67	58	1306	23	56.78	143.18
MR Ramprakash	52	92	2350	25.54	25	477	4	119.25	745.31
SL Watkin	3	5	25	5.00	5	305	11	27.72	12.59
RK Illingworth	9	14	128	9.14	13	615	19	32.36	22.14
H Morris	3	6	115	19.16					
1991-92									
DA Reeve	3	5	124	24.80	5	60	2	30.00	75.00
1992									
TA Munton	2	2	25	12.50	4	200	4	50.00	50.00
IDK Salisbury	15	25	368	14.72	24	1539	20	76.95	92.34
NA Mallender	2	3	8	2.66	3	215	10	21.50	6.45
1992-93									
JP Taylor	2	4	34	8.50	4	156	3	52.00	69.33
RJ Blakey	2	4	7	1.75					
1993									
AR Caddick	62	95	861	9.06	105	6999	234	29.91	13.42
PM Such	11	16	67	4.18	20	1242	37	33.56	18.14
MN Lathwell	2	4	78	19.50					
GP Thorpe	100	179	6744	37.67	6	37	0		
MJ McCague	3	5	21	4.20	4	390	6	65.00	43.33
MC Ilott	5	6	28	4.66	7	542	12	45.16	26.34
MP Bicknell	4	7	45	6.42	7	543	14	38.78	19.39
1994									
C White	30	50	1052	21.04	45	2220	59	37.62	28.69
SJ Rhodes	11	17	294	17.29					
D Gough	58	86	855	9.94	95	6503	229	28.39	11.77
JP Crawley	37	61	1800	29.50					
JE Benjamin	1	1	0	0.00	2	80	4	20.00	10.00
1995									
PJ Martin	8	13	115	8.84	13	580	17	34.11	26.08
DG Cork	37	56	864	15.42	62	3906	131	29.81	14.10
JER Gallian	3	6	74	12.33	2	62	0		
NV Knight	17	30	719	23.96					
M Watkinson	4	6	167	27.83	6	348	10	34.80	20.88
AP Wells	1	2	3	1.50					
1996									
RC Irani	3	5	86	17.20	4	112	3	37.33	49.77
MM Patel	2	2	45	22.50	4	180	1	180.00	720.00
AD Mullally	19	27	127	4.70	34	1812	58	31.24	18.31
MA Ealham	8	13	210	16.15	10	488	17	28.70	16.88
SJE Brown	1	2	11	5.50	2	138	2	69.00	69.00
RDB Croft	21	34	421	12.38	31	1825	49	37.24	23.55
1996-97									
CEW Silverwood	6	7	29	4.14	9	444	11	40.36	33.02
1997									
MA Butcher	71	131	4288	32.73	30	541	15	36.06	72.12
DW Headley	15	26	186	7.15	23	1671	60	27.85	10.67
AM Smith	1	2	4	2.00	1	89	0		
AJ Hollioake	4	6	65	10.83	3	67	2	33.50	50.25
BC Hollioake	2	4	44	11.00	4	199	4	49.75	49.75
1998									
SP James	2	4	71	17.75					
AF Giles	54	81	1421	17.54	88	5806	143	40.60	24.98

A Flintoff	79	130	3845	-	137	7410	226		
n/a	1	2	50	-	2	107	7		
adj	78	128	3795	29.64	135	7303	219	33.34	20.55
1998-99									
AJ Tudor	10	16	229	14.31	17	963	28	34.39	20.87
WK Hegg	2	4	30	7.50					
1999									
A Habib	2	3	26	8.66					
CMW Read	15	23	360	15.65					
DL Maddy	3	4	46	11.50	1	40	0		
ESH Giddins	4	7	10	1.42	6	240	12	20.00	10.00
1999-00									
CJ Adams	5	8	104	13.00	2	59	1	59.00	118.00
GM Hamilton	1	2	0	0.00	1	63	0		
MP Vaughan	82	147	5719	38.90	35	561	6	93.50	545.41
2000									
CP Schofield	2	3	67	22.33	1	73	0		
MJ Hoggard	67	92	473	5.14	122	7564	248	30.50	15.00
ME Trescothick	76	143	5825	40.73	10	155	1	155.00	1550.00
2001									
RJ Sidebottom	22	31	313	10.09	36	2231	79	28.24	12.86
IJ Ward	5	9	129	14.33					
U Afzaal	3	6	83	13.83	1	49	1	49.00	49.00
J Ormond	2	4	38	9.50	2	185	2	92.50	92.50
2001-02									
RKJ Dawson	7	13	114	8.76	8	677	11	61.54	44.75
JS Foster	7	12	226	18.83					
2002									
SP Jones	18	18	205	11.38	33	1666	59	28.23	15.78
RWT Key	15	26	775	29.80					
SJ Harmison	63	86	743	-	115	7192	226		
n/a	1	2	1	-	2	101	4		
adj	62	84	742	8.83	113	7091	222	31.94	16.25
2003									
A McGrath	4	5	201	40.20	2	56	4	14.00	7.00
JM Anderson	169	239	1262	5.28	314	17014	640	26.58	13.04
RL Johnson	3	4	59	14.75	6	275	16	17.18	6.44
ET Smith	3	5	87	17.39					
RJ Kirtley	4	7	32	4.57	7	561	19	29.52	10.87
Kabir Ali	1	2	10	5.00	2	136	5	27.20	10.88
2003-04									
R Clarke	2	3	96	32.00	4	60	4	15.00	15.00
GJ Batty	9	12	149	12.41	13	914	15	60.93	52.80
MJ Saggers	3	3	1	0.33	6	247	7	35.28	30.23
PD Collingwood	68	115	4259	37.03	59	1018	17	59.88	207.81
GO Jones	34	53	1172	22.11					
2004									
AJ Strauss	100	178	7037	39.53					
IR Bell	118	205	7727	37.69	6	76	1	76.00	456.00
2005									
KP Pietersen	104	181	8181	45.19	58	886	10	88.60	513.88
2005-06									
SD Udal	4	7	109	15.57	7	344	8	43.00	37.62
LE Plunkett	13	20	238	11.90	25	1536	41	37.46	22.84
AN Cook	161	291	12472	42.85	2	7	1	7.00	14.00
ID Blackwell	1	1	4	4.00	2	71	0		
MS Panesar	50	68	220	3.23	85	5797	167	34.71	17.66
OA Shah	6	10	269	26.90	2	31	0		
2006									
SI Mahmood	8	11	81	7.36	14	762	20	38.10	26.67

J Lewis	1	2	27	13.50	2	122	3	40.66	27.10
2007									
MJ Prior	79	123	4099	33.32					
CT Tremlett	12	15	113	7.53	23	1431	53	27.00	11.71
2007-08									
RS Bopara	13	19	575	30.26	10	290	1	290.00	2900.00
SCJ Broad	152	224	3412	15.23	280	14932	537	27.80	14.49
TR Ambrose	11	16	447	27.93					
2008									
DJ Pattinson	1	2	21	10.50	2	96	2	48.00	48.00
2008-09									
GP Swann	60	76	1370	18.02	109	7642	255	29.96	12.80
A Khan	1	0	-	-	2	122	1	122.00	244.00
2009									
TT Bresnan	23	26	575	22.11	41	2357	72	32.73	18.63
G Onions	9	10	30	3.00	16	957	32	29.90	14.95
IJL Trott	52	93	3835	41.23	33	400	5	80.00	528.00
2009-10									
MA Carberry	6	12	345	28.75					
ST Finn	36	47	279	5.93	66	3800	125	30.40	16.05
JC Tredwell	2	2	45	22.50	4	321	11	29.18	10.61
2010									
EJG Morgan	16	24	700	29.16					
A Shahzad	1	1	5	5.00	2	63	4	15.75	7.87
2011-12									
SR Patel	6	9	151	16.77	10	421	7	60.14	85.91
2012									
JM Bairstow	83	148	4801	32.43					
JWA Taylor	7	13	312	24.00					
2012-13									
NRD Compton	16	30	775	25.83					
JE Root	117	216	9889	45.78	112	2046	45	45.46	113.14
2013									
CR Woakes	45	74	1675	22.63	85	3996	130	30.73	20.09
SC Kerrigan	1	1	1	1.00	1	53	0		
2013-14									
BA Stokes	79	146	5061	34.66	126	5589	174	32.12	23.25
GS Ballance	23	42	1498	35.66	2	5	0		
SG Borthwick	1	2	5	2.50	2	82	4	20.50	10.25
WB Rankin [Ire]	1	2	13	6.50	2	81	1	81.00	162.00
2014									
SD Robson	7	11	336	30.54					
MM Ali	64	111	2914	26.25	112	7149	195	36.66	21.05
CJ Jordan	8	11	180	16.36	16	752	21	35.80	27.27
JC Buttler	57	100	2907	29.07					
2015									
A Lyth	7	13	265	20.38	1	0	0		
MA Wood	26	44	564	12.81	48	2617	82	31.91	18.67
2015-16									
AU Rashid	19	33	540	16.36	34	2390	60	39.83	22.57
AD Hales	11	21	573	27.28	1	2	0		
2016									
JM Vince	13	22	548	24.90	4	13	0		
JT Ball	4	8	67	8.37	6	343	3	114.33	228.66
2016-17									
BM Duckett	4	7	110	15.71					
ZS Ansari	3	5	49	9.80	5	275	5	55.00	55.00
H Hameed	10	19	439	23.10					
KK Jennings	17	32	781	24.40	4	55	0		
LA Dawson	3	6	84	14.00	5	298	7	42.57	30.40

2017									
T Westley	5	9	193	21.44	1	12	0		
DJ Malan	22	39	1074	27.53	8	131	2	65.50	262.00
TS Roland-Jones	4	6	82	13.66	8	334	17	19.64	9.24
MD Stoneman	11	20	526	26.30					
2017-18									
C Overton	8	14	182	13.00	13	760	21	36.19	22.40
TK Curran	2	3	66	22.00	3	200	2	100.00	150.00
MS Crane	1	2	6	3.00	1	193	1	193.00	193.00
MJ Leach	22	38	377	9.92	37	2519	79	31.88	14.93
2018									
DM Bess	14	19	319	16.78	22	1223	36	33.97	20.75
SM Curran	24	38	815	21.44	42	1669	47	35.51	31.73
OJ Pope	23	40	1032	25.80					
2018-19									
RJ Burns	32	59	1789	30.32					
BT Foakes	11	22	506	23.00					
JL Denly	15	28	827	29.53	12	219	2	109.50	657.00
2019									
JJ Roy	5	10	187	18.70					
OP Stone	3	6	55	9.16	5	194	10	19.40	9.70
JC Archer	13	20	155	7.75	24	1304	42	31.04	17.73
2019-20									
DP Sibley	22	39	1042	26.71	1	7	0		
Z Crawley	21	38	1087	28.60					
2020-21									
DW Lawrence	11	21	551	26.23	7	97	3	32.33	75.43
2021									
JR Bracey	2	3	8	2.66					
OE Robinson	9	16	125	7.81	17	830	39	21.28	9.27
2021-22									
SW Billings	1	2	30	15.00					
AZ Lees	3	6	126	21.00					
MD Fisher	1	1	0	0.00	2	71	1	71.00	142.00
S Mahmood	2	2	52	26.00	4	137	6	22.83	15.21

AUSTRALIA

	M	I	R	RI	IB	R	W	A	RWI
1876-77									
C Bannerman	3	6	239	39.83					
NFD Thompson	2	4	67	16.75	2	31	1	31.00	62.00
TP Horan	15	27	471	17.44	8	143	11	13.00	9.45
DW Gregory	3	5	60	12.00	1	9	0		
BB Cooper	1	2	18	9.00					
WE Midwinter [Eng]	8	14	174	12.42	12	333	14	23.78	20.38
EJ Gregory	1	2	11	5.50					
JM Blackham	35	62	800	12.90					
TW Garrett	19	33	339	10.27	30	970	36	26.94	22.44
TK Kendall	2	4	39	9.75	4	215	14	15.35	4.38
JR Hodges	2	4	10	2.50	4	84	6	14.00	9.33
TJD Kelly	2	3	64	21.33					
FR Spofforth	18	29	217	7.48	30	1731	94	18.41	5.87
WL Murdoch [Eng]	18	33	896	27.15					
1878-79									
AC Bannerman	28	50	1108	22.16	4	163	4	40.75	40.75
FE Allan	1	1	5	5.00	2	80	4	20.00	10.00
HF Boyle	12	16	153	9.56	21	641	32	20.03	13.14
1880									
TU Groube	1	2	11	5.50					

PS McDonnell	19	34	955	28.08	4	53	0		
J Slight	1	2	11	5.50					
GJ Bonnor	17	30	512	17.06	4	84	2	42.00	84.00
GE Palmer	16	25	296	11.84	30	1678	78	21.51	8.27
G Alexander	2	4	52	13.00	2	93	2	46.50	46.50
WH Moule	1	2	40	20.00	1	23	3	7.66	2.55
1881-82----------									
HH Massie	9	16	249	15.56					
G Giffen	31	53	1238	23.35	43	2791	103	27.09	11.30
E Evans	6	10	82	8.20	9	332	7	47.42	60.96
WH Cooper	2	3	13	4.33	3	226	9	25.11	8.36
SP Jones	12	24	428	17.83	7	112	6	18.66	21.76
G Coulthard	1	1	6	6.00					
1884----------									
HJH Scott	8	14	359	25.64	2	26	0		
1884-85----------									
S Morris	1	2	14	7.00	1	73	2	36.50	18.25
JW Trumble	7	13	243	18.69	6	222	10	22.20	13.32
AH Jarvis	11	21	303	14.42					
RJ Rope	1	2	3	1.50					
AP Marr	1	2	5	2.50	2	14	0		
HA Musgrove	1	2	13	6.50					
J Worrall	11	22	478	21.72	3	127	1	127.00	381.00
W Bruce	14	26	702	27.00	15	440	12	36.66	45.82
WR Robertson	1	2	2	1.00	1	24	0		
FH Walters	1	2	12	6.00					
PG McShane	3	6	26	4.33	3	48	1	48.00	144.00
1886----------									
J McIlwraith	1	2	9	4.50					
1886-87----------									
H Moses	6	10	198	19.80					
CTB Turner	17	32	323	10.09	30	1670	101	16.53	4.90
JJ Ferris [Eng]	8	16	98	6.12	14	684	48	14.25	4.15
WF Giffen	3	6	11	1.83					
JJ Lyons	14	27	731	27.07	9	149	6	24.83	37.24
RC Allen	1	2	44	22.00					
JT Cottam	1	2	4	2.00					
FJ Burton	2	4	4	1.00					
1888----------									
GHS Trott	24	42	921	21.92	29	1019	29	35.13	35.13
SMJ Woods [Eng]	3	6	32	5.33	3	121	5	24.20	14.52
JD Edwards	3	6	48	8.00					
1890----------									
JE Barrett	2	4	80	20.00					
SE Gregory	58	100	2282	22.82	3	33	0		
PC Charlton	2	4	29	7.25	2	24	3	8.00	5.33
EJK Burn	2	4	41	10.25					
H Trumble	32	57	851	14.92	57	3072	141	21.78	8.80
1891-92----------									
H Donnan	5	10	75	7.50	1	22	0		
RW McLeod	6	11	146	13.27	8	382	12	31.83	21.21
ST Callaway	3	6	87	14.50	6	142	6	23.66	23.66
1893----------									
H Graham	6	10	301	30.10					
1894-95----------									
J Darling	34	60	1657	27.61					
FA Iredale	14	23	807	35.08	1	3	0		
JC Reedman	1	2	21	10.50	2	24	1	24.00	48.00
CE McLeod	17	29	573	19.75	27	1325	33	40.15	32.85
E Jones	19	26	126	4.84	31	1857	64	29.01	14.05

A Coningham	1	2	13	6.50	2	76	2	38.00	38.00
J Harry	1	2	8	4.00					
AE Trott [Eng]	3	5	205	41.00	4	192	9	21.33	9.47
TR McKibbin	5	8	88	11.00	10	496	17	29.17	17.15
1896									
C Hill	49	89	3412	38.33					
CJ Eady	2	4	20	5.00	4	112	7	16.00	9.14
JJ Kelly	36	56	664	11.85					
1897-98									
MA Noble	42	73	1997	27.35	71	3025	121	25.00	14.66
WP Howell	18	27	158	5.85	30	1407	49	28.71	17.57
1899									
VT Trumper	48	89	3163	35.53	15	317	8	39.62	74.28
FJ Laver	15	23	196	8.52	22	964	37	26.05	15.48
1901-02									
RA Duff	22	40	1317	32.92	4	85	4	21.25	21.25
WW Armstrong	50	84	2863	34.08	80	2923	87	33.59	30.88
AJY Hopkins	20	33	509	15.42	22	696	26	26.76	22.64
JV Saunders	14	23	39	1.69	27	1796	79	22.73	7.76
JPF Travers	1	2	10	5.00	1	14	1	14.00	14.00
1903-04									
PA McAlister	8	16	252	15.75					
A Cotter	21	37	457	12.35	38	2549	89	28.64	12.22
DRA Gehrs	6	11	221	20.09	1	4	0		
1907-08									
VS Ransford	20	38	1211	31.86	3	28	1	28.00	84.00
CG Macartney	35	55	2131	38.74	45	1240	45	27.55	27.55
H Carter	28	47	873	18.57					
GR Hazlitt	9	12	89	7.41	14	623	23	27.08	16.48
MJ Hartigan	2	4	170	42.50	1	7	0		
JDA O'Connor	4	8	86	10.75	8	340	13	26.15	16.09
1909									
W Bardsley	41	66	2469	37.40					
WJ Whitty	14	19	161	8.47	25	1373	65	21.12	8.12
1910-11									
C Kelleway	26	42	1422	33.85	44	1683	52	32.36	27.38
HV Hordern	7	13	254	19.53	13	1075	46	23.36	6.60
1911-12									
RB Minnett	9	15	391	26.06	12	290	11	26.36	28.75
TJ Matthews	8	10	153	15.30	12	419	16	26.18	19.63
JW McLaren	1	2	0	0.00	2	70	1	70.00	140.00
1912									
CB Jennings	6	8	107	13.37					
SH Emery	4	2	6	3.00	4	249	5	49.80	39.84
W Carkeek	6	5	16	3.20					
DBM Smith	2	3	30	10.00					
ER Mayne	4	4	64	16.00	1	1	0		
1920-21									
HL Collins	19	31	1352	43.61	12	252	4	63.00	189.00
JM Gregory	24	34	1146	33.70	42	2648	85	31.15	15.39
JM Taylor	20	28	997	35.60	3	45	1	45.00	135.00
CE Pellew	10	14	484	34.57	3	34	0		
J Ryder	20	32	1394	43.56	28	743	17	43.70	71.97
WAS Oldfield	54	80	1427	17.83					
AA Mailey	21	29	222	7.65	34	3358	99	33.91	11.64
RL Park	1	1	0	0.00	1	9	0		
EA McDonald	11	12	116	9.66	21	1431	43	33.27	16.24
1921									
TJE Andrews	16	23	592	25.73	4	116	1	116.00	464.00

HSTL Hendry	11	18	335	18.61	19	640	16	40.00	47.50
1924-25									
WH Ponsford	29	48	2122	44.20					
AJ Richardson	9	13	403	31.00	14	521	12	43.41	50.64
VY Richardson	19	30	706	23.53					
AEV Hartkopf	1	2	80	40.00	2	134	1	134.00	268.00
AF Kippax	22	34	1192	35.05	4	19	0		
CV Grimmett	37	50	557	11.14	67	5231	216	24.21	7.50
1926									
WM Woodfull	35	54	2300	42.59					
1928-29									
DG Bradman	52	80	6996	87.45	9	72	2	36.00	162.00
H Ironmonger	14	21	42	2.00	27	1330	74	17.97	6.55
OE Nothling	1	2	52	26.00	2	72	0		
DD Blackie	3	6	24	4.00	5	444	14	31.71	11.32
EL a'Beckett	4	7	143	20.42	8	317	3	105.66	281.75
RK Oxenham	7	10	151	15.10	12	522	14	37.28	31.95
A Jackson	8	11	474	43.09					
AG Fairfax	10	12	410	34.16	18	645	21	30.71	26.32
TW Wall	18	24	121	5.04	33	2010	56	35.89	21.14
PM Hornibrook	6	7	60	8.57	11	664	17	39.05	25.26
1930									
SJ McCabe	39	62	2748	44.32	62	1543	36	42.86	73.81
1930-31									
A Hurwood	2	2	5	2.50	4	170	11	15.45	5.61
KE Rigg	8	12	401	33.41					
1931-32									
HC Nitschke	2	2	53	26.50					
PK Lee	2	3	57	19.00	4	212	5	42.40	33.92
WA Hunt	1	1	0	0.00	2	39	0		
WJ O'Reilly	27	39	410	10.51	48	3254	144	22.59	7.52
HM Thurlow	1	1	0	0.00	2	86	0		
JHW Fingleton	18	29	1189	41.00					
LJ Nash	2	2	30	15.00	4	126	10	12.60	5.04
1932-33									
LE Nagel	1	2	21	10.50	1	110	2	55.00	27.50
LPJ O'Brien	5	8	211	26.37					
LS Darling	12	18	474	26.33	5	65	0		
EH Bromley	2	4	38	9.50	1	19	0		
HSB Love	1	2	8	4.00					
HH Alexander	1	2	17	8.50	2	154	1	154.00	308.00
1934									
WA Brown	22	35	1592	45.48					
AG Chipperfield	14	20	552	27.60	14	437	5	87.40	244.72
HI Ebeling	1	2	43	21.50	2	89	3	29.66	19.77
1935-36									
EL McCormick	12	14	54	3.85	21	1079	36	29.97	17.48
LO Fleetwood-Smith	10	11	54	4.90	18	1570	42	37.38	16.02
1936-37									
CL Badcock	7	12	160	13.33					
RH Robinson	1	2	5	2.50					
MW Sievers	3	6	67	11.16	5	161	9	17.88	9.93
FA Ward	4	8	36	4.50	5	574	11	52.18	23.71
RG Gregory	2	3	153	51.00	1	14	0		
1938									
AL Hassett	43	69	3073	44.53	6	78	0		
BA Barnett	4	8	195	24.37					
MG Waite	2	3	11	3.66	3	190	1	190.00	570.00
SG Barnes	13	19	1072	56.42	9	218	4	54.50	122.62

1945-46									
KD Meuleman	1	1	0	0.00					
KR Miller	55	87	2958	34.00	95	3906	170	22.97	12.83
CL McCool	14	17	459	27.00	20	958	36	26.61	14.78
IWG Johnson	45	66	1000	15.15	74	3182	109	29.19	19.81
D Tallon	21	26	394	15.15					
RR Lindwall	61	84	1502	17.88	113	5251	228	23.03	11.41
ERH Toshack	12	11	73	6.63	23	989	47	21.04	10.29
1946-47									
AR Morris	46	79	3533	44.72	6	50	2	25.00	75.00
GE Tribe	3	3	35	11.66	6	330	2	165.00	495.00
FAW Freer	1	1	28	28.00	2	74	3	24.66	16.43
B Dooland	3	5	76	15.20	5	419	9	46.55	25.86
MR Harvey	1	2	43	21.50					
RA Hamence	3	4	81	20.25					
1947-48									
WA Johnston	40	49	273	5.57	75	3826	160	23.91	11.20
RN Harvey	79	137	6149	44.88	17	120	3	40.00	226.66
SJE Loxton	12	15	554	36.93	17	349	8	43.62	92.69
LJ Johnson	1	1	25	25.00	2	74	6	12.33	4.10
DT Ring	13	21	426	20.28	23	1305	35	37.28	24.49
1948									
RA Saggers	6	5	30	6.00					
1949-50									
J Moroney	7	12	383	31.91					
G Noblet	5	4	22	5.50	6	183	7	26.14	22.40
1950-51									
JB Iverson	5	7	3	0.42	8	320	21	15.23	5.80
KA Archer	5	9	234	26.00					
JW Burke	24	44	1280	29.09	16	230	8	28.75	57.50
GB Hole	18	33	789	23.90	14	126	3	42.00	195.99
1951-52									
GRA Langley	26	37	374	10.10					
CC McDonald	47	83	3107	37.43	1	3	0		
GR Thoms	1	2	44	22.00					
R Benaud	63	97	2201	22.69	116	6704	248	27.03	12.64
1952-53									
ID Craig	11	18	358	19.88					
RG Archer	19	30	713	23.76	35	1318	48	27.45	20.01
1953									
AK Davidson	44	61	1328	21.77	82	3819	186	20.53	9.05
JC Hill	3	6	21	3.50	5	273	8	34.12	21.32
JH de Courcy	3	6	81	13.50					
1954-55									
LE Favell	19	31	757	24.41					
LV Maddocks	7	12	177	14.75					
WJ Watson	4	7	106	15.14	1	5	0		
PJP Burge	42	68	2290	33.67					
1956									
KD Mackay	37	52	1507	28.98	53	1721	50	34.42	36.48
WPA Crawford	4	5	53	10.60	7	107	7	15.28	15.28
1956-57									
JW Rutherford	1	1	30	30.00	2	15	1	15.00	30.00
JW Wilson	1	-	-	-	2	64	1	64.00	128.00
1957-58									
RB Simpson	62	111	4869	43.86	84	3001	71	42.26	49.99
ATW Grout	51	67	890	13.28					
I Meckiff	18	20	154	7.70	34	1423	45	31.62	23.89
LF Kline	13	16	58	3.62	22	776	34	22.82	14.76
RA Gaunt	3	4	6	1.50	5	310	7	44.28	31.62

1958-59									
NCL O'Neill	42	69	2779	40.27	29	667	17	39.23	66.92
KN Slater	1	1	1	1.00	2	101	2	50.50	50.50
GF Rorke	4	4	9	2.25	7	203	10	20.30	14.21
1959-60									
GB Stevens	4	7	112	16.00					
BN Jarman	19	30	400	13.33					
1960-61									
JW Martin	8	13	214	16.46	16	832	17	48.94	46.06
FM Misson	5	5	38	7.60	10	616	16	38.50	24.06
DE Hoare	1	2	35	17.50	2	156	2	78.00	78.00
1961									
WM Lawry	67	123	5234	42.55	2	6	0		
GD McKenzie	60	89	945	10.61	113	7328	246	29.78	13.67
BC Booth	29	48	1773	36.93	12	146	3	48.66	194.64
1962-63									
BK Shepherd	9	14	502	35.85	2	9	0		
CEJ Guest	1	1	11	11.00	2	59	0		
NJN Hawke	27	37	365	9.86	50	2677	91	29.41	16.15
1963-64									
TR Veivers	21	30	813	27.10	31	1375	33	41.66	39.13
AN Connolly	29	45	260	5.77	55	2981	102	29.22	15.75
IR Redpath	66	120	4737	39.47	6	41	0		
1964									
GE Corling	5	4	5	1.25	8	447	12	37.25	24.83
RM Cowper	27	46	2061	44.80	36	1139	36	31.63	31.63
1964-65									
RHD Sellers	1	1	0	0.00	1	17	0		
IM Chappell	75	136	5345	39.30	60	1316	20	65.80	197.40
DJ Sincock	3	4	80	20.00	5	410	8	51.25	32.03
G Thomas	8	12	325	27.08					
PI Philpott	8	10	93	9.30	13	1000	26	38.46	19.23
LC Mayne	6	11	76	6.90	12	628	19	33.05	20.87
1965-66									
KD Walters	74	125	5357	42.85	72	1425	49	29.08	42.72
PJ Allan	1	-	-	-	2	83	2	41.50	41.50
KR Stackpole	43	80	2807	35.08	40	1001	15	66.73	177.94
1966-67									
HB Taber	16	27	353	13.07					
DA Renneberg	8	13	22	1.69	15	830	23	36.08	23.53
GD Watson	5	9	97	10.77	8	254	6	42.33	56.43
1967-68									
AP Sheahan	31	53	1594	30.07					
JW Gleeson	29	46	395	8.58	53	3367	93	36.20	20.63
EW Freeman	11	18	345	19.16	21	1128	34	33.17	20.48
LR Joslin	1	2	9	4.50					
1968									
RJ Inverarity	6	11	174	15.81	5	93	4	23.25	29.06
AA Mallett	38	50	430	8.60	71	3940	132	29.84	16.05
1970-71									
RW Marsh	96	150	3633	24.22	2	54	0		
TJ Jenner	9	14	208	14.85	16	749	24	31.20	20.80
AL Thomson	4	5	22	4.40	8	654	12	54.50	36.33
GS Chappell	87	151	7110	47.08	88	1913	47	40.70	76.20
KJ O'Keeffe	24	34	644	18.94	40	2018	53	38.07	28.73
JRF Duncan	1	1	3	3.00	1	30	0		
DK Lillee	70	90	905	10.05	132	8493	355	23.92	8.89
AR Dell	2	2	6	3.00	4	160	6	26.66	17.77
KH Eastwood	1	2	5	2.50	1	21	1	21.00	21.00

1972									
BC Francis	3	5	52	10.40					
DJ Colley	3	4	84	21.00	6	312	6	52.00	52.00
R Edwards	20	32	1171	36.59	1	20	0		
RAL Massie	6	8	78	9.75	11	647	31	20.87	7.40
1972-73									
J Benaud	3	5	223	44.60	1	12	2	6.00	3.00
MHN Walker	34	43	586	13.62	63	3792	138	27.47	12.54
JR Thomson	51	73	679	9.30	90	5601	200	28.00	12.60
JR Watkins	1	2	39	19.50	1	21	0		
JR Hammond	5	5	28	5.60	10	488	15	32.53	21.68
1973-74									
IC Davis	15	27	692	25.62					
GJ Gilmour	15	22	483	21.95	28	1406	54	26.03	13.49
AJ Woodcock	1	1	27	27.00					
AG Hurst	12	20	102	5.10	21	1200	43	27.90	13.62
G Dymock	21	32	236	7.35	35	2116	78	27.12	12.16
1974-75									
WJ Edwards	3	6	68	11.33					
RB McCosker	25	46	1622	35.26					
1975									
A Turner	14	27	768	28.44					
1975-76									
GJ Cosier	18	32	897	28.03	19	341	5	68.20	259.16
GN Yallop	39	70	2756	39.37	10	116	1	116.00	1160.00
1976-77									
DW Hookes	23	41	1306	31.85	7	41	1	41.00	287.00
1977									
RD Robinson	3	6	100	16.66					
CS Serjeant	12	23	522	22.69					
LS Pascoe	14	19	106	5.57	27	1668	64	26.06	10.99
RJ Bright	25	39	445	11.41	39	2180	53	41.13	30.26
KJ Hughes	70	124	4415	35.60	6	28	0		
MF Malone	1	1	46	46.00	2	77	6	12.83	4.27
1977-78									
PA Hibbert	1	2	15	7.50					
AD Ogilvie	5	10	178	17.80					
PM Toohey	15	29	893	30.79	1	4	0		
AL Mann	4	8	189	23.62	7	316	4	79.00	138.25
SJ Rixon	13	24	394	16.41					
WM Clark	10	19	98	5.15	18	1265	44	28.75	11.76
J Dyson	30	58	1359	23.43					
JB Gannon	3	5	3	0.60	5	361	11	32.81	14.91
GM Wood	59	112	3374	30.12					
WM Darling	14	27	697	25.81					
B Yardley	33	54	978	18.11	58	3986	126	31.63	14.55
IW Callen	1	2	26	13.00	2	191	6	31.83	10.60
JD Higgs	22	36	111	3.08	36	2057	66	31.16	16.99
TJ Laughlin	3	5	87	17.40	6	262	6	43.66	43.66
1978-79									
JA Maclean	4	8	79	9.87					
RM Hogg	38	58	439	7.56	66	3503	123	28.47	15.27
AR Border	156	265	11174	42.16	98	1525	39	39.10	98.25
PH Carlson	2	4	23	5.75	3	99	2	49.50	74.25
KJ Wright	10	18	219	12.16					
AMJ Hilditch	18	34	1073	31.55					
DF Whatmore	7	13	293	22.53	1	11	0		
PR Sleep	14	21	483	23.00	23	1397	31	45.06	33.43
JK Moss	1	2	60	30.00					

1979-80									
BM Laird	21	40	1341	33.52	2	12	0		
JM Wiener	6	11	281	25.54	2	41	0		
GR Beard	3	5	114	22.80	4	109	1	109.00	436.00
1980-81									
GF Lawson	46	68	894	13.14	78	5501	180	30.56	13.24
1981									
TM Chappell	3	6	79	13.16					
TM Alderman	41	53	203	3.83	73	4616	170	27.15	11.65
MF Kent	3	6	171	28.50					
MR Whitney	12	19	68	3.57	23	1325	39	33.97	20.03
DM Wellham	6	11	257	23.36					
1982-83									
GM Ritchie	30	53	1690	31.88	1	10	0		
KC Wessels [SA]	24	42	1761	41.92	6	42	0		
CG Rackemann	12	14	53	3.78	20	1137	39	29.15	14.94
RD Woolley	2	2	21	10.50					
TG Hogan	7	12	205	17.08	9	706	15	47.06	28.23
1983-84									
WB Phillips	27	48	1485	30.93					
GRJ Matthews	33	53	1849	34.88	47	2942	61	48.22	37.15
JN Maguire	3	5	28	7.00	5	323	10	32.30	16.15
SB Smith	3	5	41	8.20					
DM Jones	52	89	3631	40.79	10	64	1	64.00	640.00
1984-85									
DC Boon	107	190	7422	39.06	3	14	0		
RG Holland	11	15	35	2.33	17	1352	34	39.76	19.88
MJ Bennett	3	5	71	14.20	5	325	6	54.16	45.13
CJ McDermott	71	90	940	10.44	124	8332	291	28.63	12.19
1985									
SP O'Donnell	6	10	206	20.60	10	504	6	84.00	139.99
DR Gilbert	9	12	57	4.75	13	843	16	52.68	42.80
1985-86									
RB Kerr	2	4	31	7.75					
GR Marsh	50	93	2854	30.68					
BA Reid	27	34	93	2.73	42	2784	113	24.63	9.15
MG Hughes	53	70	1032	14.74	97	6017	212	28.38	12.98
SR Waugh	168	260	10927	42.02	150	3445	92	37.44	61.04
TJ Zoehrer	10	14	246	17.57					
SP Davis	1	1	0	0.00	1	70	0		
1986-87									
CD Matthews	3	5	54	10.00	6	313	6	52.16	52.16
GC Dyer	6	6	131	21.83					
PL Taylor	13	19	431	22.68	21	1068	27	39.55	30.76
1987-88									
MRJ Velletta	8	11	207	18.81					
TBA May	24	28	225	8.03	45	2606	75	34.74	20.84
AIC Dodemaide	10	15	202	13.46	17	953	34	28.02	14.01
1988-89									
IA Healy	119	182	4356	23.93					
MA Taylor	104	186	7525	40.45	2	26	1	26.00	52.00
TV Hohns	7	7	136	19.42	13	580	17	34.11	26.08
1989									
GD Campbell	4	4	10	2.50	8	503	13	38.69	23.80
1989-90									
TM Moody	8	14	456	32.57	9	147	2	73.50	330.75
1990-91									
ME Waugh	128	209	8029	38.41	128	2429	59	41.16	89.29

1991-92									
SK Warne	145	199	3154	-	273	17995	708		
n/a	1	2	12	-	2	71	6		
adj	144	197	3142	15.94	271	17924	702	25.53	9.85
WN Phillips	1	2	22	11.00					
PR Reiffel	35	50	955	19.10	67	2804	104	26.96	17.36
1992-93									
DR Martyn	67	109	4406	40.42	12	168	2	84.00	504.00
JL Langer	105	182	7696	-	1	3	0		
n/a	1	2	22	-	-	-	-		
adj	104	180	7674	42.63	1	3	0		
J Angel	4	7	35	5.00	7	463	10	46.30	32.41
1993									
MJ Slater	74	131	5312	40.54	3	10	1	10.00	30.00
BP Julian	7	9	128	14.22	14	599	15	39.93	37.26
1993-94									
GD McGrath	124	138	641	-	243	12186	563		
n/a	1	2	2	-	2	42	3		
adj	123	136	639	4.69	241	12144	560	21.68	9.33
ML Hayden	103	184	8625	-	3	40	0		
n/a	1	2	188	-	-	-	-		
adj	102	182	8437	46.35	3	40	0		
1994-95									
MG Bevan	18	30	785	26.16	21	703	29	24.24	17.55
DW Fleming	20	19	305	16.05	38	1942	75	25.89	13.11
PA Emery	1	1	8	8.00					
GS Blewett	46	79	2552	32.30	42	720	14	51.42	154.26
PE McIntyre	2	4	22	5.50	4	194	5	38.80	31.04
1995-96									
RT Ponting	168	287	13378	-	36	276	5		
n/a	1	2	100	-	-	-	-		
adj	167	285	13278	46.58	36	276	5	55.20	397.44
SG Law	1	1	54	54.00	1	9	0		
1996-97									
GB Hogg	7	10	186	18.60	13	933	17	54.88	41.96
MTG Elliott	21	36	1172	32.55	2	4	0		
MS Kasprowicz	38	54	445	8.24	73	3716	113	32.88	21.24
JN Gillespie	71	93	1218	13.09	137	6770	259	26.13	13.82
AJ Bichel	19	22	355	16.13	37	1870	58	32.24	20.56
1997									
S Young	1	2	4	2.00	2	13	0		
1997-98									
SH Cook	2	2	3	1.50	4	142	7	20.28	11.58
SCG MacGill	44	47	349	-	85	6038	208		
n/a	1	2	0	-	2	82	9		
adj	43	45	349	7.75	83	5956	199	29.92	12.47
GR Robertson	4	7	140	20.00	7	515	13	39.61	21.32
P Wilson	1	2	0	0.00	1	50	0		
DS Lehmann	27	42	1798	42.80	25	412	15	27.46	45.76
AC Dale	2	3	6	2.00	4	187	6	31.16	20.77
1998-99									
CR Miller	18	24	174	7.25	34	1805	69	26.15	12.88
MJ Nicholson	1	2	14	7.00	2	115	4	28.75	14.37
1999-00									
AC Gilchrist	96	137	5570	-					
n/a	1	2	95	-					
adj	95	135	5475	40.55					
SA Muller	2	2	6	3.00	4	258	7	36.85	21.05

B Lee	76	90	1451	-	150	9554	310		
n/a	1	2	4	-	2	96	2		
adj	75	88	1447	16.44	148	9458	308	30.70	14.75
2001									
SM Katich	56	99	4188	-	25	635	21		
n/a	1	2	2	-	-	-	-		
adj	55	97	4186	43.15	25	635	21	30.23	35.98
2002-03									
ML Love	5	8	233	29.12					
2003-04									
BA Williams	4	6	23	3.83	8	406	9	45.11	40.09
NW Bracken	5	6	70	11.66	10	505	12	42.08	35.06
A Symonds	26	41	1462	35.65	41	896	24	37.33	63.77
2004-05									
MJ Clarke	115	198	8643	-	65	1184	31		
n/a	1	2	44	-	-	-	-		
adj	114	196	8599	43.87	65	1184	31	38.19	80.07
NM Hauritz	17	24	426	17.75	33	2204	63	34.98	18.32
SR Watson	59	109	3731	-	93	2526	75		
n/a	1	2	34	-	1	38	0		
adj	58	107	3697	34.55	92	2488	75	33.17	40.68
2005									
SW Tait	3	5	20	4.00	5	302	5	60.40	60.40
2005-06									
MEK Hussey	79	137	6235	45.51	32	306	7	43.71	199.81
BJ Hodge	6	11	503	45.72	1	8	0		
PA Jaques	11	19	902	47.47					
SR Clark	24	26	248	9.53	48	2243	94	23.86	12.18
DJ Cullen	1	-	-	-	2	54	1	54.00	108.00
2007-08									
MG Johnson	73	109	2065	18.94	140	8891	313	28.40	12.70
CJL Rogers	25	48	2015	41.97					
2008									
BJ Haddin	66	112	3266	29.16					
B Casson	1	1	10	10.00	2	129	3	43.00	28.66
2008-09									
CL White	4	7	146	20.85	8	342	5	68.40	109.44
PM Siddle	67	94	1164	12.38	126	6777	221	30.66	17.48
JJ Krejza	2	4	71	17.75	4	562	13	43.23	13.30
AB McDonald	4	6	107	17.83	7	300	9	33.33	25.92
DE Bollinger	12	14	54	3.85	23	1296	50	25.92	11.92
PJ Hughes	26	49	1535	31.32					
MJ North	22	35	1171	33.45	19	591	14	42.21	57.28
BW Hilfenhaus	27	38	355	9.34	49	2822	99	28.50	14.10
BE McGain	1	2	2	1.00	1	149	0		
2009									
GA Manou	1	2	21	10.50					
2009-10									
CJ McKay	1	1	10	10.00	2	101	1	101.00	202.00
RJ Harris	27	39	603	15.46	52	2658	113	23.52	10.82
2010									
TD Paine	35	57	1534	26.91					
SPD Smith	85	151	8010	53.04	58	990	18	55.00	177.22
2010-11									
PR George	1	2	2	1.00	2	77	2	38.50	38.50
XJ Doherty	4	7	51	7.28	6	548	7	78.28	67.09
UT Khawaja	49	86	3638	42.30	3	8	0		
MA Beer	2	3	6	2.00	3	178	3	59.33	59.33
2011									
TA Copeland	3	4	39	9.75	6	227	6	37.83	37.83

NM Lyon	108	137	1222	8.91	204	13732	427	32.15	15.35
SE Marsh	38	68	2265	33.30					
2011-12									
PJ Cummins	41	58	833	14.36	79	4191	197	21.27	8.52
DA Warner	94	172	7753	45.07	19	269	4	67.25	319.43
JL Pattinson	21	25	417	16.68	38	2133	81	26.33	12.35
MA Starc	69	101	1805	17.87	133	7786	282	27.60	13.01
EJM Cowan	18	32	1001	31.28					
MS Wade	36	63	1613	25.60	4	28	0		
2012-13									
RJ Quiney	2	3	9	3.00	4	29	0		
JW Hastings	1	2	52	26.00	2	153	1	153.00	306.00
JM Bird	9	9	43	4.77	17	1042	34	30.64	15.32
MC Henriques	4	8	164	20.50	4	164	2	82.00	164.00
GJ Maxwell	7	14	339	24.21	9	341	8	42.62	47.94
2013									
AC Agar	4	7	195	27.85	8	410	9	45.55	40.48
JP Faulkner	1	2	45	22.50	2	98	6	16.33	5.44
2013-14									
GJ Bailey	5	8	183	22.87					
AJ Doolan	4	8	191	23.87					
2014-15									
MR Marsh	32	55	1260	22.90	54	1623	42	38.64	49.67
SNJ O'Keefe	9	13	86	6.61	16	1029	35	29.40	13.43
JR Hazlewood	57	70	445	6.35	107	5573	215	25.92	12.89
JA Burns	23	40	1442	36.05					
2015									
AC Voges	20	31	1485	47.90	6	44	0		
PM Nevill	17	23	468	20.34					
2016									
JM Holland	4	7	6	0.85	8	574	9	63.77	56.68
2016-17									
CJ Ferguson	1	2	4	2.00					
JA Mennie	1	2	10	5.00	1	85	1	85.00	85.00
MT Renshaw	11	20	636	31.80	2	13	0		
PSP Handscomb	16	29	934	32.20					
NJ Maddinson	3	4	27	6.75	2	27	0		
HWR Cartwright	2	2	55	27.50	2	31	0		
2017-18									
CT Bancroft	10	18	446	24.77					
CJ Sayers	1	2	0	0.00	2	146	2	73.00	73.00
2018-19									
AJ Finch	5	10	278	27.80	1	8	0		
TM Head	26	41	1578	38.49	12	124	0		
M Labuschagne	26	45	2390	53.11	35	663	13	51.00	137.30
MS Harris	14	26	607	23.34					
KR Patterson	2	2	144	72.00					
JA Richardson	3	3	18	6.00	6	243	11	22.09	12.04
2020-21									
C Green	12	18	619	34.38	22	494	16	30.87	42.44
WJ Pucovski	1	2	72	36.00					
2021-22									
AT Carey	8	12	362	30.16					
MG Neser	1	2	38	19.00	2	61	2	30.50	30.50
SM Boland	3	3	24	8.00	6	172	18	9.55	3.18
MJ Swepson	2	2	24	12.00	4	266	2	133.00	266.00

SOUTH AFRICA

	M	I	R	RI	IB	R	W	A	RWI
1888-89									
A Rose-Innes	2	4	14	-	3	89	5		
n/a	2	4	14	-	3	89	5		
adj	0	-	-	-	-	-	-		
AB Tancred	2	4	87	-					
n/a	2	4	87	-					
adj	0	-	-	-					
P Hutchinson	2	4	14	-					
n/a	2	4	14	-					
adj	0	-	-	-					
CH Vintcent	3	6	26	-	4	193	4		
n/a	3	6	26	-	4	193	4		
adj	0	-	-	-	-	-	-		
AE Ochse	2	4	16	0					
n/a	2	4	16	-					
adj	0	-	-	-					
WH Milton	3	6	68	-	3	48	2		
n/a	3	6	68	-	3	48	2		
adj	0	-	-	-	-	-	-		
OR Dunell	2	4	42	-					
n/a	2	4	42	-					
adj	0	-	-	-					
RB Stewart	1	2	13	-					
n/a	1	2	13	-					
adj	0	-	-	-					
FW Smith	3	6	45	-					
n/a	3	6	45	-					
adj	0	-	-	-					
CE Finlason	1	2	6	-	1	7	0		
n/a	1	2	6	-	1	7	0		
adj	0	-	-	-	-	-	-		
GA Kempis	1	2	0	-	2	76	4		
n/a	1	2	0	-	2	76	4		
WHM Richards	2	2	4	-					
n/a	1	2	4	-					
adj	0	-	-	-					
NHCD Theunissen	1	2	2	-	1	51	0		
n/a	1	2	2	-	1	51	0		
adj	0	-	-	-	-	-	-		
WH Ashley	1	2	1	-	1	95	7		
n/a	1	2	1	-	1	95	7		
adj	0	-	-	-	-	-	-		
1891-92									
TW Routledge	4	8	72	-					
n/a	4	8	72	-					
adj	0	-	-	-					
F Hearne [Eng]	4	8	121	-	1	40	2		
n/a	4	8	121	-	1	40	2		
adj	0	-	-	-	-	-	-		
CG Fichardt	2	4	15	-					
n/a	2	4	15	-					
adj	0	-	-	-					
CH Mills	1	2	25	-	1	83	2		
n/a	1	2	25	-	1	83	2		
adj	0	-	-	-	-	-	-		
EA Halliwell	8	15	188	-					
na	5	10	113	-					
adj	3	5	75	15.00					

CS Wimble	2	2	0	-					
n/a	1	2	0	-					
adj	1	-	-	-					
G Cripps	1	2	21	-	1	23	0		
n/a	1	2	21	-	1	23	0		
adj	0	-	-	-	-	-	-		
DC Parkin	1	2	6	-	1	82	3		
n/a	1	2	6	-	1	82	3		
adj	0	-	-	-	-	-	-		
JF du Toit	1	2	2	-	1	47	1		
n/a	1	2	2	-	1	47	1		
adj	0	-	-	-	-	-	-		
1895-96									
RM Poore	3	6	76	-	1	4	1		
n/a	3	6	76	-	1	4	1		
adj	0	-	-	-	-	-	-		
JH Sinclair	25	47	1069	-	41	1996	63		
n/a	5	10	303	-	6	332	17		
adj	20	37	766	20.70	35	1664	44	37.81	30.07
CFW Hime	1	2	8	-	2	31	1		
n/a	1	2	8	-	2	31	1		
adj	0	-	-	-	-	-	-		
RA Gleeson	1	2	4	-					
n/a	1	2	4	-					
adj	0	-	-	-					
FJ Cook	1	2	7	-					
n/a	1	2	7	-					
adj	0	-	-	-					
J Middleton	6	12	52	-	11	442	24		
n/a	4	8	51	-	7	271	23		
adj	2	4	1	0.25	4	71	1	71.00	284.00
JT Willoughby	2	4	8	-	3	159	6		
n/a	2	4	8	-	3	159	6		
adj	0	-	-	-	-	-	-		
CL Johnson	1	2	10	-	1	57	0		
n/a	1	2	10	-	1	57	0		
adj	0	-	-	-	-	-	-		
GH Shepstone	2	4	38	-	2	47	0		
n/a	2	4	38	-	2	47	0		
adj	0	-	-	-	-	-	-		
WHB Frank	1	2	7	-	1	52	1		
n/a	1	2	7	-	1	52	1		
adj	0	-	-	-	-	-	-		
CB Llewellyn	15	28	544	-	21	1421	48		
n/a	2	4	66	-	3	195	5		
adj	13	24	478	19.91	18	1226	43	28.51	11.93
GA Rowe	5	9	26	-	8	456	15		
n/a	4	8	22	-	6	373	14		
adj	1	1	4	4.00	2	83	1	83.00	166.00
AR Richards	1	2	6	-					
n/a	1	2	6	-					
adj	0	-	-	-					
AW Seccull	1	2	23	-	1	37	2		
n/a	1	2	23	-	1	37	2		
adj	0	-	-	-	-	-	-		
GK Glover	1	2	21	-	1	28	1		
n/a	1	2	21	-	1	28	1		

1898-99									
VM Tancred	1	2	25	-					
n/a	1	2	25	-					
adj	0	-	-	-					
HH Francis	2	4	39	-					
n/a	2	4	39	-					
adj	0	-	-	-					
RR Dower	1	2	9	-					
n/a	1	2	9	-					
adj	0	-	-	-					
M Bisset	3	6	103	-					
n/a	2	4	72	-					
adj	1	2	31	15.50					
WRT Solomon	1	2	4	-					
n/a	1	2	4	-					
adj	0	-	-	-					
R Graham	2	4	6	-	4	127	3		
n/a	2	4	6	-	4	127	3		
adj	0	-	-	-	-	-	-		
WA Shalders	12	23	355	-	1	6	1		
n/a	1	2	17	-	-	-	-		
adj	11	21	338	16.09	1	6	1	6.00	6.00
AW Powell	1	2	16	-	1	10	1		
n/a	1	2	16	-	1	10	1		
adj	0	-	-	-	-	-	-		
F Kuys	1	2	26	-	1	31	2		
n/a	1	2	26	-	1	31	2		
adj	0	-	-	-	-	-	-		
CFH Prince	1	2	6	-					
n/a	1	2	6	-					
adj	0	-	-	-					
1902-03									
LJ Tancred	14	26	530	20.38					
CMH Hathorn	12	20	325	16.25					
CJE Smith	3	6	106	17.66					
HM Taberer	1	1	2	2.00	2	48	1	48.00	96.00
AW Nourse	45	83	2234	26.91	57	1553	41	37.87	52.64
PG Thornton	1	1	1	1.00	1	20	1	20.00	20.00
JH Anderson	1	2	43	21.50					
JJ Kotze	3	5	2	0.40	5	243	6	40.50	33.74
PS Twentyman-Jones	1	2	0	0.00					
1905-06									
GC White	17	31	872	28.12	14	301	9	33.44	52.01
SJ Snooke	26	46	1008	21.91	29	702	35	20.05	16.61
GA Faulkner	25	47	1754	37.31	43	2180	82	26.58	13.93
AEE Vogler	15	26	340	13.07	28	1455	64	22.73	9.94
RO Schwarz	20	35	374	10.68	31	1417	55	25.76	14.51
PW Sherwell	13	22	427	19.40					
1907									
SD Snooke	1	1	0	0.00					
1909-10									
JW Zulch	16	32	983	30.71	2	28	0		
LA Stricker	13	24	344	14.33	9	105	1	105.00	945.00
JMM Commaille	12	22	355	16.13					
T Campbell	5	9	90	10.00					
CE Floquet	1	2	12	6.00	1	24	0		
SJ Pegler	16	28	356	12.71	23	1572	47	33.44	16.36
NO Norton	1	2	9	4.50	1	47	4	11.75	2.93
SV Samuelson	1	2	22	11.00	1	64	0		

1910-11									
COC Pearse	3	6	55	9.16	3	106	3	35.33	35.33
1912									
GPD Hartigan	5	10	114	11.40	4	141	1	141.00	564.00
HW Taylor	42	76	2936	38.63	11	156	5	31.20	68.64
F Mitchell [Eng]	3	6	28	4.66					
TA Ward	23	42	459	10.92					
CP Carter	10	15	181	12.06	12	694	28	24.78	10.62
R Beaumont	5	9	70	7.77	1	0	0		
1913-14									
PAM Hands	7	12	300	25.00	2	18	0		
PT Lewis	1	2	0	0.00					
AHC Cooper	1	2	6	3.00					
GL Tapscott	1	2	5	2.50					
HV Baumgartner	1	2	19	9.50	1	99	2	49.50	24.75
JM Blanckenberg	18	30	455	15.16	25	1817	60	30.28	12.61
JL Cox	3	6	17	2.83	4	245	4	61.25	61.25
C Newberry	4	8	62	7.75	6	268	11	24.36	13.28
CD Dixon	1	2	0	0.00	2	118	3	39.33	26.21
LR Tuckett	1	2	0	0.00	2	69	0		
D Taylor	2	4	85	21.25					
FL le Roux	1	2	1	0.50	2	24	0		
HW Chapman	2	4	39	9.75	3	104	1	104.00	312.00
RHM Hands	1	2	7	3.50					
EB Lundie	1	2	1	0.50	2	107	4	26.75	13.37
1921-22									
CN Frank	3	6	236	39.33					
WVS Ling	6	10	168	16.80	1	20	0		
WFE Marx	3	6	125	20.83	5	144	4	36.00	45.00
EP Nupen	17	31	348	11.22	31	1788	50	35.76	22.17
NV Lindsay	1	2	35	17.50					
N Reid	1	2	17	8.50	1	63	2	31.50	15.75
1922-23									
RH Catterall	24	43	1555	36.16	9	162	7	23.14	29.75
GAL Hearne	3	5	59	11.80					
WH Brann	3	5	71	14.20					
CM Francois	5	9	252	28.00	9	225	6	37.50	56.25
ID Buys	1	2	4	2.00	2	52	0		
AE Hall	7	8	11	1.37	14	886	40	22.15	7.75
DJ Meintjes	2	3	43	14.33	4	115	6	19.16	12.77
LE Tapscott	2	3	58	19.33	1	2	0		
DP Conyngham	1	2	6	3.00	2	103	2	51.50	51.50
1924									
MJ Susskind	5	8	268	33.50					
HG Deane	17	27	628	23.25					
GM Parker	2	4	3	0.75	2	273	8	34.12	8.53
1927-28									
JP Duminy	3	6	30	5.00	3	39	1	39.00	117.00
DPB Morkel	16	28	663	23.67	22	821	18	45.61	55.74
SK Coen	2	4	101	25.25	1	7	0		
HB Cameron	26	45	1239	27.53					
CL Vincent	25	38	526	13.84	40	2631	84	31.32	14.91
HLE Promnitz	2	4	14	3.50	4	161	8	20.12	10.06
AW Palm	1	2	15	7.50					
GF Bissett	4	4	38	9.50	8	469	25	18.76	6.00
IJ Siedle	18	34	977	28.73	1	7	1	7.00	7.00
JFW Nicolson	3	5	179	35.80	2	17	0		
AL Ochse	3	4	11	2.75	5	362	10	36.20	18.10

1929									
B Mitchell	42	80	3471	43.38	39	1380	27	51.11	73.82
JAJ Christy	10	18	618	34.33	6	92	2	46.00	138.00
HG Owen-Smith	5	8	252	31.50	6	113	0		
NA Quinn	12	18	90	5.00	19	1145	35	32.71	17.75
EL Dalton	15	24	698	29.08	12	490	12	40.83	40.83
Q McMillan	13	21	306	14.57	22	1243	36	34.52	21.09
AJ Bell	16	23	69	3.00	26	1567	48	32.64	17.68
EA van der Merwe	2	4	27	6.75					
1930-31									
SH Curnow	7	14	168	12.00					
KG Viljoen	27	50	1365	27.30	2	23	0		
XC Balaskas	9	13	174	13.38	11	806	22	36.63	18.31
ES Newson	3	5	30	6.00	6	265	4	66.25	99.37
JAK Cochran	1	1	4	4.00	1	47	0		
1931-32									
LS Brown	2	3	17	5.66	3	189	3	63.00	63.00
1935									
EAB Rowan	26	50	1965	39.30	2	7	0		
AD Nourse	34	62	2960	47.74	2	9	0		
HF Wade	10	18	327	18.16					
DS Tomlinson	1	1	9	9.00	1	38	0		
ACB Langton	15	23	298	12.95	23	1827	40	45.67	26.26
RJ Crisp	9	13	123	9.46	14	747	20	37.35	26.14
1935-36									
F Nicholson	4	8	76	9.50					
JB Robertson	3	6	51	8.50	5	321	6	53.50	44.58
AW Briscoe	2	3	33	11.00					
EG Bock	1	2	11	5.50	2	91	0		
RL Harvey	2	4	51	12.75					
EQ Davies	5	8	9	1.12	6	481	7	68.71	58.89
1938-39									
PGV van der Bijl	5	9	460	51.11					
A Melville	11	19	894	47.05					
N Gordon	5	6	8	1.33	8	807	20	40.35	16.14
GE Bond	1	1	0	0.00	1	16	0		
WW Wade	11	19	511	26.89					
RE Grieveson	2	2	114	57.00					
1947									
OC Dawson	9	15	293	19.53	15	578	10	57.80	86.70
TA Harris	3	5	100	20.00					
AMB Rowan	15	23	290	12.60	25	2084	54	38.59	17.86
L Tuckett	9	14	131	9.35	17	980	19	51.57	46.14
NBF Mann	19	31	400	12.90	33	1920	58	33.10	18.83
JD Lindsay	3	5	21	4.20					
VI Smith	9	16	39	2.43	12	769	12	64.08	64.08
DV Dyer	3	6	96	16.00					
JB Plimsoll	1	2	16	8.00	2	143	3	47.66	31.77
GM Fullerton	7	13	325	25.00					
1948-49									
OE Wynne	6	12	219	18.25					
DW Begbie	5	7	138	19.71	4	130	1	130.00	520.00
CN McCarthy	15	24	28	1.16	25	1510	36	41.94	29.12
MA Hanley	1	1	0	0.00	2	88	1	88.00	176.00
LA Markham	1	1	20	20.00	2	72	1	72.00	144.00
JE Cheetham	24	43	883	20.53	1	2	0		
1949-50									
JD Nel	6	11	150	13.63					
JC Watkins	15	27	612	22.66	27	816	29	28.13	26.19

HJ Tayfield	37	60	862	14.36	61	4405	170	25.91	9.29
RG Draper	2	3	25	8.33					
PL Winslow	5	9	186	20.66					
MG Melle	7	12	68	5.66	12	851	26	32.73	15.10
1951									
JHB Waite	50	86	2405	27.96					
DJ McGlew	34	64	2440	38.12	3	23	0		
CB van Ryneveld	19	33	724	21.93	20	671	17	39.47	46.43
GWA Chubb	5	9	63	7.00	8	577	21	27.47	10.46
RA McLean	40	73	2120	29.04	1	1	0		
PNF Mansell	13	22	355	16.13	18	736	11	66.90	109.47
WR Endean	28	52	1630	31.34					
1952-53									
KJ Funston	18	33	824	24.96					
ARA Murray	10	14	289	20.64	16	710	18	39.44	35.05
ERH Fuller	7	9	64	7.11	12	668	22	30.36	16.56
HJ Keith	8	16	318	19.87	2	63	0		
1953-54									
NAT Adcock	26	39	146	3.74	46	2195	104	21.10	9.33
DEJ Ironside	3	4	37	9.25	5	275	15	18.33	6.10
RJ Westcott	5	9	166	18.44	1	22	0		
1955									
TL Goddard	41	78	2516	32.25	75	3226	123	26.22	15.98
PS Heine	14	24	209	8.70	27	1455	58	25.08	11.67
1956-57									
AI Taylor	1	2	18	9.00					
AJ Pithey	17	27	819	30.33	1	5	0		
CAR Duckworth	2	4	28	7.00					
1957-58									
CGD Burger	2	4	62	15.50					
PR Carlstein	8	14	190	13.57					
1960									
S O'Linn	7	12	297	24.75					
JP Fellows-Smith	4	8	166	20.75	4	61	0		
GM Griffen	2	4	25	6.25	3	192	8	24.00	9.00
C Wesley	3	5	49	9.80					
JE Pothecary	3	4	26	6.50	6	354	9	39.33	26.21
AH McKinnon	8	13	107	8.23	15	925	26	35.57	20.52
1961-62									
EJ Barlow	30	57	2516	44.14	46	1362	40	34.05	39.15
KC Bland	21	39	1669	42.79	12	125	2	62.50	375.00
MK Elgie	3	6	75	12.50	2	46	0		
PM Pollock	28	41	607	14.80	52	2806	116	24.18	10.83
GB Lawrence	5	8	141	17.62	9	512	28	18.28	5.87
KA Walter	2	3	11	3.66	4	197	6	32.83	21.88
HD Bromfield	9	12	59	4.91	16	599	17	35.23	33.15
WS Farrer	6	10	221	22.10					
SF Burke	2	4	42	10.50	3	257	11	23.36	6.37
HR Lance	13	22	591	26.86	19	479	12	39.91	63.19
1963-64									
RG Pollock	23	41	2256	55.02	13	204	4	51.00	165.75
DT Lindsay	19	31	1130	36.45					
PL van der Merwe	15	23	533	23.17	3	22	1	22.00	66.00
DB Pithey	8	12	138	11.50	13	577	12	48.08	52.08
MA Seymour	7	10	84	8.40	9	588	9	65.33	65.33
JT Partridge	11	12	73	6.08	20	1373	44	31.20	14.18
CG Halse	3	3	30	10.00	6	260	6	43.33	43.33
1964-65									
GD Varnals	3	6	97	16.16	1	2	0		
GG Hall	1	1	0	0.00	1	94	1	94.00	94.00

MJ Macaulay	1	2	33	16.50	2	73	2	36.50	36.50
1965----------									
A Bacher	12	22	679	30.86					
R Dumbrill	5	10	153	15.30	9	336	9	37.33	37.33
JT Botten	3	6	65	10.83	6	337	8	42.12	31.59
1966-67----------									
MJ Procter	7	10	226	22.60	14	616	41	15.02	5.12
PHJ Trimborn	4	4	13	3.25	8	257	11	23.36	16.98
JH du Preez	2	2	0	0.00	3	51	3	17.00	17.00
1969-70----------									
BA Richards	4	7	508	72.57	3	26	1	26.00	78.00
BL Irvine	4	7	353	50.42					
D Gamsy	2	3	39	13.00					
GA Chevalier	1	2	0	0.00	2	100	5	20.00	8.00
AJ Traicos [Zim]	3	4	8	2.00	6	207	4	51.75	77.62

1991-92----------									
MW Rushmere	1	2	6	3.00					
AC Hudson	35	63	2007	31.85					
KC Wessels [Aus]	16	29	1027	35.41					
PN Kirsten	12	22	626	28.45	3	30	0		
WJ Cronje	68	111	3714	33.45	84	1288	43	29.95	58.50
AP Kuiper	1	2	34	17.00					
DJ Richardson	42	64	1359	21.23					
RP Snell	5	8	95	11.87	9	538	19	28.31	13.40
MW Pringle	4	6	67	11.16	5	270	5	54.00	54.00
AA Donald	72	94	652	6.93	129	7344	330	22.25	8.69
T Bosch	1	2	5	2.50	2	104	3	34.66	23.10
1992-93----------									
SJ Cook	3	6	107	17.83					
JN Rhodes	52	80	2532	31.65	2	5	0		
BM McMillan	38	62	1968	31.74	64	2537	75	33.82	28.85
O Henry	3	3	53	17.66	4	189	3	63.00	83.99
BN Schultz	9	8	9	1.12	14	749	37	20.24	7.65
CR Matthews	18	25	348	13.92	33	1502	52	28.88	18.32
DJ Cullinan	70	115	4554	39.60	8	71	2	35.50	142.00
1993-94----------									
PL Symcox	20	27	741	27.44	34	1603	37	43.32	39.80
CE Eksteen	7	11	91	8.27	14	494	8	61.75	108.06
G Kirsten	101	176	7289	41.41	15	142	2	71.00	532.50
PS de Villiers	18	26	359	13.80	34	2063	85	24.27	9.70
1994-95----------									
JB Commins	3	6	125	20.83					
SD Jack	2	2	7	3.50	4	196	8	24.50	12.25
PJR Steyn	3	6	127	21.16					
1995-96----------									
JH Kallis	166	280	13289	-	272	9535	292		
n/a	1	2	83	-	2	38	1		
adj	165	278	13206	47.50	270	9497	291	32.63	30.27
SM Pollock	108	156	3781	24.23	202	9733	421	23.11	11.08
PR Adams	45	55	360	6.54	76	4405	134	32.87	18.64
1996-97----------									
HH Gibbs	90	154	6167	40.04	1	4	0		
L Klusener	49	69	1906	27.62	84	3033	80	37.91	39.80
AM Bacher	19	33	833	25.24	1	4	0		
1997-98----------									
MV Boucher	147	206	5515	-	1	6	1		
n/a	1	2	17	-	-	-	-		
adj	146	204	5498	26.95	1	6	1	6.00	6.00
HD Ackerman	4	8	161	20.12					

M Ntini	101	116	699	6.02	190	11242	390	28.82	14.04
GFJ Liebenberg	5	8	104	13.00					
1998									
S Elworthy	4	5	72	14.40	8	444	13	34.15	21.01
1998-99									
DJ Terbrugge	7	8	16	2.00	13	517	20	25.85	16.80
1999-00									
HH Dippenaar	38	62	1718	27.70	1	1	0		
M Hayward	16	17	66	3.88	29	1609	54	29.79	15.99
PC Strydom	2	3	35	11.66	1	27	0		
N Boje	43	62	1312	21.61	72	4265	100	42.65	30.70
2000									
ND McKenzie	58	94	3253	34.60	6	68	0		
2000-01									
M Ngam	3	1	1	1.00	5	189	11	17.18	7.80
JM Kemp	4	6	80	13.33	8	222	9	24.66	21.91
2001-02									
CW Henderson	7	7	65	9.28	12	928	22	42.18	23.00
A Nel	36	42	337	8.02	69	3919	123	31.86	17.87
JL Ontong	2	4	57	14.25	3	133	1	133.00	399.00
AG Prince	66	104	3665	35.24	4	47	1	47.00	188.00
GC Smith	117	205	9265	-	34	885	8		
n/a	1	2	12	-	-	-	-		
adj	116	203	9253	45.58	37	885	8	110.62	511.61
AJ Hall	21	33	760	23.03	38	1617	45	35.93	30.34
D Pretorius	4	4	22	5.50	8	430	6	71.66	95.54
2002-03									
M van Jaarsveld	9	15	397	26.46	1	28	0		
JA Rudolph	48	83	2622	31.59	19	432	4	108.00	513.00
AC Dawson	2	1	10	10.00	4	117	5	23.40	18.72
CM Willoughby	2	-	-	-	3	125	1	125.00	375.00
RJ Peterson	15	20	464	23.20	27	1416	38	37.26	26.47
2003									
M Zondeki	6	5	82	16.40	11	480	19	25.26	14.62
2004-05									
Z de Bruyn	3	5	155	31.00	3	92	3	30.66	30.66
TL Tsolekile	3	5	47	9.40					
HM Amla	124	215	9282	43.17	5	37	0		
AB de Villiers	114	191	8765	45.89	5	104	2	52.00	130.00
DW Steyn	93	119	1251	10.51	171	10077	439	22.95	8.93
CK Langeveldt	6	4	16	4.00	10	593	16	37.06	23.16
2005-06									
J Botha	5	6	83	13.83	10	573	17	33.70	19.82
2006-07									
M Morkel	86	104	944	9.07	160	8550	309	27.66	14.32
PL Harris	37	48	460	9.58	63	3901	103	37.87	23.16
2008-09									
JP Duminy	46	74	2103	28.41	57	1601	42	38.11	51.72
I Khan	1	1	20	20.00					
JA Morkel	1	1	58	58.00	2	132	1	132.00	264.00
2009-10									
F de Wet	2	2	20	10.00	4	186	6	31.00	20.66
R McLaren	2	3	47	15.66	4	162	3	54.00	71.99
WD Parnell	6	4	67	16.75	10	414	15	27.60	18.39
AN Petersen	36	64	2093	32.70	7	62	1	62.00	434.00
2010									
LL Tsotsobe	5	5	19	3.80	9	448	9	49.77	49.77
2011-12									
VD Philander	64	94	1779	18.92	119	5000	224	22.32	11.85
Imran Tahir	20	23	130	5.65	37	2294	57	40.24	26.12

M de Lange	2	2	9	4.50	4	277	9	30.77	13.67
2012-13									
RK Kleinveldt	4	5	27	5.40	7	422	10	42.20	29.54
F du Plessis	69	118	4163	35.27	5	69	0		
D Elgar	76	134	4864	36.29	45	673	15	44.86	134.58
KJ Abbott	11	14	95	6.78	21	886	39	22.71	12.22
2013-14									
Q de Kock	54	91	3300	36.26					
2014									
DL Piedt	9	12	131	10.91	15	1175	26	45.19	26.07
2014-15									
S van Zyl	12	17	395	23.23	11	148	6	24.66	45.20
T Bavuma	51	87	2612	30.02	5	61	1	61.00	305.00
SR Harmer	7	9	136	15.11	12	785	33	23.78	8.64
2015									
DJ Villas	6	9	94	10.44					
2015-16									
K Rabada	52	79	786	9.94	95	5446	243	22.41	8.76
CH Morris	4	7	173	24.71	8	459	12	38.25	25.49
GC Viljoen	1	2	26	13.00	2	94	1	94.00	188.00
SC Cook	11	19	632	33.26					
2016-17									
KA Maharaj	42	66	953	14.43	76	4601	150	30.67	15.53
T Shamsi	2	4	20	5.00	4	278	6	46.33	30.88
D Olivier	15	19	50	2.63	27	1294	59	21.93	10.03
TB de Bruyn	12	23	428	18.60	4	74	0		
2017									
HG Kuhn	4	8	113	14.12					
2017-18									
AK Markram	31	57	1973	34.61	12	130	2	65.00	390.00
AL Phehlukwayo	4	4	19	4.75	8	147	11	13.36	9.71
L Ngidi	13	20	52	2.60	25	971	47	20.65	10.98
2018-19									
Zubayr Hamza	6	12	212	17.66					
PWA Mulder	10	17	255	15.00	18	464	18	25.77	25.77
2019-20									
S Mathusamy	2	4	98	24.50	3	180	2	90.00	135.00
A Nortje	12	21	115	5.47	21	1321	47	28.10	12.55
H Klaasen	1	2	11	5.50					
GF Linde	3	6	135	22.50	5	252	9	28.00	15.55
HE van der Dussen	15	27	824	30.51					
D Pretorius	3	6	83	13.83	6	252	7	36.00	30.85
PJ Malan	3	6	156	26.00	1	5	0		
D Paterson	2	4	43	10.75	3	166	4	41.50	31.12
BE Hendricks	1	2	9	4.50	2	175	6	29.16	9.71
2020-21									
L Sipamla	3	4	15	3.75	6	245	11	22.27	12.14
2021									
KD Peterson	7	13	453	34.84					
K Verreynne	8	13	343	26.38					
2021-22									
M Jansen	5	8	118	14.75	9	570	28	20.35	6.54
SJ Erwee	4	8	240	30.00					
GA Stuurman	2	2	11	5.50	1	124	1	124.00	124.00
RD Rickelton	2	4	114	28.50					
LB Williams	2	3	25	8.33	2	105	3	35.00	23.33
K Zondo	1	-	-	-					

WEST INDIES

	M	I	R	RI	IB	R	W	A	RWI
1928									
G Challenor	3	6	101	16.33					
FR Martin	9	18	486	27.00	11	619	8	77.37	106.38
MP Fernandes	2	4	49	12.25					
RK Nunes	4	8	245	30.62					
WH St Hill	3	6	117	19.50	1	9	0		
CA Roach	16	32	952	29.75	5	103	2	51.50	128.75
LN Constantine	18	33	635	19.24	29	1746	58	30.10	15.05
JA Small	3	6	79	13.16	4	184	3	61.33	81.77
CR Browne	4	8	176	22.00	6	288	6	48.00	48.00
GN Francis	10	18	81	4.50	13	763	23	33.17	18.74
HC Griffith	13	23	91	3.95	18	1243	44	28.25	11.55
ELG Hoad	4	8	98	12.25					
OC Scott	8	13	171	13.15	11	925	22	42.04	21.02
EL Bartlett	5	8	131	16.37					
CV Wight	2	4	67	16.75	1	6	0		
1929-30									
GA Headley	22	40	2190	54.75	14	230	0		
FI de Caires	3	6	232	38.66	1	9	0		
JED Sealy	11	19	478	25.15	6	94	3	31.33	62.66
LA Walcott	1	2	40	20.00	2	32	1	32.00	64.00
EL St Hill	2	4	18	4.50	4	221	3	73.66	98.21
EAC Hunte	3	6	166	27.66					
MG Grell	1	2	34	17.00	2	17	0		
N Betancourt	1	2	52	26.00					
EE Achong	6	11	81	7.36	8	378	8	47.25	47.25
CEL Jones	4	7	63	9.00	3	11	0		
CC Passailaigue	1	2	46	23.00	1	15	0		
IM Barrow	11	19	276	14.52					
OC Da Costa	5	9	153	17.00	7	175	3	58.33	136.10
G Gladstone	1	1	12	12.00	2	189	1	189.00	378.00
1930-31									
LS Birkett	4	8	136	17.00	4	71	1	71.00	284.00
GC Grant	12	22	413	18.77	3	18	0		
1933									
CA Merry	2	4	34	8.50					
EA Martindale	10	14	58	4.14	17	804	37	21.72	9.97
CA Wiles	1	2	2	1.00					
VA Valentine	2	4	35	8.75	2	104	1	104.00	208.00
BJ Sealey	1	2	41	20.50	1	10	1	10.00	10.00
1934-35									
GM Carew	4	7	170	24.28	1	2	0		
RS Grant	7	11	220	20.00	11	353	11	32.09	32.09
LG Hylton	6	8	70	8.75	12	418	16	26.12	19.59
CM Christiani	4	7	98	14.00					
KL Wishart	1	2	52	26.00					
JM Neblett	1	2	16	8.00	2	75	1	75.00	150.00
GH Mudie	1	1	5	5.00	2	40	3	13.33	8.88
RL Fuller	1	1	1	1.00	2	12	0		
1939									
JB Stollmeyer	32	56	2159	38.55	23	507	13	39.00	69.00
KH Weekes	2	3	173	57.66					
JH Cameron	2	3	6	2.00	2	88	3	29.33	19.55
CB Clarke	3	4	3	0.75	4	261	6	43.50	28.99
GE Gomez	29	46	1243	27.02	46	1590	58	27.41	21.73
EAV Williams	4	6	113	18.33	7	241	9	26.77	20.82
TF Johnson	1	1	9	9.00	2	129	3	43.00	28.66
VH Stollmeyer	1	1	96	96.00					

1947-48									
CL Walcott	44	74	3798	51.32	22	408	11	37.09	74.18
ED Weekes	48	81	4455	55.00	10	77	1	77.00	770.00
RJ Christiani	22	37	896	24.21	6	108	3	36.00	72.00
JDC Goddard	27	39	859	22.02	36	1050	33	31.81	34.70
W Ferguson	8	10	200	20.00	15	1165	34	34.26	15.11
PEW Jones	9	11	47	4.27	17	751	25	30.04	20.42
BBM Gaskin	2	3	17	5.66	4	158	2	79.00	158.00
AG Ganteaume	1	1	112	112.00					
FMM Worrell	51	87	3860	44.36	82	2672	69	38.72	46.01
J Trim	4	5	21	4.20	8	291	18	16.16	7.18
LR Pierre	1	-	-	-	2	28	0		
KR Rickards	2	3	104	34.66					
HHH Johnson	3	4	38	9.50	5	238	13	18.30	7.03
ESM Kentish	2	2	1	0.50	4	178	8	22.25	11.12
1948-49									
AF Rae	15	24	1016	42.33					
FJ Cameron	5	7	151	21.57	7	278	3	92.66	216.20
DS Atkinson	22	35	922	26.34	39	1647	47	35.04	29.07
1950									
S Ramadhin	43	58	361	6.22	76	4579	158	28.98	13.93
AL Valentine	36	51	141	2.76	63	4215	139	30.32	13.74
1951-52									
RE Marshall	4	7	143	20.42	2	15	0		
SC Guillen [NZ]	5	6	104	17.33					
1952-53									
BH Pairaudeau	13	21	454	21.61	1	3	0		
AP Binns	5	8	64	8.00					
FM King	14	17	116	6.82	23	1159	29	39.96	31.69
RA Legall	4	5	50	10.00					
GL Wight	1	1	21	21.00					
RC Miller	1	1	23	23.00	1	28	0		
AHP Scott	1	1	5	5.00	2	140	0		
1953-54									
MC Fredrick	1	2	30	15.00					
JKC Holt	17	31	1066	34.38	3	20	1	20.00	
CA McWatt	6	9	202	22.44	1	16	1	16.00	16.00
GS Sobers	93	160	8032	50.20	159	7999	235	34.03	23.02
1954-55									
GL Gibbs	1	2	12	6.00	2	7	0		
OG Smith	26	42	1331	31.69	37	1625	48	33.85	26.09
LS Butler	1	1	16	16.00	1	151	2	75.50	37.75
CC Depeiaza	5	8	187	23.37	2	15	0		
NE Marshall	1	2	8	4.00	2	62	2	31.00	31.00
DT Dewdney	9	12	17	1.41	16	807	21	38.42	29.27
HA Furlonge	3	5	99	19.80					
1955-56									
AT Roberts	1	2	28	14.00					
1957									
RB Kanhai	79	137	6227	45.45	9	85	0		
R Gilchrist	13	14	60	4.28	23	1521	57	26.68	10.76
NS Asgarali	2	4	62	15.50					
FCM Alexander	25	38	961	25.28					
1957-58									
CC Hunte	44	78	3245	41.60	8	110	2	55.00	220.00
ES Atkinson	8	9	126	14.00	15	589	25	23.56	14.13
EDAS McMorris	13	21	564	26.85					
IS Madray	2	3	3	1.00	4	108	0		
LR Gibbs	79	109	488	4.47	148	8989	309	29.09	13.93

JO Taylor	3	5	4	0.80	5	273	10	27.30	13.65
1958-59---									
BF Butcher	44	78	3104	39.79	6	90	5	18.00	21.60
WW Hall	48	66	818	12.39	92	5066	192	26.38	12.64
JS Solomon	27	46	1326	28.82	14	268	4	67.00	234.50
MR Bynoe	4	6	111	18.50	1	5	1	5.00	5.00
1959-60---									
RO Scarlett	3	4	54	13.50	6	209	2	104.50	313.50
CD Watson	7	6	12	2.00	13	724	19	38.10	26.08
CK Singh	2	3	11	3.66	4	166	5	33.20	26.56
SM Nurse	29	54	2523	46.72	3	7	0		
CC Griffith	28	42	530	12.61	50	2683	94	28.54	15.18
1960-61---									
CW Smith	5	10	222	22.20					
PD Lashley	4	7	159	22.71	1	1	1	1.00	1.00
1961-62---									
SC Stayers	4	4	58	14.50	8	364	9	40.44	35.94
JL Hendriks	20	32	447	13.96					
WV Rodriguez	5	7	96	13.71	8	374	7	53.42	61.05
IL Mendonca	2	2	81	40.50					
DW Allen	5	7	75	10.71					
LA King	2	4	41	10.25	4	154	9	17.11	7.60
1963---									
MC Carew	19	36	1127	31.30	22	437	8	54.62	150.20
DL Murray	62	96	1993	20.76					
1964-65---									
AW White	2	4	71	17.75	3	152	3	50.66	50.66
BA Davis	4	8	245	30.62					
1966---									
DAJ Holford	24	39	768	19.69	35	2009	51	39.39	27.03
1966-67---									
CH Lloyd	110	175	7515	42.94	45	622	10	62.20	279.90
1967-68---									
GS Camacho	11	22	640	29.09	1	12	0		
1968-69---									
RC Fredericks	59	109	4334	39.76	43	548	7	78.28	480.86
CA Davis	15	29	1301	44.86	20	330	2	165.00	1650.00
RM Edwards	5	8	65	8.12	9	626	18	34.77	17.38
1969---									
MLC Foster	14	24	580	24.16	23	600	9	66.66	170.35
JN Shepherd	5	8	77	9.62	8	479	19	25.21	10.61
VA Holder	40	59	682	11.55	72	3627	109	33.27	21.97
TM Findlay	10	16	212	13.25					
GC Shillingford	7	8	57	7.12	12	537	15	35.80	28.64
1970-71---									
AG Barrett	6	7	40	5.71	10	603	13	46.38	35.67
JM Noreiga	4	5	11	2.20	7	493	17	29.00	11.94
DM Lewis	3	5	259	51.80					
KD Boyce	21	30	657	21.90	39	1801	60	30.01	19.50
Inshan Ali	12	18	172	9.55	23	1621	34	47.67	32.24
UG Dowe	4	3	8	2.66	8	534	12	44.50	29.66
1971-72---									
LG Rowe	30	49	2047	41.77	5	44	0		
GA Greenidge	5	9	209	23.22	4	75	0		
AI Kallicharran	66	109	4399	40.35	16	158	4	39.50	158.00
AB Howard	1	-	-	-	1	140	2	70.00	35.00
RR Jumadeen	12	14	84	6.00	22	1141	29	39.34	29.84
1972-73---									
ET Willett	5	8	74	9.25	10	482	11	43.81	39.82

1973									
RGA Headley	2	4	62	15.50					
BD Julien	24	34	866	25.47	45	1868	50	37.36	33.62
1973-74									
AME Roberts	47	62	762	12.29	90	5174	202	25.61	11.41
1974-75									
CG Greenidge	108	185	7558	40.85	2	4	0		
IVA Richards	121	182	8540	46.92	103	1964	32	61.37	197.53
L Baichan	3	6	184	30.66					
1975-76									
MA Holding	60	76	910	11.97	113	5898	249	23.68	10.74
Imtiaz Ali	1	1	1	1.00	2	89	2	44.50	44.50
AL Padmore	2	2	8	4.00	3	135	1	135.00	405.00
WW Daniel	10	11	46	4.18	19	910	36	25.27	13.33
1976									
HA Gomes	60	91	3171	34.84	51	930	15	62.00	210.80
CL King	9	16	418	26.12	11	282	3	94.00	344.66
1976-77									
J Garner	58	68	672	9.88	111	5433	259	20.97	8.98
CEH Croft	27	37	158	4.27	52	2913	125	23.30	9.69
IT Shillingford	4	7	218	31.14					
1977-78									
DL Haynes	116	202	7487	37.06	3	8	1	8.00	24.00
RA Austin	2	2	22	11.00	1	5	0		
DR Parry	12	20	381	19.05	17	936	23	40.69	30.07
AE Greenidge	6	10	222	22.20					
AB Williams	7	12	469	39.08					
DA Murray	19	31	601	19.38					
S Shivnarine	8	14	379	27.07	10	167	1	167.00	1670.00
N Phillip	9	15	297	19.80	15	1041	28	37.17	19.91
ST Clarke	11	16	172	10.75	19	1170	42	27.85	12.59
SFAF Bacchus	19	30	782	26.06	1	3	0		
1978-79									
MD Marshall	81	107	1810	16.91	151	7876	376	20.94	8.40
HS Chang	1	2	8	4.00					
1980-81									
R Nanan	1	2	16	8.00	2	91	4	22.75	11.37
EH Mattis	4	5	145	29.00	2	14	0		
1981-82									
PJL Dujon	81	115	3322	28.88					
1982-83									
AL Logie	52	78	2470	31.66	2	4	0		
WW Davis	14	17	202	11.88	28	1472	45	32.71	20.35
1983-84									
EAE Baptiste	10	11	233	21.18	19	563	16	35.18	41.77
RB Richardson	86	146	5949	40.74	7	18	0		
RA Harper	25	32	535	16.71	39	1291	46	28.06	23.78
MA Small	2	1	3	3.00	4	153	4	38.25	38.25
1984-85									
CA Walsh	132	185	936	5.05	242	12688	519	24.44	11.39
CG Butts	7	8	108	13.50	10	595	10	59.50	59.50
1985-86									
CA Best	8	13	342	26.30	2	21	0		
BP Patterson	28	38	145	3.81	53	2874	93	30.90	17.60
TRO Payne	1	1	5	5.00					
1986-87									
AH Gray	5	8	48	6.00	10	377	22	17.13	7.78
1987-88									
WKM Benjamin	21	26	470	18.07	35	1648	61	27.01	15.49
CL Hooper	102	173	5762	33.30	145	5635	114	49.42	62.85

CEL Ambrose	98	145	1439	9.92	179	8501	405	20.99	9.27
1988									
KLT Arthurton	33	50	1382	27.64	19	183	1	183.00	3477.00
1988-89									
PV Simmons	26	47	1002	21.31	16	257	4	64.25	257.00
IR Bishop	43	63	632	10.03	76	3909	161	24.27	11.45
1989-90									
EA Moseley	2	4	35	8.75	4	261	6	43.50	28.99
1990-91									
BC Lara	131	232	11953	-	4	28	0		
n/a	1	2	41	-	-	-	-		
adj	130	230	11912	51.79	4	28	0		
1991									
IBA Allen	2	2	5	2.50	3	180	5	36.00	21.60
CB Lambert	5	9	284	31.55	2	5	1	5.00	10.00
1991-92									
JC Adams	54	90	3012	33.46	60	1336	27	49.48	109.95
D Williams	11	19	242	12.73					
KCG Benjamin	26	36	222	6.16	48	2785	92	30.27	15.79
1992-93									
JR Murray	33	45	918	20.40					
AC Cummins	5	6	98	16.33	8	342	8	42.75	42.75
1993-94									
S Chanderpaul	164	280	11867	42.38	43	883	9	98.11	468.74
SC Williams	31	52	1183	22.75	1	19	0		
1994-95									
R Dhanraj	4	4	17	4.25	8	595	8	74.37	74.37
CE Cuffy	15	23	58	2.52	26	1455	43	33.83	20.45
SL Campbell	52	93	2882	30.98					
CO Browne	20	30	387	12.90					
OD Gibson	2	4	93	23.25	4	275	3	91.66	122.21
1995-96									
RG Samuels	6	12	372	31.00					
PIC Thompson	2	3	17	5.66	3	215	5	43.00	25.80
1996-97									
AFG Griffith	14	27	638	23.62					
RIC Holder	11	17	380	22.35					
FA Rose	19	28	344	12.28	31	1637	53	30.88	18.06
M Dillon	38	68	549	8.07	66	4398	131	33.57	16.91
FL Reifer	6	12	111	9.25					
1997-98									
PA Wallace	7	13	279	21.46					
RN Lewis	5	10	89	8.90	8	456	4	114.00	228.00
NAM McLean	19	32	368	11.50	32	1873	44	42.56	30.95
D Ramnarine	12	21	106	5.04	22	1383	45	30.73	15.02
1998-99									
RD Jacobs	65	112	2577	23.00					
D Ganga	48	86	2160	25.11	8	106	1	106.00	848.00
RD King	19	27	66	2.44	33	1733	53	32.69	20.35
S Ragoonath	2	4	13	3.25					
DRE Joseph	4	7	141	20.14					
PT Collins	32	47	235	5.00	61	3671	106	34.63	19.92
LA Roberts	1	1	0	0.00					
NO Perry	4	7	74	10.57	7	446	10	44.60	31.22
CD Collymore	30	52	197	3.78	53	3004	93	32.30	18.40
1999-00									
RL Powell	2	3	53	17.66	2	49	0		
CH Gayle	103	182	7214	39.63	104	3120	73	42.73	60.87
WW Hinds	45	80	2608	32.60	25	590	16	36.87	57.60

2000									
RR Sarwan	87	154	5842	37.93	56	1163	23	50.56	123.10
MV Nagamootoo	5	8	185	23.12	8	637	12	53.08	35.38
MI Black	6	11	21	1.90	9	597	12	49.75	37.31
MN Samuels	71	127	3917	30.84	69	2445	41	59.63	100.35
CEL Stuart	6	9	24	2.66	12	628	20	31.40	18.84
NC McGarrell	4	6	61	10.16	7	453	17	26.64	10.96
LV Garrick	1	2	27	13.50					
2001-02									
RO Hinds	15	25	505	20.20	22	870	13	66.92	113.24
A Sanford	11	17	72	4.23	18	1316	30	43.86	26.31
2002									
DBL Powell	37	57	407	7.14	66	4068	85	47.85	37.15
2002-03									
GR Breese	1	2	5	2.50	2	135	2	67.50	67.50
JJC Lawson	13	21	52	2.47	25	1512	51	29.64	14.52
VC Drakes	12	20	386	19.30	21	1362	33	41.27	26.26
DS Smith	43	76	1760	23.15	1	3	0		
DE Bernard	3	6	202	33.66	5	185	4	46.25	57.81
CS Baugh	21	36	610	16.94					
OAC Banks	10	16	318	19.87	20	1367	28	48.82	34.87
TL Best	25	38	401	10.55	45	2291	57	40.19	31.72
2003									
JE Taylor	46	73	856	11.72	78	4480	130	34.46	20.67
FH Edwards	55	88	394	4.47	97	6249	165	37.87	22.26
2003-04									
DR Smith	10	14	320	22.85	13	344	7	49.14	91.25
D Mohammed	5	8	225	28.12	9	668	13	51.38	35.57
2004									
DJ Bravo	40	71	2200	30.98	61	3426	86	39.83	28.25
SC Joseph	5	10	147	14.70	1	8	0		
2004-05									
DJ Pagon	2	3	37	12.33					
N Deonarine	18	30	725	24.16	25	713	24	29.70	30.93
DM Washington	1	1	7	7.00	2	93	0		
2005									
XM Marshall	7	12	243	20.25	1	0	0		
RS Morton	15	27	573	21.22	5	50	0		
D Ramdin	74	126	2898	23.00					
RR Ramdass	1	2	26	13.00					
2005-06									
IDR Bradshaw	5	8	96	12.00	7	540	9	60.00	46.66
2007									
DJG Sammy	38	63	1323	21.00	65	3007	84	35.79	27.69
2007-08									
BA Parchment	2	4	55	13.75					
SJ Benn	25	39	486	12.46	42	3402	87	39.10	18.87
S Chattergoon	4	7	127	18.14					
2008									
AS Jaggernauth	1	2	0	0.00	2	96	1	96.00	192.00
2008-09									
BP Nash	21	33	1103	33.42	14	247	2	123.50	864.50
LS Baker	4	6	23	3.83	5	395	5	79.00	79.00
LMP Simmons	8	16	278	17.37	5	147	1	147.00	735.00
2009									
DM Richards	3	6	125	20.83					
OJ Phillips	2	4	160	40.00					
TM Dowlin	6	11	343	31.18	1	3	0		
CAK Walton	2	4	13	3.25					
NO Miller	1	2	5	2.50	2	67	0		

RA Austin	2	4	39	9.75	4	155	3	51.66	68.87
KAJ Roach	71	114	1083	9.50	128	6578	242	27.18	14.37
2009-10-----									
AB Barath	15	28	657	23.46	1	4	0		
R Rampaul	18	31	335	10.80	33	1705	49	34.79	23.42
GC Tonge	1	2	25	12.50	2	113	1	113.00	226.00
2010-----									
S Shillingford	16	26	266	10.23	27	2419	70	34.55	13.32
NT Pascal	2	2	12	6.00	2	59	0		
BJ Bess	1	2	11	5.50	2	92	1	92.00	184.00
2010-11-----									
DM Bravo	56	102	3538	34.68	1	2	0		
AD Russell	1	1	2	2.00	2	104	1	104.00	208.00
2011-----									
D Bishoo	36	61	707	11.59	59	4350	117	37.17	18.74
KC Brathwaite	77	148	4743	32.04	59	1321	25	52.84	124.70
KOA Powell	44	83	2113	25.45	1	0	0		
KA Edwards	17	32	986	30.81	1	19	0		
2012-----									
ST Gabriel	56	84	221	2.63	98	5127	161	31.84	19.38
AB Fudadin	3	5	122	24.40	1	11	0		
SP Narine	6	7	40	5.71	11	851	21	40.52	21.22
2012-13-----									
V Permaul	9	13	145	11.15	17	1183	31	38.16	20.92
2013-14-----									
SS Cottrell	2	4	11	2.75	2	196	2	98.00	98.00
2014-----									
J Blackwood	46	84	2437	29.01	18	242	4	60.50	272.25
JO Holder	56	100	2571	25.71	98	3981	142	28.03	19.34
LR Johnson	9	16	403	25.18	1	9	0		
2014-15-----									
KK Peters	1	1	0	0.00	1	69	2	34.50	17.25
2015-----									
SD Hope	38	72	1726	23.97					
SO Dowrich	35	62	1570	25.32					
R Chandrika	5	10	140	14.00					
2015-16-----									
JA Warrican	13	23	163	7.08	23	1444	41	35.21	19.75
CR Brathwaite	3	5	181	36.20	4	242	1	242.00	968.00
2016-----									
RL Chase	43	79	2009	25.43	61	3377	79	42.74	33.00
ML Cummins	14	22	114	5.18	23	1084	27	40.14	34.19
AS Joseph	20	31	443	14.29	37	1971	50	39.42	29.17
2017-----									
SO Hetmyer	16	30	838	27.93					
VA Singh	3	6	63	10.50					
KA Hope	5	9	101	11.22					
2017-18-----									
SW Ambris	6	12	166	13.83					
RA Reifer	1	2	52	26.00	2	88	2	44.00	44.00
2018-----									
KMA Paul	3	6	96	16.00	5	189	6	31.50	26.24
2018-19-----									
SH Lewis	2	4	24	6.00	2	162	3	54.00	35.99
JD Campbell	18	36	752	20.88	2	30	0		
2019-----									
SSJ Brooks	11	20	501	25.05					
JN Hamilton	1	2	5	2.50					
RRS Cornwall	9	15	238	15.86	17	1284	34	37.76	18.88

2020-21									
JA da Silva	14	25	640	25.60					
CK Holder	1	2	21	10.50	1	110	2	55.00	27.50
S Moseley	2	4	28	7.00					
NE Bonner	12	21	754	35.90	8	82	1	82.00	656.00
KR Mayers	11	21	664	31.61	18	358	20	17.90	16.11
2021									
JNT Seales	7	11	30	2.72	13	632	27	23.40	11.26
2021-22									
JL Solozano	1	-	-	-					

NEW ZEALAND

	M	I	R	RI	IB	R	W	A	RWI
1929-30									
CS Dempster	10	15	723	48.20	1	10	0		
H Foley	1	2	4	2.00					
AW Roberts	5	10	248	24.80	4	209	7	29.85	17.05
ML Page	14	20	492	24.60	12	231	5	46.20	110.88
RC Blunt	9	13	330	25.38	14	472	12	39.33	45.88
TC Lowry	7	8	223	27.87	2	5	0		
KC James	11	13	52	4.00					
FT Badcock	7	9	137	15.22	9	610	16	38.12	21.44
GR Dickinson	3	5	31	6.20	6	245	8	30.62	22.96
WE Merritt	6	8	73	9.12	9	617	12	51.41	38.55
M Henderson	1	2	8	4.00	2	64	2	32.00	32.00
JE Mills	7	10	241	24.10					
EG McLeod	1	2	18	9.00	1	5	0		
GL Weir	11	16	416	26.00	8	209	7	29.85	34.11
CFW Allcott	6	7	113	16.14	8	541	6	90.16	120.21
HM McGirr	2	1	51	51.00	3	115	1	115.00	345.00
AM Matheson	2	1	7	7.00	3	136	2	68.00	102.00
1931									
JL Kerr	7	12	212	17.66					
IB Cromb	5	8	123	15.37	7	442	8	55.25	48.34
HG Vivian	7	10	421	42.10	10	633	17	37.23	21.90
1931-32									
DC Cleverley	2	4	19	4.75	2	130	0		
J Newman	3	4	33	8.25	3	254	2	127.00	190.50
1932-33									
PE Whitelaw	2	4	64	16.00					
HD Smith	1	1	4	4.00	1	113	1	113.00	113.00
DL Freeman	2	2	2	1.00	2	169	1	169.00	338.00
JA Dunning	4	6	38	6.33	7	493	5	98.60	138.04
1937									
WA Hadlee	11	19	543	28.57					
WM Wallace	13	21	439	20.90	1	5	0		
MP Donnelly	7	12	582	48.50	1	20	0		
DAR Moloney	3	6	156	26.00	1	9	0		
EWT Tindill	5	9	73	8.11					
J Cowie	9	13	90	6.92	13	969	45	21.53	6.21
N Gallichan	1	2	32	16.00	2	113	3	37.66	25.10
1945-46									
WM Anderson	1	2	5	2.50					
VJ Scott	10	17	458	26.94	2	4	0		
CG Rowe	1	2	0	0.00					
LA Butterfield	1	2	0	0.00	1	24	0		
DAN McRae	1	2	8	4.00	1	44	0		
C Burke	1	2	4	2.0	1	30	2	15.00	7.50

1946-47									
B Sutcliffe	42	76	2727	35.88	20	344	4	86.00	430.00
DD Taylor	3	5	77	15.40					
FB Smith	4	6	237	39.50					
RH Scott	1	1	18	18.00	1	74	1	74.00	74.00
TB Burtt	10	15	252	16.80	14	1170	33	35.45	15.03
CA Snedden	1	-	-	-	1	46	0		
1949									
GO Rabone	12	20	562	28.10	14	635	16	39.68	34.72
FLH Mooney	14	22	343	15.59	1	0	0		
HB Cave	19	31	229	7.38	25	1849	62	29.82	12.02
JR Reid	58	108	3428	31.74	72	2835	85	33.35	28.24
GF Cresswell	3	5	14	2.80	4	292	13	22.46	6.91
1950-51									
AR MacGibbon	26	46	814	17.69	37	2160	70	30.85	16.30
AM Moir	17	30	327	10.90	19	1418	28	50.64	34.36
JA Hayes	15	22	73	3.31	19	1217	30	40.56	25.68
1951-52									
RWG Emery	2	4	46	11.50	1	52	2	26.00	13.00
DD Beard	4	7	101	14.42	7	302	9	33.55	26.09
JG Leggat	9	18	351	19.50					
1952-53									
FE Fisher	1	2	23	11.50	1	78	1	78.00	78.00
EM Meuli	1	2	38	19.00					
LSM Miller	13	25	346	13.84	1	1	0		
RW Blair	19	34	189	5.55	28	1515	43	35.23	22.94
ME Chapple	14	27	497	18.40	5	84	1	84.00	420.00
MB Poore	14	24	355	14.79	11	367	9	40.77	49.82
EW Dempster	5	8	106	13.25	6	219	2	109.50	328.50
1953-54									
GWF Overton	3	6	8	1.33	4	258	9	28.66	12.73
JEF Beck	8	15	394	26.26					
IB Leggat	1	1	0	0.00	1	6	0		
W Bell	2	3	21	7.00	4	235	2	117.50	235.00
1954-55									
SN McGregor	25	47	892	18.97					
L Watt	1	2	2	1.00					
IA Colquhoun	2	4	1	0.25					
1955-56									
PGZ Harris	9	18	378	21.00	1	14	0		
JC Alabaster	21	34	272	8.00	32	1863	49	38.02	24.82
TG McMahon	5	7	7	1.00					
NS Harford	8	15	229	15.26					
EC Petrie	14	25	258	10.32					
JW Guy	12	23	440	19.13					
AF Lissette	2	4	2	0.50	2	124	3	41.33	27.55
SC Guillen [WI]	3	6	98	16.33					
IM Sinclair	2	4	25	6.25	2	120	1	120.00	240.00
RT Barber	1	2	17	8.50					
1958									
JW D'Arcy	5	10	136	13.60					
WR Playle	8	15	151	10.06					
T Meale	2	4	21	5.25					
JT Sparling	11	20	229	11.45	10	327	5	65.40	130.80
1958-59									
BA Bolton	2	3	59	19.66					
RM Harris	2	3	31	10.33					
KW Hough	2	3	62	20.66	2	175	6	29.16	9.71
1961-62									
PT Barton	7	14	285	20.35					

AE Dick	17	30	370	12.33					
RC Motz	32	56	612	10.92	55	3148	100	31.48	17.31
GA Bartlett	10	18	263	14.61	18	792	24	33.00	24.75
FJ Cameron	19	30	116	3.86	35	1849	62	29.82	16.83
GT Dowling	39	77	2306	29.84	1	19	1	19.00	19.00
1962-63									
BW Sinclair	21	40	1148	28.70	1	32	2	16.00	8.00
BW Yuile	17	33	481	14.57	26	1213	34	35.67	27.27
BD Morrison	1	2	10	5.00	1	129	2	64.50	32.25
MJF Shrimpton	10	19	265	13.94	6	158	5	31.60	37.92
1963-64									
SG Gedye	4	8	193	24.12					
JT Ward	8	12	75	6.25					
WP Bradburn	2	4	62	15.50					
RS Cunis	20	31	295	9.51	38	1887	51	37.00	27.56
1964-65									
BE Congdon	61	114	3448	30.24	66	2154	59	36.50	40.83
RO Collinge	35	50	533	10.66	62	3393	116	29.25	15.63
RW Morgan	20	34	734	21.58	20	609	5	121.80	487.20
PB Truscott	1	2	29	14.50					
TW Jarvis	13	22	625	28.40	2	3	0		
V Pollard	32	59	1266	21.45	49	1853	40	46.32	56.74
BR Taylor	30	50	898	17.96	53	2953	111	26.60	12.70
GE Vivian	5	6	110	18.33	6	107	1	107.00	642.00
1965-66									
GP Bilby	2	4	55	13.75					
N Puna	3	5	31	6.20	5	240	4	60.00	75.00
1967-68									
BAG Murray	13	26	598	23.00	1	0	1	0.00	0.00
MG Burgess	50	92	2684	29.17	15	212	6	35.33	88.32
RI Harford	3	5	7	1.40					
K Thomson	2	4	94	23.50	1	9	1	9.00	9.00
1968-69									
GM Turner	41	73	2991	40.97	1	5	0		
BF Hastings	31	56	1510	26.96	2	9	0		
BD Milburn	3	3	8	2.66					
1969									
KJ Wadsworth	33	51	1010	19.80					
DR Hadlee	26	42	530	12.61	44	2389	71	33.64	20.84
HJ Howarth	30	42	291	6.92	50	3178	86	36.95	21.48
1970-71									
MG Webb	3	2	12	6.00	6	471	4	117.75	176.62
1972-73									
JM Parker	36	63	1498	23.77	1	24	1	24.00	24.00
RJ Hadlee	86	134	3124	23.31	150	9611	431	22.29	7.75
DR O'Sullivan	11	21	158	7.52	15	1224	18	68.00	56.66
RE Redmond	1	2	163	81.50					
1973-74									
JFM Morrison	17	29	656	22.62	5	71	2	35.50	88.75
B Andrews	2	3	22	7.33	3	154	2	77.00	115.50
JV Coney	52	85	2668	31.38	53	966	27	35.77	70.21
BL Cairns	43	65	928	14.27	72	4280	130	32.92	18.23
1974-75									
GP Howarth	47	83	2531	30.49	20	271	3	90.33	602.20
EJ Chatfield	43	54	180	3.33	73	3958	123	32.17	19.09
1975-76									
ADG Roberts	7	12	254	21.16	8	182	4	45.50	91.00
1976-77									
RW Anderson	9	18	423	23.50					
WK Lees	21	37	778	21.02	1	4	0		

PJ Petherick	6	11	34	3.09	10	681	16	42.56	26.60
NM Parker	3	6	89	14.83					
GB Troup	15	18	55	3.05	26	1454	39	37.28	24.85
GN Edwards	8	15	377	25.13					
1977-78									
JG Wright	82	148	5334	36.04	3	5	0		
SL Boock	30	41	207	5.04	48	2564	74	34.64	22.46
1978									
BA Edgar	39	68	1958	28.79	1	3	0		
BP Bracewell	6	12	24	2.00	11	585	14	41.78	32.82
1978-79									
JF Reid	19	31	1296	41.80	2	7	0		
1979-80									
PN Webb	2	3	11	3.66					
PE McEwan	4	7	96	13.71	2	13	0		
1980-81									
IDS Smith	63	88	1815	20.62	1	5	0		
JG Bracewell	41	60	1001	16.68	67	3653	102	35.81	23.52
MC Snedden	25	30	327	10.90	41	2199	58	37.91	26.79
1981-82									
MD Crowe	77	131	5444	41.55	35	676	14	48.28	120.70
1982-83									
JJ Crowe	39	65	1601	24.63	2	9	0		
1983									
EJ Gray	10	16	248	15.50	16	886	17	52.11	49.04
TJ Franklin	21	37	828	22.37					
1984-85									
DA Stirling	6	9	108	12.00	10	601	13	46.23	35.56
KR Rutherford	56	99	2465	24.89	11	161	1	161.00	1771.00
1985-86									
VR Brown	2	3	51	17.00	4	176	1	176.00	704.00
SR Gillespie	1	1	28	28.00	1	79	1	79.00	79.00
GK Robertson	1	1	12	12.00	1	91	1	91.00	91.00
1986									
W Watson	15	18	60	3.33	25	1387	40	34.67	21.66
TE Blain	11	20	456	22.80					
1986-87									
DN Patel	37	66	1200	18.18	53	3154	75	42.05	29.71
PA Horne	4	7	71	10.14					
AH Jones	39	74	2922	39.48	14	194	1	194.00	2716.00
1987-88									
DK Morrison	48	71	379	5.33	76	5549	160	34.68	16.47
MJ Greatbatch	41	71	2021	28.46	1	0	0		
RH Vance	4	7	207	29.57					
1988-89									
CM Kuggeleijn	2	4	7	1.75	3	67	1	67.00	201.00
1989-90									
CL Cairns	62	104	3320	31.92	104	6410	218	29.40	14.02
SA Thomson	19	35	958	27.37	26	953	19	50.15	68.62
1990									
MW Priest	3	4	56	14.00	5	158	3	52.66	87.76
AC Parore	78	128	2865	22.38					
1990-91									
DJ White	2	4	31	7.75	1	5	0		
GE Bradburn	7	10	105	10.50	7	460	6	76.66	89.43
C Pringle	14	21	175	8.33	22	1389	30	46.30	33.95
1991-92									
BR Hartland	9	18	303	16.83					
ML Su'a	12	18	165	9.16	22	1377	36	38.25	23.37
RT Latham	4	7	219	31.28	1	6	0		

1992-93									
SB Doull	32	50	570	11.40	51	2872	98	29.30	15.24
MJ Haslam	4	2	4	2.00	5	245	2	122.50	306.25
DJ Nash	32	45	729	16.20	53	2649	93	28.48	16.23
CZ Harris	23	42	777	18.50	29	1170	16	73.12	132.53
JTC Vaughan	6	12	201	16.75	8	450	11	40.90	29.74
MB Owens	8	12	16	1.33	12	585	17	34.41	24.28
1993-94									
BA Pocock	15	29	665	22.93	2	20	0		
BA Young	35	68	2034	29.91					
RP de Groen	5	10	45	4.50	7	505	11	45.90	29.20
MN Hart	14	24	353	14.70	22	1438	29	49.58	37.61
SP Fleming	111	189	7172	37.94					
1994									
GR Larsen	8	13	127	9.76	14	689	24	28.70	16.74
HT Davis	5	7	20	2.85	9	499	17	29.35	15.53
1994-95									
DJ Murray	8	16	303	18.93					
KP Walmsley	3	5	13	2.60	6	391	9	43.44	28.95
1995-96									
LK Germon	12	21	382	18.19					
RG Twose	16	27	628	23.25	6	130	3	43.33	86.66
CM Spearman	19	37	922	24.91					
NJ Astle	81	137	4702	34.32	94	2143	51	42.01	77.43
GR Loveridge	1	1	4	4.00					
RJ Kennedy	4	5	28	5.60	8	380	6	63.33	84.43
GI Allott	10	15	27	1.80	16	1111	19	58.47	49.23
1996-97									
DL Vettori	113	174	4531	-	187	12441	362		
n/a	1	2	8	-	2	111	1		
adj	112	172	4523	26.29	185	12330	361	34.15	17.50
MJ Horne	35	65	1788	27.50	3	26	0		
1997-98									
SB O'Connor	19	27	103	3.81	34	1724	53	32.52	20.86
DG Sewell	1	1	1	1.00	2	90	0		
CD McMillan	55	91	3116	34.24	50	1257	28	44.89	80.16
PJ Wiseman	25	34	366	10.76	45	2903	61	47.59	35.10
1998-99									
MD Bell	18	32	729	22.78					
GR Stead	5	8	278	34.75	1	1	0		
1999-00									
MS Sinclair	33	56	1635	29.19	2	14	0		
DR Tuffey	26	36	427	11.86	45	2445	77	31.75	18.55
2000-01									
MH Richardson	38	65	2776	42.70	3	21	1	21.00	63.00
CS Martin	71	104	123	1.18	126	7878	233	33.81	18.28
BGK Walker	5	8	118	14.75	7	399	5	79.80	111.72
HJH Marshall	13	19	652	34.31	1	4	0		
JEC Franklin	31	46	808	17.56	54	2786	82	33.97	22.37
CJ Drum	5	5	10	2.00	9	482	16	30.12	16.94
2001-02									
SE Bond	18	20	168	8.40	32	1922	87	22.09	8.12
L Vincent	23	40	1332	33.30	1	2	0		
IG Butler	8	10	76	7.60	14	884	24	36.83	21.48
AR Adams	1	2	18	9.00	2	105	6	17.50	5.83
2002									
RG Hart	11	19	260	13.68					
SB Styris	29	48	1586	33.04	36	1015	20	50.75	91.35
2002-03									
JDP Oram	33	59	1780	30.16	55	1983	60	33.05	30.29

2003-04									
RA Jones	1	2	23	11.50					
MHW Papps	8	16	246	15.37					
BB McCullum	101	176	6453	36.66	8	88	1	88.00	704.00
MJ Mason	1	2	3	1.50	2	105	0		
2004									
KD Mills	19	30	289	9.63	31	1453	44	33.02	23.26
2004-05									
CD Cumming	11	19	441	23.21					
IE O'Brien	22	34	219	6.44	37	2429	73	33.27	16.86
JAH Marshall	7	11	218	19.81					
2005-06									
JM How	19	35	772	22.05	2	4	0		
PG Fulton	23	39	967	24.79					
JS Patel	24	38	381	10.02	42	3078	65	47.35	30.59
2007-08									
LRPL Taylor	112	196	7683	39.19	8	48	3	16.00	42.66
MR Gillespie	5	8	76	9.50	8	631	22	28.68	10.42
GD Elliott	5	9	86	9.55	6	140	4	35.00	52.50
TG Southee	85	120	1769	14.74	160	9530	338	28.19	13.34
2008									
AJ Redmond	8	16	325	20.31	5	80	3	26.66	44.43
DR Flynn	24	45	1038	23.06	1	0	0		
GJ Hopkins	4	7	71	10.14					
2008-09									
JD Ryder	18	33	1269	38.45	15	280	5	56.00	168.00
TG McIntosh	17	33	854	25.87					
MJ Guptill	47	89	2586	29.05	18	298	8	37.25	83.81
2009-10									
BJ Watling	75	117	3790	32.39					
PJ Ingram	2	4	61	15.25					
BJ Arnel	6	12	45	3.75	11	566	9	62.88	76.85
2010-11									
KS Williamson	86	150	7272	48.48	67	1207	30	40.23	89.84
HK Bennett	1	1	4	4.00	1	47	0		
AJ McKay	1	2	25	12.50	1	120	1	120.00	120.00
RA Young	5	10	169	16.90					
2011-12									
DG Brownlie	14	25	711	28.44	5	52	1	52.00	260.00
DAJ Bracewell	27	45	568	12.62	49	2796	72	38.83	26.42
TA Boult	75	88	704	8.00	143	8254	301	27.42	13.02
RJ Nicol	2	4	28	7.00	3	13	0		
CFK van Wyk	9	17	341	20.05					
2012									
N Wagner	58	74	775	10.47	110	6464	244	26.49	11.94
2012-13									
TD Astle	5	6	98	16.33	8	368	7	52.57	60.07
C Munro	1	2	15	7.50	1	40	2	20.00	10.00
HD Rutherford	16	29	755	26.03	1	2	0		
BP Martin	5	6	74	12.33	9	646	12	53.83	40.37
2013-14									
CJ Anderson	13	22	683	31.04	23	659	16	41.18	59.19
IS Sodhi	17	25	448	17.92	31	1992	41	48.58	36.73
TWM Latham	65	113	4502	39.84					
JDS Neesham	12	22	709	32.22	21	675	14	48.21	72.31
2014									
MD Craig	15	25	589	23.56	29	2326	50	46.52	26.98
2015									
MJ Henry	16	20	294	14.70	31	1938	51	38.00	23.09
L Ronchi	4	8	319	39.87					

2015-16									
MJ Santner	24	32	766	23.93	40	1871	41	45.63	44.51
HM Nicholls	46	69	2544	36.86					
2016-17									
C de Grandhomme	28	42	1390	33.09	51	1588	48	33.08	35.14
JA Raval	24	39	1143	29.30	2	34	1	34.00	68.00
NT Broom	2	3	32	10.66					
2017-18									
TA Blundell	17	27	809	29.96	1	13	0		
2018-19									
AY Patel	11	15	80	5.33	20	1167	43	27.13	12.61
WER Somerville	6	10	115	11.50	12	724	15	48.26	38.60
2019-20									
DJ Mitchell	9	11	403	36.63	8	160	2	80.00	320.00
LH Ferguson	1	2	1	0.50	1	47	0		
GD Phillips	1	2	52	26.00					
KA Jamieson	14	18	351	19.50	28	1236	66	18.72	7.94
2020-21									
WA Young	9	14	439	31.35					
2021									
DP Conway	7	12	767	63.91					
2021-22									
R Ravindra	3	6	73	12.16	5	188	3	62.66	104.43

INDIA

	M	I	R	RI	IB	R	W	A	RWI
1932									
JG Navle	2	4	42	10.50					
Naoomal Jaoomal	3	5	108	21.60	4	68	2	34.00	68.00
S Wazir Ali	7	14	237	16.92	3	25	0		
CK Nayudu	7	14	350	25.00	10	386	9	42.88	47.64
SHM Colah	2	4	69	17.25					
S Nazir Ali	2	4	30	7.50	1	83	4	20.75	5.18
PE Palia	2	4	29	7.25	2	13	0		
Lall Singh	1	2	44	22.00					
M Jahangir Khan	4	7	39	5.57	6	255	4	63.75	95.62
L Amar Singh	7	14	292	20.85	13	858	28	30.64	14.22
Mohammad Nissar	6	11	55	5.00	11	707	25	28.28	12.44
1933-34									
L Amarnath	24	40	878	21.95	35	1481	45	32.91	25.59
LP Jai	1	2	19	9.50					
VM Merchant	10	18	859	47.22	2	40	0		
L Ramji	1	2	1	0.50	1	64	0		
RJD Jamshedji	1	2	5	2.50	1	137	3	45.66	15.21
Dilawar Hussain	3	6	254	42.33					
S Mushtaq Ali	11	20	612	30.60	5	202	3	67.33	112.21
CS Nayudu	11	19	147	7.73	12	359	2	179.50	1077.00
MJ Gopalan	1	2	18	9.00	1	39	1	39.00	39.00
Yuvraj of Patiala	1	2	84	42.00					
1936									
DD Hindlekar	4	7	71	10.14					
Maharaj of Vizianagram	3	6	33	5.50					
C Ramaswami	2	4	170	42.50					
KR Meherhomji	1	1	0	0.00					
M Baqa Jilani	1	2	16	8.00	1	55	0		
1946									
MH Mankad	44	72	2109	29.29	70	5236	162	32.32	13.96

VS Hazare	30	52	2192	42.15	43	1220	20	61.00	131.15
RS Modi	10	17	736	43.29	1	14	0		
IAK Pataudi [Eng]	3	5	55	11.00					
Gul Mohammad [Pak]	8	15	166	11.06	4	24	2	12.00	24.00
Abdul Hafeez (AH Kardar [Pak])	3	5	80	16.00					
SG Shinde	7	11	85	7.27	10	717	12	59.75	49.79
SW Sohoni	4	7	83	11.85	5	202	2	101.00	252.50
CT Sarwate	9	17	208	12.23	10	374	3	124.66	415.53
1947-48									
HR Adhikari	21	36	872	24.22	3	82	3	27.33	27.33
G Kishenchand	5	10	89	8.90					
KM Rangnekar	3	6	33	5.50					
JK Irani	2	3	3	1.00					
DG Phadkar	31	45	1229	27.31	48	2285	62	36.85	28.52
Amir Elahi [Pak]	1	2	17	8.50					
K Rai Singh	1	2	26	13.00					
PK Sen	14	18	165	9.16					
CR Rangachari	4	6	8	1.33	4	493	9	54.77	24.34
1948-49									
KC Ibrahim	4	8	169	21.12					
KK Tarapore	1	1	2	2.00	1	72	0		
PR Umrigar	59	94	3631	38.62	50	1473	35	42.08	60.11
Ghulam Ahmed	22	31	192	6.19	36	2052	68	30.17	15.97
SA Banerjee	1	1	0	0.00	2	181	5	36.20	14.48
MR Rege	1	2	15	7.50					
NR Chowdhury	2	2	3	1.50	3	205	1	205.00	615.00
SN Banerjee	1	2	13	6.50	2	127	5	25.40	10.16
1951-52									
Pankaj Roy	43	79	2442	30.91	7	66	1	66.00	462.00
PG Joshi	12	20	207	10.35					
MK Mantri	4	8	67	8.37					
CD Gopinath	8	12	242	20.16	1	11	1	11.00	11.00
VL Manjrekar	55	92	3208	34.86	6	44	1	44.00	264.00
RV Divecha	5	5	60	12.00	7	361	11	32.81	20.87
SP Gupte	36	42	183	4.35	61	4403	149	29.55	12.09
1952									
DK Gaekwad	11	20	350	17.50	2	12	0		
GS Ramchand	33	53	1180	22.26	56	1899	41	46.31	63.25
1952-53									
HG Gaekwad	1	2	22	11.00	1	47	0		
S Nyalchand	1	2	7	3.50	1	97	3	32.33	10.77
ML Apte	7	13	542	41.69	1	3	0		
HT Dani	1	-	-	-	2	19	1	19.00	38.00
V Rajindernath	1	-	-	-					
ES Maka	2	1	2	2.00					
RH Shodhan	3	4	181	45.25	3	26	0		
CV Gadkari	6	10	129	12.90	3	45	0		
JM Ghorpade	8	15	229	15.26	5	131	0		
1954-55									
PH Punjabi	5	10	164	16.40					
NS Tamhane	21	27	225	8.33					
P Bhandari	3	4	77	19.25	2	39	0		
JM Patel	7	10	25	2.50	11	637	29	21.96	8.32
1955-56									
AG Kripal Singh	14	20	422	21.10	15	584	10	58.40	87.60
VN Swamy	1	-	-	-	2	45	0		
VL Mehra	8	14	329	23.50	3	6	0		
NJ Contractor	31	52	1611	30.98	10	80	1	80.00	800.00
SR Patil	1	1	14	14.00	2	51	2	25.50	25.50

RG Nadkarni	41	67	1414	21.10	65	2559	88	29.07	21.47
GR Sunderam	2	1	3	3.00	4	166	3	55.33	73.77
CT Patankar	1	2	14	7.00					
1958-59									
MS Hardikar	2	4	56	14.00	3	55	1	55.00	165.00
CG Borde	55	97	3061	31.55	54	2417	52	46.48	48.26
GM Guard	2	2	11	5.50	4	182	3	60.66	80.87
VB Ranjane	7	9	40	4.44	13	649	19	34.15	23.36
RB Kenny	5	10	245	24.50					
Surendranath	11	20	136	6.80	17	1053	26	40.50	26.48
AK Sengupta	1	2	9	4.50					
RB Desai	28	44	418	9.50	45	2761	74	37.31	22.68
1959									
ML Jaisimha	39	71	2056	28.95	51	829	9	92.11	521.95
AL Apte	1	2	15	7.50					
AA Baig	10	18	428	23.77	2	15	0		
1959-60									
VM Muddiah	2	3	11	3.66	3	134	3	44.66	44.66
BK Kunderan	18	34	981	28.85	1	13	0		
SA Durani	29	50	1202	24.04	46	2657	75	35.42	21.72
AG Milkha Singh	4	6	92	15.33	1	2	0		
MM Sood	1	2	3	1.50					
1960-61									
RF Surti	26	48	1263	26.31	45	1962	42	46.71	50.04
BP Gupte	3	3	28	9.33	5	349	3	116.33	193.88
VV Kumar	2	2	6	3.00	3	202	7	28.85	12.36
1961-62									
DN Sardesai	30	55	2001	36.38	5	45	0		
FM Engineer	46	87	2611	30.01					
MAK Pataudi	46	83	2793	33.65	10	88	1	88.00	880.00
EAS Prasanna	49	84	735	8.75	86	5742	189	30.38	13.82
1963-64									
Rajinder Pal	1	2	6	3.00	2	22	0		
BS Chandrasekhar	58	80	167	2.08	97	7199	242	29.74	11.92
Hanumant Singh	14	24	686	28.58	3	51	0		
1964-65									
KS Indrajitsinhji	4	7	51	7.28					
S Venkataraghavan	57	76	748	9.84	96	5634	156	36.11	22.22
V Subramanya	9	15	263	17.53	14	201	3	67.00	312.66
1966-67									
AL Wadekar	37	71	2113	29.76	7	55	0		
BS Bedi	67	101	656	6.49	118	7637	266	28.71	12.73
1967									
RC Saxena	1	2	25	12.50	1	11	0		
S Guha	4	7	17	2.42	8	311	3	103.66	276.42
1967-68									
S Abid Ali	29	53	1018	19.20	49	1980	47	42.12	43.91
UN Kulkarni	4	8	13	1.62	7	238	5	47.60	66.64
1969-70									
CPS Chauhan	40	68	2084	30.64	10	106	2	53.00	265.00
AV Mankad	22	42	991	23.59	3	43	0		
AM Pai	1	2	10	5.00	2	31	2	15.50	15.50
AK Roy	4	7	91	13.00					
A Gandotra	2	4	54	13.50	1	5	0		
ED Solkar	27	48	1068	22.25	44	1070	18	59.44	145.29
GR Viswanath	91	155	6080	39.22	7	46	1	46.00	322.00
M Amarnath	69	113	4378	38.74	71	1782	32	55.68	123.54
1970-71									
HK Jayantilal	1	1	5	5.00					
P Krishnamurthy	5	6	33	5.50					

SM Gavaskar	125	214	10122	47.29	29	206	1	206.00	5974.00
1972-73									
RD Parkar	2	4	80	20.00					
1974									
BP Patel	21	38	972	25.57					
S Madan Lal	39	62	1042	16.80	63	2846	71	40.08	35.56
SS Naik	3	6	141	23.50					
1974-75									
HS Kanitkar	2	4	111	27.75					
PH Sharma	5	10	187	18.70	2	8	0		
AD Gaekwad	40	70	1985	28.35	17	187	2	93.50	794.75
KD Ghavri	39	57	913	16.01	69	3656	109	33.54	21.23
1975-76									
DB Vengsarkar	116	185	6868	37.12	6	36	0		
S Amarnath	10	18	550	30.55	1	5	1	5.00	5.00
SMH Kirmani	88	124	2759	22.25	3	13	1	13.00	39.00
1976-77									
Yajurvindra Singh	4	7	109	15.57	4	50	0		
1978-79									
Kapil Dev	131	184	5248	28.52	227	12867	434	29.64	15.50
MV Narasimha Rao	4	6	46	7.66	6	227	3	75.66	151.32
DD Parsana	2	2	1	0.50	3	50	1	50.00	150.00
1979									
B Reddy	4	5	38	7.60					
Yashpal Sharma	37	59	1606	27.22	3	17	1	17.00	51.00
1979-80									
DR Doshi	33	38	129	3.39	55	3502	114	30.71	14.81
NS Yadav	35	40	403	10.07	61	3580	102	35.09	20.98
RMH Binny	27	41	830	20.24	38	1534	47	32.63	26.38
SM Patil	29	47	1588	33.78	15	240	9	26.66	44.43
1980-81									
KBJ Azad	7	12	135	11.25	10	373	3	124.33	414.43
RJ Shastri	80	121	3830	31.65	125	6185	151	40.96	33.90
B Yograj Singh	1	2	10	5.00	1	63	1	63.00	63.00
TE Srinivasan	1	2	48	24.00					
1981-82									
K Srikkanth	43	72	2062	28.63	16	114	0		
P Roy	2	3	71	23.66					
AO Malhotra	7	10	226	22.60	2	3	0		
1982									
GAHM Parkar	1	2	7	3.50					
SV Nayak	2	3	19	6.33	3	132	1	132.00	396.00
1982-83									
J Arun Lal	16	29	729	25.13	3	7	0		
RS Shukla	1	-	-	-	2	152	2	76.00	76.00
Maninder Singh	35	38	99	2.60	52	3288	88	37.36	22.07
BS Sandhu	8	11	214	19.45	10	557	10	55.70	55.70
TAP Sekhar	2	1	0	0.00	2	129	0		
L Sivaramakrishnan	9	9	130	14.44	16	1145	26	44.03	27.09
1983-84									
AR Bhat	2	3	6	2.00	2	151	4	37.75	18.87
NS Sidhu	51	78	3202	41.05	1	9	0		
1984-85									
C Sharma	23	27	396	14.66	39	2163	61	35.45	22.66
M Prabhakar	39	58	1600	27.58	68	3581	96	37.30	26.42
M Azharuddin	99	147	6215	42.27	3	16	0		
G Sharma	5	4	11	2.75	8	418	10	41.80	33.44
1985-86									
LS Rajput	2	4	105	26.25					
S Viswanath	3	5	31	6.20					

1986									
KS More	49	64	1285	20.07	1	12	0		
CS Pandit	5	8	171	21.37					
1986-87									
RR Kulkarni	3	2	2	1.00	6	227	5	45.40	54.48
R Lamba	4	5	102	20.40					
B Arun	2	2	4	2.00	3	116	4	29.00	21.75
1987-88									
SV Manjrekar	37	61	2043	33.49	3	15	0		
A Ayub	13	19	257	13.52	22	1438	41	35.07	18.81
WV Raman	11	19	448	23.57	7	129	2	64.50	225.75
AK Sharma	1	2	53	26.50	9	0			
ND Hirwani	17	22	54	2.45	28	1987	66	30.10	12.76
1988-89									
RGM Patel	1	2	0	0.00	2	51	0		
SK Sharma	2	3	56	18.66	4	247	6	41.16	27.43
M Venkataramana	1	2	0	0.00	2	58	1	58.00	116.00
1989-90									
SR Tendulkar	200	329	15921	48.39	145	2492	46	54.17	170.75
SA Ankola	1	1	6	6.00	2	128	2	64.00	64.00
V Razdan	2	2	6	3.00	2	141	5	28.00	11.28
SLV Raju	28	34	240	7.05	51	2857	93	30.72	16.84
AS Wassan	4	5	94	18.80	6	504	10	50.40	30.24
Gurusharan Singh	1	1	18	18.00					
1990									
A Kumble	132	173	2506	14.48	236	18355	619	29.65	11.30
1991-92									
J Srinath	67	92	1009	10.96	121	7196	236	30.49	15.63
ST Banerjee	1	1	3	3.00	1	47	3	15.66	5.21
1992-93									
A Jadeja	15	24	576	24.00					
PK Amre	11	13	425	32.69					
VG Kambli	17	21	1084	51.61					
RK Chauhan	21	17	98	5.76	34	1857	47	39.51	28.58
V Yadav	1	1	30	30.00					
1993-94									
NR Mongia	44	68	1442	21.20					
1994-95									
AR Kapoor	4	6	97	16.16	7	255	6	42.50	49.58
1996									
V Rathour	6	10	131	13.10					
SB Joshi	15	19	352	18.52	26	1470	41	35.85	22.73
PL Mhambrey	2	3	58	19.33	3	148	2	74.00	111.00
BKV Prasad	33	47	203	4.31	58	3360	96	35.00	21.14
SC Ganguly	113	188	7212	38.36	99	1681	32	52.53	162.51
RS Dravid	164	286	13288	-	5	39	1	-	-
n/a	1	2	23	-	-	-	-	-	-
adj	163	284	13265	46.70	5	39	1	39.00	195.00
1996-97									
DJ Johnson	2	3	8	2.66	4	143	3	47.66	63.54
VVS Laxman	134	225	8781	39.02	13	126	2	63.00	409.50
D Ganesh	4	7	25	3.57	7	287	5	57.40	80.36
A Kuruvilla	10	11	66	6.00	15	892	25	35.68	21.40
1997									
NM Kulkarni	3	2	5	2.50	3	332	2	166.00	249.00
DS Mohanty	2	1	0	0.00	4	239	4	59.75	59.75
1997-98									
Harvinder Singh	3	4	6	1.50	6	185	4	46.25	69.37
Harbhajan Singh	103	145	2224	15.33	190	13537	417	32.46	14.78

1998-99									
RR Singh	1	2	27	13.50	2	32	0		
AB Agarkar	26	39	571	14.64	46	2745	58	47.32	37.52
R Singh	1	1	0	0.00	2	176	3	58.66	39.10
S Ramesh	19	37	1367	36.94	3	43	0		
A Nehra	17	25	77	3.08	29	1866	44	42.40	27.94
1999-00									
DJ Gandhi	4	7	204	29.14					
MSK Prasad	6	10	106	10.60					
R Vijay Bharadwaj	3	3	28	9.33	4	107	1	107.00	428.00
W Jaffer	31	58	1944	33.51	1	18	2	9.00	4.50
M Kartik	8	10	88	8.80	15	820	24	34.16	21.35
N Chopra	1	2	7	3.50	1	78	0		
M Kaif	13	22	624	28.36	1	4	0		
HH Kanitkar	2	4	74	18.50	1	2	0		
2000-01									
SS Das	23	40	1326	33.15	2	35	0		
SS Karim	1	1	15	15.00					
Z Khan	92	127	1231	9.69	165	10247	311	32.94	17.47
V Dahiya	2	1	2	2.00					
Sarandeep Singh	3	2	43	21.50	4	340	10	34.00	13.60
RL Sanghvi	1	2	2	1.00	2	78	2	39.00	39.00
SV Bahutule	2	4	39	9.75	3	203	3	67.66	67.66
SS Dighe	6	10	141	14.10					
2001									
HK Badani	4	7	94	13.42	1	17	0		
2001-02									
D Dasgupta	8	13	344	26.46					
V Sehwag	104	180	8586	-	91	1894	40	-	-
n/a	1	2	83	-	-	-	-	-	-
adj	103	178	8503	47.76	91	1894	40	47.35	107.72
SB Bangar	12	18	470	26.11	14	343	7	49.00	98.00
IR Siddiqui	1	2	29	14.50	2	48	1	48.00	96.00
T Yohannan	3	4	13	3.25	6	256	5	51.20	61.44
A Ratra	6	10	163	16.30	1	1	0		
2002									
PA Patel	25	38	934	24.57					
2003-04									
A Chopra	10	19	437	23.00					
L Balaji	8	9	51	5.66	15	1004	27	37.18	20.65
Yuvraj Singh	40	62	1900	30.64	35	547	9	60.77	236.37
IK Pathan	29	40	1105	27.62	54	3226	100	32.26	17.42
2004-05									
G Gambhir	58	104	4154	39.94	1	4	0		
KD Karthik	26	42	1025	24.40					
2005-06									
MS Dhoni	90	144	4876	33.86	7	67	0		
RP Singh	14	19	116	6.10	25	1682	40	42.05	26.28
S Sreesanth	27	40	281	7.02	50	3271	87	37.59	21.60
PP Chawla	3	3	6	2.00	6	270	7	38.57	33.05
MM Patel	13	14	60	4.28	25	1349	35	38.54	27.52
VRV Singh	5	6	47	7.83	10	427	8	53.37	66.71
2007									
RR Powar	2	2	13	6.50	4	118	6	19.66	13.10
I Sharma	105	142	785	5.52	188	10078	311	32.40	19.58
2008-09									
A Mishra	22	32	648	20.25	40	2715	76	35.72	18.79
M Vijay	61	105	3982	37.92	18	198	1	198.00	3564.00
2009-10									
PP Ojha	24	27	89	3.29	48	3420	113	30.26	12.85

S Badrinath	2	3	63	21.00					
WP Saha	40	56	1353	24.16					
2010									
A Mithun	4	5	120	24.00	8	456	9	50.66	45.03
SK Raina	18	31	768	24.77	22	603	13	46.38	78.48
2010-11									
CA Pujara	95	162	6713	41.43	1	2	0		
JD Unadkat	1	2	2	1.00	1	101	0		
2011									
A Mukund	7	14	320	22.85	1	14	0		
V Kohli	101	171	8043	47.03	11	84	0		
P Kumar	6	10	149	14.90	11	697	27	25.81	10.51
2011-12									
R Ashwin	86	123	2931	23.82	162	10666	442	24.13	8.84
UT Yadav	52	61	408	6.68	102	4867	158	30.80	19.88
VR Aaron	9	14	35	2.50	14	947	18	52.61	40.91
R Vinay Kumar	1	2	11	5.50	1	73	1	73.00	73.00
2012-13									
RA Jadeja	59	87	2396	27.54	112	5915	242	24.44	11.31
B Kumar	21	29	552	19.03	37	1644	63	26.09	15.32
S Dhawan	34	58	2315	39.91	5	18	0		
AM Rahane	82	140	4931	35.22					
2013-14									
RG Sharma	45	77	3137	40.74	16	224	2	112.00	896.00
Mohammed Shami	59	82	656	8.00	112	5789	214	27.05	14.15
2014									
STR Binny	6	10	194	19.40	7	258	3	86.00	200.66
Pankaj Singh	2	4	10	2.50	3	292	2	146.00	219.00
2014-15									
KV Sharma	1	2	8	4.00	2	238	4	59.50	29.75
KL Rahul	43	74	2547	34.41					
2015									
NV Ojha	1	2	56	28.00					
2016-17									
J Yadav	6	9	248	27.55	12	465	16	29.06	21.79
KK Nair	6	7	374	53.42	2	11	0		
Kuldeep Yadav	7	8	54	6.75	12	620	26	23.84	11.00
2017									
HH Pandya	11	18	532	29.55	19	528	17	31.05	34.70
2017-18									
JJ Bumrah	29	44	174	3.95	56	2673	123	21.73	9.89
2018									
RR Pant	30	51	1920	37.64					
GH Vihari	15	26	808	31.07	10	180	5	36.00	72.00
2018-19									
PP Shaw	5	9	339	37.66					
SN Thakur	7	12	249	20.75	13	547	26	21.03	10.51
MA Agarwal	21	36	1488	41.33					
2019-20									
S Nadeem	2	3	1	0.33	4	273	8	34.12	17.06
2020-21									
Shubman Gill	10	19	558	29.36					
Mohammed Siraj	12	17	62	3.64	23	1067	36	29.63	18.93
NA Saini	2	3	8	2.66	4	172	4	43.00	43.00
Washington Sundar	4	6	265	44.16	7	299	6	49.83	58.13
T Natarajan	1	1	1	1.00	2	119	3	39.66	26.43
AR Patel	6	10	197	19.70	12	485	39	12.43	3.82
2021-22									
SS Iyer	4	7	388	55.42					

PAKISTAN

	M	I	R	RI	IB	R	W	A	RWI
1952-53									
Nazar Mohammad	5	8	277	34.62	1	4	0		
Hanif Mohammad	55	97	3915	40.36	13	95	1	95.00	1235.00
Israr Ali	4	8	33	4.12	5	165	6	27.50	22.91
Imtiaz Ahmed	41	72	2079	28.87	1	0	0		
Maqsood Ahmed	16	27	507	18.77	15	191	3	63.66	318.30
AH Kardar (Abdul Hafeez [Ind])	23	37	847	22.89	26	954	21	45.42	56.23
Anwar Hussain	4	6	42	7.00	2	29	1	29.00	58.00
Waqar Hasan	21	35	1071	30.60	1	10	0		
Fazal Mahmood	34	50	620	12.40	53	3434	139	24.70	9.41
Khan Mohammad	13	17	100	5.88	22	1292	54	23.92	9.74
Amir Elahi [Ind]	5	7	65	9.28	4	248	7	35.42	20.23
Zulfiqar Ahmed	9	10	200	20.00	10	366	20	18.30	9.15
Mahmood Hussain	27	39	336	8.61	42	2628	68	38.64	23.86
Wazir Mohammad	20	33	801	24.27	3	15	0		
1954									
Alimuddin	25	45	1091	24.24	4	75	1	75.00	300.00
Khalid Wazir	2	3	14	4.66					
Shujauddin	19	32	395	12.34	25	801	20	40.05	50.06
MEZ Ghazali	2	4	32	8.00	1	18	0		
Mohammad Aslam	1	2	34	17.00					
Khalid Hassan	1	2	17	8.50	1	116	2	58.00	29.00
1954-55									
Miran Bakhsh	2	3	1	0.33	3	115	2	57.50	86.25
1955-56									
W Mathias	21	36	783	21.75	1	20	0		
Agha Saadat Ali	1	1	8	8.00					
1956-57									
Gul Mohammad [Ind]	1	2	39	19.50					
1957-58									
Saeed Ahmed	41	78	2991	38.34	41	802	22	36.45	67.92
Nasim-ul-Ghani	29	50	747	14.94	40	1959	52	37.67	28.97
Haseeb Ahsan	12	16	61	3.81	17	1330	27	49.25	31.00
SF Rehman	1	2	10	5.00	2	99	1	99.00	198.00
1958-59									
Ijaz Butt	8	16	279	17.43					
A D'Souza	6	10	76	7.60	9	745	17	43.82	23.19
Mushtaq Mohammad	57	100	3643	36.43	70	2309	79	29.22	25.89
1959-60									
DA Sharpe	3	6	134	22.33					
Mohammad Munaf	4	7	63	9.00	7	341	11	31.00	19.72
Intikhab Alam	47	77	1493	19.38	78	4494	125	35.95	22.43
Munir Malik	3	4	7	1.75	4	358	9	39.77	17.67
1960-61									
Javed Burki	25	48	1341	27.93	5	23	0		
Mohammad Farooq	7	9	85	9.44	11	682	21	32.47	17.00
1961-62									
Afaq Hussain	2	4	66	16.50	3	106	1	106.00	318.00
1962									
Javed Akhtar	1	2	4	2.00	1	52	0		
Shahid Mahmood	1	2	25	12.50	1	23	0		
1964-65									
Khalid Ibadulla	4	8	253	31.62	6	99	1	99.00	594.00
Abdul Kadir	4	8	272	34.00					
Shafqat Rana	5	7	221	31.57	3	9	1	9.00	27.00
Majid Khan	63	106	3931	37.08	60	1456	27	53.92	119.82
Asif Iqbal	58	99	3575	36.11	54	1502	53	28.33	28.86

Pervez Sajjad	19	20	123	6.15	35	1410	59	23.89	14.17
Mohammad Ilyas	10	19	441	23.21	5	63	0		
Arif Butt	3	5	59	11.80	6	288	14	20.57	8.81
Farooq Hamid	1	2	3	1.50	2	107	1	107.00	214.00
Naushad Ali	6	11	156	14.18					
Mufasir-ul-Haq	1	1	8	8.00	2	84	3	28.00	18.66
Salahuddin	5	8	117	14.62	5	187	7	26.71	19.07
1967									
Saleem Altaf	21	31	276	8.90	39	1710	46	37.17	31.51
Wasim Bari	81	112	1366	12.19	1	2	0		
Niaz Ahmed	2	3	17	5.66	3	94	3	31.33	31.33
Ghulam Abbas	1	2	12	6.00					
1968-69									
Aftab Gul	6	8	182	22.75	1	4	0		
Asif Masood	16	19	93	4.89	27	1568	38	41.26	29.31
Sarfraz Nawaz	55	72	1045	14.51	95	5798	177	32.75	17.57
1969-70									
Sadiq Mohammad	41	74	2579	34.85	11	98	0		
Younis Ahmed	4	7	177	25.28	1	6	0		
Zaheer Abbas	78	124	5062	40.82	14	132	3	44.00	205.33
Mohammad Nazir	14	18	144	8.00	23	1123	34	33.02	22.33
Aftab Baloch	2	3	97	32.33	2	17	0		
1971									
Imran Khan	88	126	3807	30.21	142	8258	362	22.81	8.94
1972-73									
Talat Ali	10	18	370	20.55	2	7	0		
Wasim Raja	57	92	2821	30.66	69	1826	51	35.80	48.43
1974									
Shafiq Ahmed	6	10	99	9.90	1	1	0		
1974-75									
Agha Zahid	1	2	15	7.50					
Liaqat Ali	5	7	28	4.00	6	359	6	59.83	59.83
1976-77									
Javed Miandad	124	189	8832	46.73	36	682	17	40.11	84.93
Farrukh Zaman	1	-	-	-	2	15	0		
Shahid Israr	1	1	7	7.00					
Sikander Bakht	26	35	146	4.17	45	2412	67	36.00	24.17
Mudassar Nazar	76	116	4114	35.46	96	2532	66	38.36	55.79
Iqbal Qasim	50	57	549	9.63	86	4807	171	28.11	14.13
Haroon Rasheed	23	36	1217	33.80	1	3	0		
1977-78									
Abdul Qadir	67	77	1029	13.36	111	7742	236	32.80	15.42
Mohsin Khan	48	79	2709	34.29	6	30	0		
1978-79									
Anwar Khan	1	2	15	7.50	1	12	0		
1979-80									
Ehteshamuddin	5	3	2	0.66	7	375	16	23.43	10.25
Taslim Arif	6	10	501	50.10	1	28	1	28.00	28.00
Tauseef Ahmed	34	38	318	8.36	58	2950	93	31.72	19.78
Azmat Rana	1	1	49	49.00					
Azhar Khan	1	1	14	14.00	2	2	1	2.00	4.00
1980-81									
Mansoor Akhtar	19	29	655	22.58					
Ijaz Faqih	5	8	183	22.87	7	299	4	74.75	130.81
1981-82									
Rizwan-uz-Zaman	11	19	345	18.15	3	46	4	11.50	8.62
Saleem Malik	103	154	5768	37.45	30	414	5	82.80	496.80
Saleem Yousuf	32	44	1055	23.97					
Tahir Naqqash	15	19	300	15.78	27	1398	34	41.11	32.64
Rashid Khan	4	6	155	25.83	7	360	8	45.00	39.37

Ashraf Ali	8	8	229	28.62					
1982-83									
Jalal-ud-Din	6	3	2	0.66	9	537	11	48.81	39.93
1983-84									
Azeem Hafeez	18	21	134	6.38	28	2204	63	34.98	15.54
Shoaib Mohammad	45	68	2705	39.77	26	170	5	34.00	176.80
Qasim Umar	26	43	1502	34.93	1	0	0		
Rameez Raja	57	94	2833	30.13					
Anil Dalpat	9	12	167	13.91					
Mohsin Kamal	9	11	37	3.36	12	822	24	34.25	17.12
1984-85									
Manzoor Elahi	6	10	123	12.30	7	194	7	27.71	27.71
Wasim Akram	104	147	2898	19.71	181	9779	414	23.62	10.32
1985-86									
Zulqarnain	3	4	24	6.00					
Zakir Khan	2	2	9	4.50	4	259	5	51.80	41.44
1986-87									
Asif Mujtaba	25	41	928	22.63	16	303	4	75.75	303.00
Saleem Jaffar	14	14	42	3.00	23	1139	36	31.63	20.20
Ijaz Ahmed	60	92	3315	36.03	6	77	2	38.50	115.50
1987-88									
Aamer Malik	14	19	565	29.73	9	89	1	89.00	801.00
1988-89									
Aaqib Javed	22	27	101	3.74	37	1874	54	34.70	23.77
1989-90									
Shahid Saeed	1	1	12	12.00	2	43	0		
Waqar Younis	87	120	1010	8.41	154	8788	373	23.56	9.72
Naved Anjum	2	3	44	14.66	3	162	4	40.50	30.37
Nadeem Abbasi	3	2	46	23.00					
Akram Raza	9	12	153	12.75	14	732	13	56.30	60.63
Shahid Mahboob	1	-	-	-	1	131	2	65.50	32.75
Mushtaq Ahmed	52	72	656	9.11	89	6100	185	32.97	15.86
Nadeem Ghauri	1	1	0	0.00	1	20	0		
1990-91									
Zahid Fazal	9	16	288	18.00					
Saeed Anwar	55	91	4052	44.52	4	23	0		
Moin Khan	69	104	2741	26.35					
Masood Anwar	1	2	39	19.50	2	102	3	34.00	22.66
1992									
Aamer Sohail	47	83	2823	34.01	46	1049	25	41.96	77.20
Inzamam-ul-Haq	120	200	8830		1	8	0		
n/a	1	2	1	-	-	-	-		
adj	119	198	8829	44.59	1	8	0		
Ata-ur-Rehman	13	15	76	5.06	22	1071	31	34.54	24.51
Rashid Latif	37	57	1381	24.22	1	10	0		
1992-93									
Basit Ali	19	33	858	26.00	1	6	0		
Aamer Nazir	6	11	31	2.81	12	597	20	29.85	17.91
Nadeem Khan	2	3	34	11.33	4	230	2	115.00	230.00
Shakeel Ahmed	3	5	74	14.80					
1993-94									
Ashfaq Ahmed	1	2	1	0.50	2	53	2	26.50	26.50
Atif Rauf	1	2	25	12.50					
Kabir Khan	4	5	24	4.80	6	370	9	41.11	27.40
1995-96									
Ijaz Ahmed	2	3	29	9.66	1	6	0		
Saqlain Mushtaq	49	78	927	11.88	86	6206	208	29.83	12.33
Mohammad Akram	9	15	24	1.60	15	859	17	50.52	44.57
Saleem Elahi	13	24	436	18.16					

1996									
Shadab Kabir	5	7	148	21.14	1	9	0		
1996-97									
Azam Khan	1	1	14	14.00					
Shahid Nazir	15	19	194	10.21	28	1272	36	35.33	27.47
Hasan Raza	7	10	235	23.50	1	1	0		
Mohammad Hussain	2	3	18	6.00	3	87	3	29.00	29.00
Zahoor Elahi	2	3	30	10.00					
Mohammad Wasim	18	28	783	27.96					
Mohammad Zahid	5	6	7	1.16	8	502	15	33.46	17.84
1997-98									
Ali Naqvi	5	9	242	26.88	1	11	0		
Mohammad Ramzan	1	2	36	18.00					
Azhar Mahmood	21	34	900	26.47	35	1402	39	35.94	32.25
Ali Hussain Rizvi	1	-	-	-	1	72	2	36.00	11.99
Arshad Khan	9	8	31	3.87	17	960	32	30.00	15.93
Shoaib Akhtar	46	67	544	8.11	82	4574	178	25.69	11.83
Mohammad Yousuf	90	156	7530	48.26	1	3	0		
Fazl-e-Akbar	5	8	52	6.50	8	511	11	46.45	33.78
1998-99									
Shahid Afridi	27	48	1716	35.75	47	1709	48	35.60	34.85
Shakeel Ahmed	1	1	1	1.00	2	139	4	34.75	17.37
Naved Ashraf	2	3	64	21.33					
Wajahatullah Wasti	6	10	329	32.90	3	8	0		
Imran Nazir	8	13	427	32.84					
1999-00									
Abdul Razzaq	46	77	1946	25.27	76	3694	100	36.94	28.07
Younis Khan	118	213	10099	47.41	31	491	9	54.55	187.89
Atiq-uz-Zaman	1	2	26	13.00					
Irfan Fazil	1	2	4	2.00	2	65	2	32.50	32.50
2000									
Qaiser Abbas	1	1	2	2.00	1	35	0		
Danish Kaneria	61	84	360	4.28	112	9082	261	34.79	14.92
2000-01									
Imran Farhat	40	77	2400	31.16	15	284	3	94.66	473.30
Misbah-ul-Haq	75	132	5222	39.56					
Faisal Iqbal	26	44	1124	25.54	1	7	0		
Mohammad Sami	36	56	487	8.69	66	4483	85	52.74	40.95
Humayun Farhat	1	2	54	27.00					
2001-02									
Taufeeq Umar	44	83	2963	35.69	7	44	0		
Shoaib Malik	35	60	1898	31.63	43	1519	32	47.46	63.77
Naved Latif	1	2	20	10.00					
2002-03									
Kamran Akmal	53	92	2648	28.78					
2003									
Mohammad Hafeez	55	105	3652	34.78	77	1808	53	34.11	49.55
Yasir Hameed	25	49	1491	30.42	4	72	0		
Shabbir Ahmed	10	15	88	5.86	19	1175	51	23.03	8.57
Umar Gul	47	67	577	8.61	90	5553	163	34.06	18.80
Salman Butt	33	62	1889	30.46	5	106	1	106.00	530.00
Farhan Adil	1	2	33	16.50					
Yasir Ali	1	2	1	0.50	2	55	2	27.50	27.50
2003-04									
Asim Kamal	12	20	717	35.85					
2004-05									
Riaz Afridi	1	1	9	9.00	2	87	2	43.50	43.50
Naved-ul-Hasan	9	15	239	15.93	16	1044	18	58.00	51.55
Mohammad Khalil	2	4	9	2.25	4	200	0		
Mohammad Asif	23	38	141	3.71	44	2583	106	24.36	10.11

Bazid Khan	1	2	32	16.00					
2005-06									
Iftikhar Anjum	1	1	9	9.00	2	62	0		
2007-08									
Abdur Rehman	22	31	395	12.74	43	2910	99	29.39	12.76
Sohail Thanvir	2	3	17	5.66	4	316	5	63.20	50.56
Yasir Arafat	3	3	94	31.33	5	438	9	48.66	27.03
2008-09									
Khurram Manzoor	16	30	817	27.23					
Sohail Khan	9	12	252	21.00	17	1125	27	41.66	26.23
Mohammad Talha	4	5	34	6.80	6	504	9	56.00	37.33
2009									
Abdur Rauf	3	6	52	8.66	6	278	6	46.33	46.33
Mohammad Amir	36	67	751	11.20	67	3627	119	30.47	17.15
Saeed Ajmal	35	53	451	8.50	67	5003	178	28.10	10.57
Fawad Alam	18	28	986	35.21	3	54	2	27.00	40.50
2009-10									
Umar Akmal	16	30	1003	33.43					
Sarfaraz Ahmed	49	86	2657	30.89					
2010									
Azhar Ali	94	174	7021	40.35	37	621	8	77.62	358.99
Umar Amin	4	8	99	12.37	5	63	3	21.00	34.99
Zulqarnain Haider	1	2	88	44.00					
Wahab Riaz	27	41	306	7.46	49	2864	83	34.50	20.36
2010-11									
Adnan Akmal	21	29	591	20.37					
Asad Shafiq	77	128	4660	36.40	15	196	3	65.33	326.65
Tanvir Ahmed	5	7	170	24.28	10	453	17	26.64	15.67
2010									
Mohammad Salman	2	4	25	6.25					
2011-12									
Junaid Khan	21	28	122	4.35	41	2253	71	31.73	18.32
Aizaz Cheema	7	5	1	0.20	14	638	20	31.90	22.33
2012									
Mohammad Ayub	1	2	47	23.50					
2012-13									
Nasir Jamshed	2	4	51	12.75					
Rahat Ali	21	31	136	4.38	39	2264	58	39.03	26.24
Mohammad Irfan	4	7	28	4.00	6	389	10	38.90	23.34
Ehsan Adil	3	4	21	5.25	5	263	5	52.60	52.60
2013-14									
Shan Masood	25	47	1378	29.31	10	92	2	46.00	230.00
Zulfiqar Babar	15	18	144	8.00	28	2139	54	39.61	20.53
Ahmed Shehzad	13	25	982	39.28	2	28	0		
Bilawal Bhatti	2	3	70	23.33	3	291	6	48.50	24.25
2014-15									
Yasir Shah	46	69	847	12.27	85	7306	235	31.08	11.24
Imran Khan	10	10	16	1.60	18	917	29	31.62	19.62
2015									
Sami Aslam	13	25	758	30.32					
2016									
Iftikhar Ahmed	4	6	61	10.16	5	161	1	161.00	805.00
2016-17									
Babar Azam	40	71	2851	40.15	5	16	2	8.00	20.00
Mohammad Nawaz	3	4	50	12.50	6	147	5	29.40	35.28
Mohammad Rizwan	22	33	1112	33.69					
Sharjeel Khan	1	2	44	22.00					
2017									
Mohammad Abbas	25	36	110	3.05	44	2072	90	23.02	11.25
Shadab Khan	6	11	300	27.27	11	513	14	36.64	28.78

Hasan Ali	19	28	312	11.14	36	1747	74	23.60	11.48
2017-18									
Haris Sohail	16	27	847	31.37	17	294	13	22.61	29.56
2018									
Imam-ul-Haq	14	27	855	31.66					
Faheem Ashraf	14	21	636	30.28	25	818	24	34.08	35.49
Usman Salahuddin	1	2	37	18.50					
2018-19									
Bilal Asif	5	8	73	9.12	10	424	16	26.50	16.56
Fakhar Zaman	3	6	192	32.00					
Mir Hamza	1	2	4	2.00	2	67	1	67.00	134.00
Shaheen Shah Afridi	24	31	145	4.67	40	2383	95	25.08	10.55
2019-20									
Naseem Shah	11	14	29	2.07	16	1019	26	39.19	24.11
Muhammad Musa	1	2	16	8.00	1	114	0		
Abid Ali	16	26	1180	45.38					
Usman Shinwari	1	0	-	-	1	54	1	54.00	54.00
2020-21									
Zafar Gohar	1	2	71	35.00	1	159	0		
Imran Butt	6	10	178	17.80					
Nauman Ali	10	11	203	18.45	19	909	28	32.46	22.02
2021									
Sajid Khan	7	7	73	10.42	13	832	22	37.81	22.34
Tabish Khan	1	0	-	-	2	68	1	68.00	136.00
2021-22									
Abdullah Shafique	5	9	547	60.77					

SRI LANKA

	M	I	R	RI	IB	R	W	A	RWI
1981-82									
B Warnapura	4	8	96	12.00	4	46	0		
S Wettimuny	23	43	1221	28.39	2	37	0		
RL Dias	20	36	1285	35.69	1	17	0		
LRD Mendis	24	43	1329	30.90					
RS Madugalle	21	39	1029	26.38	5	38	0		
A Ranatunga	93	155	5105	32.93	56	1040	16	65.00	227.50
DS de Silva	12	22	406	18.45	19	1347	37	36.40	18.69
ALF de Mel	17	28	326	11.64	27	2180	59	36.94	16.90
LWS Kaluperuma	2	4	12	3.00	3	93	0		
HM Goonatilleke	5	10	177	17.70					
GRA de Silva	4	7	41	5.85	7	385	7	55.00	55.00
JR Ratnayeke	22	38	807	21.23	31	1972	56	35.21	19.49
AN Ranasinghe	2	4	88	22.00	3	69	1	69.00	207.00
RSA Jayasekera	1	2	2	1.00					
RGCE Wijesuriya	4	7	22	3.14	5	294	1	294.00	1470.00
1982-83									
MD Wettimuny	2	4	28	7.00					
ERNS Fernando	5	10	112	11.20					
Y Goonasekera	2	4	48	12.00					
RG de Alwis	11	19	152	8.00					
S Jeganathan	2	4	19	4.75	1	12	0		
RJ Ratnayake	23	36	433	12.02	35	2563	73	35.10	16.82
VB John	6	10	53	5.30	9	614	28	21.92	7.04
SAR Silva	9	16	353	22.06					
RPW Guneratne	1	2	0	0.00	1	84	0		
1983-84									
SMS Kaluperuma	4	8	88	11.00	6	124	2	62.00	186.00
AMJG Amerasinghe	2	4	54	13.50	3	150	3	50.00	50.00

1984									
PA de Silva	93	159	6361	40.00	58	1208	29	41.65	83.30
1985-86									
EAR de Silva	10	16	185	11.56	15	1032	8	129.00	241.87
FS Ahangama	3	3	11	3.66	6	348	18	19.33	6.44
CDUS Weerasinghe	1	1	3	3.00	2	36	0		
BR Jurangpathy	2	4	1	0.25	2	93	1	93.00	186.00
AP Gurusinha	41	70	2452	35.02	39	681	20	34.05	66.39
KPJ Warnaweera	10	12	39	3.25	15	1021	32	31.90	14.95
RS Mahanama	52	89	2576	28.94	2	30	0		
SD Anurasiri	18	22	91	4.13	27	1548	41	37.75	24.85
AK Kuruppuarachchi	2	2	0	0.00	3	149	8	18.62	6.98
KN Amalean	2	3	9	3.00	2	156	7	22.28	6.36
1986-87									
GF Labrooy	9	14	158	11.28	15	1194	27	44.22	24.56
DSBP Kuruppu	4	7	320	45.71					
1987-88									
CPH Ramanayake	18	24	143	5.95	29	1880	44	42.72	28.15
1988									
MAR Samarasekera	4	7	118	16.85	2	104	3	34.66	23.10
MAWR Madurasinghe	3	6	24	4.00	4	172	3	57.33	76.43
1989-90									
D Ranatunga	2	3	87	29.00					
AGD Wickremasinghe	3	3	17	5.66					
HP Tillakaratne	83	131	4545	34.69	10	25	0		
1990-91									
MS Atapattu	90	156	5502	35.26	5	24	1	24.00	120.00
CP Senanayake	3	5	97	19.40					
UC Hathurusingha	26	44	1274	28.95	32	789	17	46.41	87.35
ST Jayasuriya	110	189	6973	36.89	140	3366	98	34.34	49.05
1991									
KIW Wijegunawardene	2	4	14	3.50	4	147	7	21.00	11.99
1991-92									
GP Wickramasinghe	40	64	555	8.67	63	3559	85	41.87	31.03
1992-93									
RS Kaluwitharana	49	78	1933	24.78					
DK Liyanage	9	9	69	7.66	15	666	17	39.17	34.56
M Muralitharan	133	164	1261	-	230	18180	800	-	-
n/a	1	2	2	-	2	157	5	-	-
adj	132	162	1259	7.77	228	18023	795	22.67	6.50
AM de Silva	3	3	10	3.33					
1993-94									
RS Kalpage	11	18	294	16.33	16	774	12	64.50	85.99
PB Dassanayake	11	17	196	11.52					
PK Wijetunge	1	2	10	5.00	2	118	2	59.00	59.00
HDPK Dharmasena	31	51	868	17.01	53	2920	69	42.31	32.49
DP Samaraweera	7	14	211	15.07					
1994-95									
S Ranatunga	9	17	531	31.23					
WPUJC Vaas	111	162	3089	19.06	194	10501	355	29.58	16.16
KR Pushpakumara	23	31	166	5.35	38	2242	58	38.65	25.32
CI Dunusinghe	5	10	160	16.00					
1995-96									
KJ Silva	7	4	6	1.50	11	647	20	32.35	17.79
1996-97									
DNT Zoysa	30	40	288	7.20	51	2157	64	33.70	26.85
KSC de Silva	8	12	65	5.41	14	889	16	55.56	48.61
RP Arnold	44	69	1821	26.39	28	598	11	54.36	138.37

1997									
DPMD Jayawardene	149	252	11814	46.88	22	310	6	51.66	189.41
1997-98									
SKL de Silva	3	4	36	9.00					
MRCN Bandaratilleke	7	9	93	10.33	14	698	23	30.34	18.46
HMCM Bandara	8	11	124	11.27	14	633	16	39.56	34.61
1998									
ASA Perera	3	4	77	19.25	5	180	1	180.00	900.00
1998-99									
KEA Upashantha	2	3	10	3.33	3	200	4	50.00	37.50
PDRL Perera	8	9	33	3.66	14	661	17	38.88	32.01
DA Gunawardene	6	11	181	16.45					
UDU Chandana	16	24	616	25.66	29	1535	37	41.48	32.51
1999-00									
HMRKB Herath	93	144	1699	11.79	170	12157	433	28.07	11.02
SI de Saram	4	5	117	23.40					
TM Dilshan	87	145	5492	37.87	76	1711	39	43.87	85.49
IS Gallage	1	1	3	3.00	2	77	0		
2000									
CRD Fernando	40	47	249	5.29	68	3784	100	37.84	25.73
HAPW Jayawardene	58	83	2124	25.59					
KC Sangakkara	134	233	12400	53.21	4	49	0		
2000-01									
D Hettiarachchi	1	2	0	0.00	2	41	2	20.50	20.50
2001									
TT Samaraweera	81	132	5462	41.37	35	689	15	45.93	107.16
2001-02									
MG Vandort	20	33	1144	34.66					
TCB Fernando	9	8	132	16.50	17	792	18	44.00	41.55
2002									
WRS de Silva	3	2	10	5.00	6	209	11	19.00	10.36
MKGCP Lakshitha	2	3	42	14.00	4	158	5	31.60	25.28
J Mubarak	13	23	385	16.73	6	66	0		
MN Nawaz	1	2	99	49.50					
2002-03									
KHRK Fernando	2	4	38	9.50	2	108	4	27.00	13.50
KS Lokuarachchi	4	5	94	18.80	6	295	5	59.00	70.80
RAP Nissanka	4	5	18	3.60	7	366	10	36.60	25.62
2003									
T Thushara	10	14	94	6.71	18	1040	28	37.14	23.87
2003-04									
KADM Fernando	2	3	56	18.66	4	107	1	107.00	428.00
MF Maharoof	22	34	556	16.35	35	1631	25	65.24	91.33
2004									
SL Malinga	30	37	275	7.43	59	3349	101	33.15	19.36
2004-05									
KMDN Kulasekara	21	28	391	13.96	38	1794	48	37.37	29.58
S Kalavitigoda	1	2	8	4.00					
2005									
G Wijekoon	2	3	38	12.66	3	66	2	33.00	49.50
2005-06									
WU Tharanga	31	58	1754	30.24					
2006									
CK Kapugedera	8	15	418	27.86	1	9	0		
2006-07									
LPC Silva	11	17	537	31.58	3	65	1	65.00	195.00
2007									
BSM Warnapura	14	24	821	34.20					
2007-08									
UWMBCA Welegedara	21	30	218	7.26	35	2273	55	41.32	26.29

MKDI Amerasinghe	1	2	0	0.00	2	105	1	105.00	210.00
2008									
BAW Mendis	19	19	213	11.21	31	2434	70	34.77	15.39
KTGD Prasad	25	39	476	12.20	44	2698	75	35.97	21.10
2008-09									
NT Paranavitana	32	60	1792	29.86	6	86	1	86.00	516.00
2009									
AD Mathews	94	169	6432	38.05	83	1766	33	53.51	134.58
2010									
S Randiv	12	17	147	8.64	21	1613	43	37.51	18.31
2010-11									
RAS Lakmal	70	109	934	8.56	122	6232	171	36.44	25.99
2011									
NLTC Perera	6	10	203	20.30	8	653	11	59.36	43.17
HDRL Thirimanne	44	85	2088	24.56	5	51	0		
S Prasanna	1	1	5	5.00	1	80	0		
RMS Eranga	19	26	193	7.42	35	2138	57	37.50	23.02
2011-12									
Nuwan Pradeep	28	50	132	2.64	53	3003	70	42.90	32.48
JK Silva	39	74	2099	28.36					
CKB Kulasekara	1	2	22	11.00	2	80	1	80.00	160.00
LD Chandimal	64	117	4217	36.04					
2012-13									
FDM Karunaratne	76	147	5620	38.23	13	191	2	95.50	620.75
KDK Vithanage	10	16	370	23.12	5	133	1	133.00	665.00
2013-14									
SMSM Senanayake	1	1	5	5.00	2	96	0		
MDK Perera	43	77	1303	16.92	78	5780	161	35.90	17.39
2014									
N Dickwella	47	84	2529	30.10					
2014-15									
PHT Kaushal	7	12	106	8.83	14	1105	25	44.20	24.75
2015									
PVD Chameera	12	21	104	4.95	21	1321	32	41.28	27.09
MDKJ Perera	22	41	1177	28.70					
2015-16									
TAM Siriwardana	5	9	298	33.11	9	257	11	23.36	19.11
BKG Mendis	48	93	3078	33.09	8	110	1	110.00	880.00
MDUS Jayasundera	2	4	30	7.50	2	45	0		
2016									
MD Shanaka	6	12	140	11.66	8	431	13	33.15	20.39
DM de Silva	40	72	2517	34.95	59	1623	29	55.96	113.84
PADLR Sandakan	11	17	117	6.88	20	1276	37	34.48	18.63
MVT Fernando	16	24	68	2.83	26	1604	43	37.30	22.55
2016-17									
DAS Gunaratne	6	10	455	45.50	6	114	3	38.00	76.00
CBRLS Kumara	24	32	56	1.75	39	2694	70	38.48	21.43
2017									
MD Gunathilaka	8	16	299	18.68	6	111	1	111.00	666.00
PM Pushpakumara	4	8	102	12.75	6	520	14	37.14	15.91
2017-18									
S Samarawickrama	4	8	125	15.62					
PLS Gamage	5	8	6	0.75	9	573	10	57.30	51.57
ARS Silva	12	23	702	30.52					
A Dananjaya	6	10	135	13.50	12	819	33	24.81	9.02
2018									
ML Udawatte	2	4	23	5.75					
CAK Rajitha	9	12	35	2.91	15	779	25	31.16	18.69
2018-19									
C Karunaratne	1	2	22	11.00	2	148	1	148.00	296.00

BOP Fernando	13	24	726	30.25	3	19	0		
L Embuldeniya	15	23	183	7.95	26	2434	70	34.77	12.91
2020-21----------									
PWH de Silva	4	7	196	28.00	7	403	4	100.75	176.31
M Bhanuka	1	2	6	3.00					
AM Fernando	3	6	4	0.66	4	156	4	39.00	39.00
WRT Mendis	4	7	100	14.28	8	560	26	21.53	6.62
P Nissanka	7	12	494	41.16					
2021----------									
P Jayawickrama	4	5	12	2.40	7	487	25	19.48	5.45
2021-22----------									
KIC Asalanka	3	6	88	14.66	2	16	0		

ZIMBABWE

	M	I	R	RI	IB	R	W	A	RWI
1992-93----------									
KJ Arnott	4	8	302	37.75					
GW Flower	67	123	3457	28.10	60	1537	25	61.48	147.55
ADR Campbell	60	109	2858	26.22	6	28	0		
AJ Pycroft	3	5	152	30.40					
MG Burmester	3	4	54	13.50	4	227	3	75.66	100.87
DL Houghton	22	36	1464	40.66	1	0	0		
A Flower	63	112	4794	42.80	2	4	0		
GJ Crocker	3	4	69	17.25	5	217	3	72.33	120.54
EA Brandes	10	15	121	8.06	18	951	26	36.57	25.31
AJ Traicos [SA]	4	6	11	1.83	6	562	14	40.14	17.20
MP Jarvis	5	3	4	1.33	8	393	11	35.00	25.45
AH Omarshah	3	5	122	24.40	3	125	1	125.00	375.00
DH Brain	9	13	115	8.84	16	915	30	30.50	16.26
GA Briant	1	2	17	8.50					
U Ranchod	1	2	8	4.00	1	45	1	45.00	45.00
1993-94----------									
MH Dekker	14	22	333	15.13	2	15	0		
GJ Whittall	46	82	2207	26.91	52	2088	51	40.94	41.74
GK Bruk-Jackson	2	4	39	9.75					
SG Peall	4	6	60	10.00	6	303	4	75.75	113.62
HH Streak	65	107	1990	18.59	102	6079	216	28.14	13.28
JA Rennie	4	6	62	10.33	8	293	3	97.66	260.42
WR James	4	4	61	15.25					
1994-95----------									
PA Strang	24	41	839	20.46	38	2522	70	36.02	19.55
SV Carlisle	37	66	1615	24.46					
HK Olonga	30	45	184	4.08	47	2620	68	38.52	26.62
BC Strang	26	45	465	10.33	44	2203	56	39.33	30.90
IP Butchart	1	2	23	11.50	1	11	0		
1995-96----------									
CB Wishart	27	50	1098	21.96					
ACI Lock	1	2	8	4.00	2	105	5	21.00	8.40
1996-97----------									
CN Evans	3	6	52	8.66	2	35	0		
AR Whittall	10	18	114	6.33	12	736	7	105.14	180.02
M Mbangwa	15	25	34	1.36	24	1006	32	31.43	23.57
EZ Matambanadzo	3	5	17	3.40	5	250	4	62.50	78.12
AC Waller	2	3	69	23.00					
1997-98----------									
GJ Rennie	23	46	1023	22.23	4	84	1	84.00	336.00
AG Huckle	8	14	74	5.28	13	872	25	34.88	18.13
MW Goodwin	19	37	1414	38.21	8	69	0		
DP Viljoen	2	4	57	14.25	2	65	1	65.00	130.00

TN Madondo	3	4	90	22.50					
1998-99									
NC Johnson	13	23	532	23.13	14	594	15	39.60	36.95
1999-00									
GB Brent	4	6	35	5.83	6	314	7	44.85	38.44
RW Price	22	38	261	6.86	35	2885	80	36.06	15.77
BA Murphy	11	15	123	8.20	19	1113	18	61.83	65.26
TR Gripper	20	38	809	21.28	20	509	6	84.83	282.76
2000									
ML Nkala	10	15	187	12.46	15	727	11	66.09	90.12
2000-01									
DT Mutendera	1	2	10	5.00	1	29	0		
DA Marillier	5	7	186	26.57	6	322	11	29.27	15.96
AM Blignaut	19	36	886	24.61	30	1964	53	37.05	20.97
DD Ebrahim	29	55	1225	22.27					
BT Watambwa	6	8	11	1.37	9	490	14	35.00	22.49
2001									
TJ Friend	13	19	447	23.52	19	1090	25	43.60	33.13
T Taibu	28	54	1546	28.62	1	27	1	27.00	27.00
H Masakadza	38	76	2223	29.25	24	489	16	30.56	45.84
2001-02									
DT Hondo	9	15	83	5.53	13	774	21	36.85	22.81
2002-03									
NB Mahwire	10	17	147	8.64	14	915	18	50.83	39.53
MA Vermeulen	9	18	449	24.94	1	5	0		
2003									
SM Ervine	5	8	261	32.62	6	388	9	43.11	28.73
2003-04									
GM Ewing	3	6	108	18.00	5	260	2	130.00	325.00
V Sibanda	14	28	591	21.10					
S Matsikenyeri	8	16	351	21.93	8	345	2	172.50	690.00
BRM Taylor	34	68	2320	34.11	4	38	0		
E Chigumbura	14	27	569	21.07	22	966	21	46.00	48.19
A Maregwede	2	4	74	18.50					
P Utseya	4	8	107	13.37	6	410	10	41.00	24.60
T Panyangara	9	18	201	11.16	16	813	31	26.22	13.53
T Mupariwa	1	2	15	7.50	1	136	0		
2004-05									
BG Rogers	4	8	90	11.25	1	17	0		
AG Cremer	19	38	540	14.21	27	2604	57	45.68	21.63
CB Mpofu	15	28	105	3.75	23	1392	29	48.00	38.00
2005									
NR Ferreira	1	2	21	10.50					
KM Dabengwa	3	6	90	15.00	3	249	5	49.80	29.88
CK Coventry	2	4	88	22.00					
T Duffin	2	4	80	20.00					
W Mwayenga	1	2	15	7.50	1	79	1	79.00	79.00
2011									
TMK Mawoyo	11	22	615	27.95					
CR Ervine	18	36	1208	33.55					
KM Jarvis	13	24	128	5.33	22	1354	46	29.43	14.07
BV Vitori	4	7	52	7.42	7	464	12	38.66	22.55
GA Lamb	1	2	46	23.00	2	141	3	47.00	31.33
2011-12									
MN Waller	14	28	577	20.60	9	218	8	27.25	30.65
RW Chakabva	22	43	1061	24.67					
N Ncube	1	2	17	8.50	2	121	1	121.00	242.00
F Mutizwa	1	2	24	12.00					
SW Masakadza	5	9	88	9.77	9	515	16	32.18	18.10

2012-13									
TL Chatara	9	16	90	5.62	16	663	24	27.62	18.41
SC Williams	14	27	1034	38.29	22	1072	21	51.04	53.47
2013									
T Maruma	4	7	68	9.71					
R Mutumbami	6	12	217	18.08					
KO Meth	2	4	72	18.00	3	98	4	24.50	18.37
Sikandar Raza	17	33	1187	35.96	25	1441	34	42.38	31.16
2014									
J Nyumbu	3	6	38	6.33	6	379	5	75.80	90.96
DT Tiripano	15	29	508	17.51	24	1247	26	47.96	44.27
2014-015									
TP Kamungozi	1	2	5	2.50	2	58	1	58.00	116.00
BB Chari	7	14	254	18.14	2	12	0		
N M'shangwe	2	4	8	2.00	4	435	7	62.14	35.50
2016									
CJ Chibhabha	3	6	124	20.66	4	162	1	162.00	648.00
PS Masvaure	8	15	346	23.06	2	61	0		
MT Chinouya	2	4	1	0.25	3	188	3	62.66	62.66
PJ Moor	8	16	533	33.31					
2016-17									
CT Mumba	3	5	25	5.00	6	354	10	35.40	21.24
2017									
TK Musakanda	5	9	134	14.88					
2017-18									
SF Mire	2	4	78	19.50	3	32	1	32.00	96.00
TS Chisoro	3	5	27	5.40	3	333	6	55.50	27.75
RP Burl	3	5	24	4.80	4	107	4	26.75	26.75
B Muzarabani	6	11	102	9.27	9	473	19	24.89	11.78
2018-19									
BA Mavuta	2	4	9	2.25	4	237	4	59.25	59.25
WP Masakadza	1	2	21	10.50	2	54	2	27.00	27.00
2019-20									
KT Kasuza	7	12	249	20.75					
A Ndlovu	2	4	9	2.25	2	277	2	138.50	138.50
VM Nyauchi	6	10	40	4.00	11	567	15	37.80	27.71
BS Mudzinganyama	1	1	16	16.00					
CT Mutombodzi	1	2	41	20.50	2	67	0		
CK Tshuma	1	2	3	1.50	1	85	1	85.00	85.00
2020-21									
WN Madhevere	2	3	0	0.00	2	42	0		
2021									
M Shumba	3	6	101	16.83	4	233	1	233.00	932.00
R Kaia	3	6	59	9.83	3	165	0		
R Ngarava	3	6	31	5.16	4	281	5	56.20	44.96
LM Jongwe	1	2	56	28.00	1	68	1	68.00	68.00
T Kaitano	1	2	94	47.00					
D Myers	1	2	53	26.50	1	13	0		

BANGLADESH

	M	I	R	RI	IB	R	W	A	RWI
2000-01									
Shahriar Hossain	3	5	99	19.80					
Mehrab Hossain	9	18	241	13.38	1	5	0		
Habibul Bashar	50	99	3026	30.56	9	217	0		
Aminul Islam	13	26	530	20.38	5	149	1	149.00	745.00
Akram Khan	8	16	259	16.18					
Al Sahariar	15	30	683	22.76					
Naimur Rahman	8	15	210	14.00	10	718	12	59.83	49.85

Khaled Mashud	44	84	1409	16.77					
Mohammad Rafique	33	63	1059	16.80	48	4076	100	40.76	19.56
Hasibul Hossain	5	10	97	9.70	6	571	6	95.16	95.16
Ranjan Das	1	2	2	1.00	2	72	1	72.00	144.00
Javed Omar	40	80	1720	21.50	1	12	0		
Manjural Islam	17	33	81	2.45	22	1605	28	57.32	45.03
Mohammad Sharif	10	20	122	6.10	11	1106	14	79.00	62.07
Mushfiqur Rahman	10	19	232	12.21	15	823	13	63.30	73.03
Enamul Haque	10	19	180	9.47	12	1027	18	57.05	38.03
2001-02									
Mohammad Ashraful	61	119	2737	23.00	67	1271	21	60.52	193.08
Khaled Mahmud	12	23	266	11.56	17	832	13	64.00	83.69
Mashrafe Mortaza	36	67	797	11.89	51	3239	78	41.52	27.14
Sanwar Hossain	9	18	345	19.16	6	310	5	62.00	74.40
Fahim Muntasir	3	6	52	8.66	4	342	5	68.40	54.72
2002									
Alamgir Kabir	3	5	8	1.60	4	221	0		
Ehsanul Haque	1	2	7	3.50	1	18	0		
Hannan Sarkar	17	33	662	20.06					
Talha Jubair	7	14	52	3.71	9	771	14	55.07	35.40
Alok Kapali	17	34	584	17.17	19	709	6	118.16	374.17
Tapash Baisya	21	40	384	9.60	29	2137	36	59.36	47.81
Tushar Imran	5	10	89	8.90	1	48	0		
2002-03									
Rafiqul Islam	1	2	7	3.50					
Anwar Hossain	1	2	14	7.00					
2003									
Mohammad Salim	2	4	49	12.25					
Anwar Hossain Monir	3	6	22	3.66	3	307	0		
Rajin Saleh	24	46	1141	24.80	16	268	2	134.00	1072.00
2003-04									
Enamul Haque, jr	15	26	59	2.26	26	1787	44	40.61	23.99
Manjural Islam Rana	6	11	257	23.36	7	401	5	80.20	112.28
2004									
Faisal Hossain	1	2	7	3.50					
Tareq Aziz	3	6	22	3.66	4	261	1	261.00	1044.00
2004-05									
Nafees Iqbal	11	22	518	23.54					
Aftab Ahmed	16	31	582	18.77	9	237	5	47.40	85.32
Nazmul Hossain	2	4	16	4.00	3	194	5	38.80	23.28
2005									
Mushfiqur Rahim	80	148	4932	33.32					
Shahadat Hossain	38	69	521	7.55	60	3731	72	51.81	43.17
2005-06									
Shahriar Nafees	24	48	1267	26.39					
Syed Rasel	6	12	37	3.08	8	573	12	47.75	31.83
Abdur Razzak	13	22	248	11.27	20	1673	28	59.75	42.67
2007									
Shakib Al Hasan	59	109	4029	36.96	99	6731	215	31.30	14.41
Mehrab Hossain, jr	7	13	243	18.69	11	281	4	70.25	193.18
2007-08									
Tamim Iqbal	65	125	4848	38.78	5	20	0		
Junaid Siddique	19	37	969	26.18	2	11	0		
Sajedul Islam	3	6	18	3.00	5	232	3	77.33	128.88
2008-09									
Naeem Islam	8	15	416	27.73	14	303	1	303.00	4242.00
Raqibul Hasan	9	18	336	18.66	4	17	1	17.00	68.00
Imrul Kayes	39	76	1797	23.64	4	12	0		
Mahbubul Alam	4	7	5	0.71	6	314	5	62.80	75.36

2009									
Mahmudullah	50	94	2914	31.00	66	1958	43	45.53	69.88
Rubel Hossain	27	47	265	5.63	44	2764	36	76.77	93.82
2009-10									
Shafiul Islam	11	21	211	10.04	19	942	17	55.41	61.92
Jahurul Islam	7	14	347	24.78					
2010									
Robiul Islam	9	17	99	5.82	17	992	25	39.68	26.98
2011-12									
Nasir Hossain	19	32	1044	32.62	25	442	8	55.25	172.65
Elias Sunny	4	6	38	6.33	7	518	12	43.16	25.17
Suhrawadi Shuvo	1	2	15	7.50	2	146	4	36.50	18.25
Nazimuddin	3	6	125	20.83					
2012-13									
Sohag Gazi	10	16	325	20.31	18	1599	38	42.07	19.92
Abul Hasan	3	5	165	33.00	5	371	3	123.66	206.09
Anamul Haque	4	8	73	9.12					
Mominul Haque	51	95	3514	36.98	35	473	7	67.57	337.85
2013									
Ziaur Rahman	1	2	14	7.00	2	71	4	17.75	8.87
2013-14									
Marshall Ayub	3	6	125	20.83	2	53	0		
Al-Amin Hossain	7	11	90	8.18	10	545	9	60.55	67.27
Shamsur Rahman	6	12	305	25.41	1	5	0		
2014									
Shuvagata Hom	8	15	244	16.26	11	506	8	63.25	86.96
Taijul Islam	36	61	488	8.00	62	4899	153	32.01	12.97
2014-15									
Jubair Hossain	6	5	13	2.60	9	493	16	30.81	17.33
2015									
Soumya Sarkar	16	30	831	27.70	12	336	4	84.00	252.00
Mohammad Shahid	5	6	57	9.50	6	288	5	57.60	69.12
Liton Das	31	53	1730	32.64					
Mustafizur Rahman	14	20	59	2.95	23	1102	30	36.73	28.15
2016-17									
Sabbir Rahman	11	22	481	21.86	7	98	0		
Mehidy Hasan Miraz	33	61	1072	17.57	56	4451	128	34.77	15.21
Kamrul Islam	7	14	51	3.64	11	504	8	63.00	86.62
Taskin Ahmed	11	19	187	9.84	20	1398	25	55.92	44.73
Subashis Roy	4	6	14	2.33	7	465	9	51.66	40.17
Najmul Hossain Shanto	15	29	817	28.17	5	50	0		
Nurul Hasan	5	9	207	23.00					
Mosaddek Hossain	3	6	164	27.33	5	49	0		
2017-18									
Sunzamul Islam	1	1	24	24.00	1	153	1	153.00	153.00
2018									
Abu Jayed	13	22	36	1.63	18	1118	30	37.26	22.35
2018-19									
Ariful Haque	2	4	88	22.00	3	24	1	24.00	72.00
Nazmul Islam	1	2	4	2.00	2	76	4	19.00	9.50
Mohammad Mithun	10	18	333	18.50					
Khaled Ahmed	5	8	4	0.50	8	554	9	61.55	54.71
Nayeem Hasan	7	10	109	10.90	12	656	25	26.24	12.59
Shadman Islam	13	25	559	22.36					
Ebadot Hossain	14	22	8	0.36	20	1437	25	57.48	45.98
2019-20									
Saif Hassan	6	11	159	14.45	2	27	1	27.00	54.00
2021									
Shoriful Islam	3	5	9	1.80	5	277	6	46.16	38.46

2021-22									
Yasir Ali	5	9	196	21.77					
Mahmudul Hasan Joy	4	7	225	32.14					
Mohammad Naim	1	2	24	12.00					

IRELAND

	M	I	R	RI	IB	R	W	A	RWI
2018									
EC Joyce	1	2	47	23.50					
WTS Porterfield	3	6	58	9.66					
A Balbirnie	3	6	146	24.33	1	8	0		
NJ O'Brien	1	2	18	9.00					
PR Stirling	3	6	104	17.33	1	11	0		
KJ O'Brien	3	6	258	43.00	2	31	0		
SR Thompson	3	6	64	10.66	6	204	10	20.40	12.24
TE Kane	1	2	14	7.00	2	103	0		
GC Wilson	2	4	45	11.25					
WB Rankin [Eng]	2	4	30	7.50	4	223	7	31.85	18.19
TJ Murtagh	3	6	109	18.16	6	213	13	16.38	7.55
2018-19									
JA McCollum	2	4	73	18.25					
SW Poynter	1	2	1	0.50					
AR McBrine	2	4	18	4.50	3	159	3	53.00	53.00
J Cameron-Dow	1	2	41	20.50	2	118	3	39.33	26.21
GH Dockrell	1	2	64	32.00	2	121	2	60.50	60.50
2019									
MR Adair	1	2	11	5.50	2	98	6	16.33	5.44

AFGHANISTAN

	M	I	R	RI	IB	R	W	A	RWI
2018									
Mohammad Shahzad	2	4	69	17.25					
Javed Ahmadi	3	6	113	18.83	3	69	1	69.00	207.00
Rahmat Shah	6	12	385	32.08	1	9	0		
Afsar Zazai	5	8	172	21.50					
Hashmatullah Shahidi	5	10	353	35.30					
Asghar Afghan	6	10	440	44.00	2	17	0		
Mohammad Nabi	3	6	33	5.50	5	254	8	31.75	19.84
Rashid Khan	5	7	106	15.14	9	760	34	22.35	5.91
Yamin Ahmadzai	5	9	32	3.55	9	264	11	24.00	19.63
Mujeed-Ur-Rahman	1	2	18	9.00	1	75	1	75.00	75.00
Wafadar Momand	2	3	12	4.00	3	155	2	77.50	116.25
2018-19									
Ihsanullah	3	6	110	18.33					
Ikram Alikhil	1	1	7	7.00					
Waqar Salamkheil	1	1	1	1.00	2	101	4	25.25	12.62
2019									
Ibrahim Zadran	4	8	356	44.50	1	13	1	13.00	13.00
Qais Ahmad	1	2	23	11.50	2	28	1	28.00	56.00
Zahir Khan	3	6	0	0.00	4	239	7	34.14	19.50
2019-20									
Nasir Jamal	2	4	76	19.00					
Amir Hamza	3	4	72	18.00	6	342	16	21.37	8.01
2020-21									
Abdul Malik	1	2	0	0.00					
Munir Ahmad	1	2	13	6.50					
Abdul Wasi	1	2	12	6.00	1	23	0		

Sayed Shirzad	1	0	-	-	2	97	3	32.33	21.55
Shahidullah	1	1	0	0.00	1	6	0		

Printed in Great Britain
by Amazon

18806165R00160